# Frieren

## Beyond Journey's End

### 3

Story by Kanehito Yamada    Art by **Tsukasa Abe**

# CONTENTS

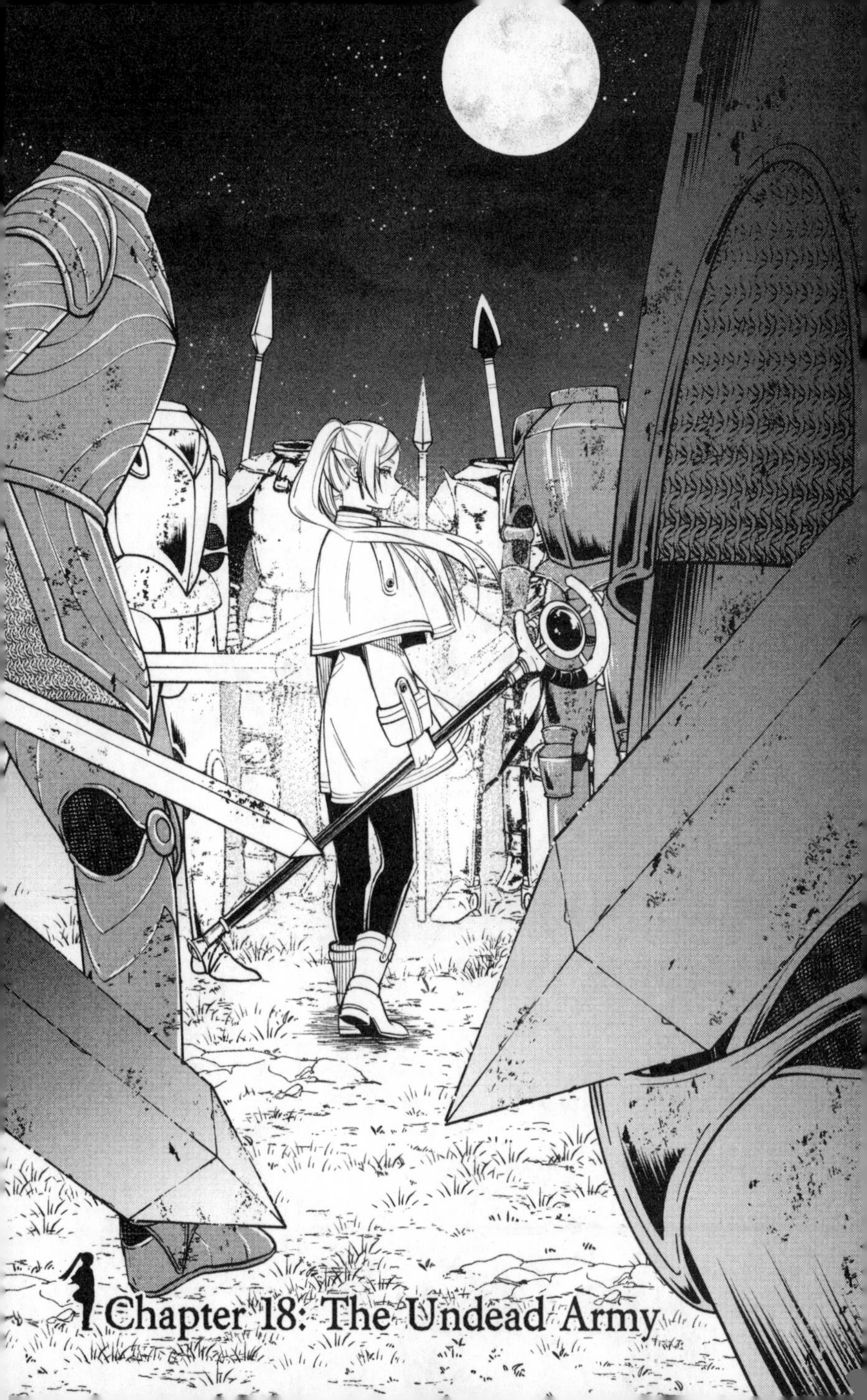

# Chapter 18: The Undead Army

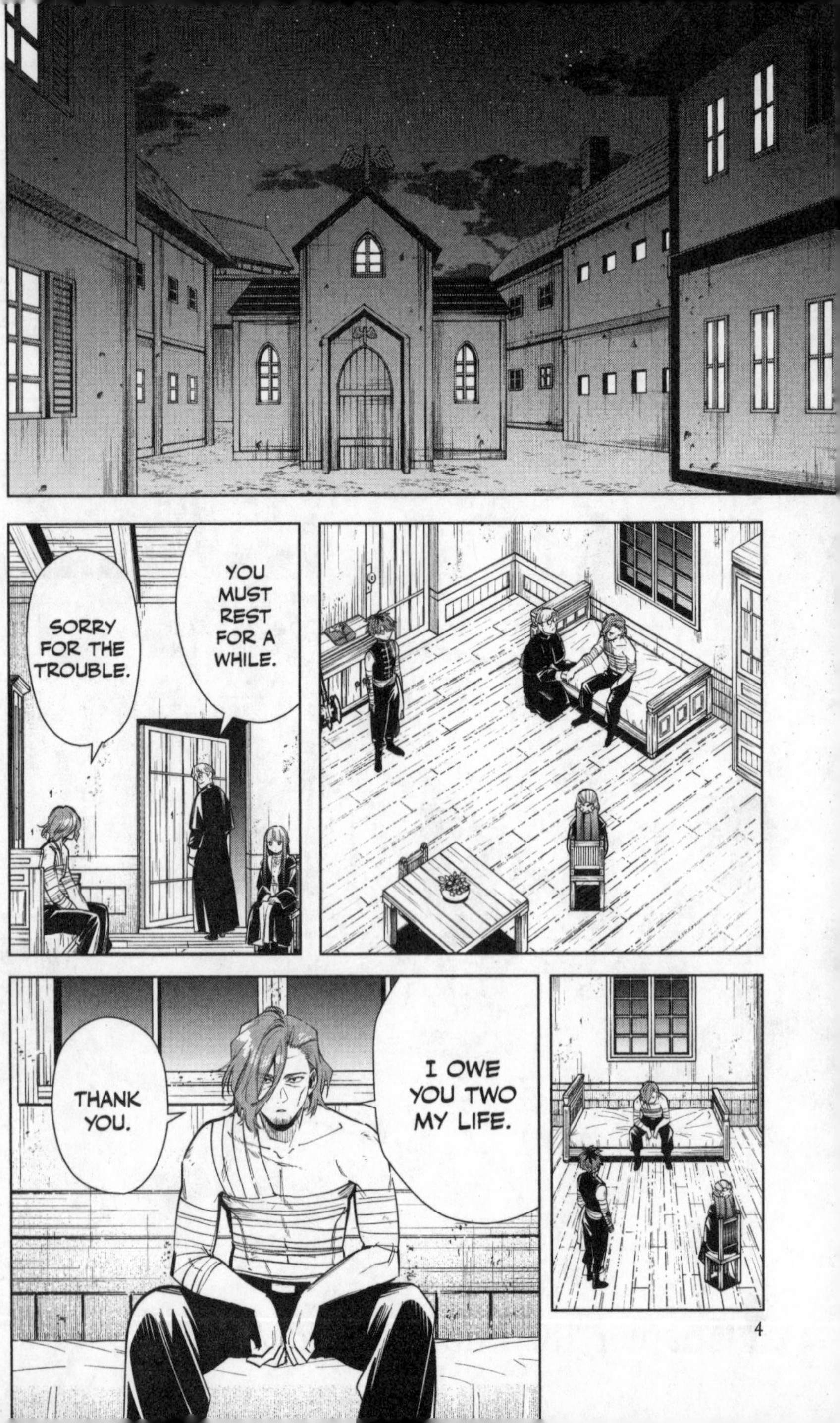
YOU MUST REST FOR A WHILE.
SORRY FOR THE TROUBLE.
I OWE YOU TWO MY LIFE.
THANK YOU.

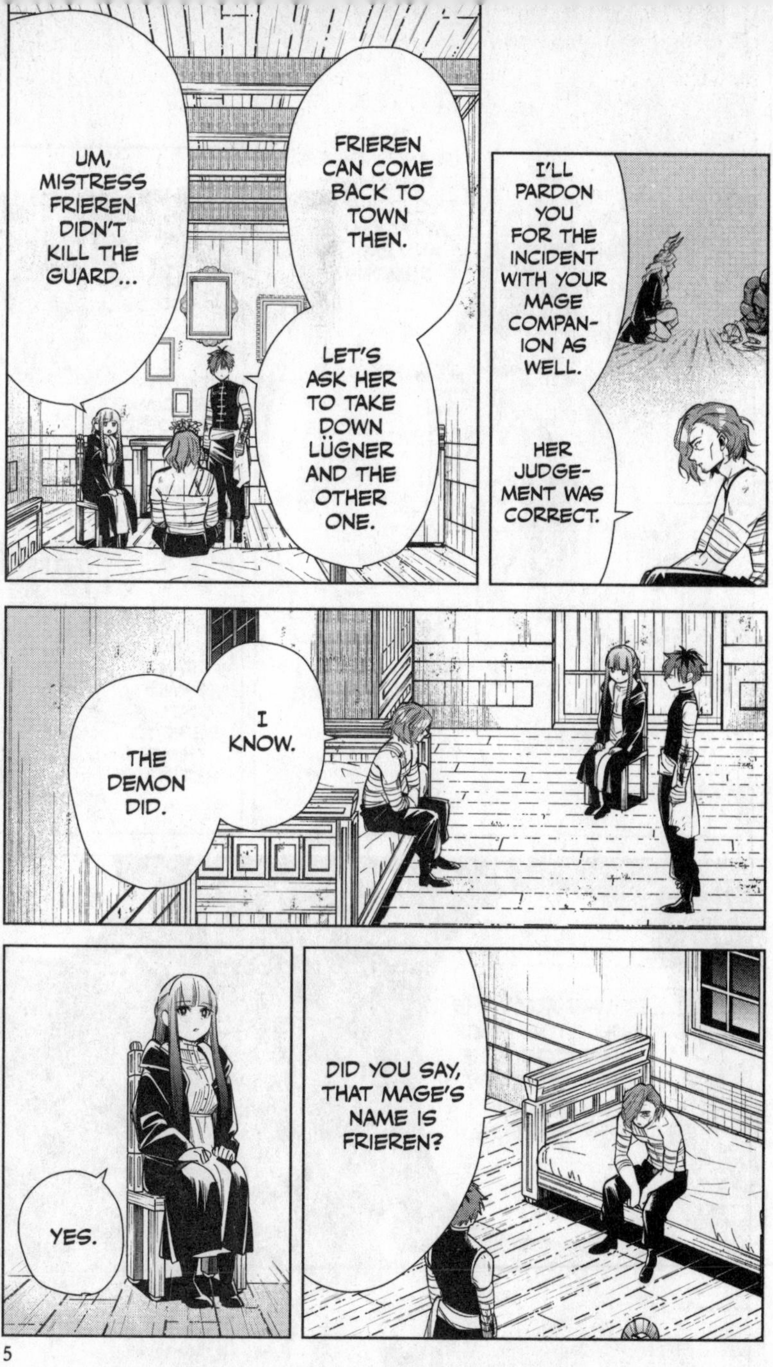
I'LL PARDON YOU FOR THE INCIDENT WITH YOUR MAGE COMPANION AS WELL.
HER JUDGEMENT WAS CORRECT.
FRIEREN CAN COME BACK TO TOWN THEN.
LET'S ASK HER TO TAKE DOWN LÜGNER AND THE OTHER ONE.
UM, MISTRESS FRIEREN DIDN'T KILL THE GUARD...
I KNOW.
THE DEMON DID.
DID YOU SAY, THAT MAGE'S NAME IS FRIEREN?
YES.

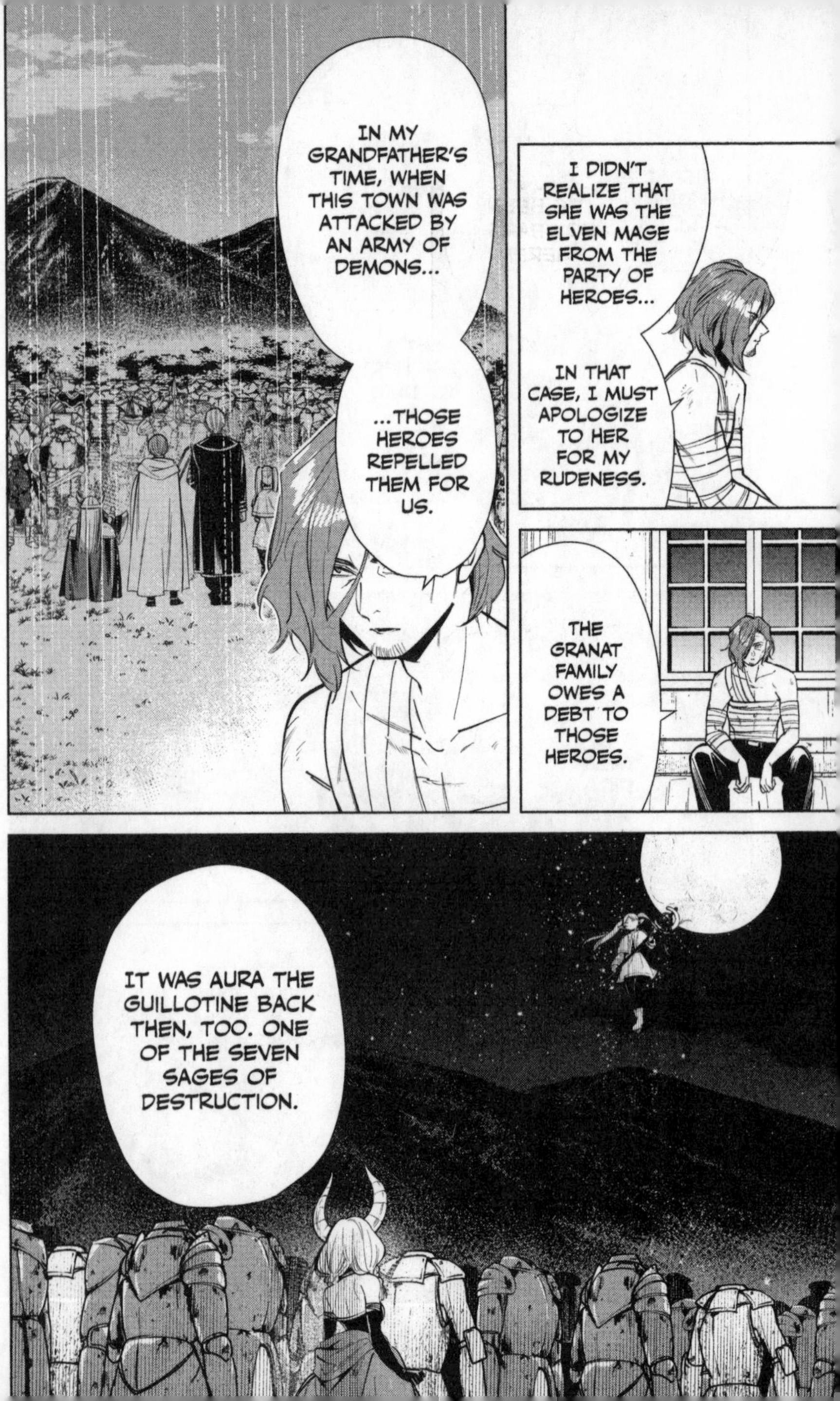
I DIDN'T REALIZE THAT SHE WAS THE ELVEN MAGE FROM THE PARTY OF HEROES...
IN THAT CASE, I MUST APOLOGIZE TO HER FOR MY RUDENESS.
THE GRANAT FAMILY OWES A DEBT TO THOSE HEROES.
IN MY GRANDFATHER'S TIME, WHEN THIS TOWN WAS ATTACKED BY AN ARMY OF DEMONS...
...THOSE HEROES REPELLED THEM FOR US.
IT WAS AURA THE GUILLOTINE BACK THEN, TOO. ONE OF THE SEVEN SAGES OF DESTRUCTION.

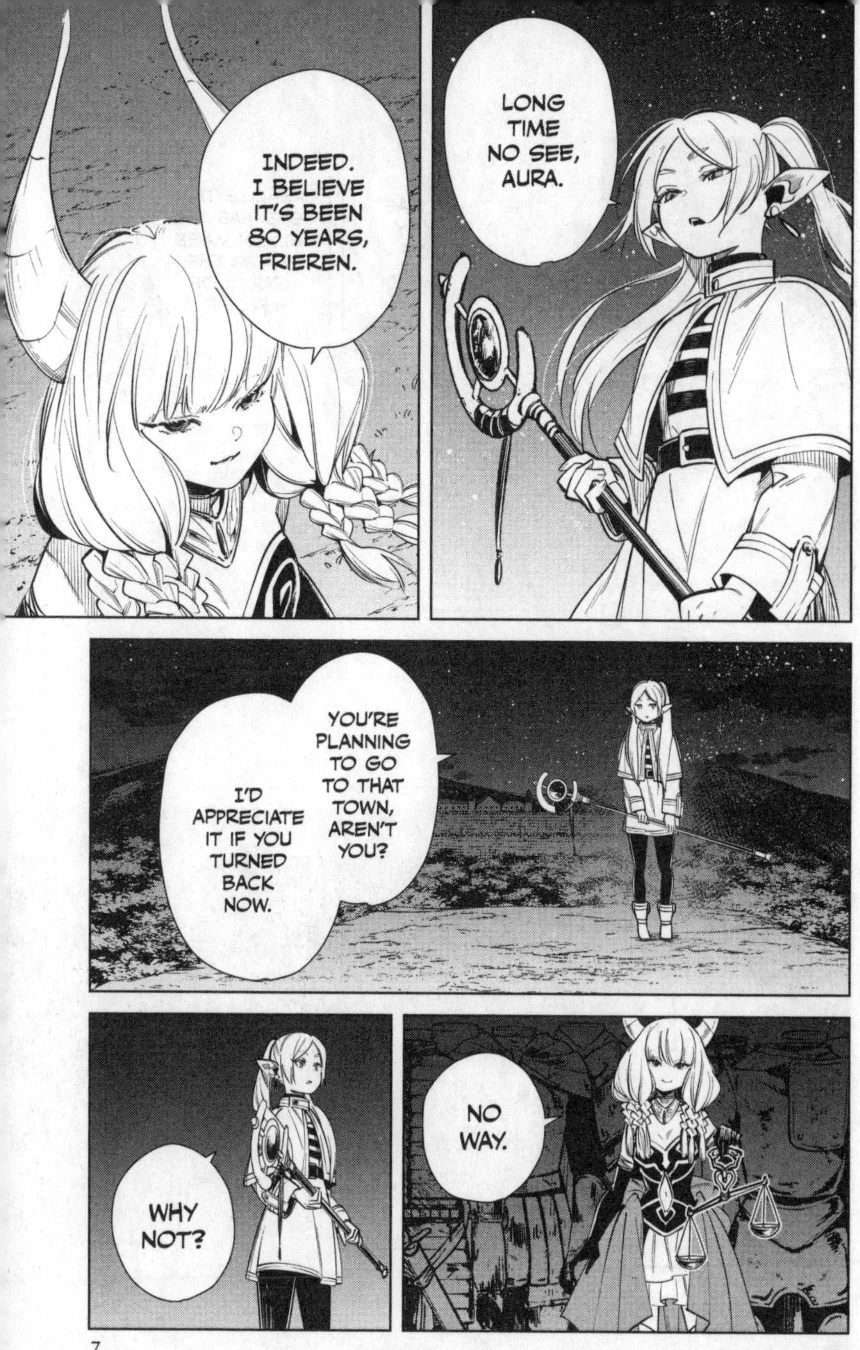
LONG TIME NO SEE, AURA.
INDEED. I BELIEVE IT'S BEEN 80 YEARS, FRIEREN.
YOU'RE PLANNING TO GO TO THAT TOWN, AREN'T YOU?
I'D APPRECIATE IT IF YOU TURNED BACK NOW.
NO WAY.
WHY NOT?

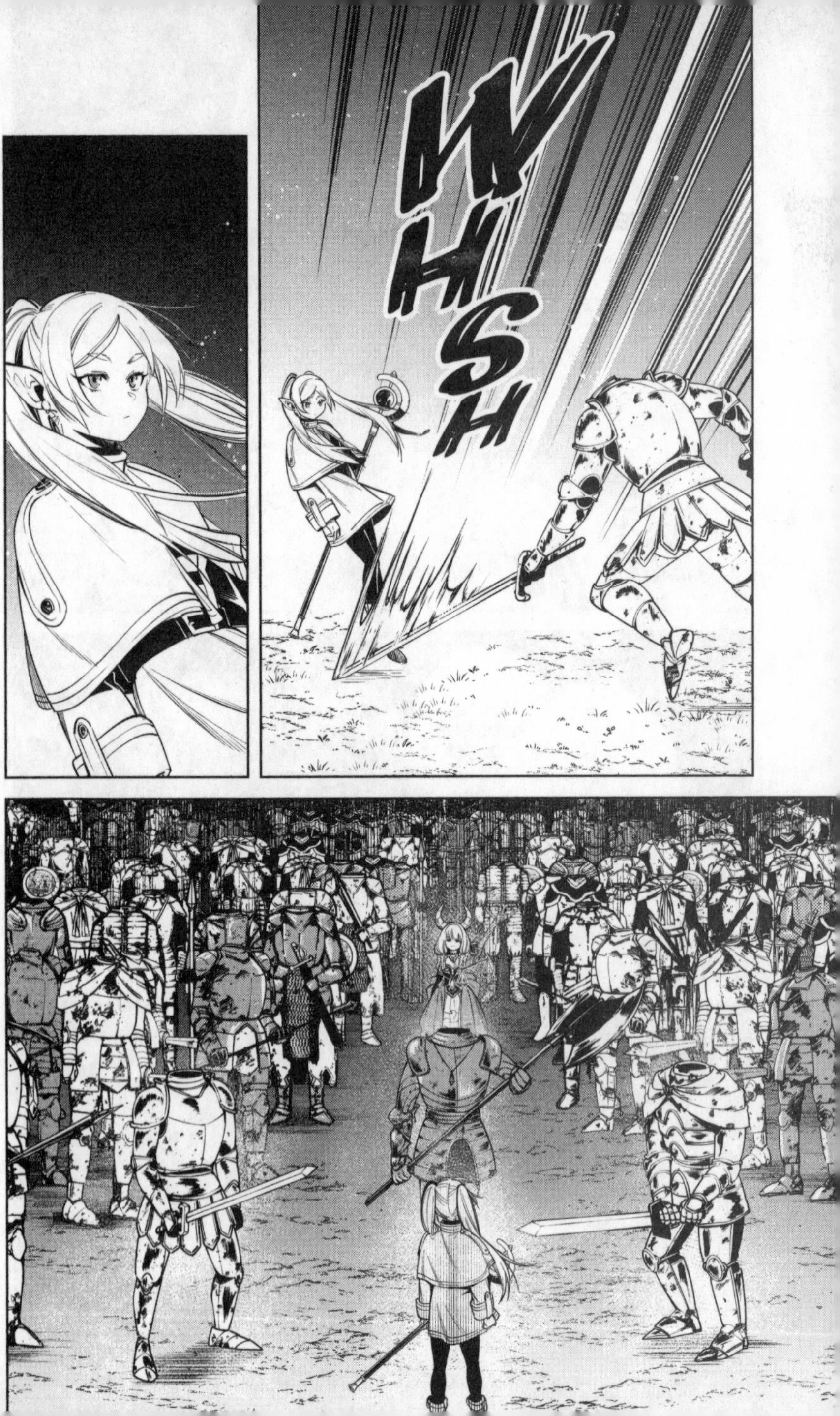
WHSH

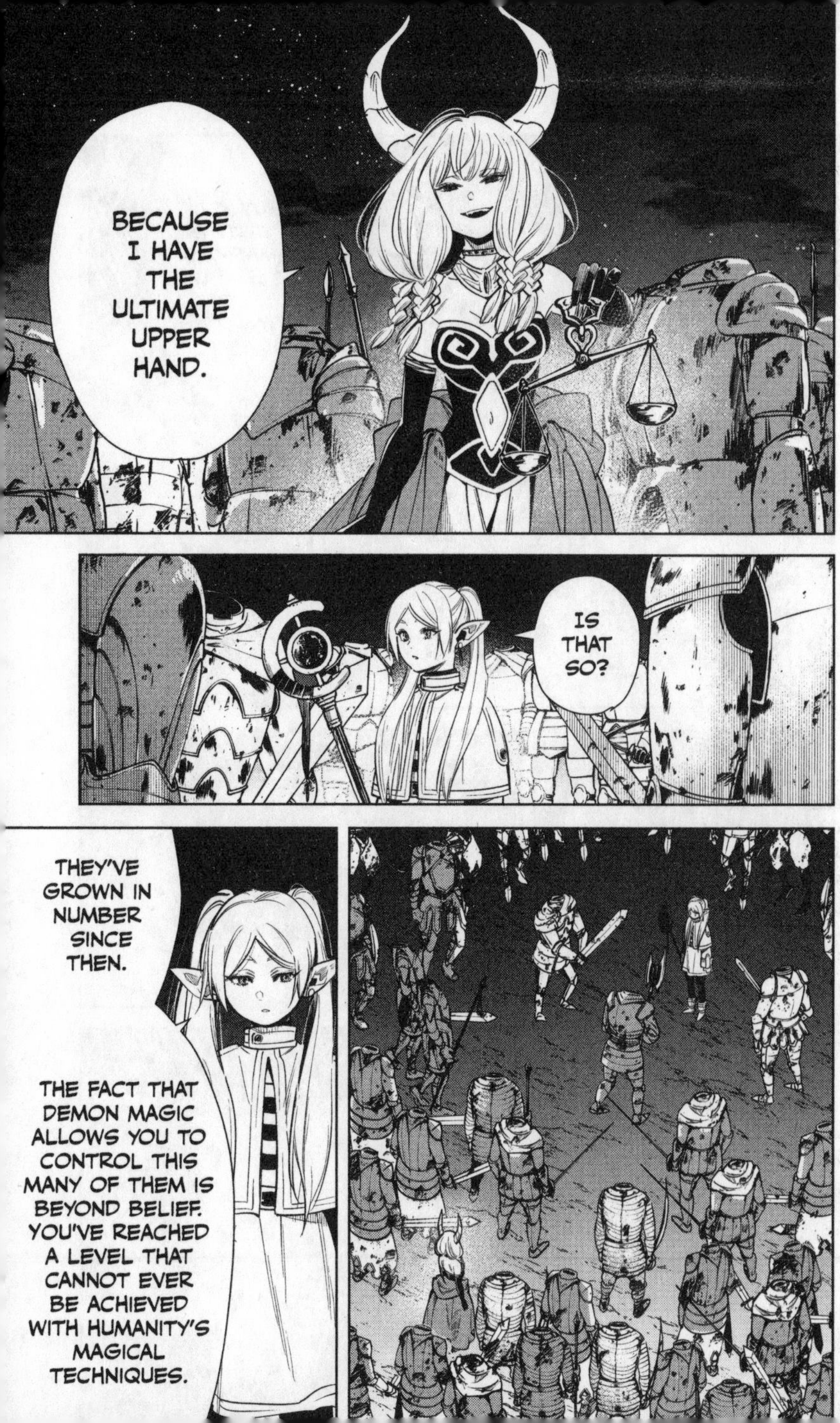
BECAUSE I HAVE THE ULTIMATE UPPER HAND.
IS THAT SO?
THEY'VE GROWN IN NUMBER SINCE THEN.
THE FACT THAT DEMON MAGIC ALLOWS YOU TO CONTROL THIS MANY OF THEM IS BEYOND BELIEF. YOU'VE REACHED A LEVEL THAT CANNOT EVER BE ACHIEVED WITH HUMANITY'S MAGICAL TECHNIQUES.

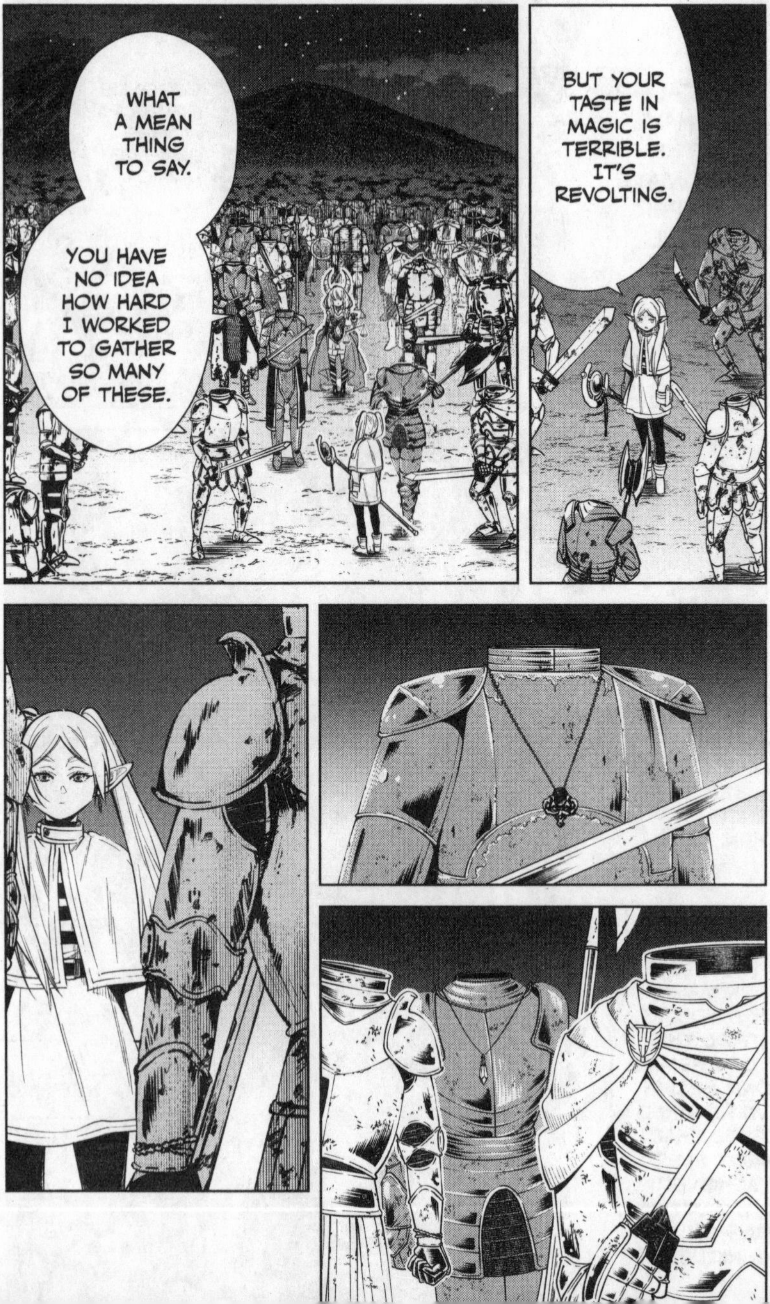
BUT YOUR TASTE IN MAGIC IS TERRIBLE. IT'S REVOLTING.
WHAT A MEAN THING TO SAY.
YOU HAVE NO IDEA HOW HARD I WORKED TO GATHER SO MANY OF THESE.

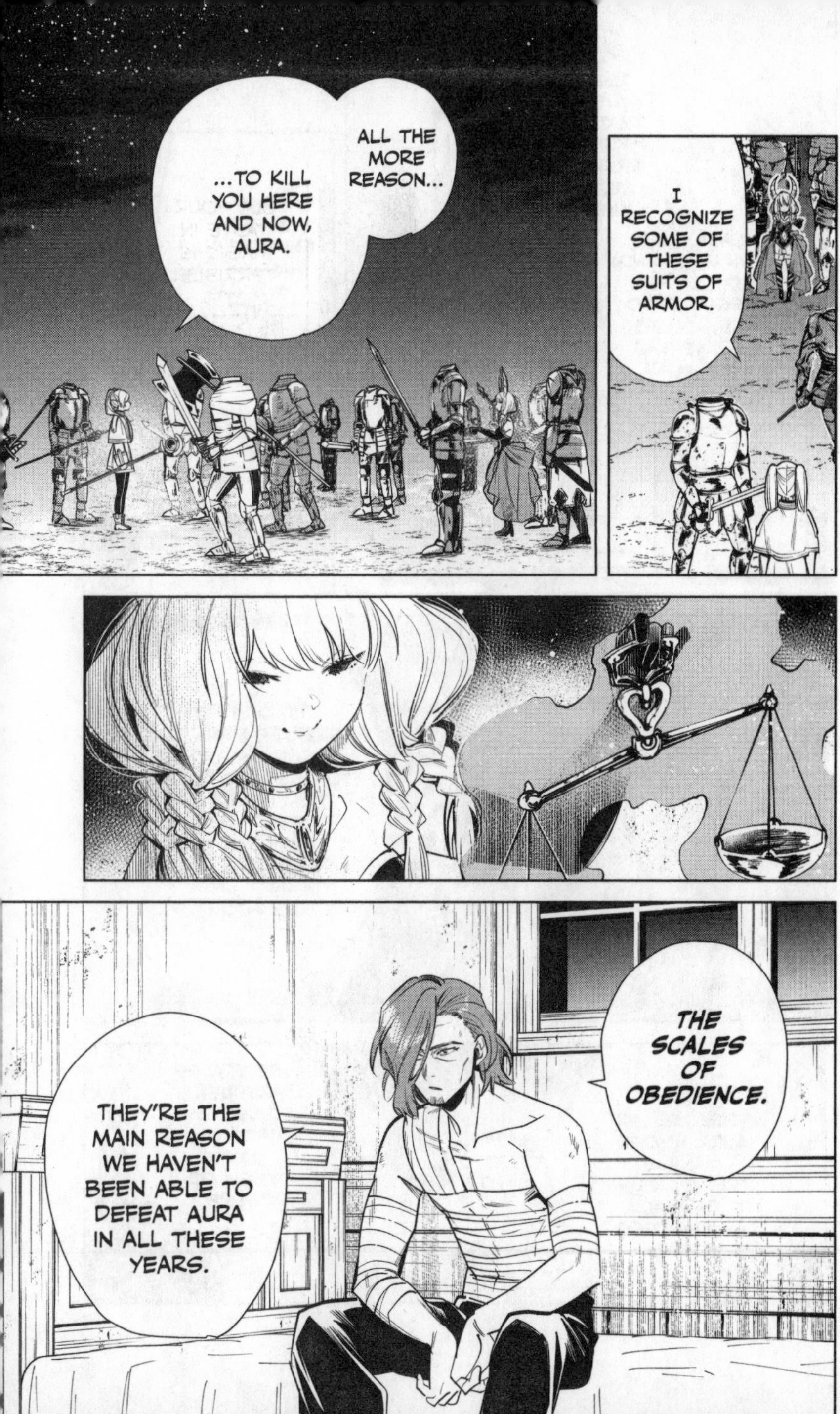
I RECOGNIZE SOME OF THESE SUITS OF ARMOR.
ALL THE MORE REASON...
...TO KILL YOU HERE AND NOW, AURA.
THE SCALES OF OBEDIENCE.
THEY'RE THE MAIN REASON WE HAVEN'T BEEN ABLE TO DEFEAT AURA IN ALL THESE YEARS.

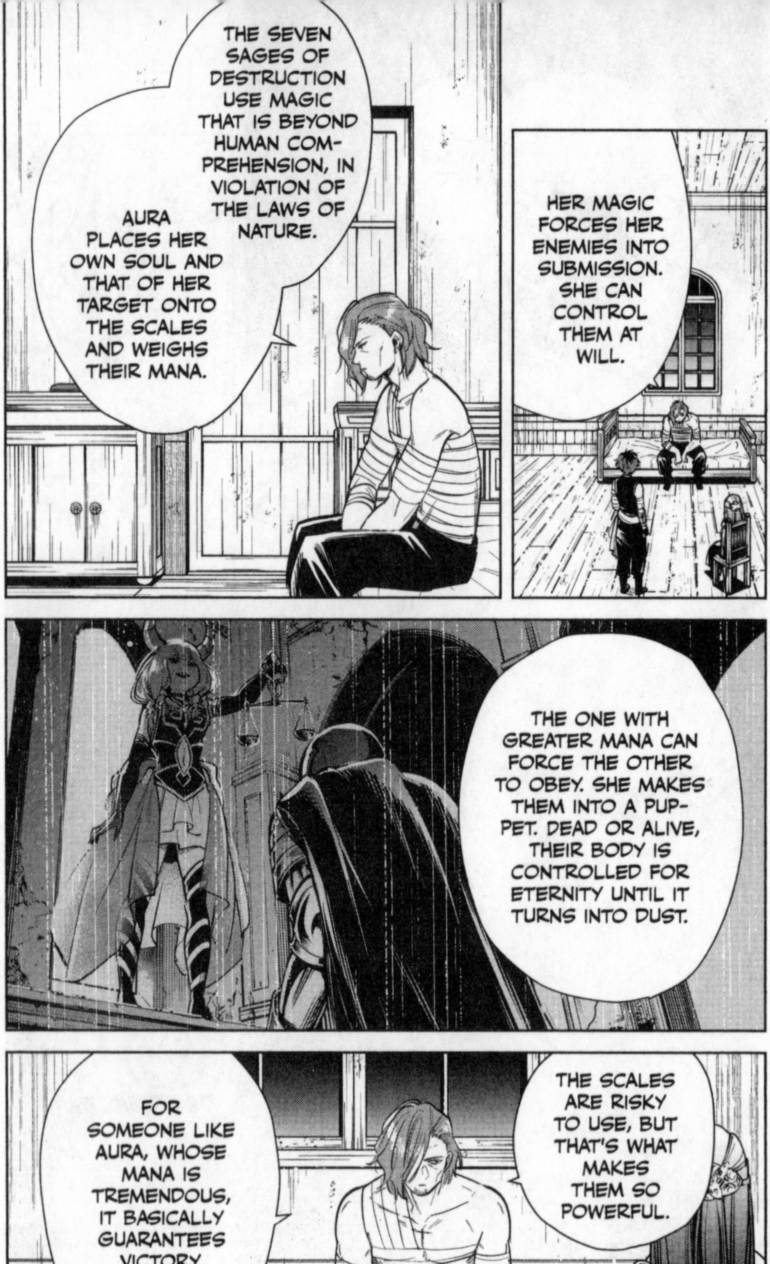
HER MAGIC FORCES HER ENEMIES INTO SUBMISSION. SHE CAN CONTROL THEM AT WILL.
THE SEVEN SAGES OF DESTRUCTION USE MAGIC THAT IS BEYOND HUMAN COMPREHENSION, IN VIOLATION OF THE LAWS OF NATURE.
AURA PLACES HER OWN SOUL AND THAT OF HER TARGET ONTO THE SCALES AND WEIGHS THEIR MANA.
THE ONE WITH GREATER MANA CAN FORCE THE OTHER TO OBEY. SHE MAKES THEM INTO A PUPPET. DEAD OR ALIVE, THEIR BODY IS CONTROLLED FOR ETERNITY UNTIL IT TURNS INTO DUST.
THE SCALES ARE RISKY TO USE, BUT THAT'S WHAT MAKES THEM SO POWERFUL.
FOR SOMEONE LIKE AURA, WHOSE MANA IS TREMENDOUS, IT BASICALLY GUARANTEES VICTORY.

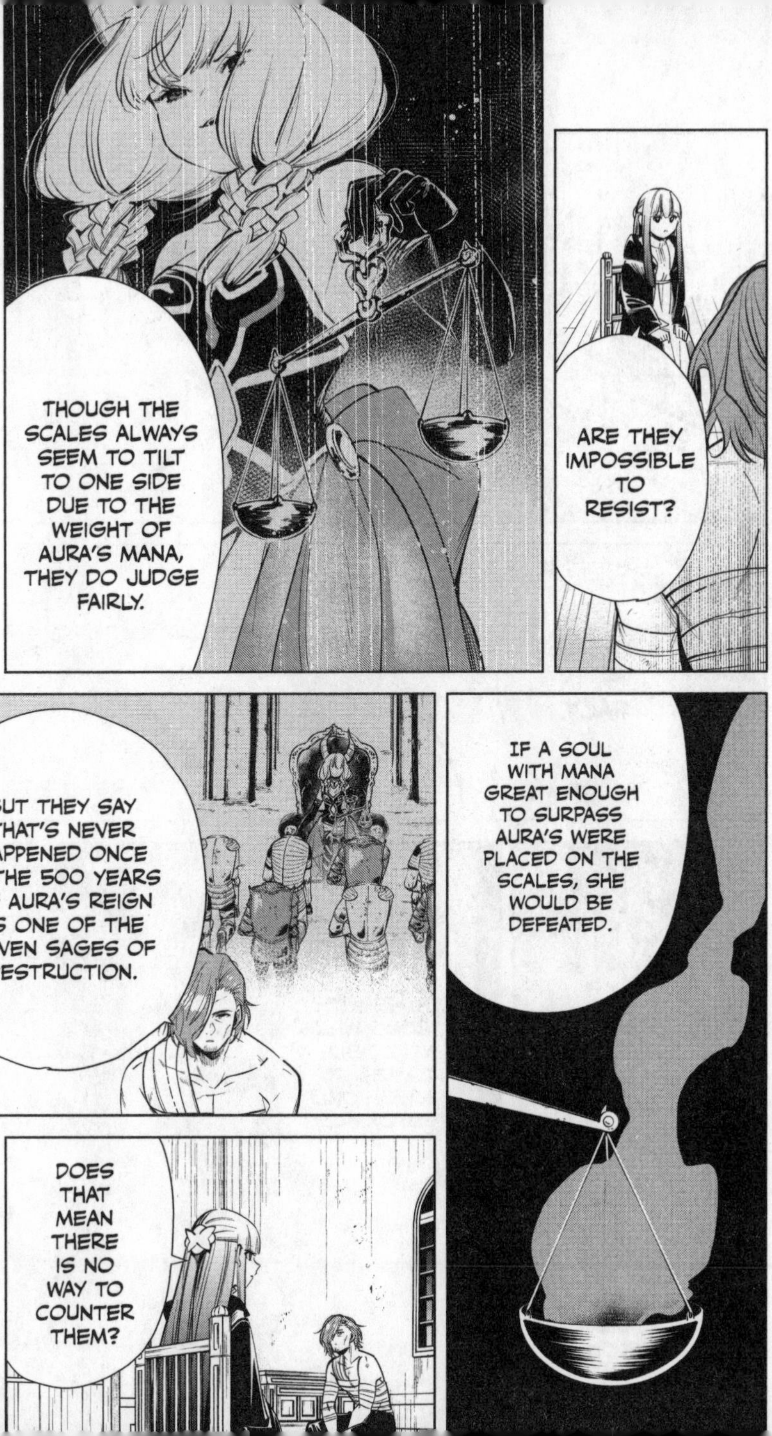
ARE THEY IMPOSSIBLE TO RESIST?
THOUGH THE SCALES ALWAYS SEEM TO TILT TO ONE SIDE DUE TO THE WEIGHT OF AURA'S MANA, THEY DO JUDGE FAIRLY.
IF A SOUL WITH MANA GREAT ENOUGH TO SURPASS AURA'S WERE PLACED ON THE SCALES, SHE WOULD BE DEFEATED.
BUT THEY SAY THAT'S NEVER HAPPENED ONCE IN THE 500 YEARS OF AURA'S REIGN AS ONE OF THE SEVEN SAGES OF DESTRUCTION.
DOES THAT MEAN THERE IS NO WAY TO COUNTER THEM?

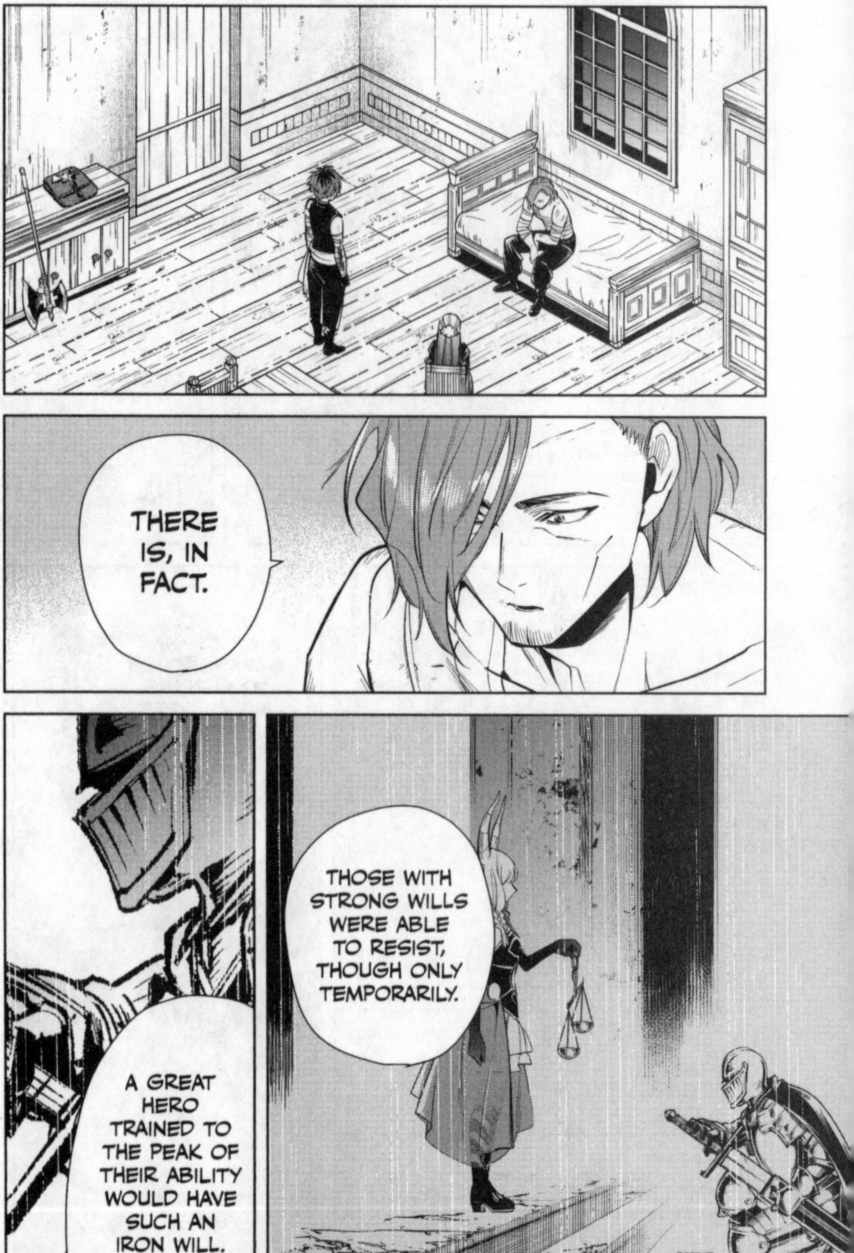
THERE IS, IN FACT.
THOSE WITH STRONG WILLS WERE ABLE TO RESIST, THOUGH ONLY TEMPORARILY.
A GREAT HERO TRAINED TO THE PEAK OF THEIR ABILITY WOULD HAVE SUCH AN IRON WILL.

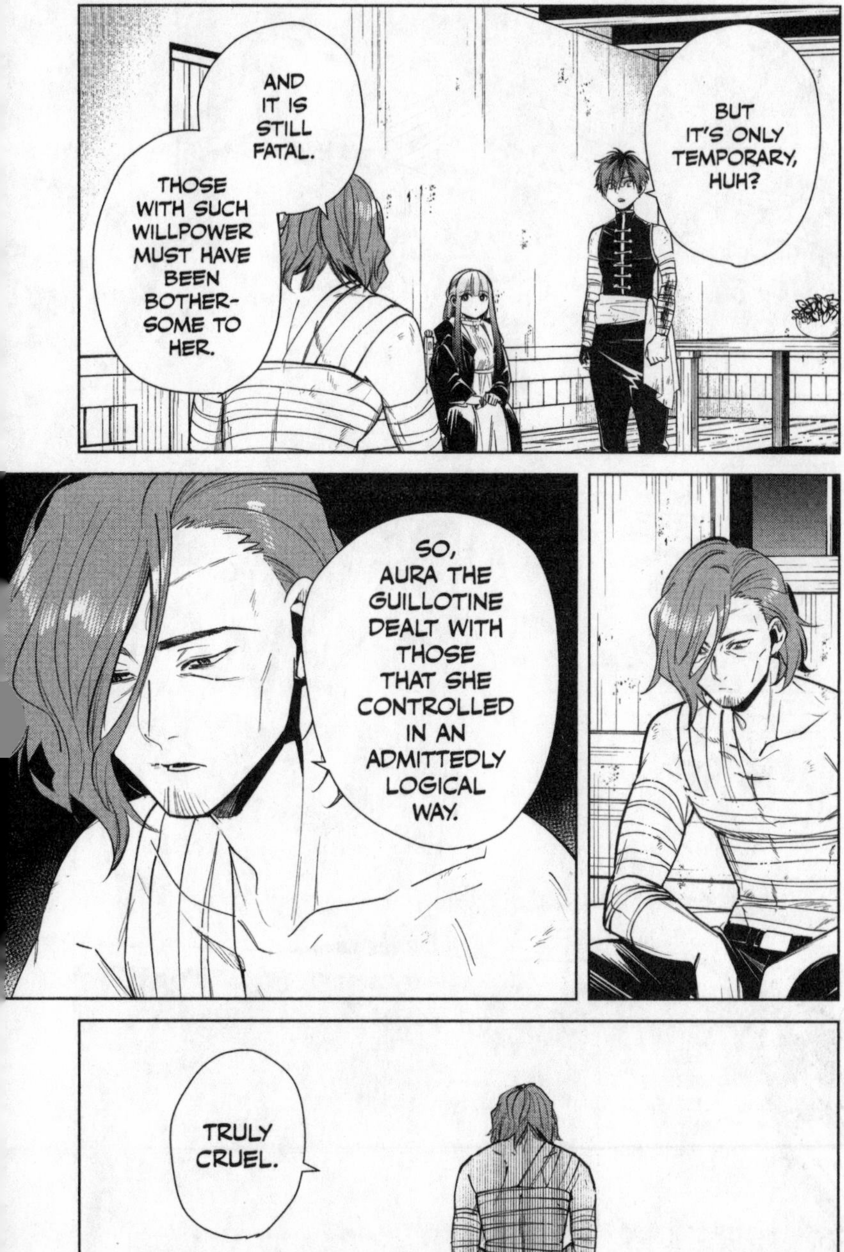
BUT IT'S ONLY TEMPORARY, HUH?
AND IT IS STILL FATAL.
THOSE WITH SUCH WILLPOWER MUST HAVE BEEN BOTHER-SOME TO HER.
SO, AURA THE GUILLOTINE DEALT WITH THOSE THAT SHE CONTROLLED IN AN ADMITTEDLY LOGICAL WAY.
TRULY CRUEL.

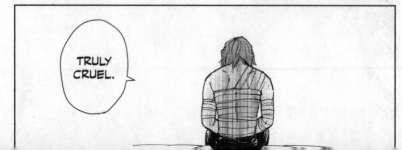

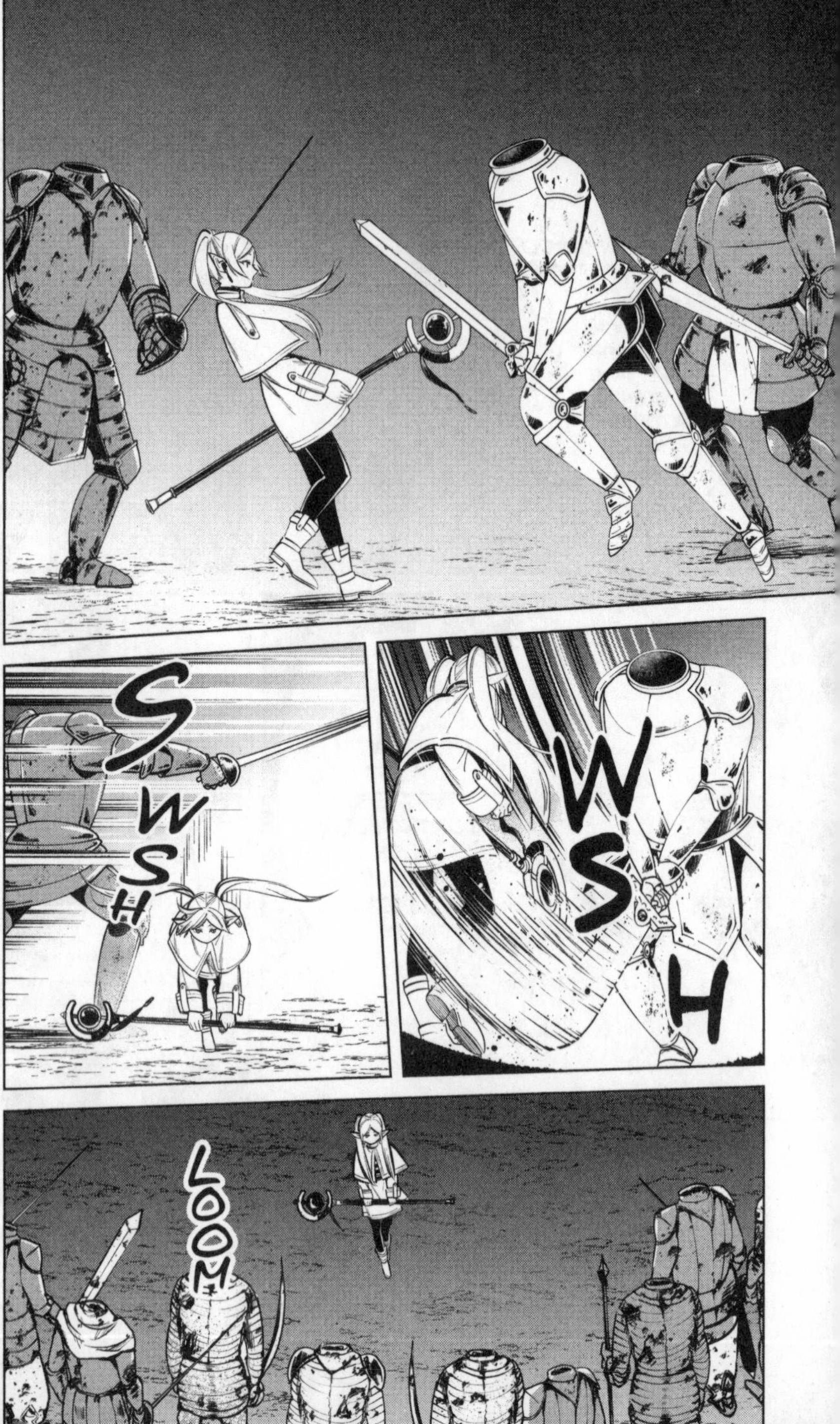
WSH
SWSH
LOOM

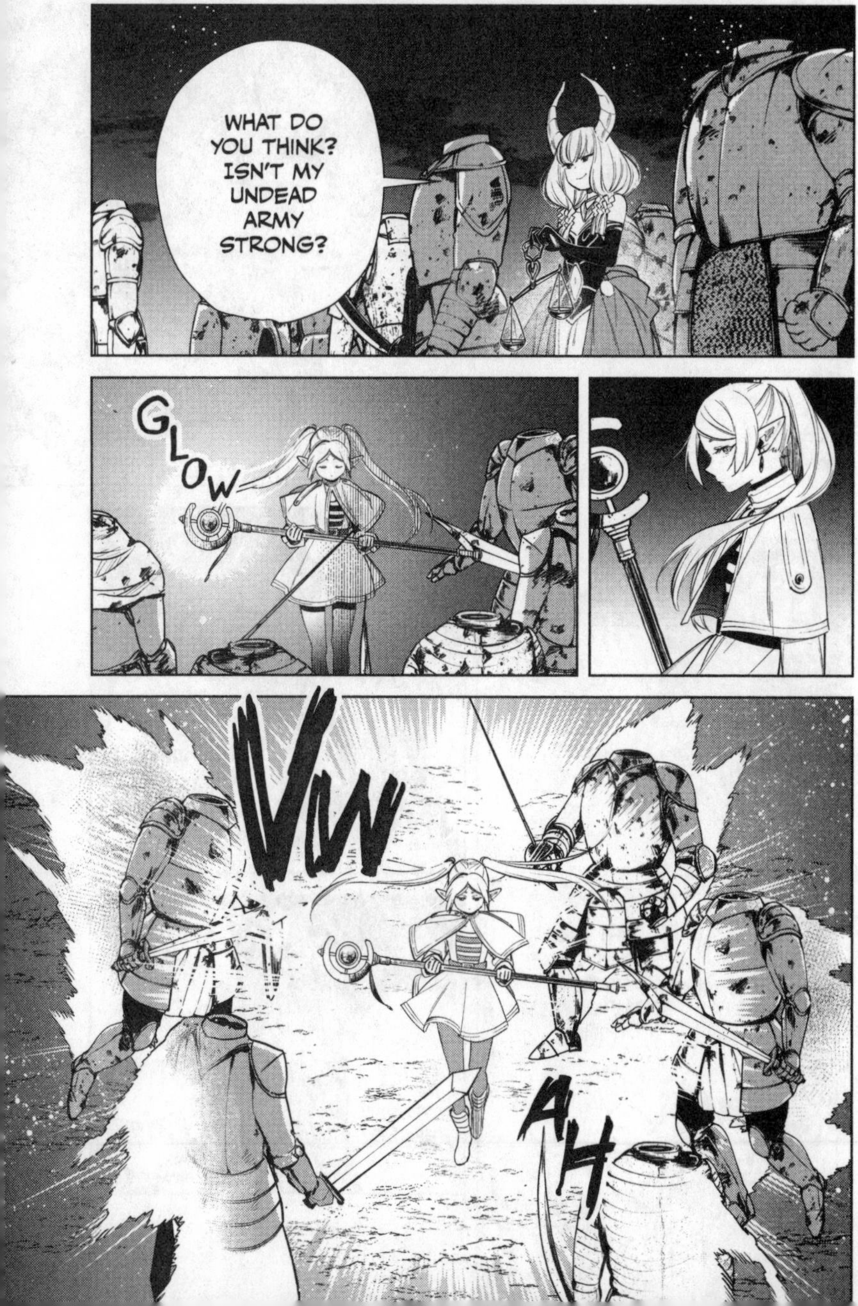
WHAT DO YOU THINK? ISN'T MY UNDEAD ARMY STRONG?
GLOW
VW
AH

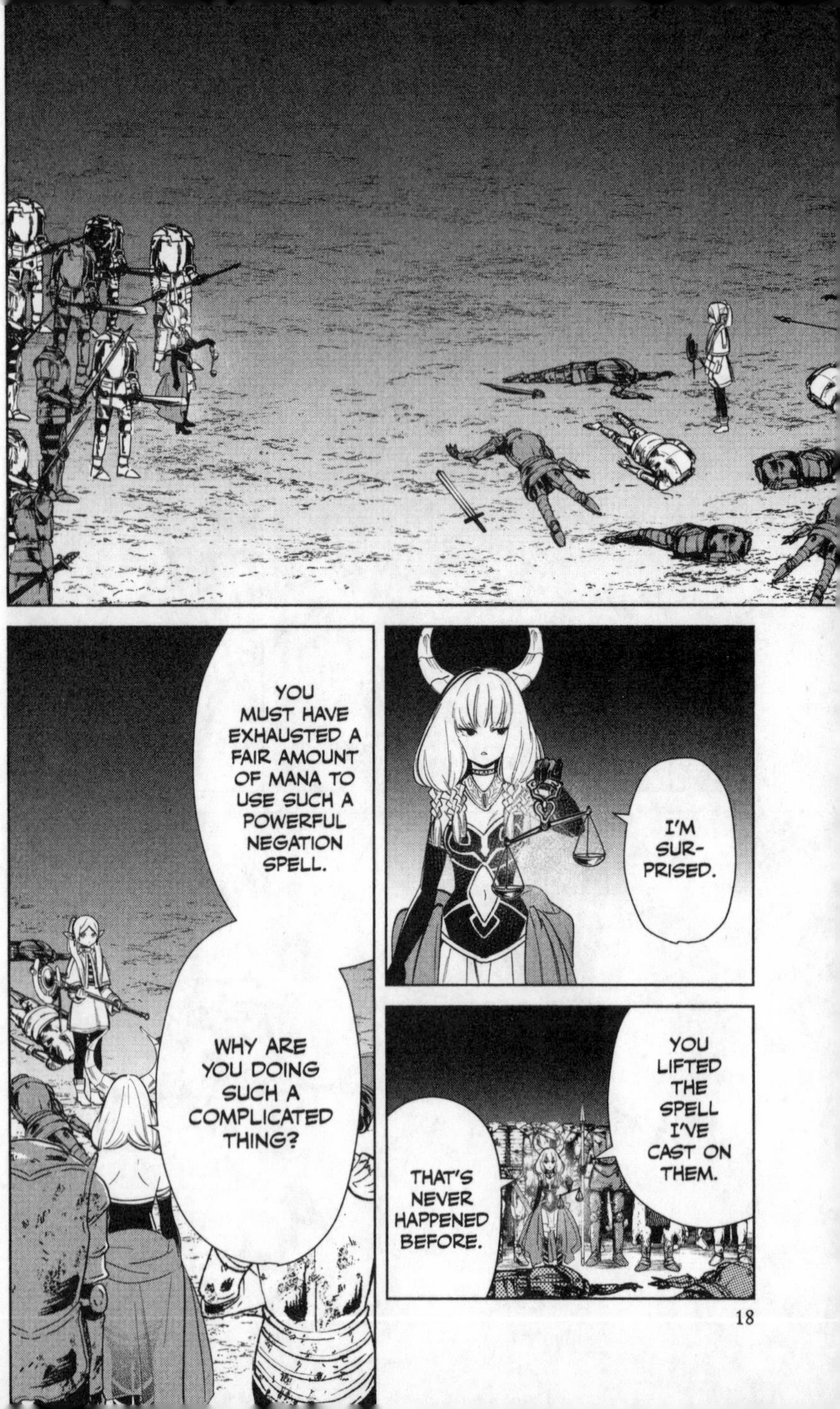
I'M SUR-PRISED.
YOU LIFTED THE SPELL I'VE CAST ON THEM.
THAT'S NEVER HAPPENED BEFORE.
YOU MUST HAVE EXHAUSTED A FAIR AMOUNT OF MANA TO USE SUCH A POWERFUL NEGATION SPELL.
WHY ARE YOU DOING SUCH A COMPLICATED THING?

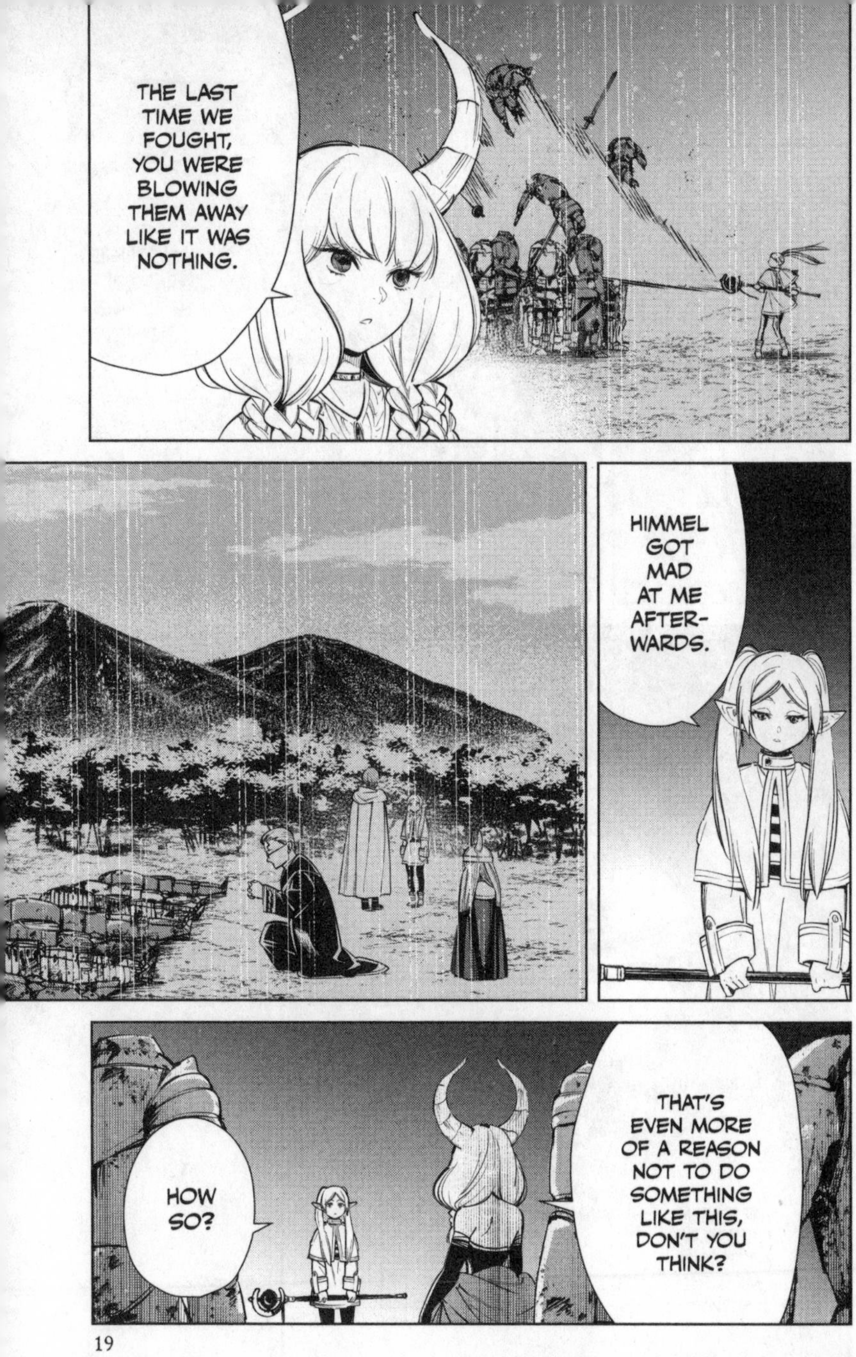
THE LAST TIME WE FOUGHT, YOU WERE BLOWING THEM AWAY LIKE IT WAS NOTHING.
HIMMEL GOT MAD AT ME AFTER-WARDS.
THAT'S EVEN MORE OF A REASON NOT TO DO SOMETHING LIKE THIS, DON'T YOU THINK?
HOW SO?

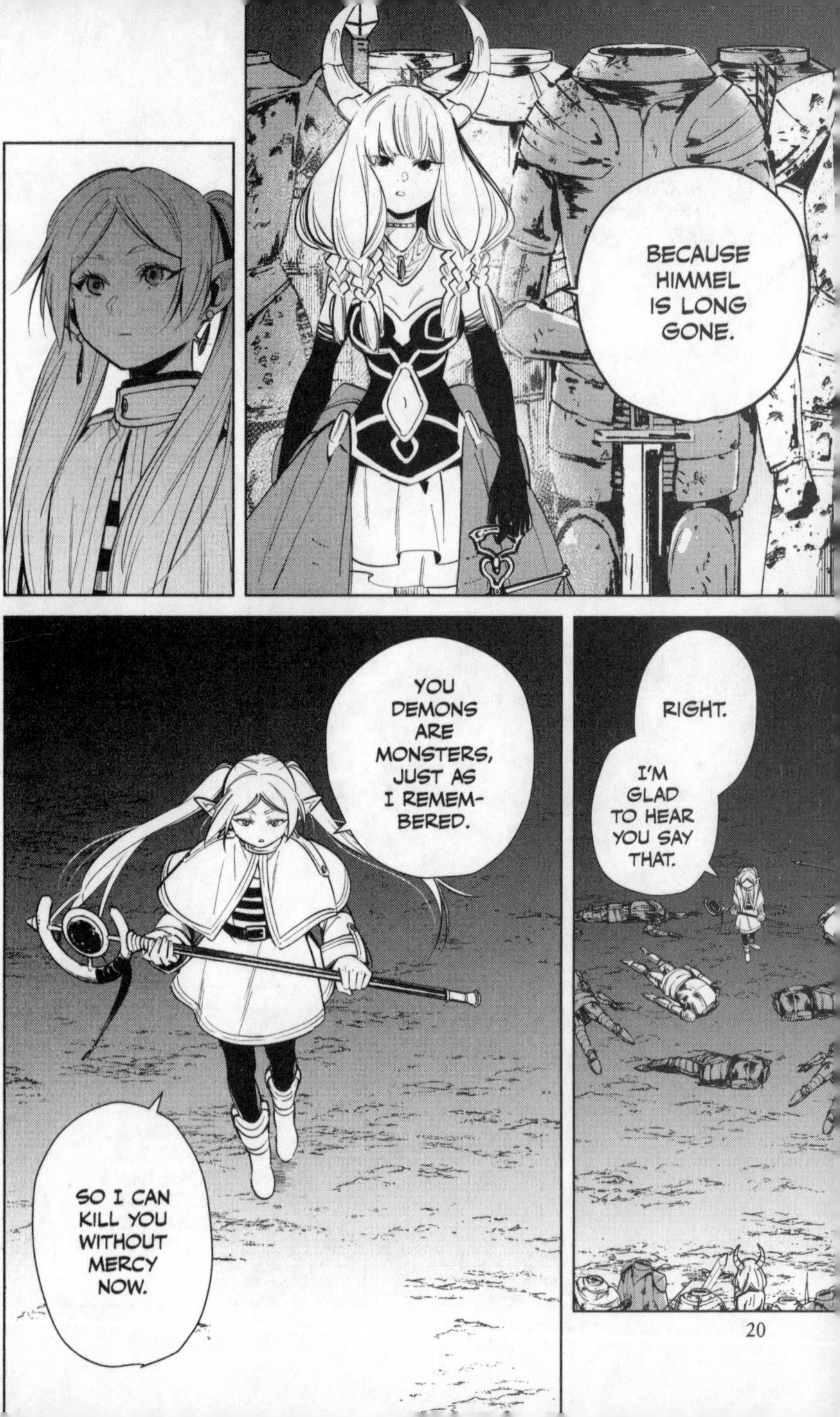
BECAUSE HIMMEL IS LONG GONE.
RIGHT.
I'M GLAD TO HEAR YOU SAY THAT.
YOU DEMONS ARE MONSTERS, JUST AS I REMEM-BERED.
SO I CAN KILL YOU WITHOUT MERCY NOW.

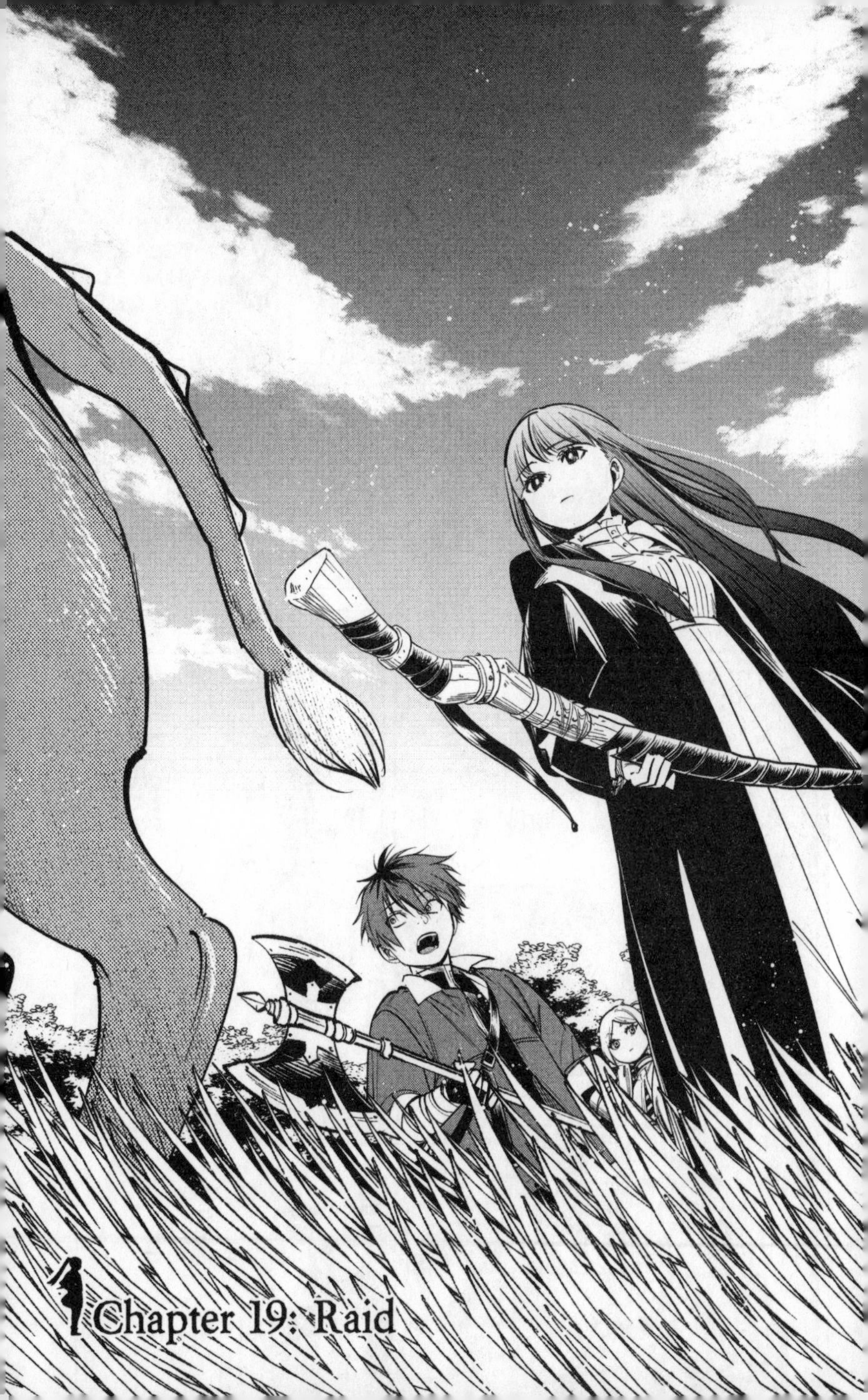
Chapter 19: Raid

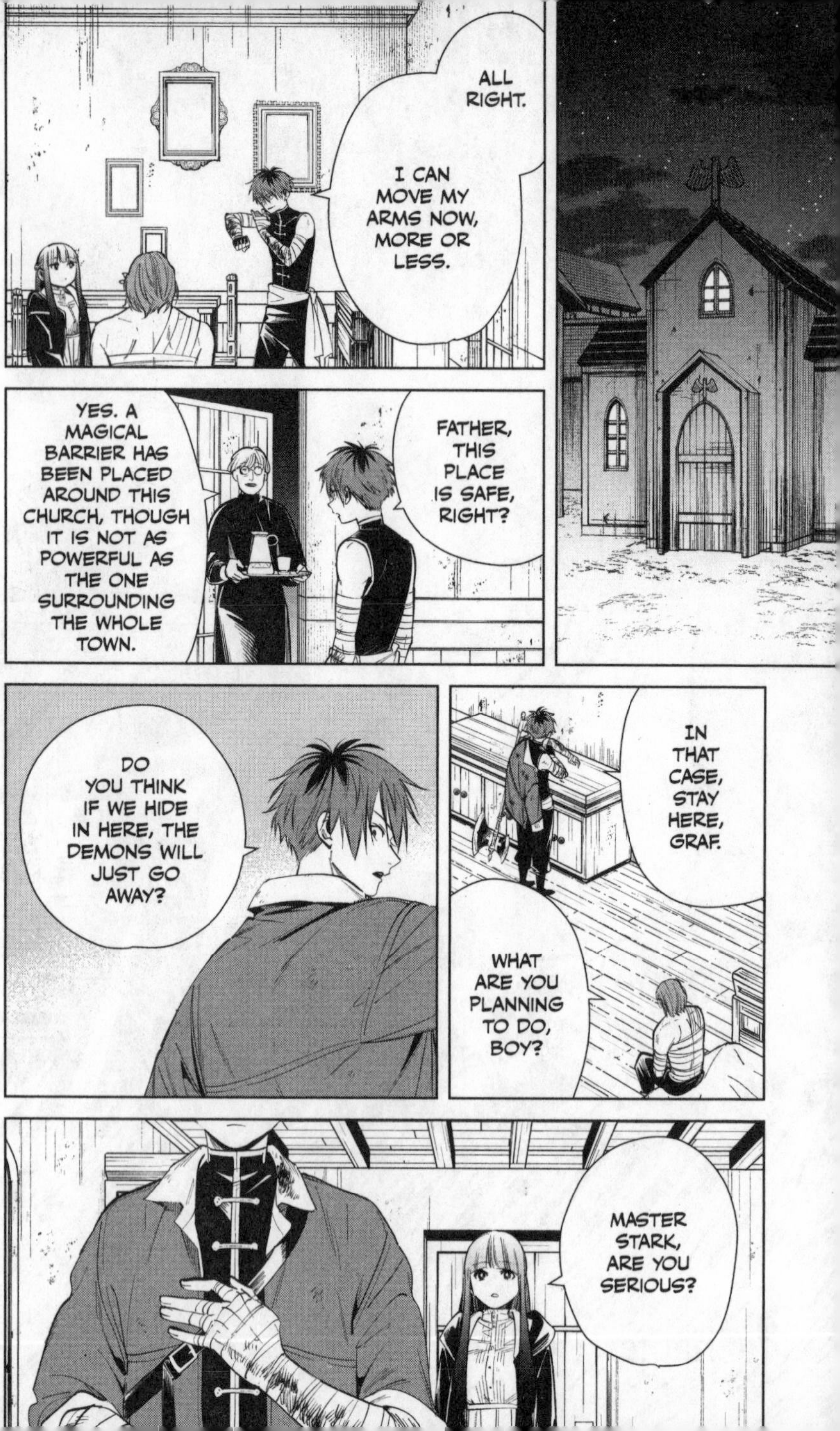
ALL RIGHT.
I CAN MOVE MY ARMS NOW, MORE OR LESS.
FATHER, THIS PLACE IS SAFE, RIGHT?
YES. A MAGICAL BARRIER HAS BEEN PLACED AROUND THIS CHURCH, THOUGH IT IS NOT AS POWERFUL AS THE ONE SURROUNDING THE WHOLE TOWN.
IN THAT CASE, STAY HERE, GRAF.
WHAT ARE YOU PLANNING TO DO, BOY?
DO YOU THINK IF WE HIDE IN HERE, THE DEMONS WILL JUST GO AWAY?
MASTER STARK, ARE YOU SERIOUS?

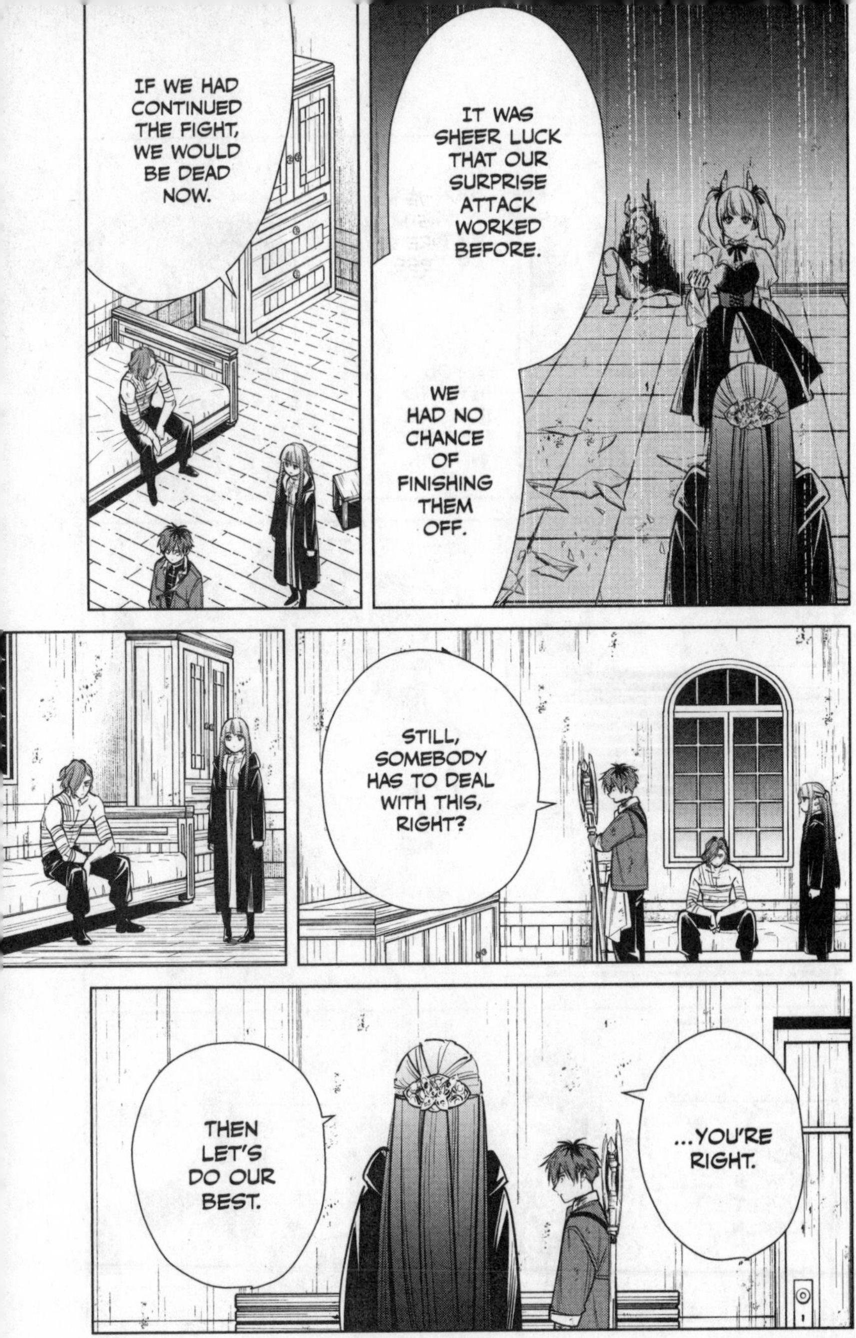
IT WAS SHEER LUCK THAT OUR SURPRISE ATTACK WORKED BEFORE.
WE HAD NO CHANCE OF FINISHING THEM OFF.
IF WE HAD CONTINUED THE FIGHT, WE WOULD BE DEAD NOW.
STILL, SOMEBODY HAS TO DEAL WITH THIS, RIGHT?
...YOU'RE RIGHT.
THEN LET'S DO OUR BEST.

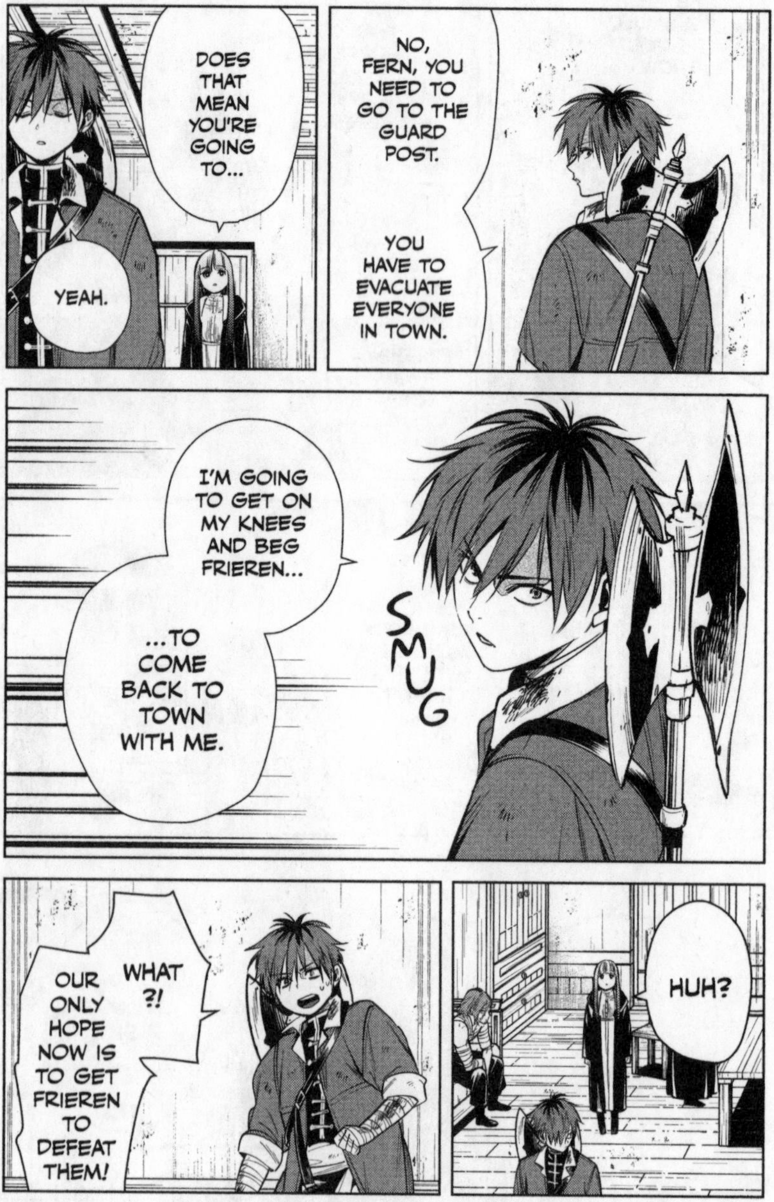
NO, FERN, YOU NEED TO GO TO THE GUARD POST.
YOU HAVE TO EVACUATE EVERYONE IN TOWN.
DOES THAT MEAN YOU'RE GOING TO...
YEAH.
I'M GOING TO GET ON MY KNEES AND BEG FRIEREN...
...TO COME BACK TO TOWN WITH ME.
SMUG
HUH?
WHAT?!
OUR ONLY HOPE NOW IS TO GET FRIEREN TO DEFEAT THEM!

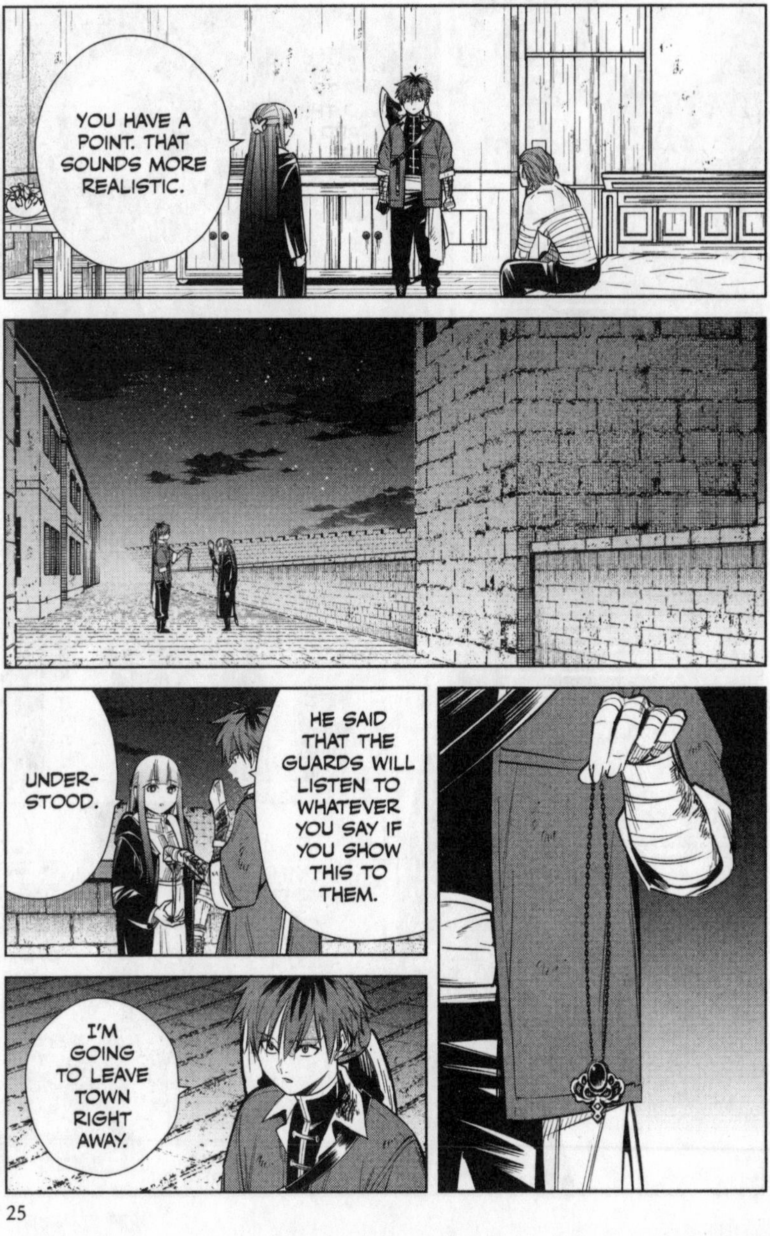
YOU HAVE A POINT. THAT SOUNDS MORE REALISTIC.
HE SAID THAT THE GUARDS WILL LISTEN TO WHATEVER YOU SAY IF YOU SHOW THIS TO THEM.
UNDER-STOOD.
I'M GOING TO LEAVE TOWN RIGHT AWAY.

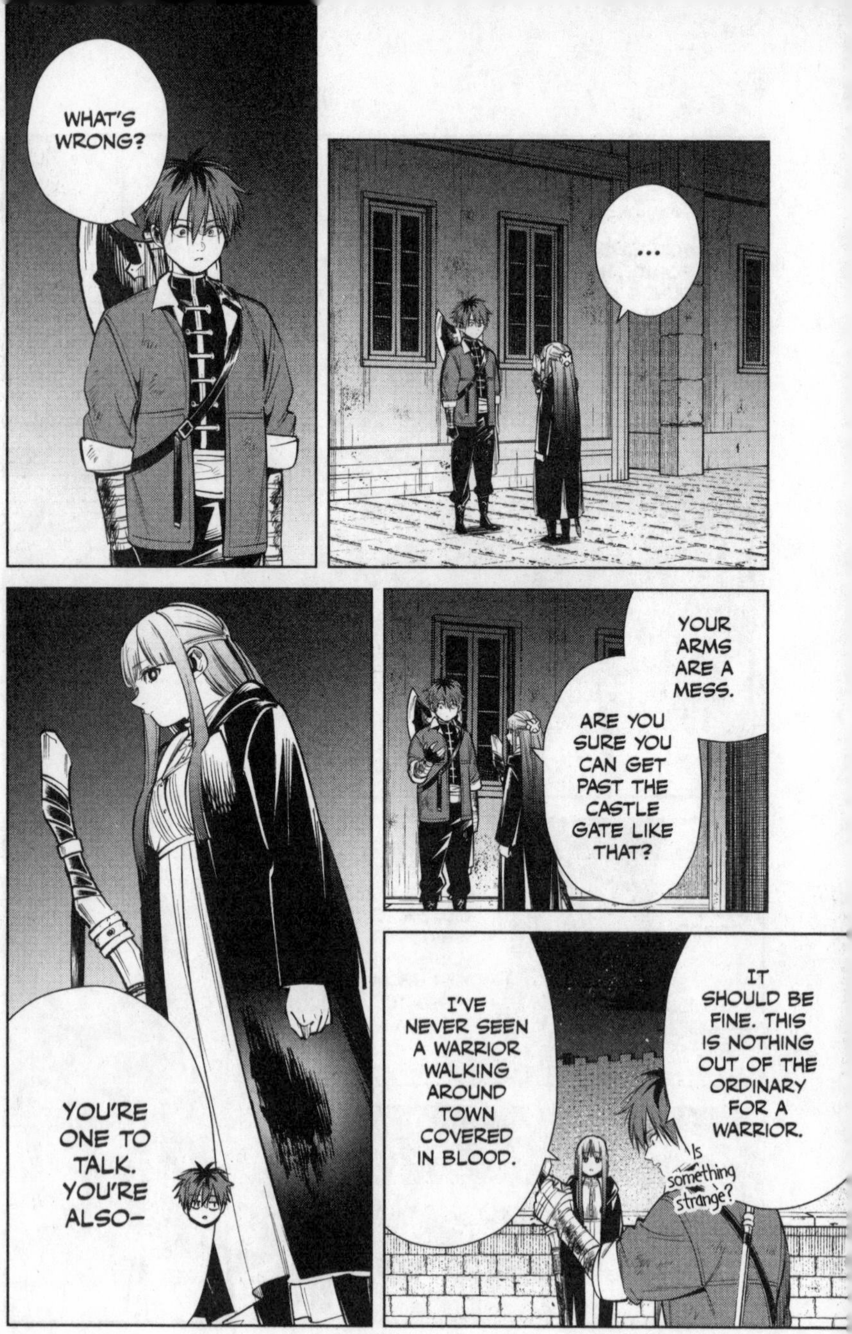
...
WHAT'S WRONG?
YOUR ARMS ARE A MESS.
ARE YOU SURE YOU CAN GET PAST THE CASTLE GATE LIKE THAT?
IT SHOULD BE FINE. THIS IS NOTHING OUT OF THE ORDINARY FOR A WARRIOR.
Is something strange?
I'VE NEVER SEEN A WARRIOR WALKING AROUND TOWN COVERED IN BLOOD.
YOU'RE ONE TO TALK. YOU'RE ALSO—

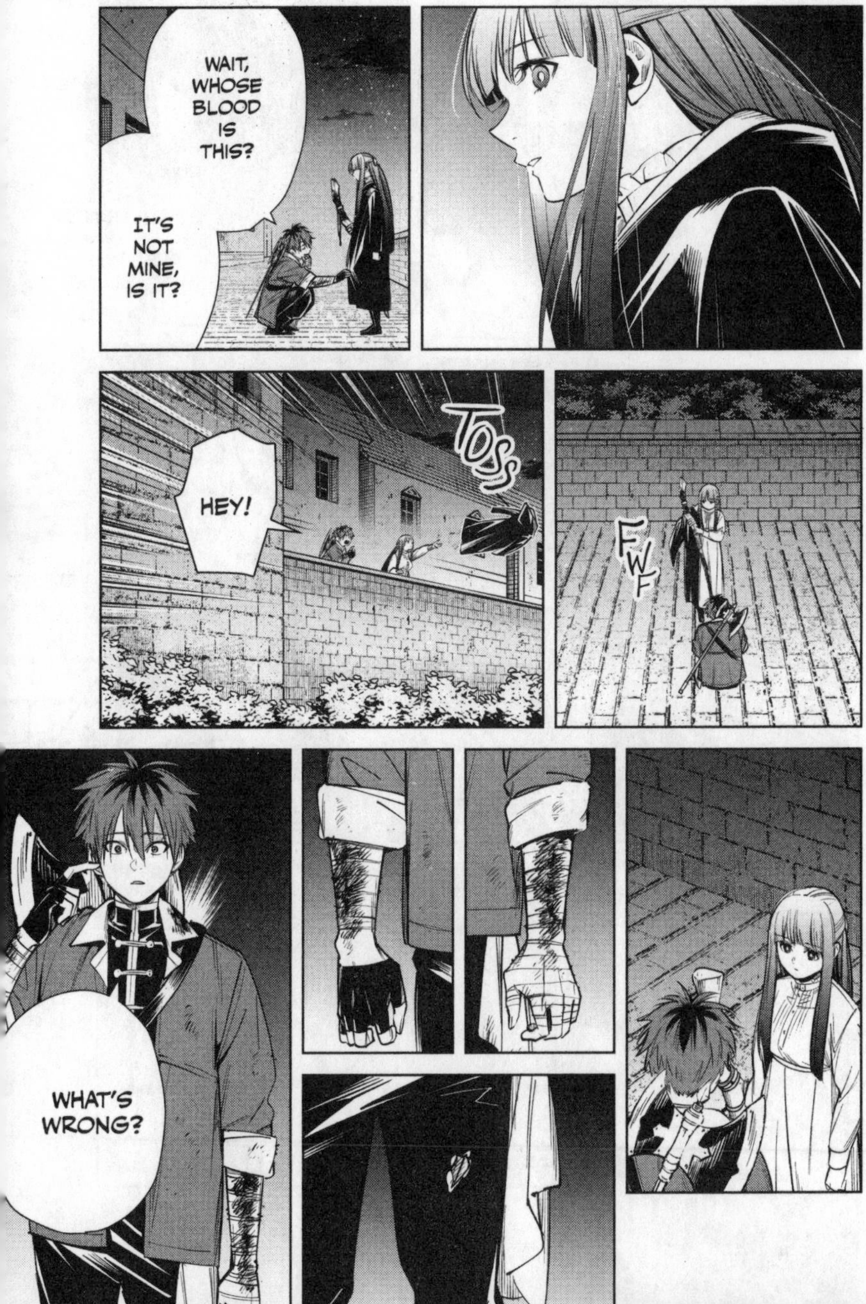
WAIT, WHOSE BLOOD IS THIS?
IT'S NOT MINE, IS IT?
FWF
TOSS
HEY!
WHAT'S WRONG?

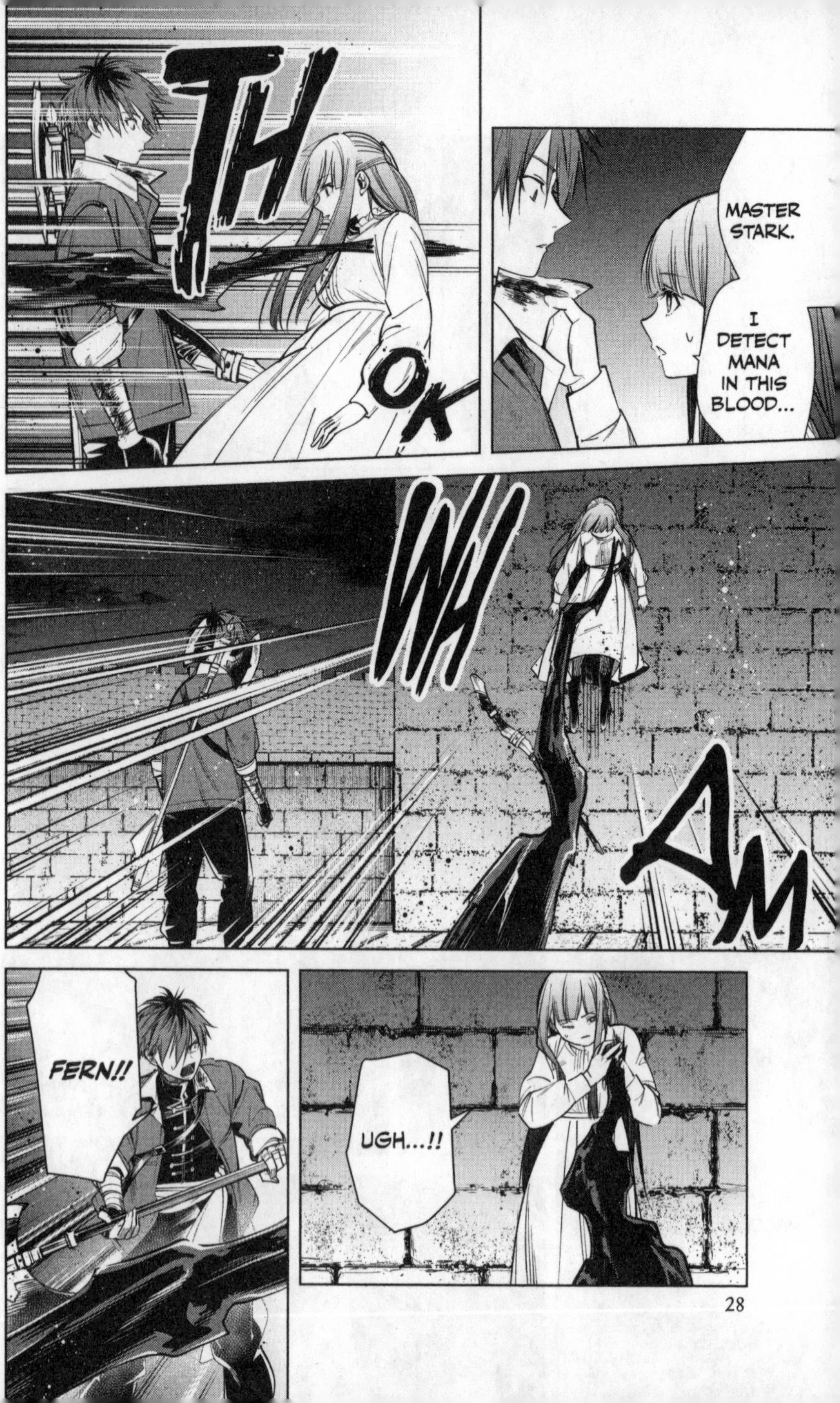
MASTER STARK.
I DETECT MANA IN THIS BLOOD...
THOK
WHAM
UGH...!!
FERN!!

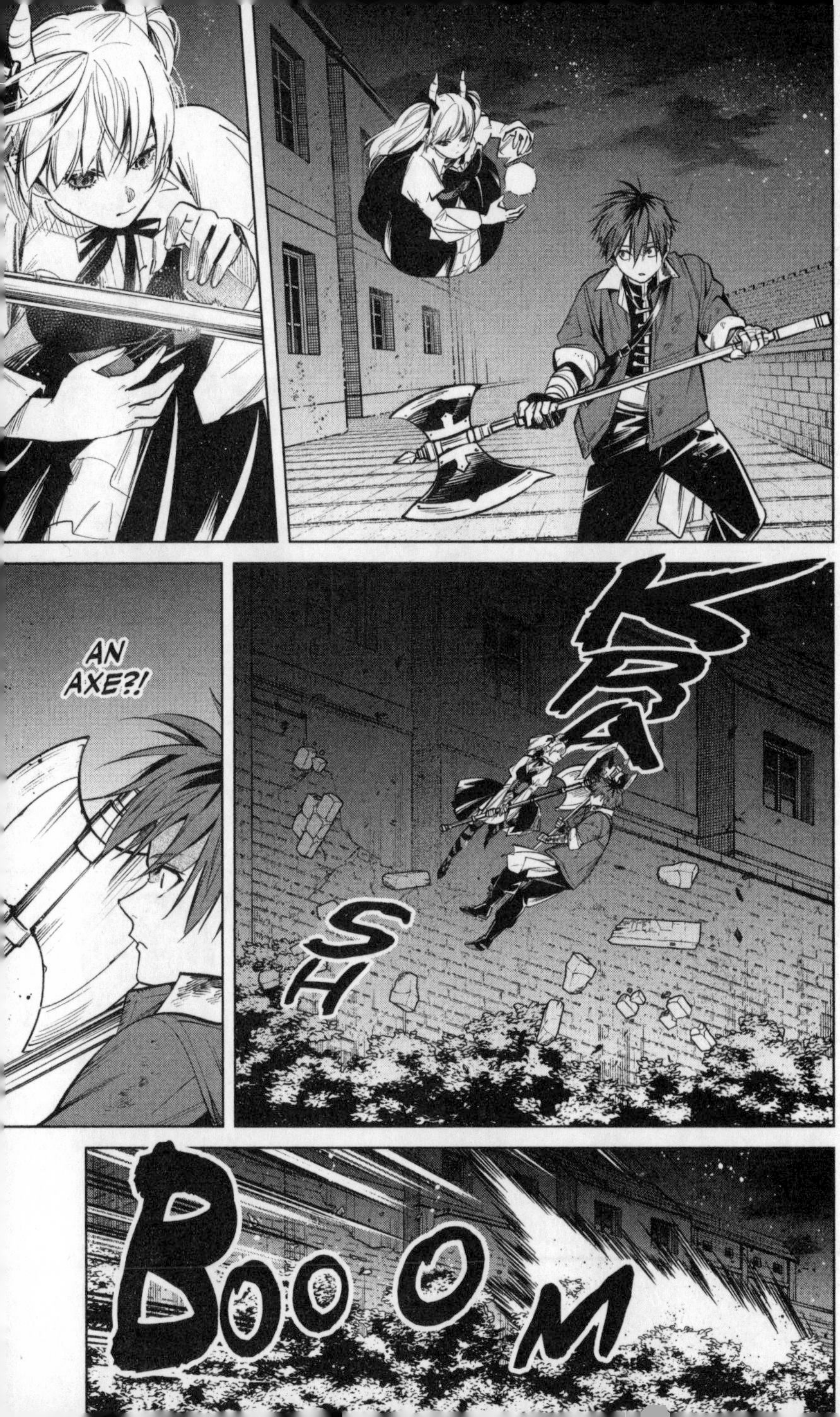
KRASH
AN AXE?!
BOOOM

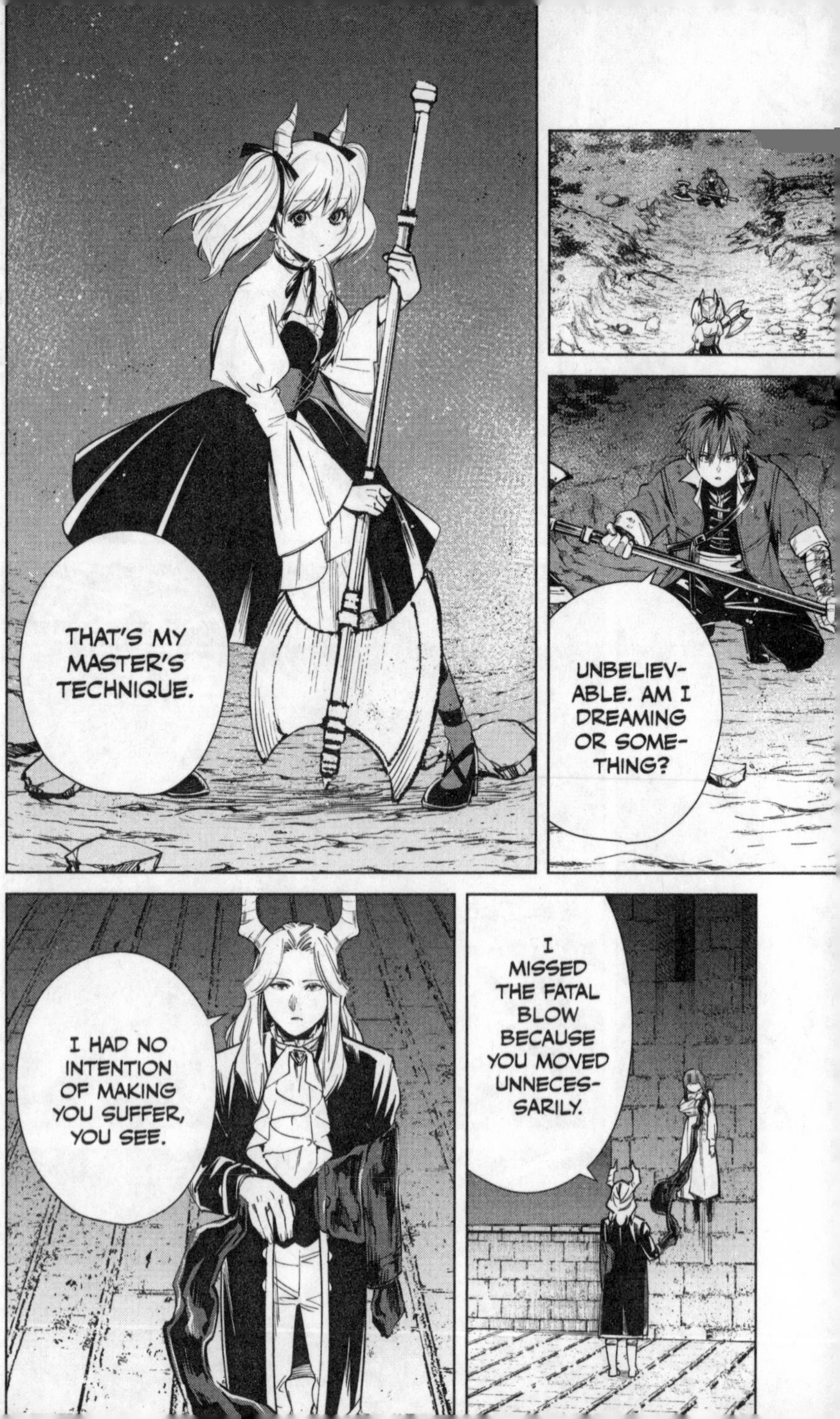
UNBELIEV-ABLE. AM I DREAMING OR SOME-THING?
THAT'S MY MASTER'S TECHNIQUE.
I MISSED THE FATAL BLOW BECAUSE YOU MOVED UNNECES-SARILY.
I HAD NO INTENTION OF MAKING YOU SUFFER, YOU SEE.

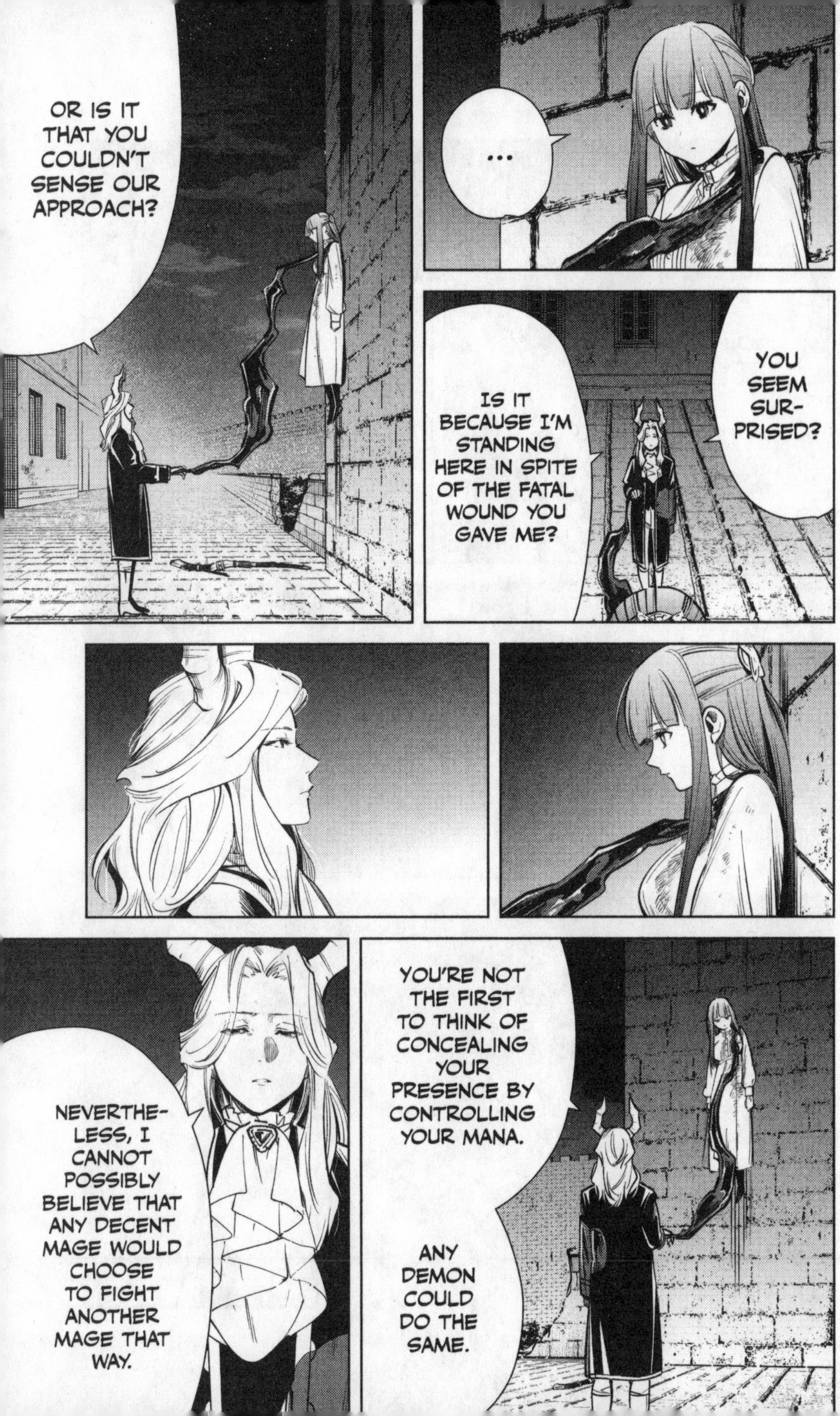
...
YOU SEEM SURPRISED?
IS IT BECAUSE I'M STANDING HERE IN SPITE OF THE FATAL WOUND YOU GAVE ME?
OR IS IT THAT YOU COULDN'T SENSE OUR APPROACH?
YOU'RE NOT THE FIRST TO THINK OF CONCEALING YOUR PRESENCE BY CONTROLLING YOUR MANA.
ANY DEMON COULD DO THE SAME.
NEVERTHELESS, I CANNOT POSSIBLY BELIEVE THAT ANY DECENT MAGE WOULD CHOOSE TO FIGHT ANOTHER MAGE THAT WAY.

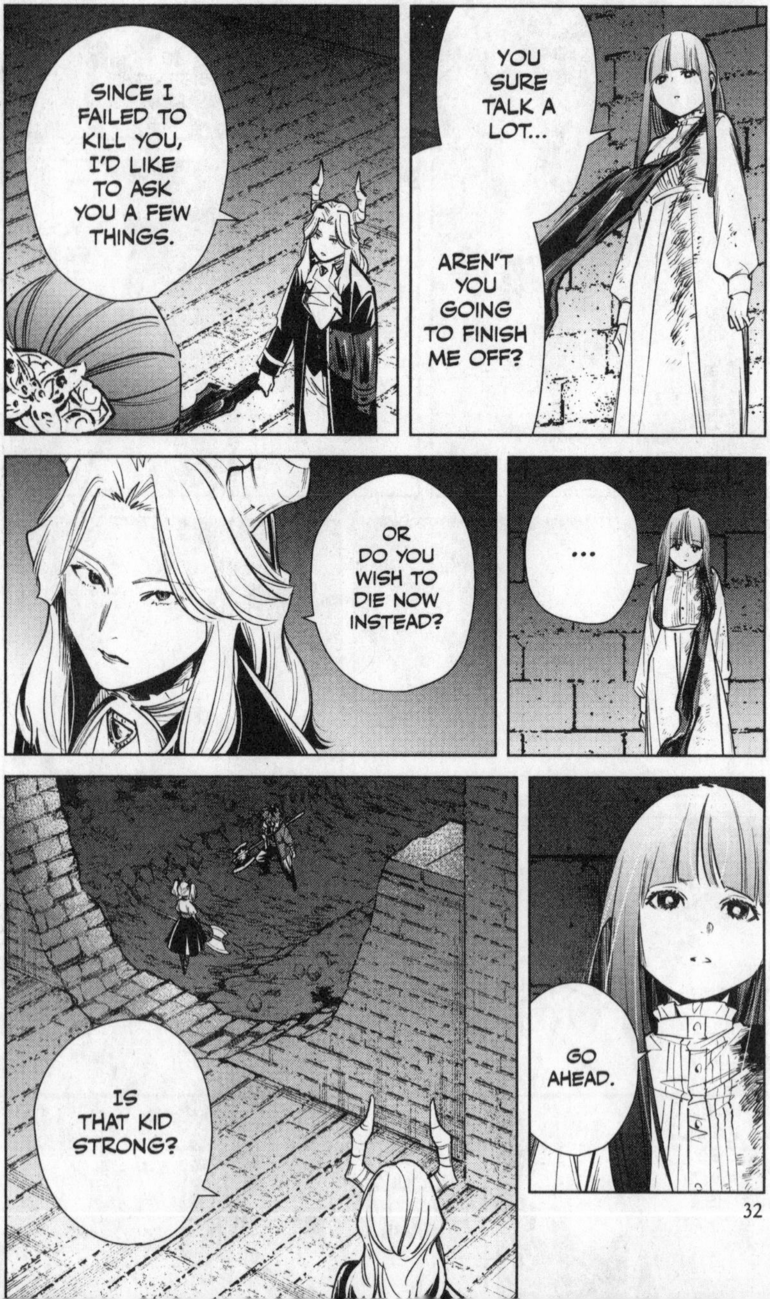
YOU SURE TALK A LOT...
AREN'T YOU GOING TO FINISH ME OFF?
SINCE I FAILED TO KILL YOU, I'D LIKE TO ASK YOU A FEW THINGS.
...
OR DO YOU WISH TO DIE NOW INSTEAD?
GO AHEAD.
IS THAT KID STRONG?

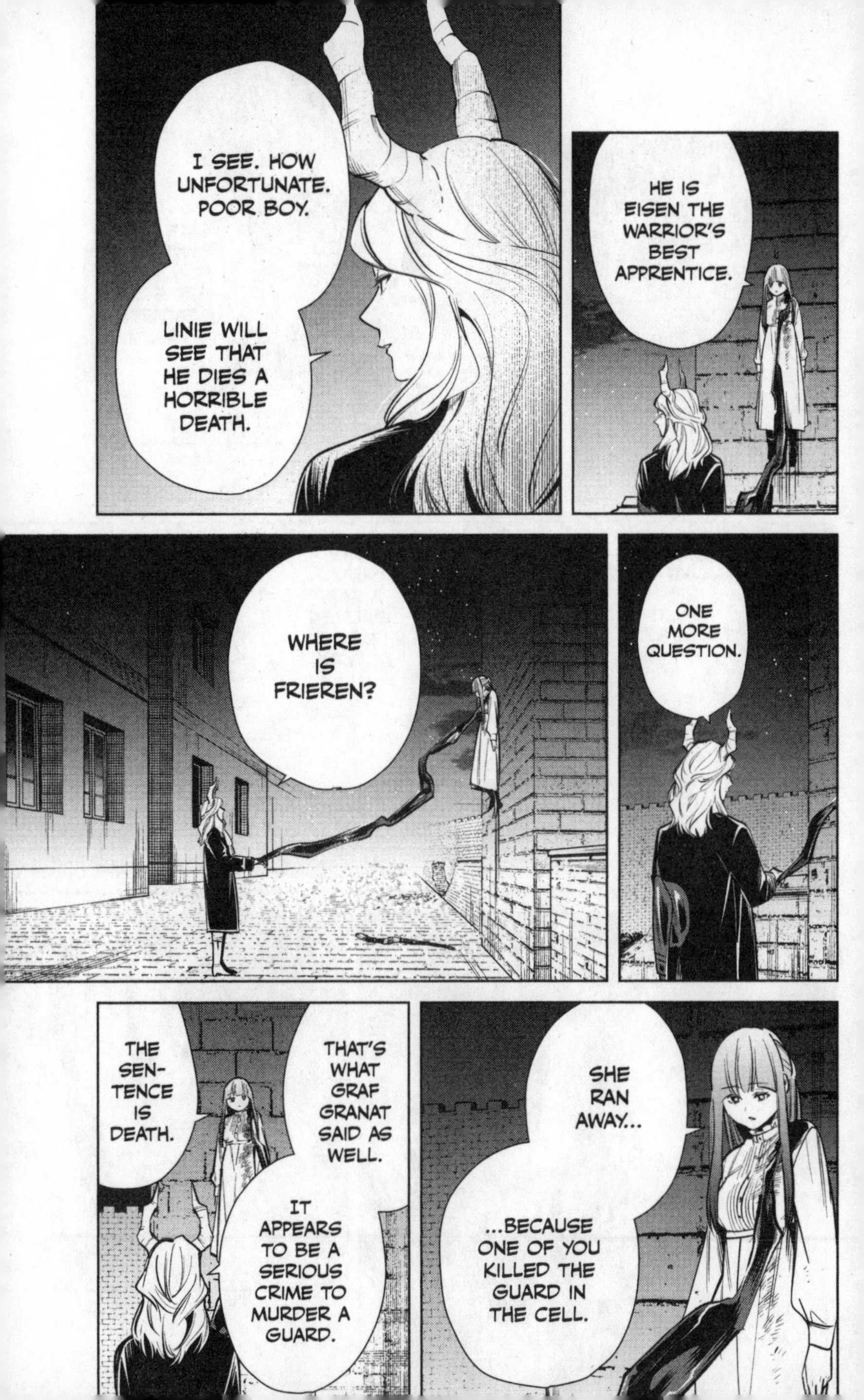
HE IS EISEN THE WARRIOR'S BEST APPRENTICE.
I SEE. HOW UNFORTUNATE. POOR BOY.
LINIE WILL SEE THAT HE DIES A HORRIBLE DEATH.
ONE MORE QUESTION.
WHERE IS FRIEREN?
SHE RAN AWAY...
...BECAUSE ONE OF YOU KILLED THE GUARD IN THE CELL.
THAT'S WHAT GRAF GRANAT SAID AS WELL.
IT APPEARS TO BE A SERIOUS CRIME TO MURDER A GUARD.
THE SEN-TENCE IS DEATH.

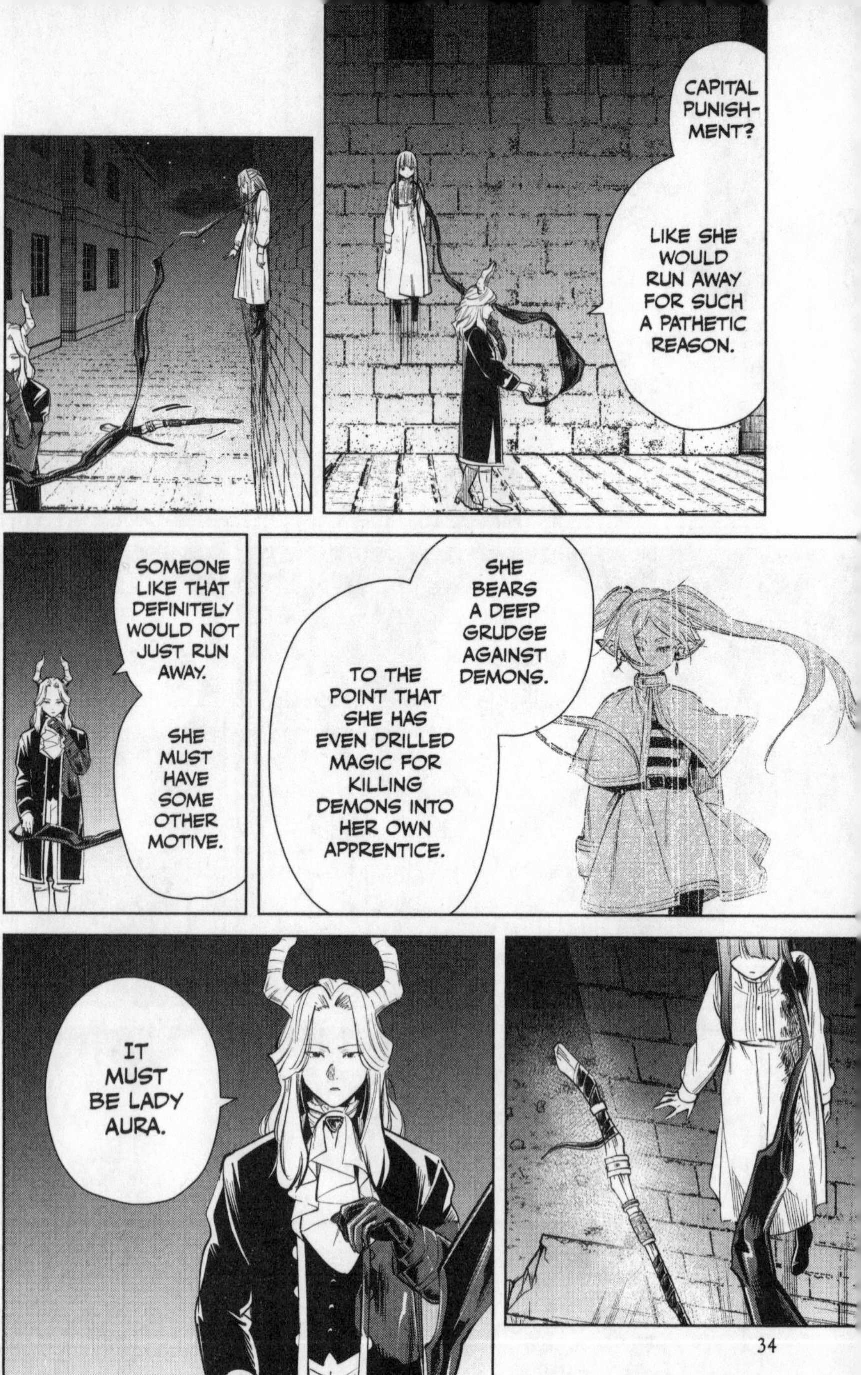
CAPITAL PUNISHMENT?
LIKE SHE WOULD RUN AWAY FOR SUCH A PATHETIC REASON.
SHE BEARS A DEEP GRUDGE AGAINST DEMONS.
TO THE POINT THAT SHE HAS EVEN DRILLED MAGIC FOR KILLING DEMONS INTO HER OWN APPRENTICE.
SOMEONE LIKE THAT DEFINITELY WOULD NOT JUST RUN AWAY.
SHE MUST HAVE SOME OTHER MOTIVE.
IT MUST BE LADY AURA.

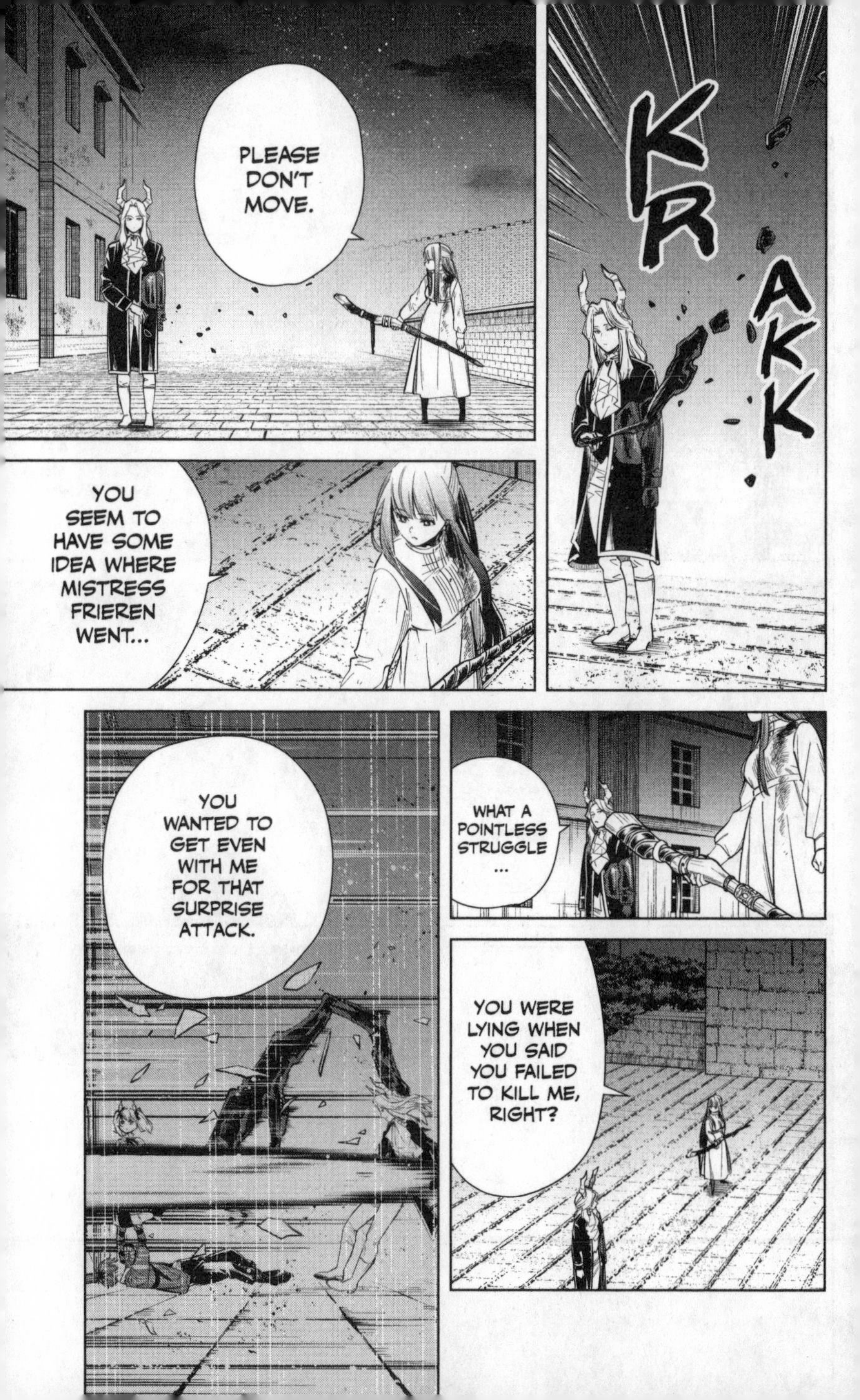
KRAKK
PLEASE DON'T MOVE.
YOU SEEM TO HAVE SOME IDEA WHERE MISTRESS FRIEREN WENT...
WHAT A POINTLESS STRUGGLE ...
YOU WERE LYING WHEN YOU SAID YOU FAILED TO KILL ME, RIGHT?
YOU WANTED TO GET EVEN WITH ME FOR THAT SURPRISE ATTACK.

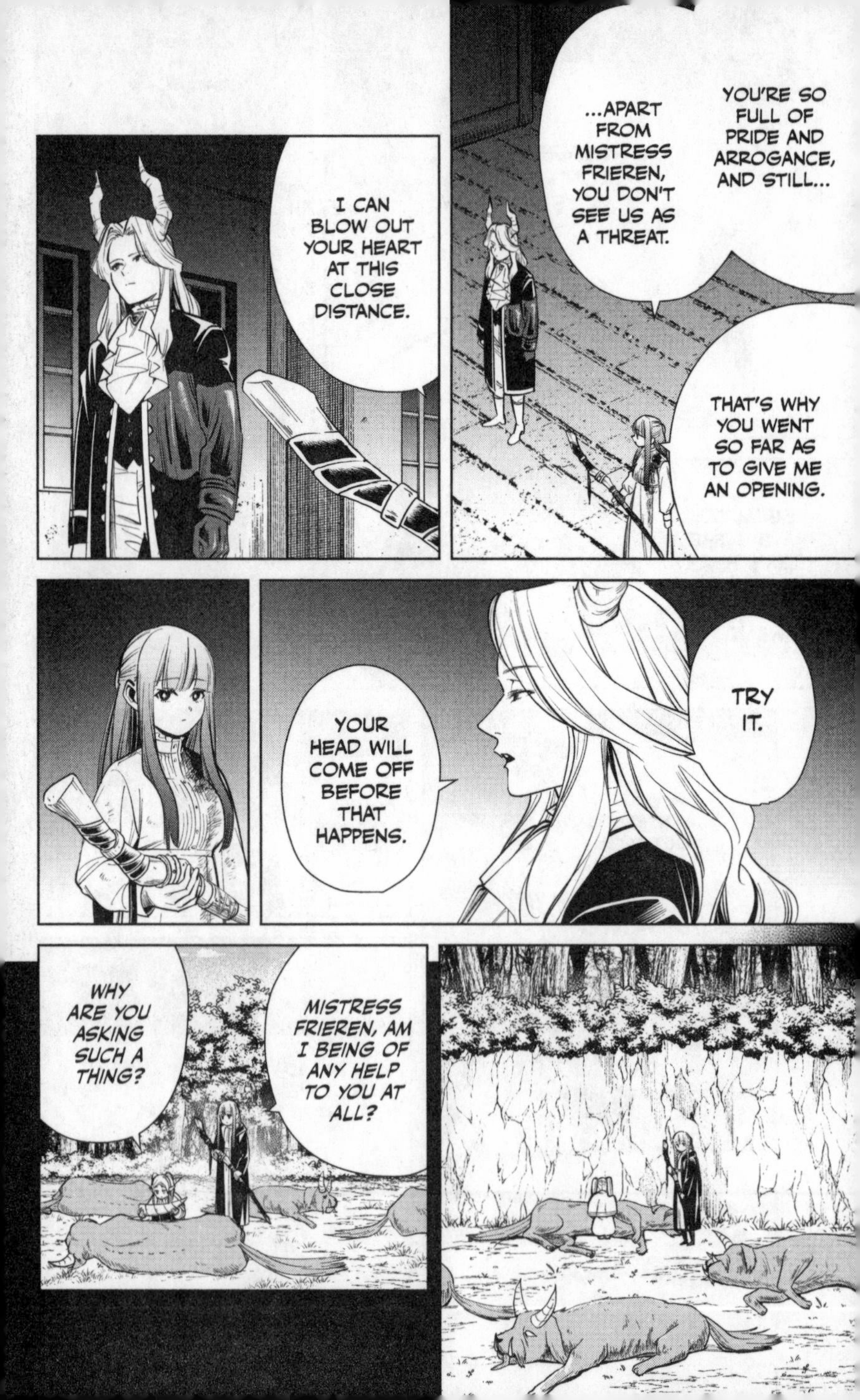
YOU'RE SO FULL OF PRIDE AND ARROGANCE, AND STILL...
...APART FROM MISTRESS FRIEREN, YOU DON'T SEE US AS A THREAT.
THAT'S WHY YOU WENT SO FAR AS TO GIVE ME AN OPENING.
I CAN BLOW OUT YOUR HEART AT THIS CLOSE DISTANCE.
TRY IT.
YOUR HEAD WILL COME OFF BEFORE THAT HAPPENS.
MISTRESS FRIEREN, AM I BEING OF ANY HELP TO YOU AT ALL?
WHY ARE YOU ASKING SUCH A THING?

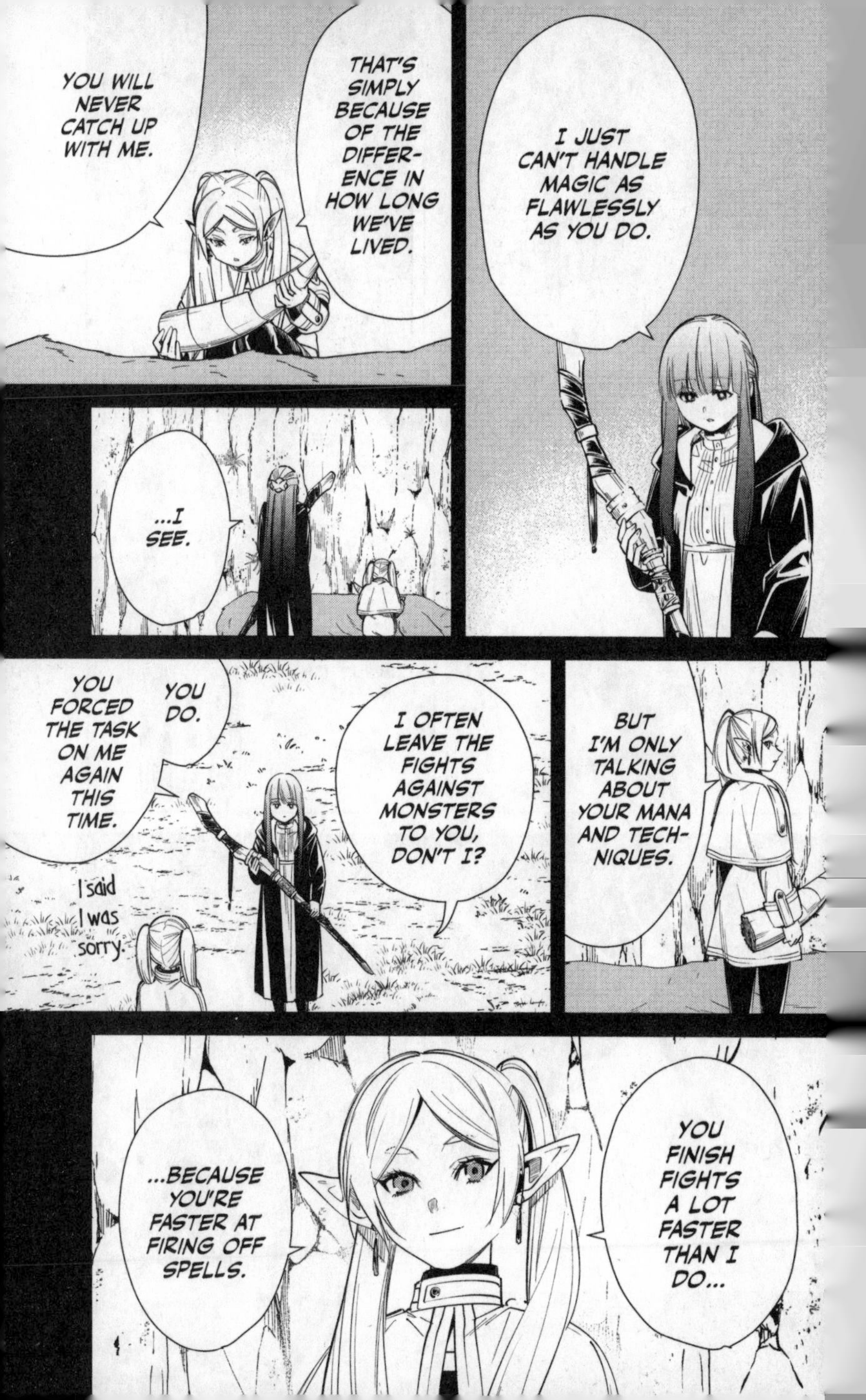
I JUST CAN'T HANDLE MAGIC AS FLAWLESSLY AS YOU DO.
THAT'S SIMPLY BECAUSE OF THE DIFFER-ENCE IN HOW LONG WE'VE LIVED.
YOU WILL NEVER CATCH UP WITH ME.
...I SEE.
BUT I'M ONLY TALKING ABOUT YOUR MANA AND TECH-NIQUES.
I OFTEN LEAVE THE FIGHTS AGAINST MONSTERS TO YOU, DON'T I?
YOU DO.
YOU FORCED THE TASK ON ME AGAIN THIS TIME.
I said I was sorry.
YOU FINISH FIGHTS A LOT FASTER THAN I DO...
...BECAUSE YOU'RE FASTER AT FIRING OFF SPELLS.

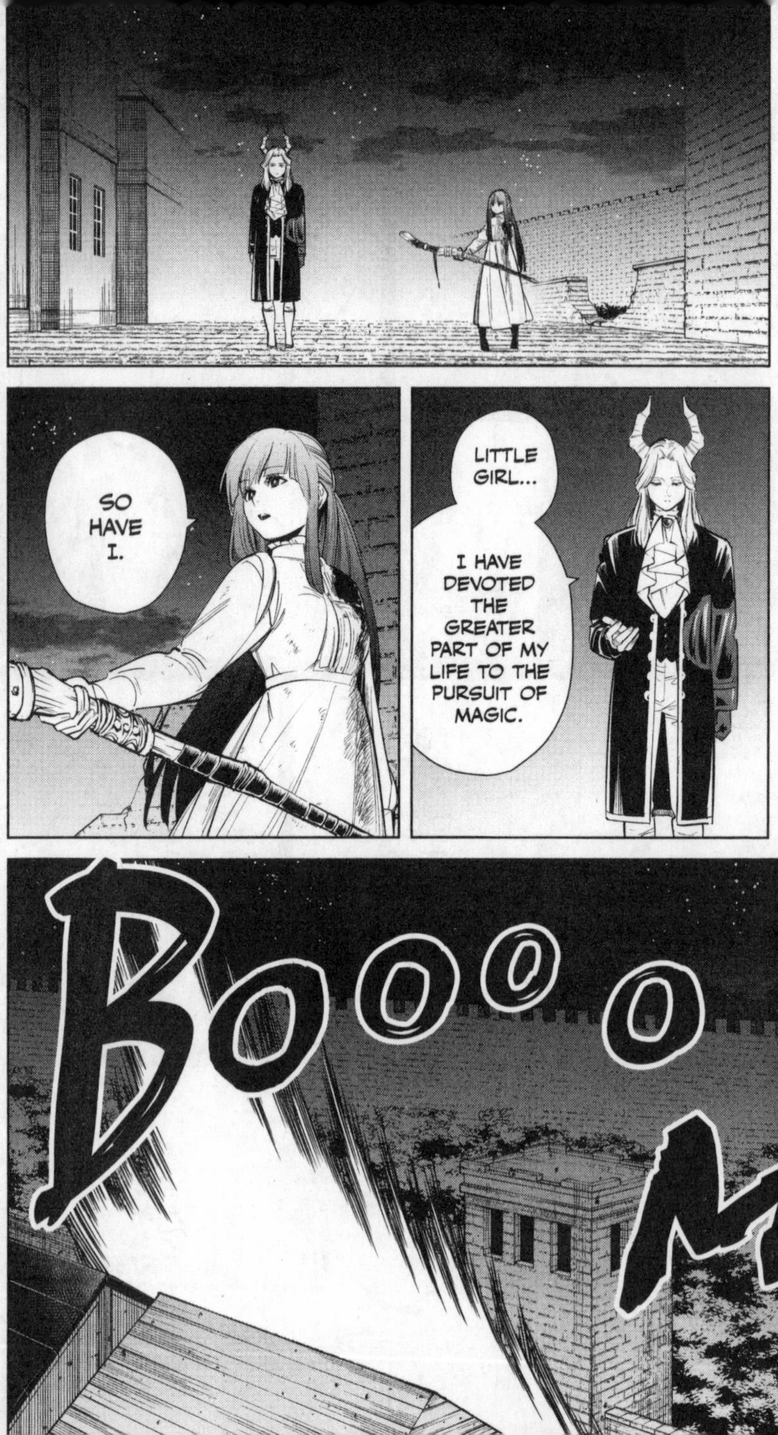
LITTLE GIRL...
I HAVE DEVOTED THE GREATER PART OF MY LIFE TO THE PURSUIT OF MAGIC.
SO HAVE I.
BOOOOM

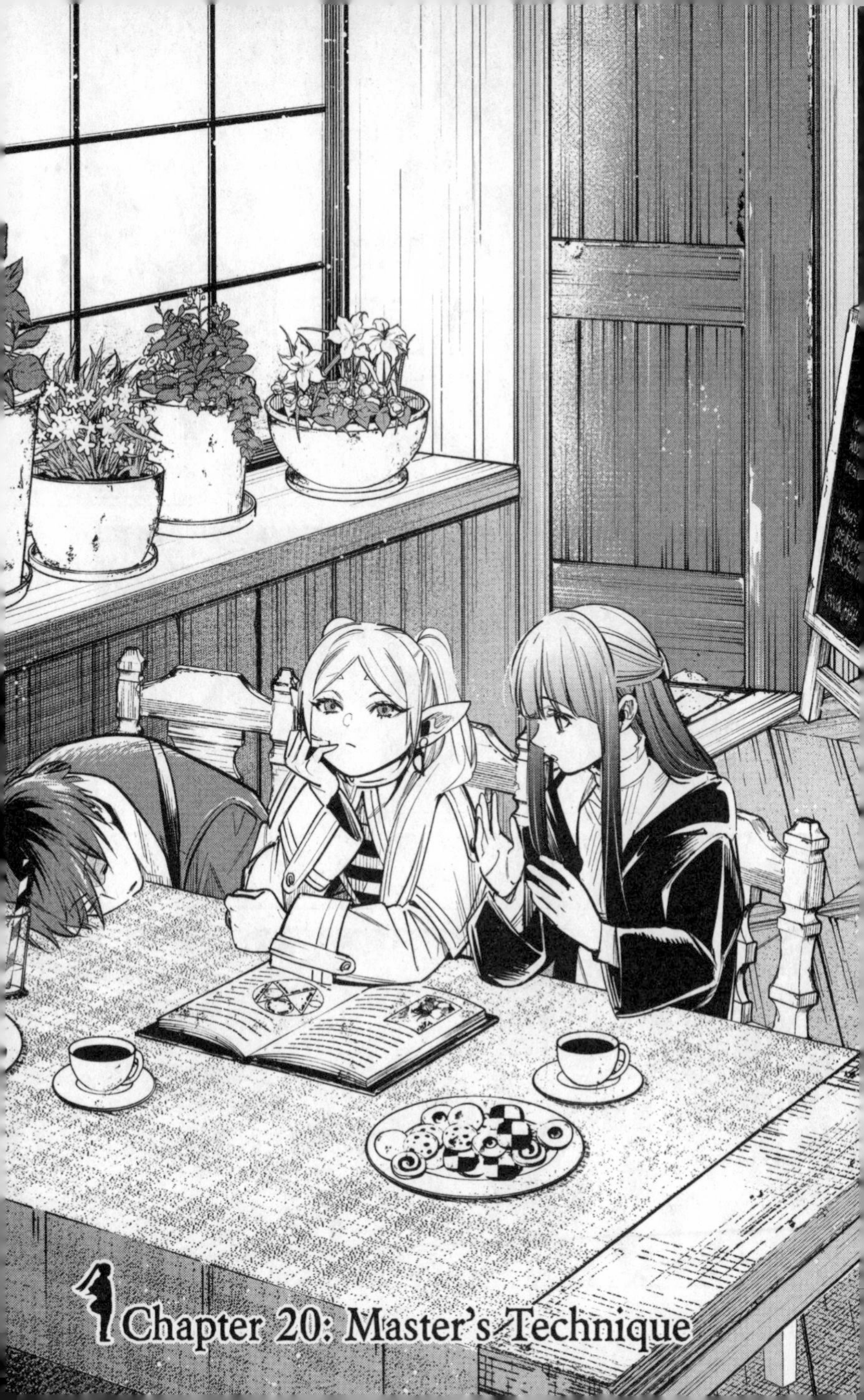

# Chapter 20: Master's Technique

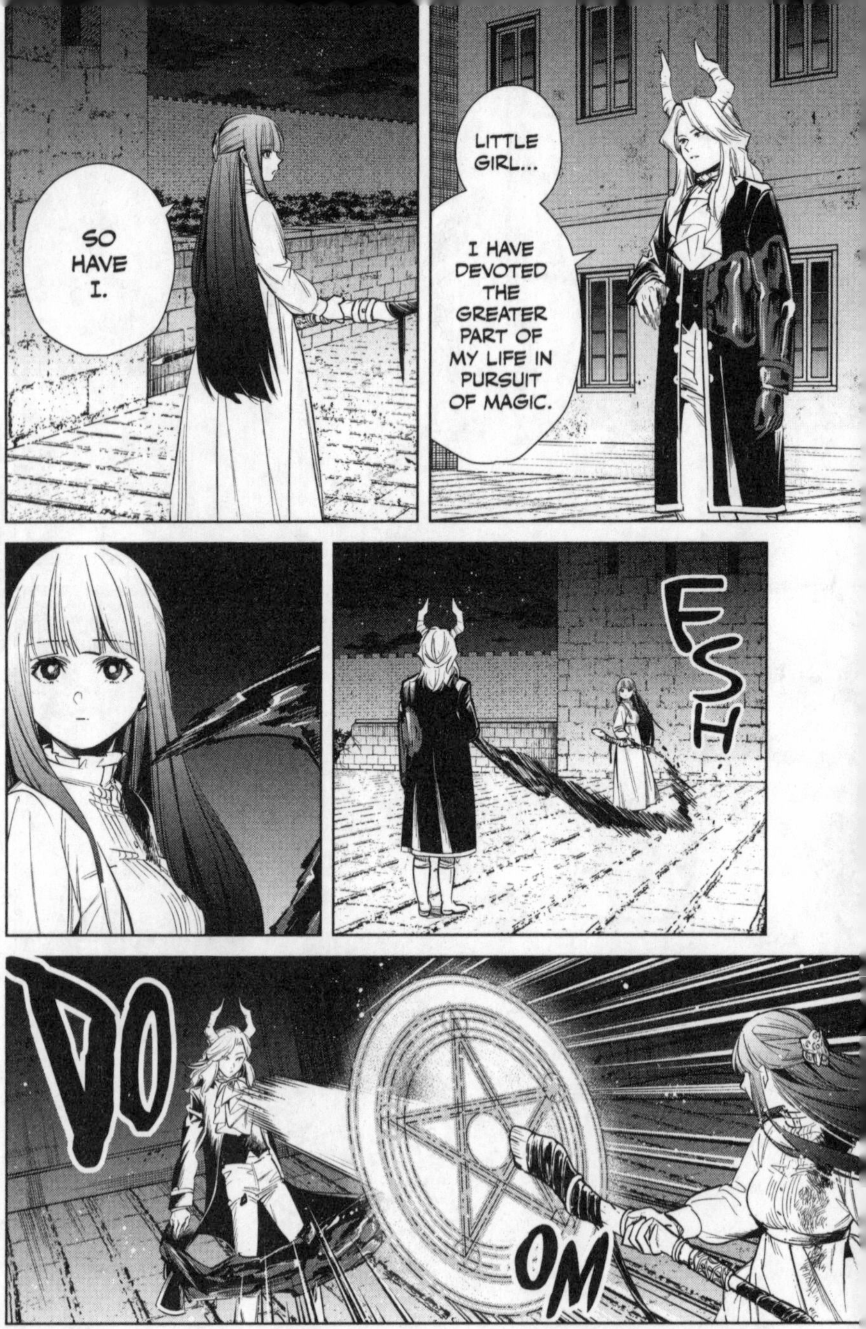
LITTLE GIRL...
I HAVE DEVOTED THE GREATER PART OF MY LIFE IN PURSUIT OF MAGIC.
SO HAVE I.
FSH
DO
OM

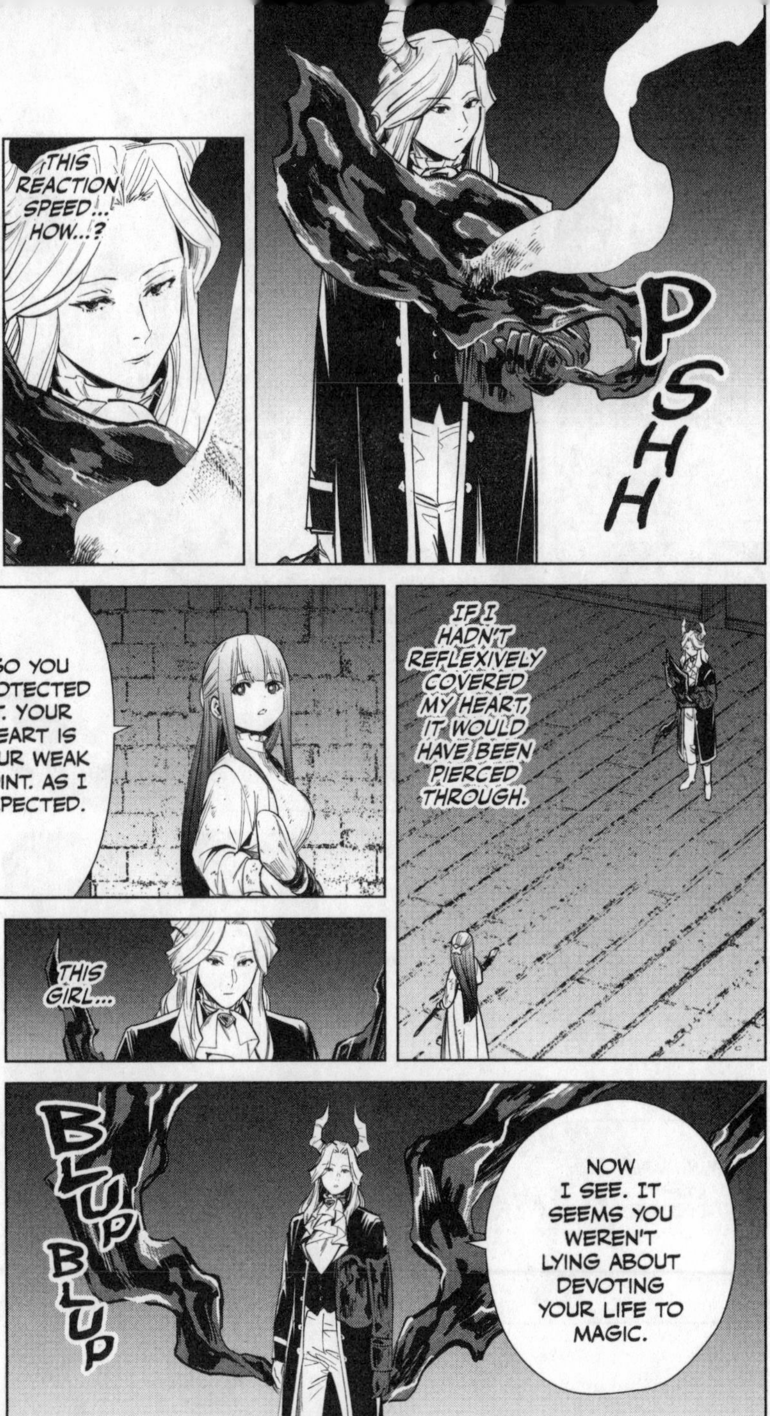
PSHH
THIS REACTION SPEED... HOW...?
IF I HADN'T REFLEXIVELY COVERED MY HEART, IT WOULD HAVE BEEN PIERCED THROUGH.
SO YOU PROTECTED IT. YOUR HEART IS YOUR WEAK POINT. AS I EXPECTED.
THIS GIRL...
NOW I SEE. IT SEEMS YOU WEREN'T LYING ABOUT DEVOTING YOUR LIFE TO MAGIC.
BLUP BLUP BLUP

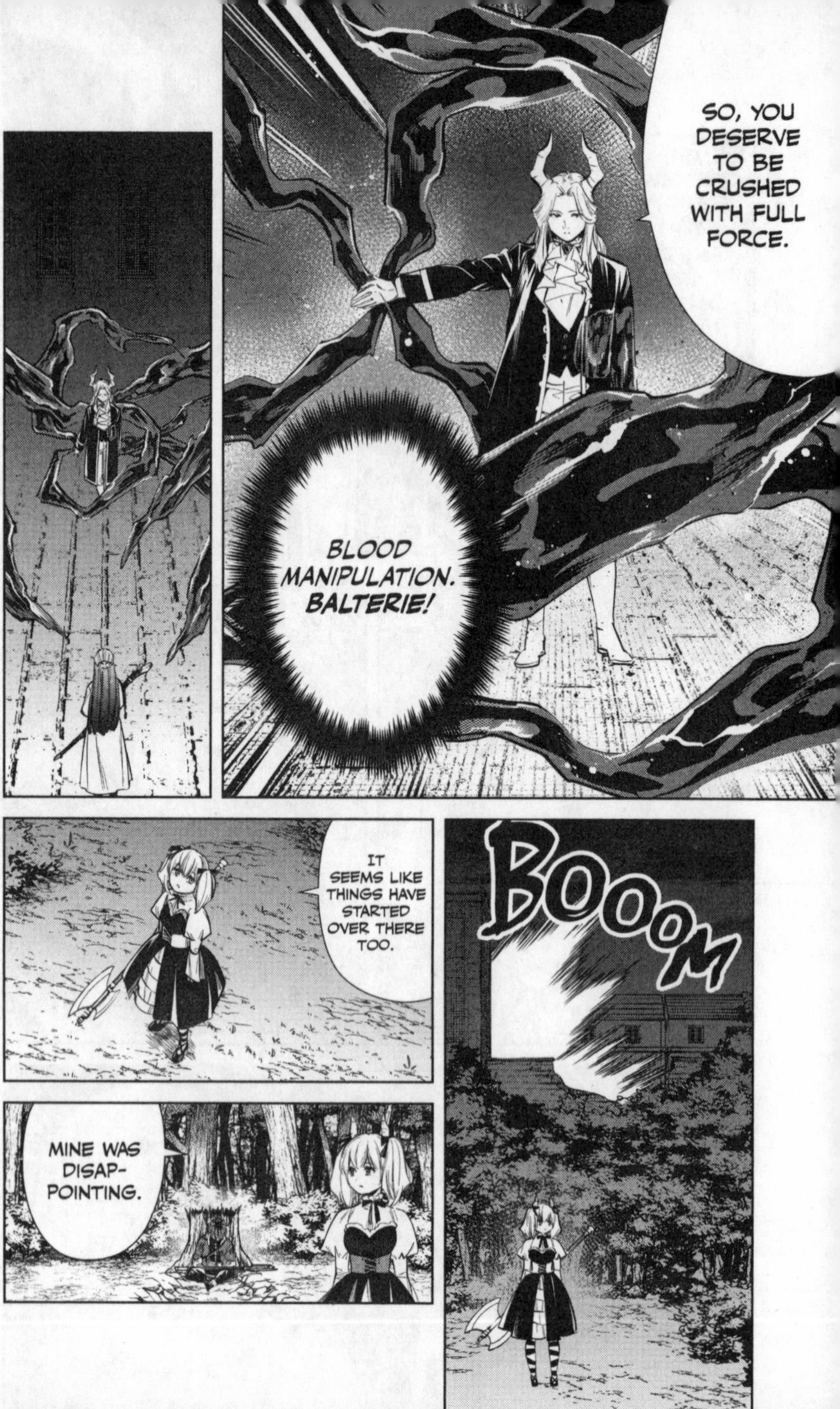
SO, YOU DESERVE TO BE CRUSHED WITH FULL FORCE.
BLOOD MANIPULATION. BALTERIE!
BOOOOM
IT SEEMS LIKE THINGS HAVE STARTED OVER THERE TOO.
MINE WAS DISAP-POINTING.

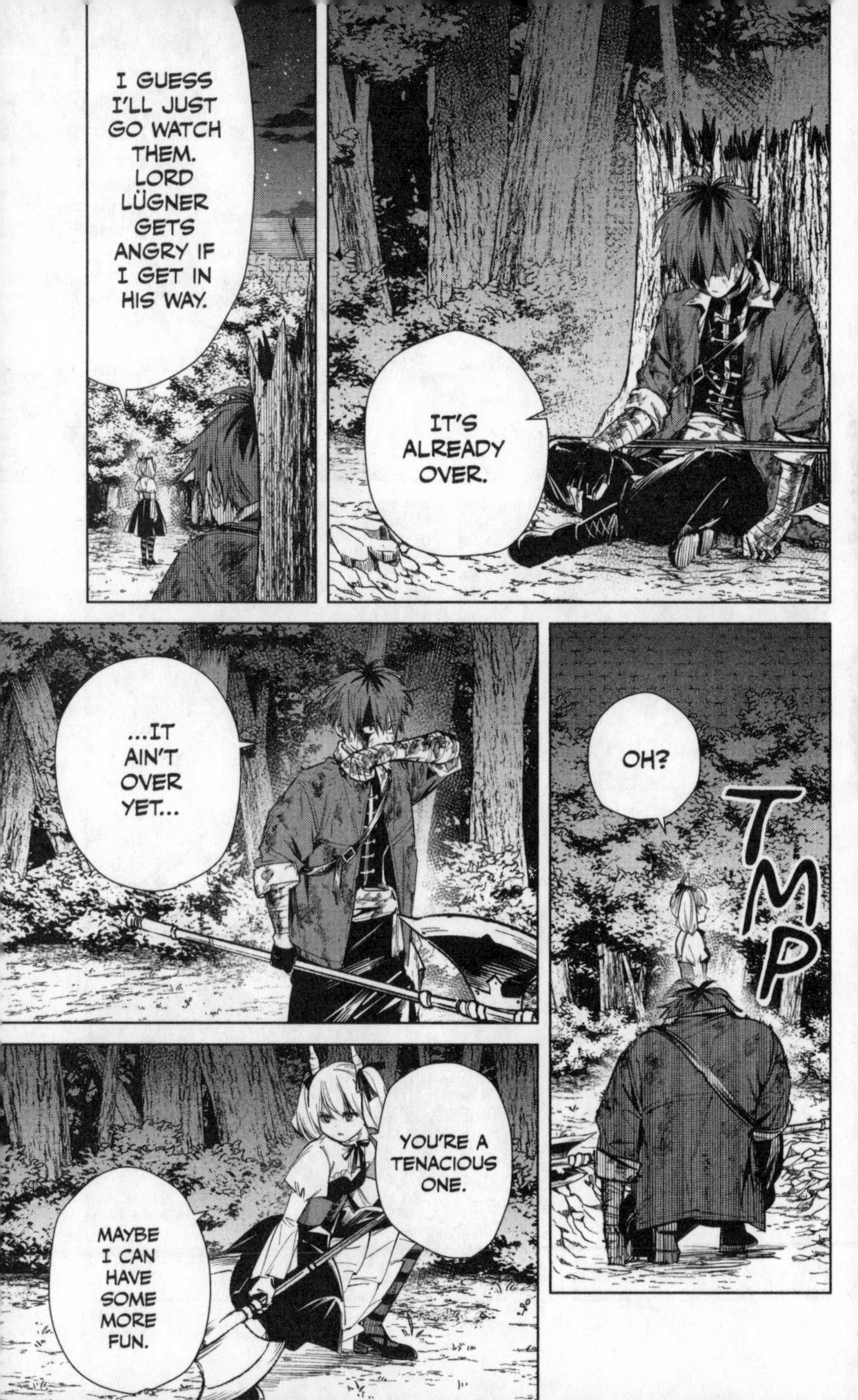
IT'S ALREADY OVER.
I GUESS I'LL JUST GO WATCH THEM. LORD LÜGNER GETS ANGRY IF I GET IN HIS WAY.
OH?
TMP
...IT AIN'T OVER YET...
YOU'RE A TENACIOUS ONE.
MAYBE I CAN HAVE SOME MORE FUN.

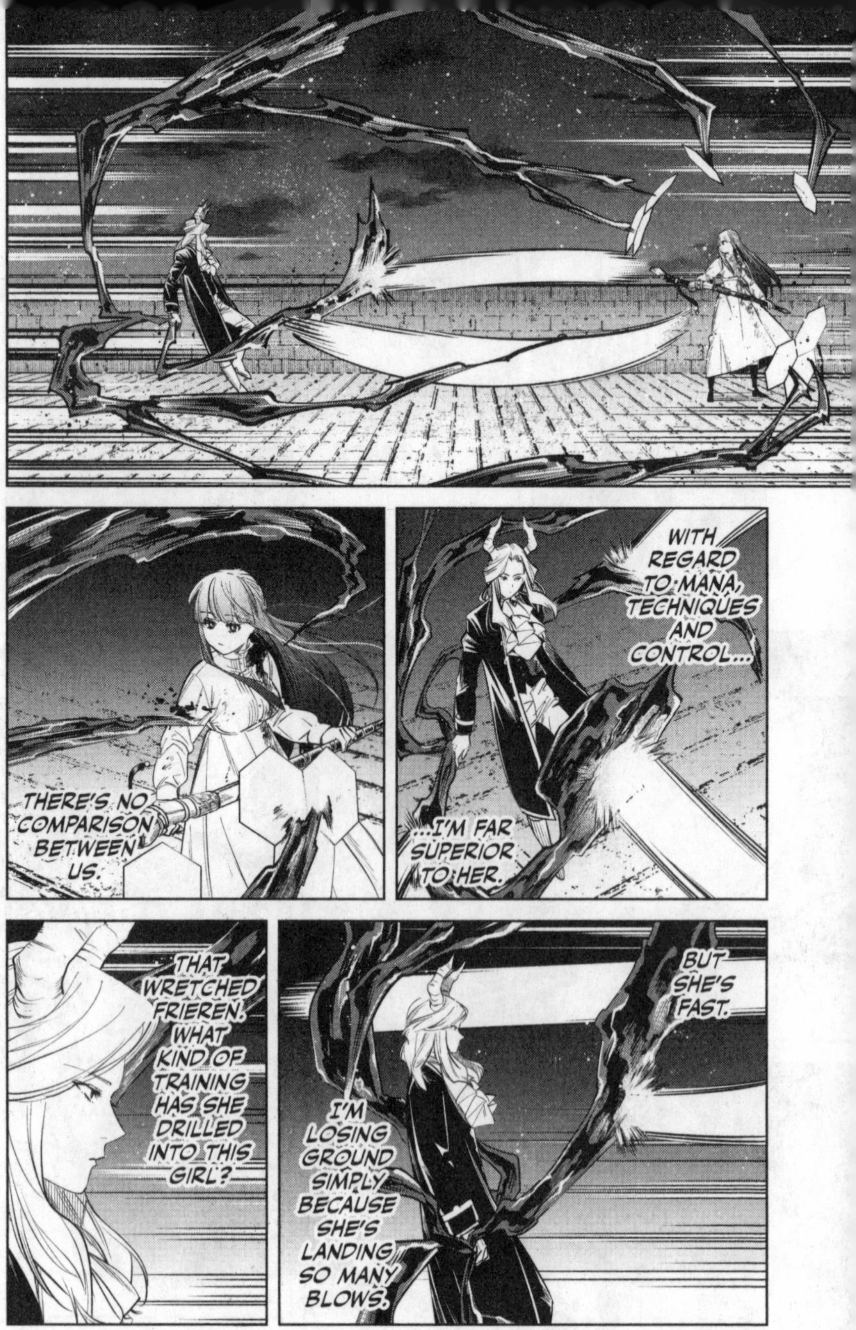
WITH REGARD TO MANA, TECHNIQUES AND CONTROL...
...I'M FAR SUPERIOR TO HER.
THERE'S NO COMPARISON BETWEEN US.
BUT SHE'S FAST.
I'M LOSING GROUND SIMPLY BECAUSE SHE'S LANDING SO MANY BLOWS.
THAT WRETCHED FRIEREN. WHAT KIND OF TRAINING HAS SHE DRILLED INTO THIS GIRL?

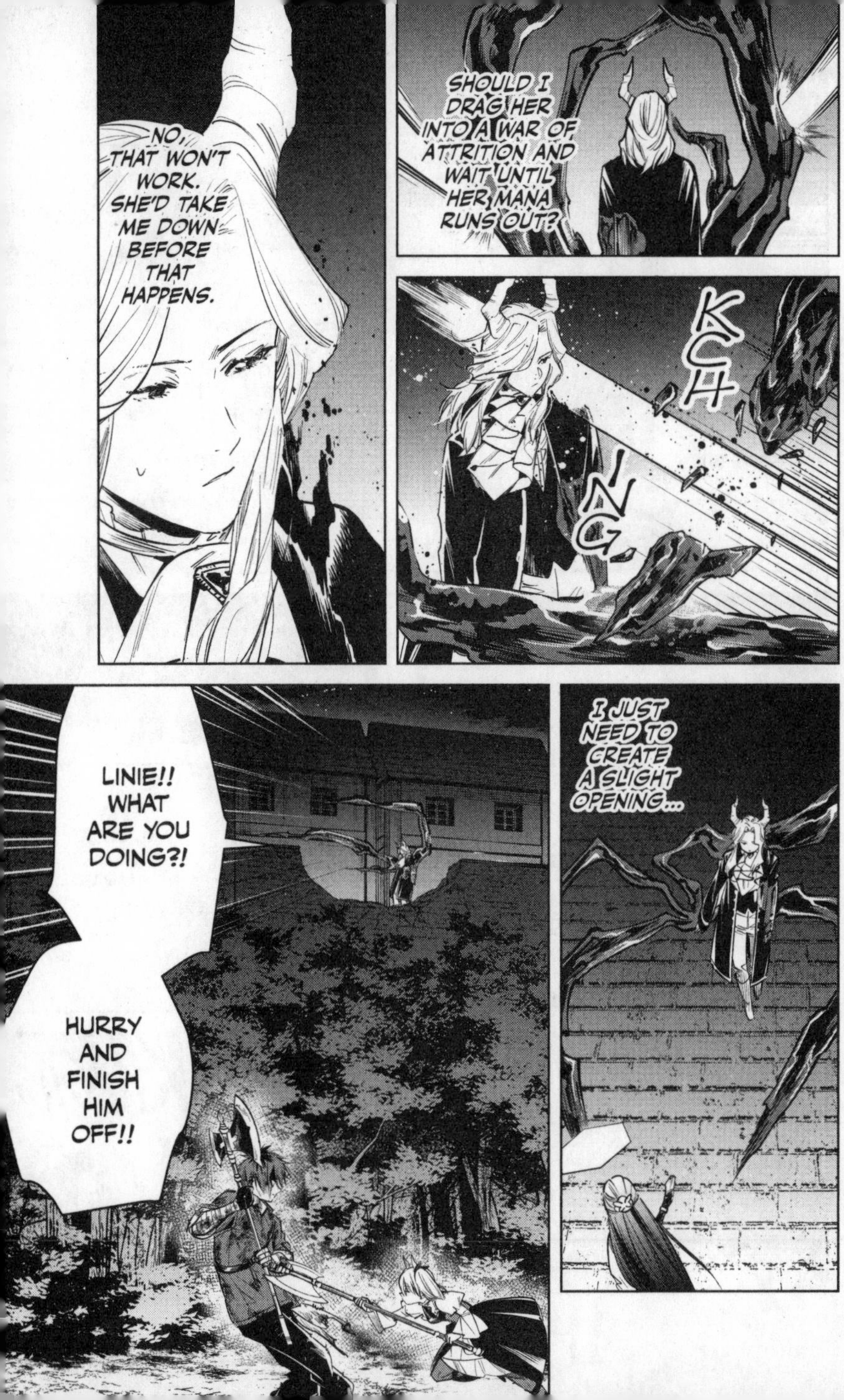
SHOULD I DRAG HER INTO A WAR OF ATTRITION AND WAIT UNTIL HER MANA RUNS OUT?
KCH ING
NO, THAT WON'T WORK. SHE'D TAKE ME DOWN BEFORE THAT HAPPENS.
I JUST NEED TO CREATE A SLIGHT OPENING...
LINIE!! WHAT ARE YOU DOING?!
HURRY AND FINISH HIM OFF!!

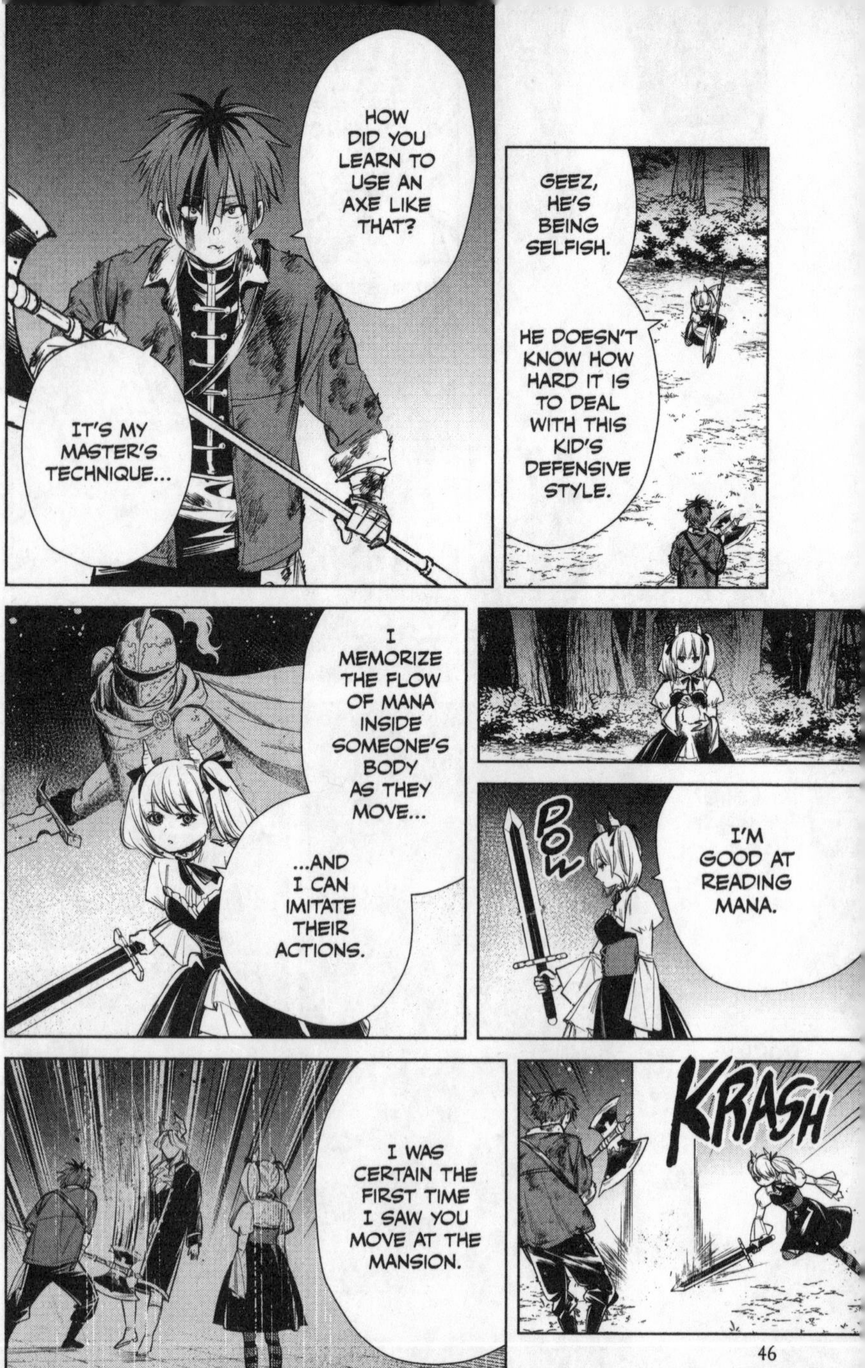
GEEZ, HE'S BEING SELFISH.
HE DOESN'T KNOW HOW HARD IT IS TO DEAL WITH THIS KID'S DEFENSIVE STYLE.
HOW DID YOU LEARN TO USE AN AXE LIKE THAT?
IT'S MY MASTER'S TECHNIQUE...
POW
I'M GOOD AT READING MANA.
I MEMORIZE THE FLOW OF MANA INSIDE SOMEONE'S BODY AS THEY MOVE...
...AND I CAN IMITATE THEIR ACTIONS.
KRASH
I WAS CERTAIN THE FIRST TIME I SAW YOU MOVE AT THE MANSION.

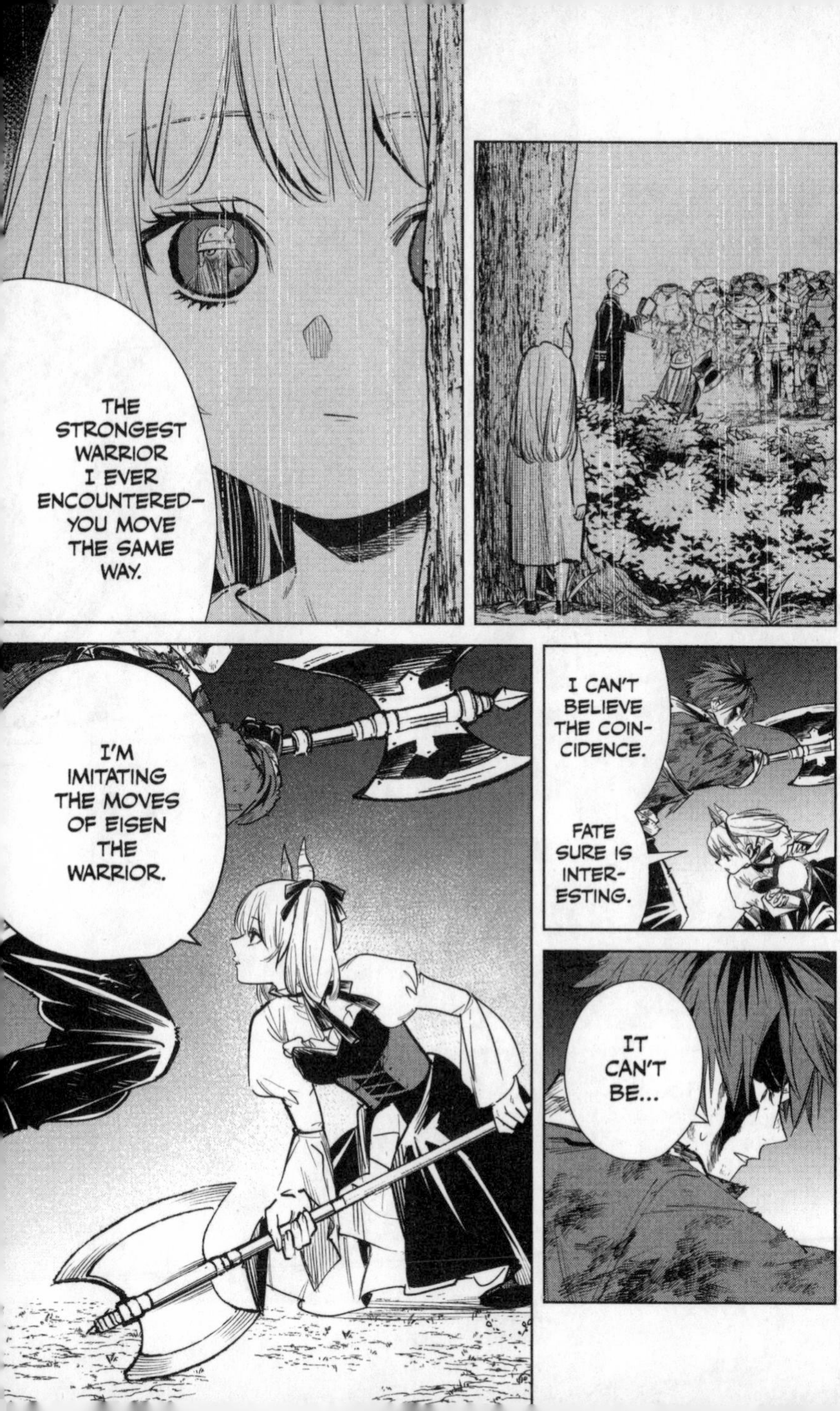
THE STRONGEST WARRIOR I EVER ENCOUNTERED— YOU MOVE THE SAME WAY.
I CAN'T BELIEVE THE COIN- CIDENCE.
FATE SURE IS INTER- ESTING.
IT CAN'T BE...
I'M IMITATING THE MOVES OF EISEN THE WARRIOR.

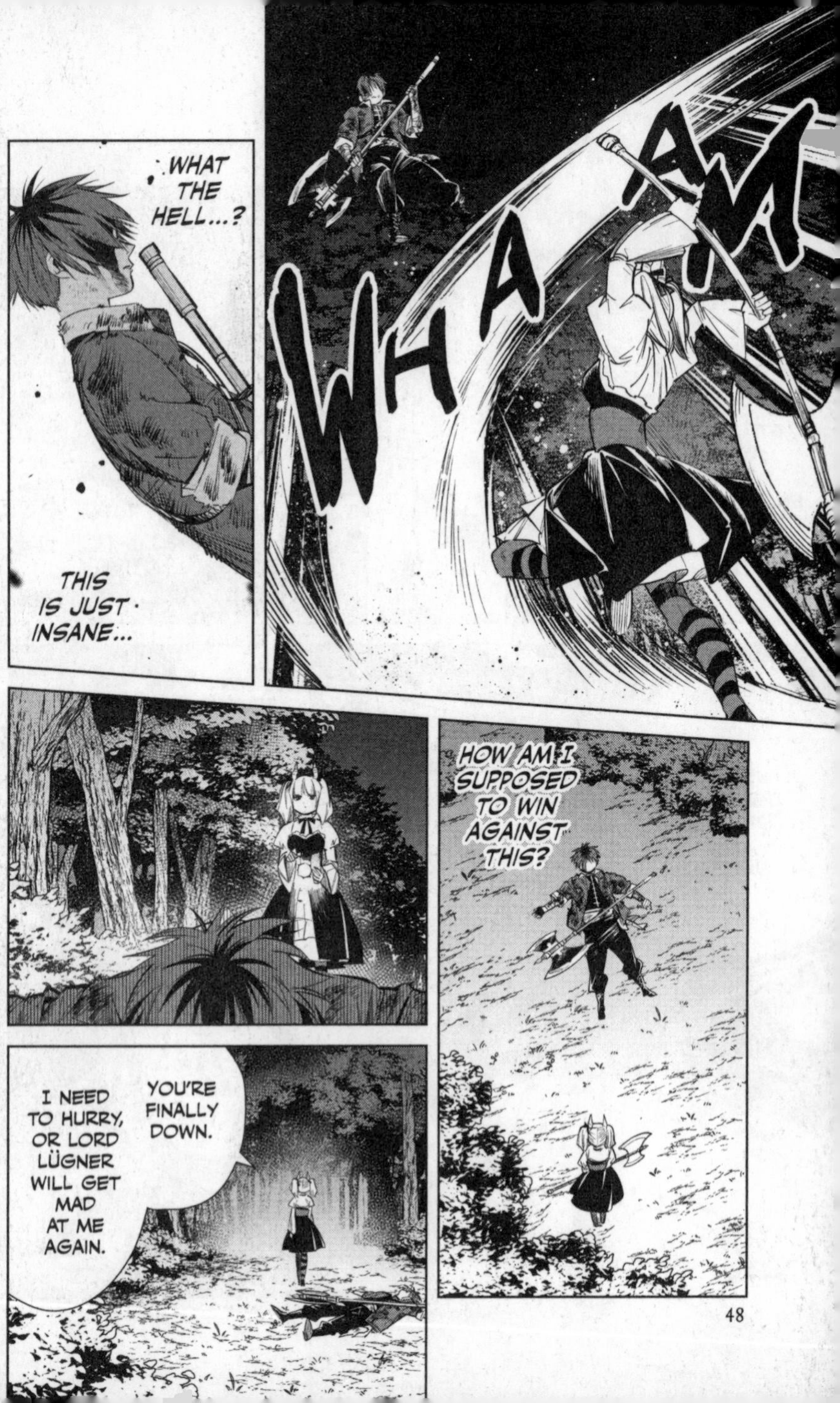
WHAAM
...WHAT THE HELL...?
THIS IS JUST INSANE...
HOW AM I SUPPOSED TO WIN AGAINST THIS?
YOU'RE FINALLY DOWN.
I NEED TO HURRY, OR LORD LÜGNER WILL GET MAD AT ME AGAIN.

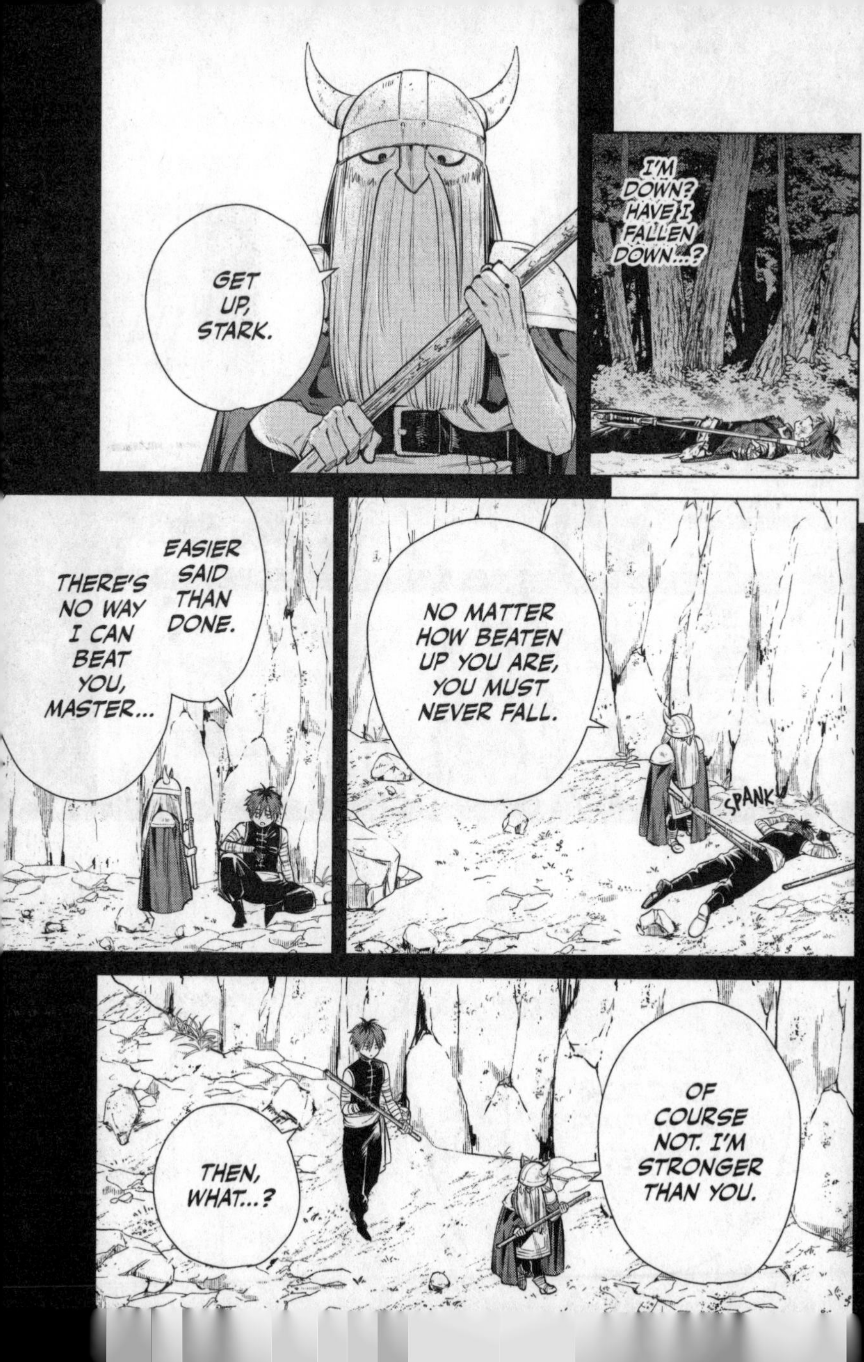
I'M DOWN? HAVE I FALLEN DOWN...?
GET UP, STARK.
NO MATTER HOW BEATEN UP YOU ARE, YOU MUST NEVER FALL.
SPANK
EASIER SAID THAN DONE.
THERE'S NO WAY I CAN BEAT YOU, MASTER...
OF COURSE NOT. I'M STRONGER THAN YOU.
THEN, WHAT...?

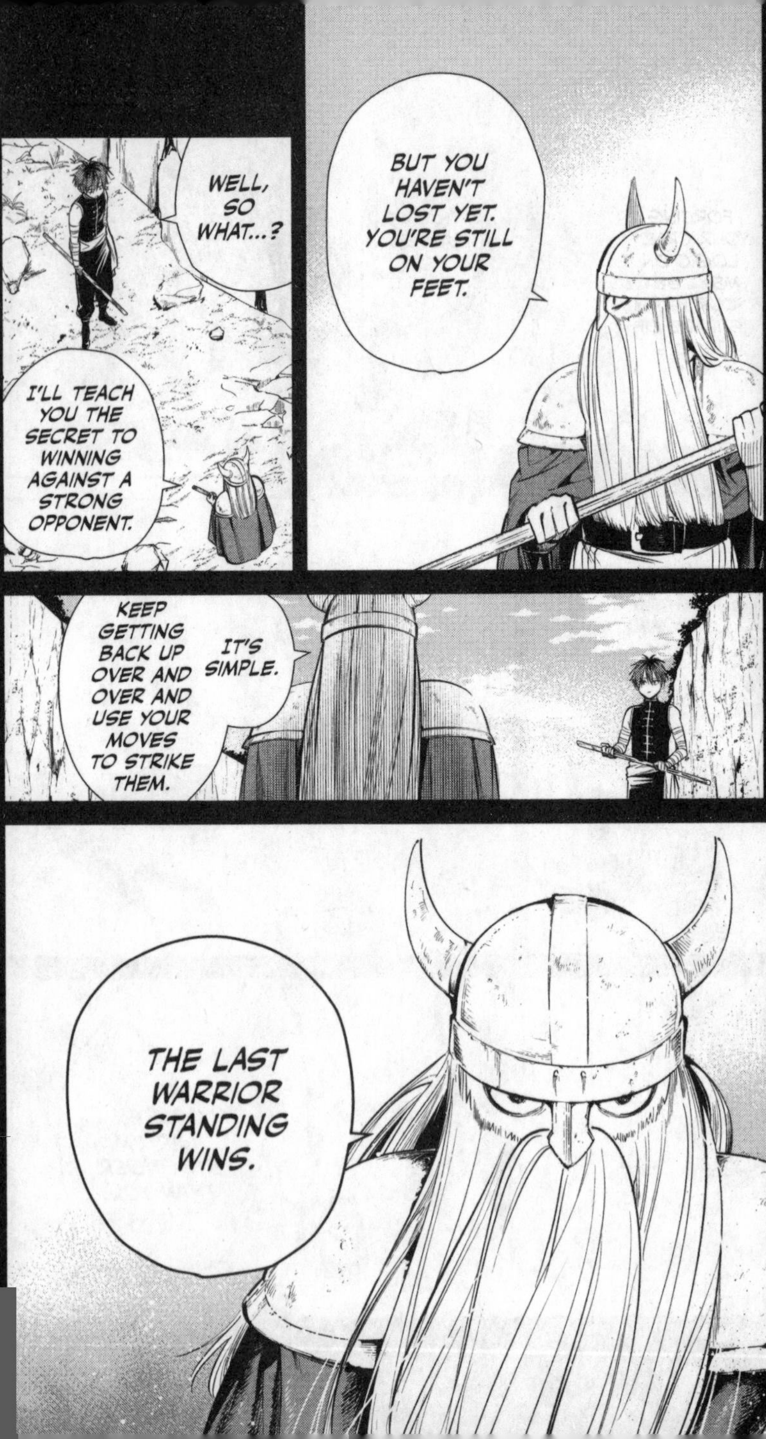
BUT YOU HAVEN'T LOST YET. YOU'RE STILL ON YOUR FEET.
WELL, SO WHAT...?
I'LL TEACH YOU THE SECRET TO WINNING AGAINST A STRONG OPPONENT.
IT'S SIMPLE.
KEEP GETTING BACK UP OVER AND OVER AND USE YOUR MOVES TO STRIKE THEM.
THE LAST WARRIOR STANDING WINS.

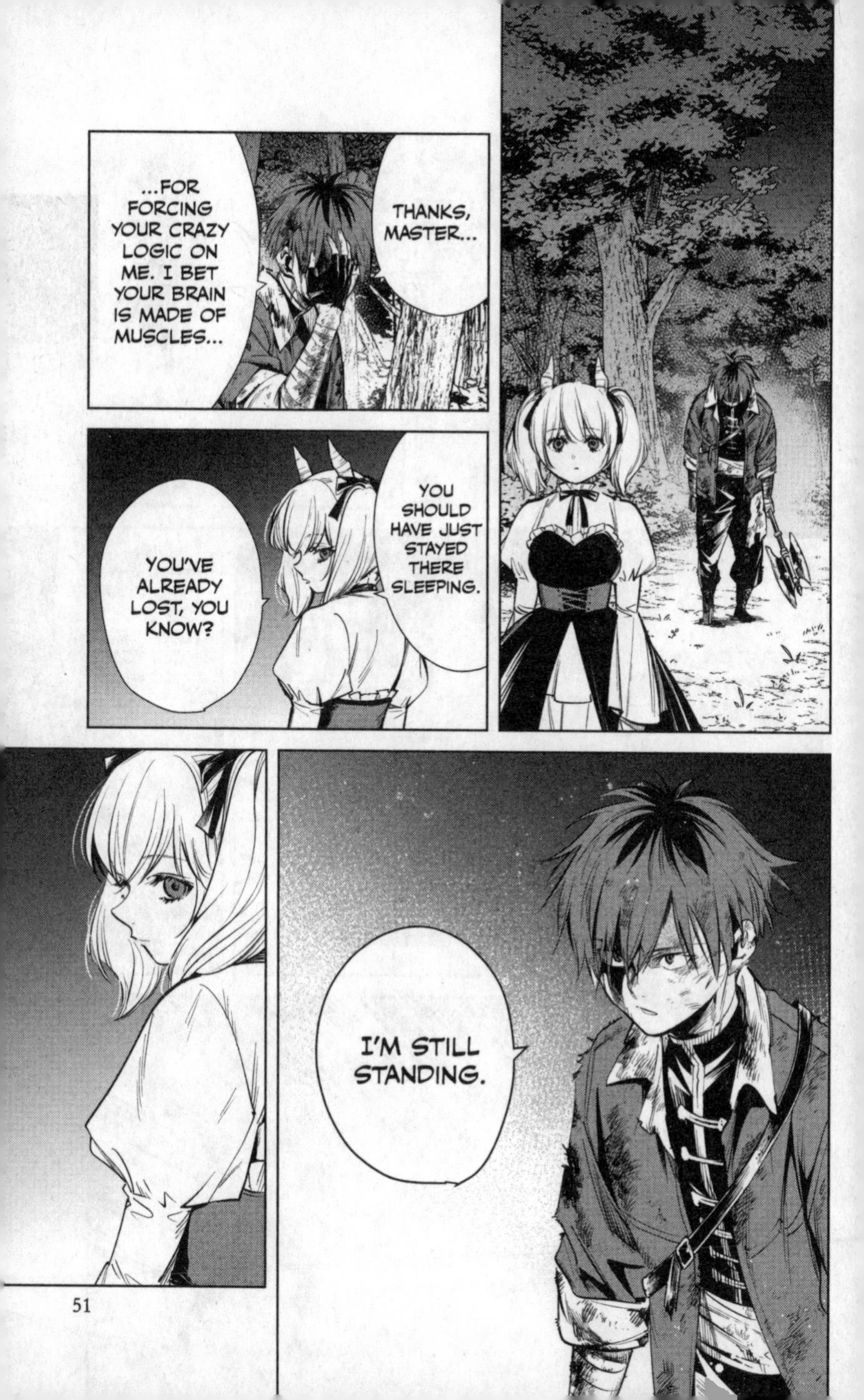
THANKS, MASTER...
...FOR FORCING YOUR CRAZY LOGIC ON ME. I BET YOUR BRAIN IS MADE OF MUSCLES...
YOU SHOULD HAVE JUST STAYED THERE SLEEPING.
YOU'VE ALREADY LOST, YOU KNOW?
I'M STILL STANDING.

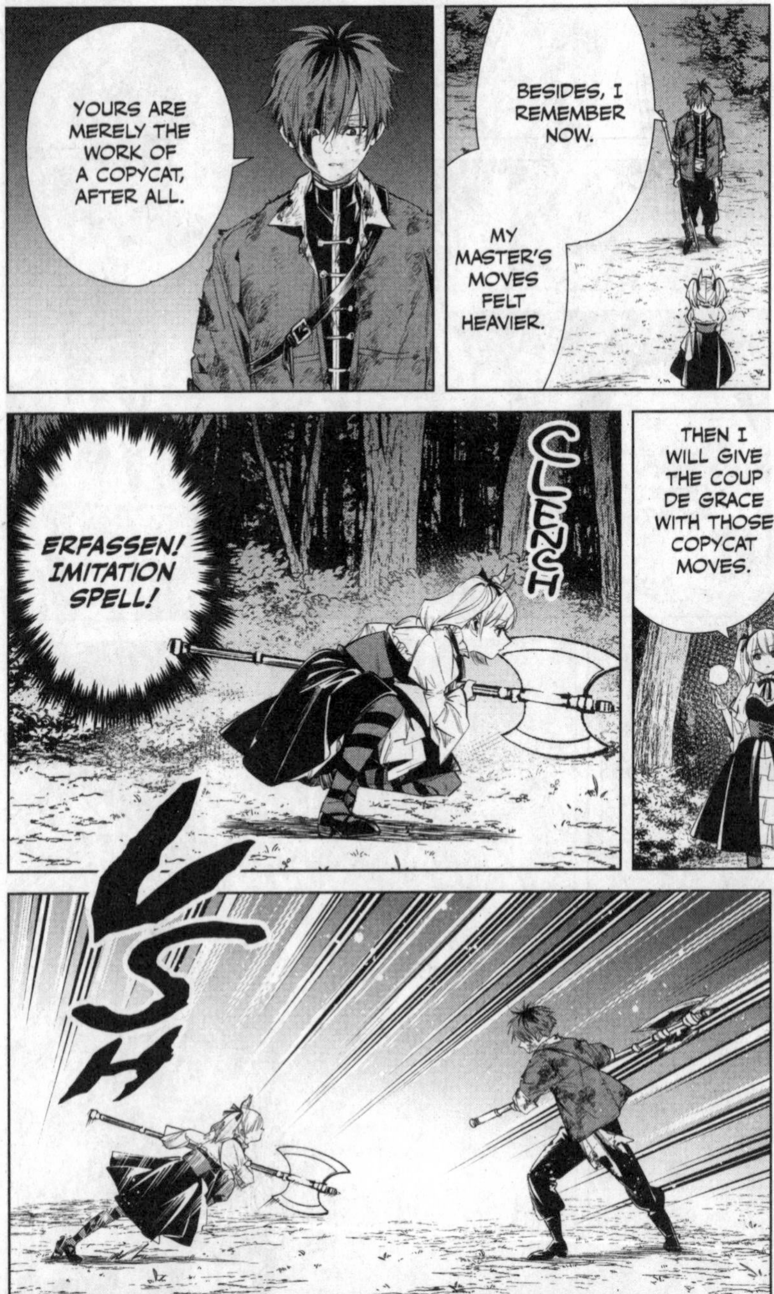
BESIDES, I REMEMBER NOW.
MY MASTER'S MOVES FELT HEAVIER.
YOURS ARE MERELY THE WORK OF A COPYCAT, AFTER ALL.
THEN I WILL GIVE THE COUP DE GRACE WITH THOSE COPYCAT MOVES.
CLENCH
ERFASSEN! IMITATION SPELL!
VSH

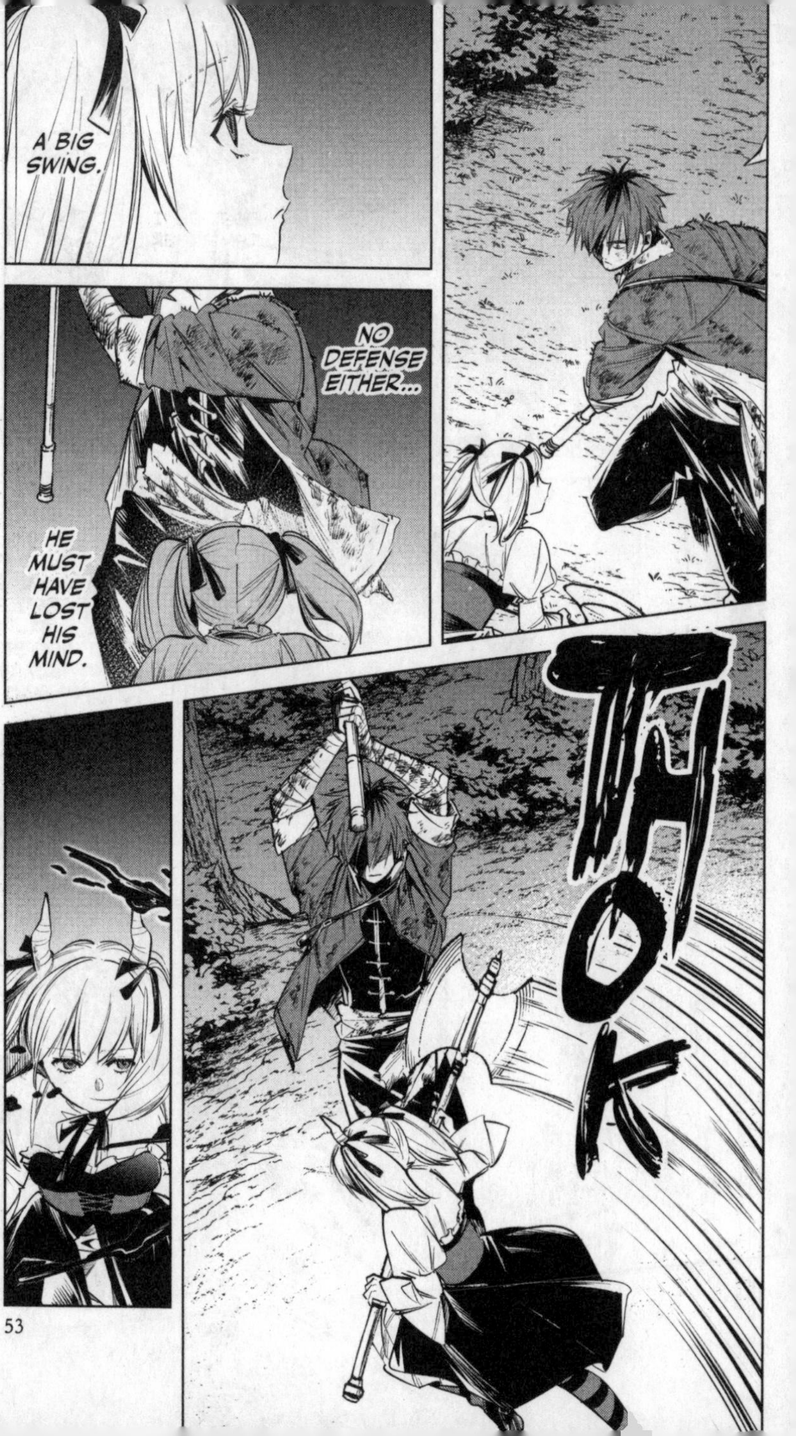
A BIG SWING.
NO DEFENSE EITHER...
HE MUST HAVE LOST HIS MIND.
THOK

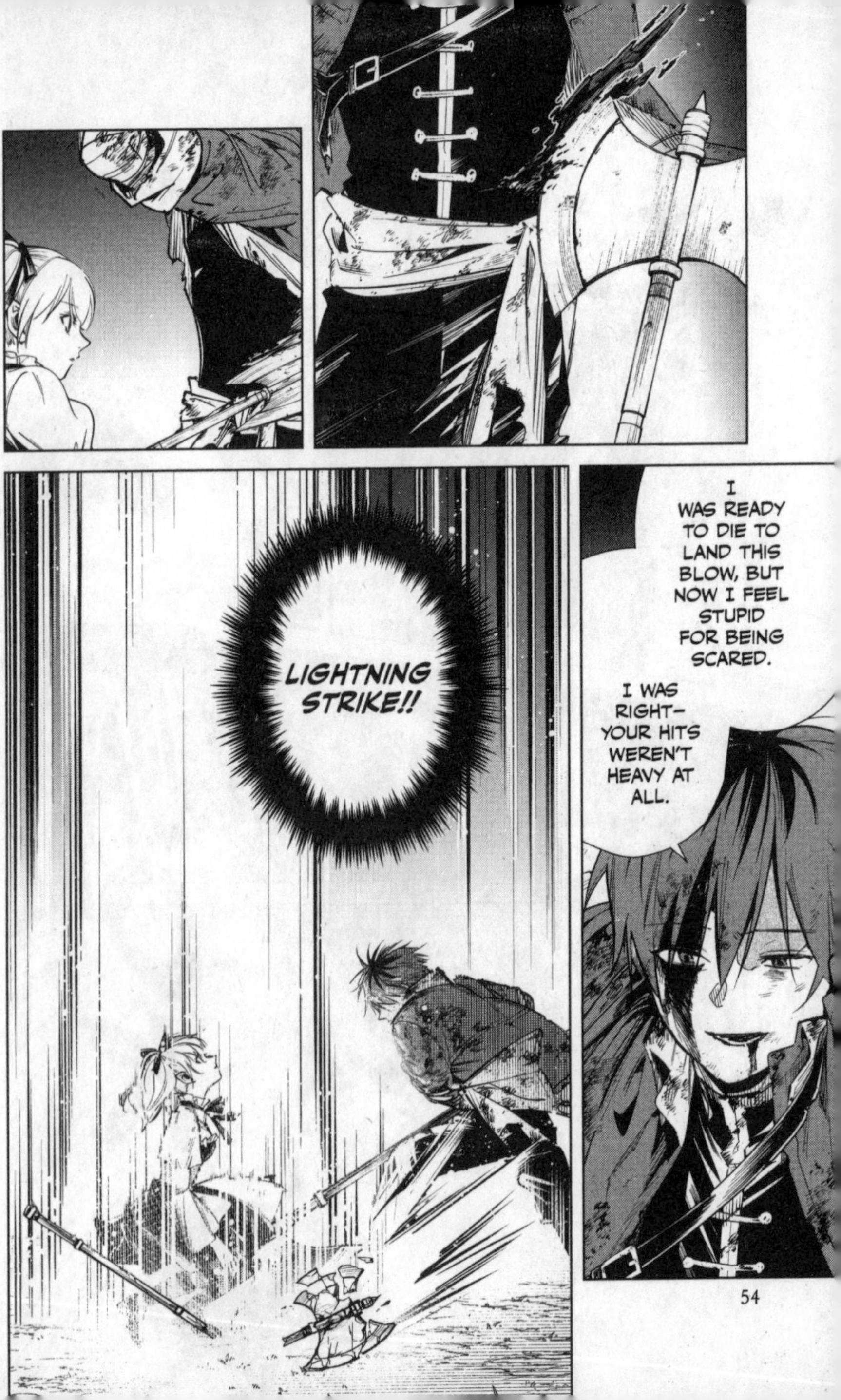
I WAS READY TO DIE TO LAND THIS BLOW, BUT NOW I FEEL STUPID FOR BEING SCARED.
I WAS RIGHT—YOUR HITS WEREN'T HEAVY AT ALL.
LIGHTNING STRIKE!!

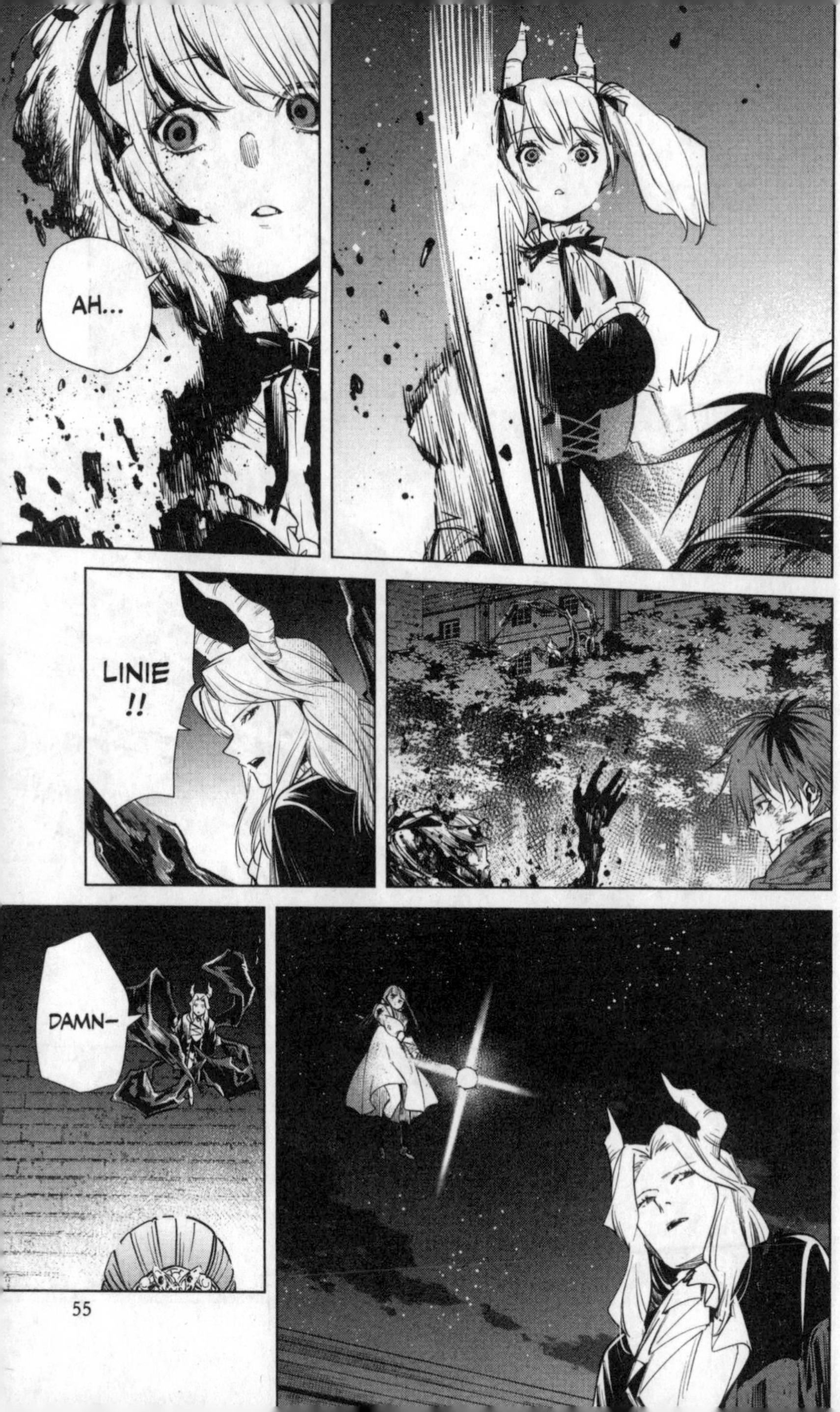
AH...
LINIE !!
DAMN–

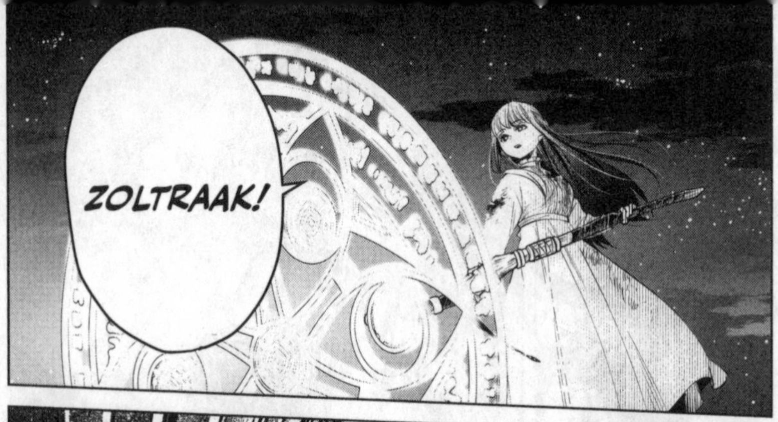
ZOLTRAAK!
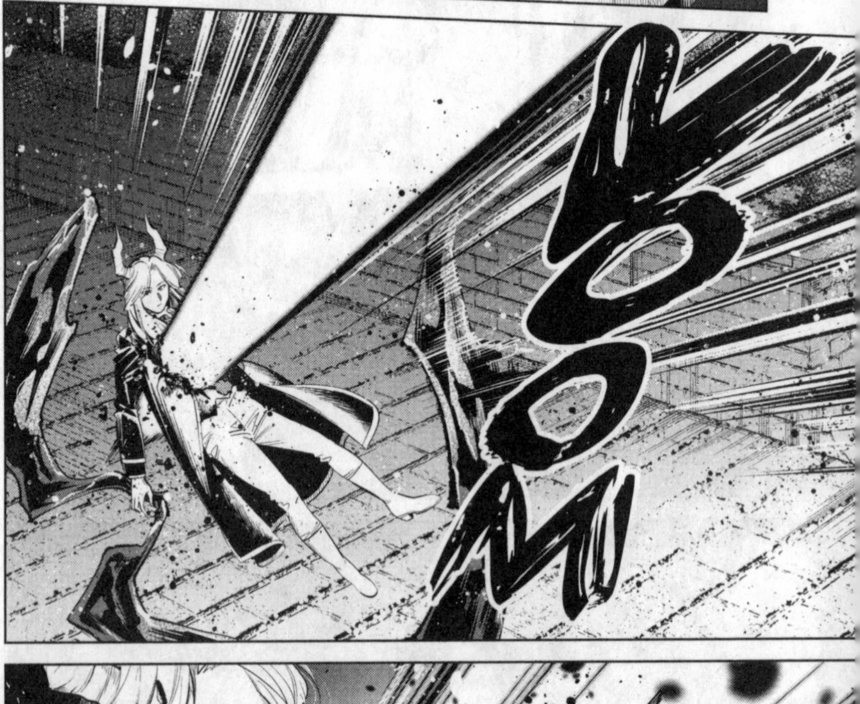
BOOM
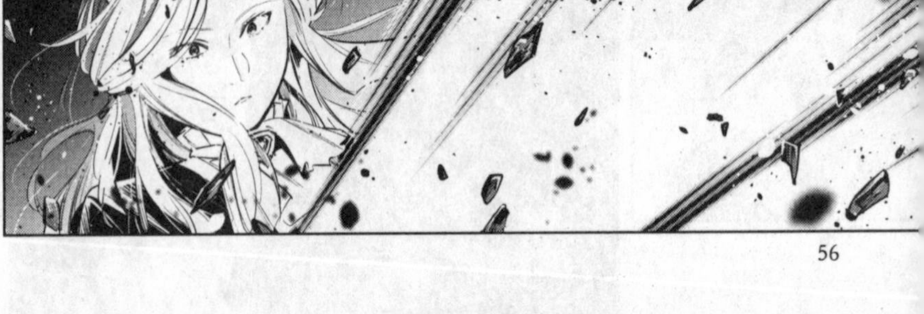

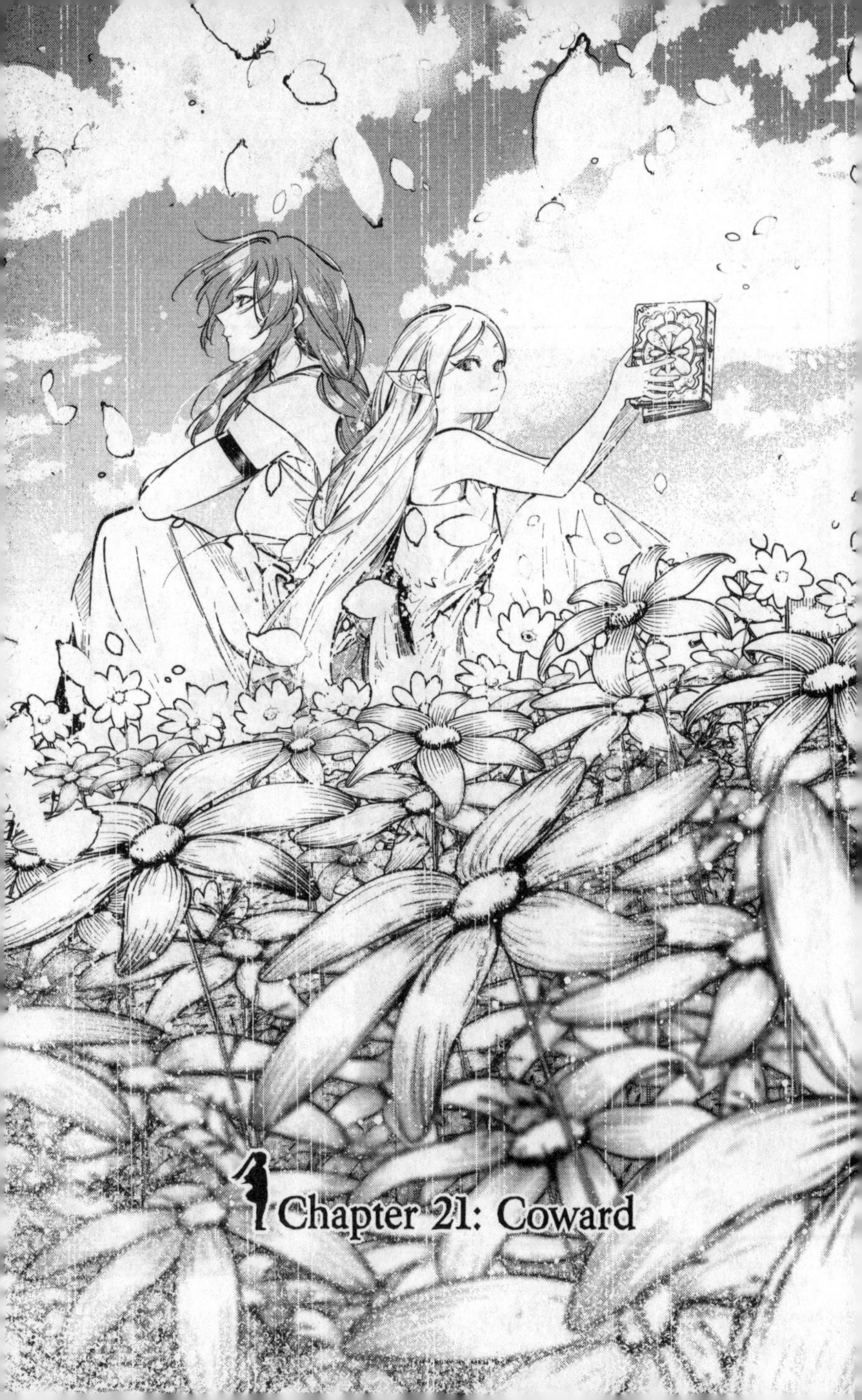

# Chapter 21: Coward

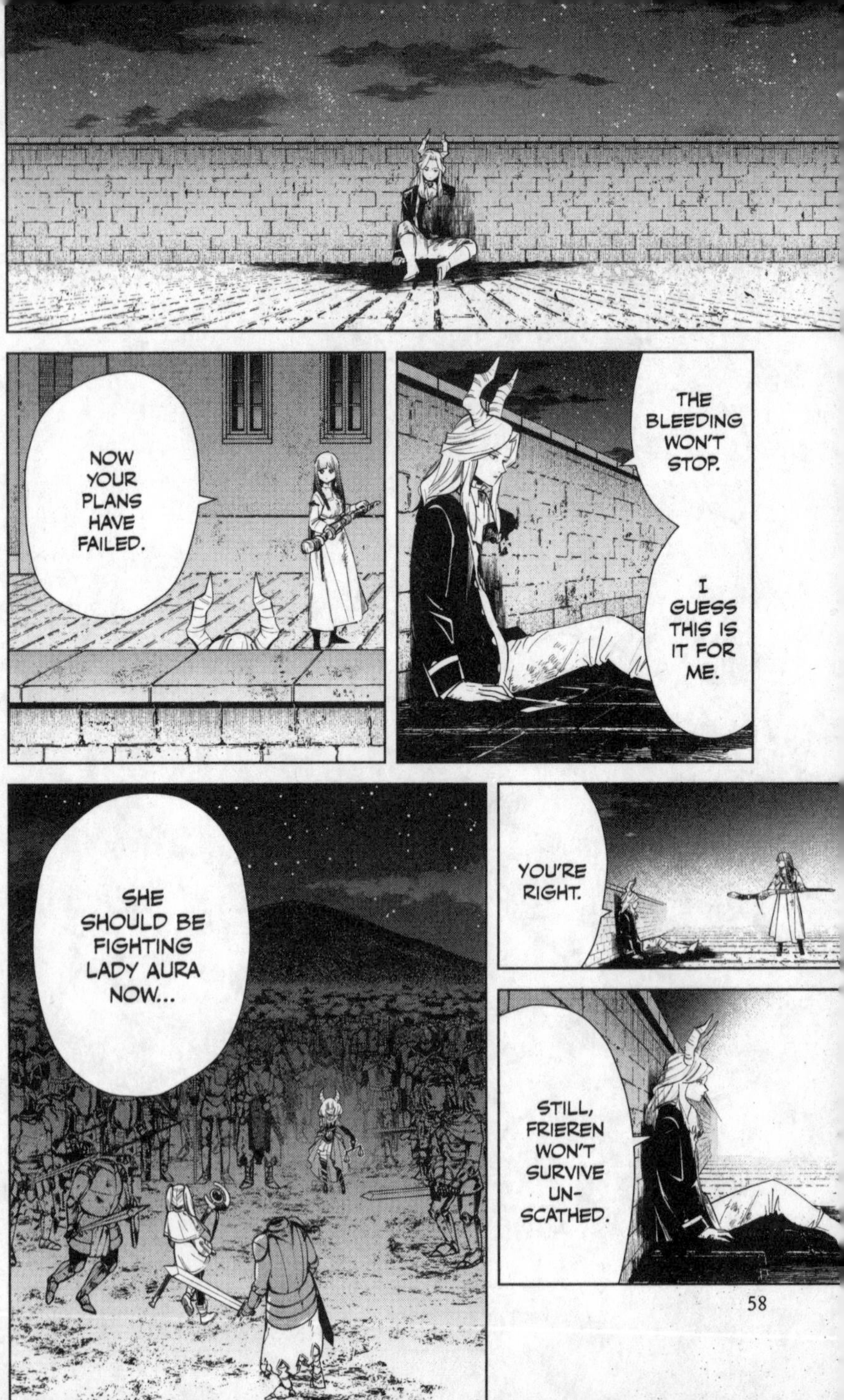
THE BLEEDING WON'T STOP.
I GUESS THIS IS IT FOR ME.
NOW YOUR PLANS HAVE FAILED.
YOU'RE RIGHT.
STILL, FRIEREN WON'T SURVIVE UN-SCATHED.
SHE SHOULD BE FIGHTING LADY AURA NOW...

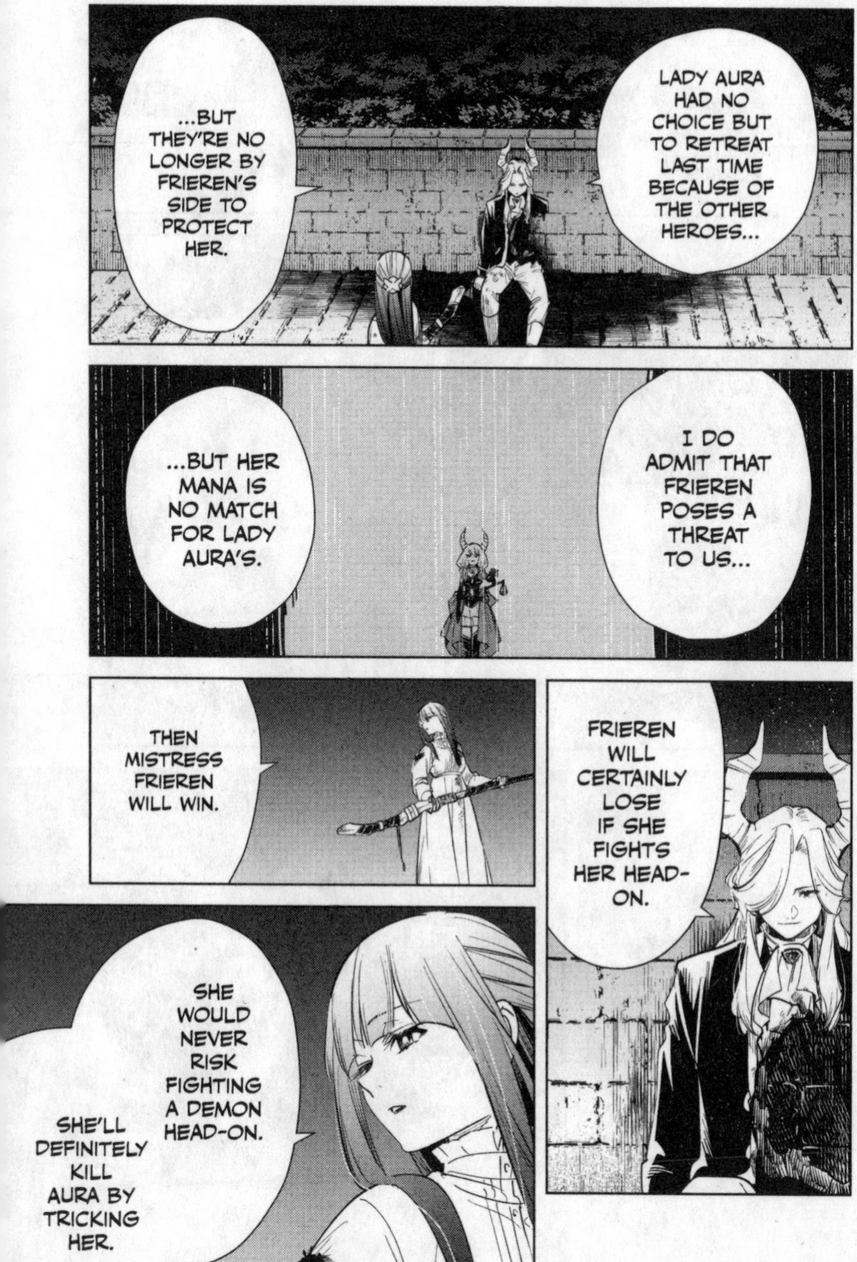
LADY AURA HAD NO CHOICE BUT TO RETREAT LAST TIME BECAUSE OF THE OTHER HEROES...
...BUT THEY'RE NO LONGER BY FRIEREN'S SIDE TO PROTECT HER.
I DO ADMIT THAT FRIEREN POSES A THREAT TO US...
...BUT HER MANA IS NO MATCH FOR LADY AURA'S.
FRIEREN WILL CERTAINLY LOSE IF SHE FIGHTS HER HEAD-ON.
THEN MISTRESS FRIEREN WILL WIN.
SHE WOULD NEVER RISK FIGHTING A DEMON HEAD-ON.
SHE'LL DEFINITELY KILL AURA BY TRICKING HER.

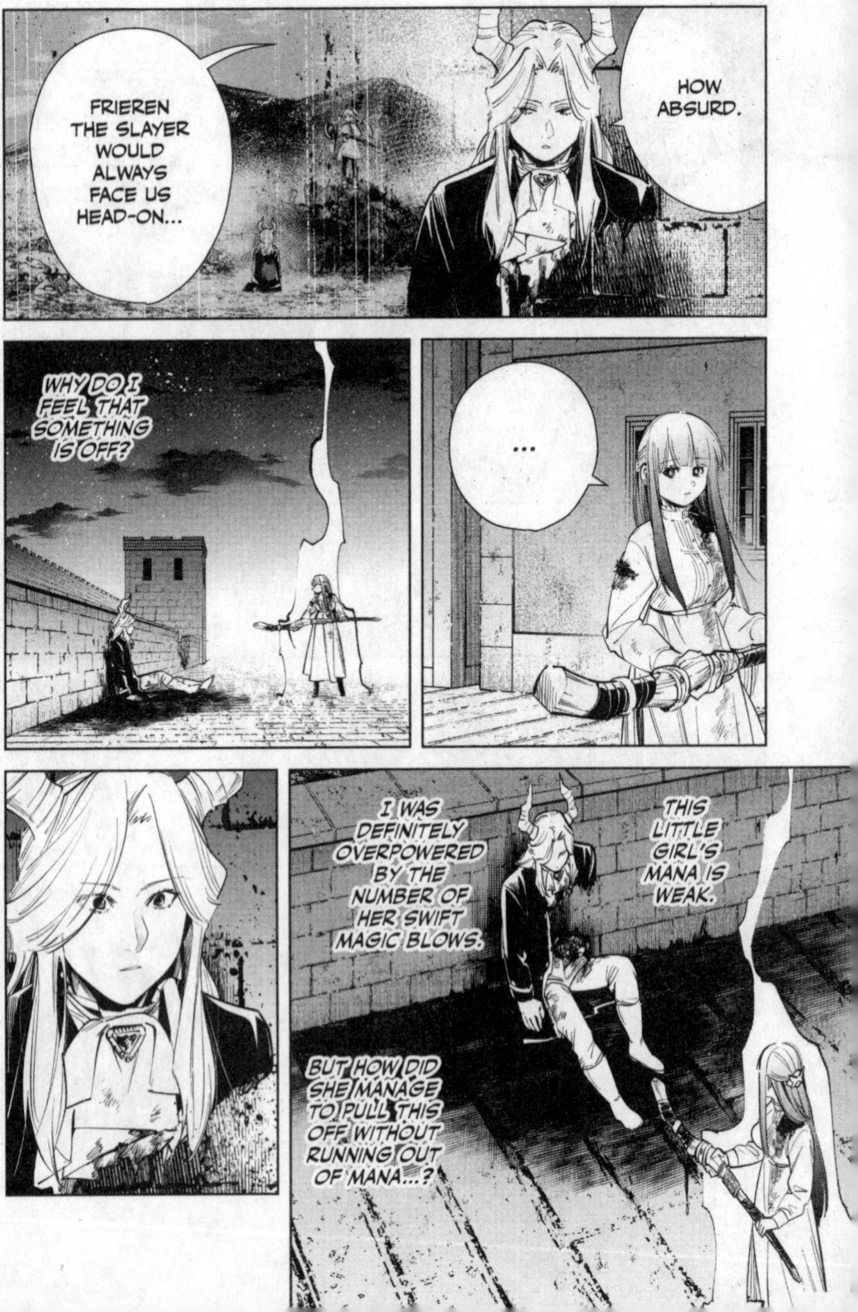
HOW ABSURD.
FRIEREN THE SLAYER WOULD ALWAYS FACE US HEAD-ON...
...
WHY DO I FEEL THAT SOMETHING IS OFF?
THIS LITTLE GIRL'S MANA IS WEAK.
I WAS DEFINITELY OVERPOWERED BY THE NUMBER OF HER SWIFT MAGIC BLOWS.
BUT HOW DID SHE MANAGE TO PULL THIS OFF WITHOUT RUNNING OUT OF MANA...?

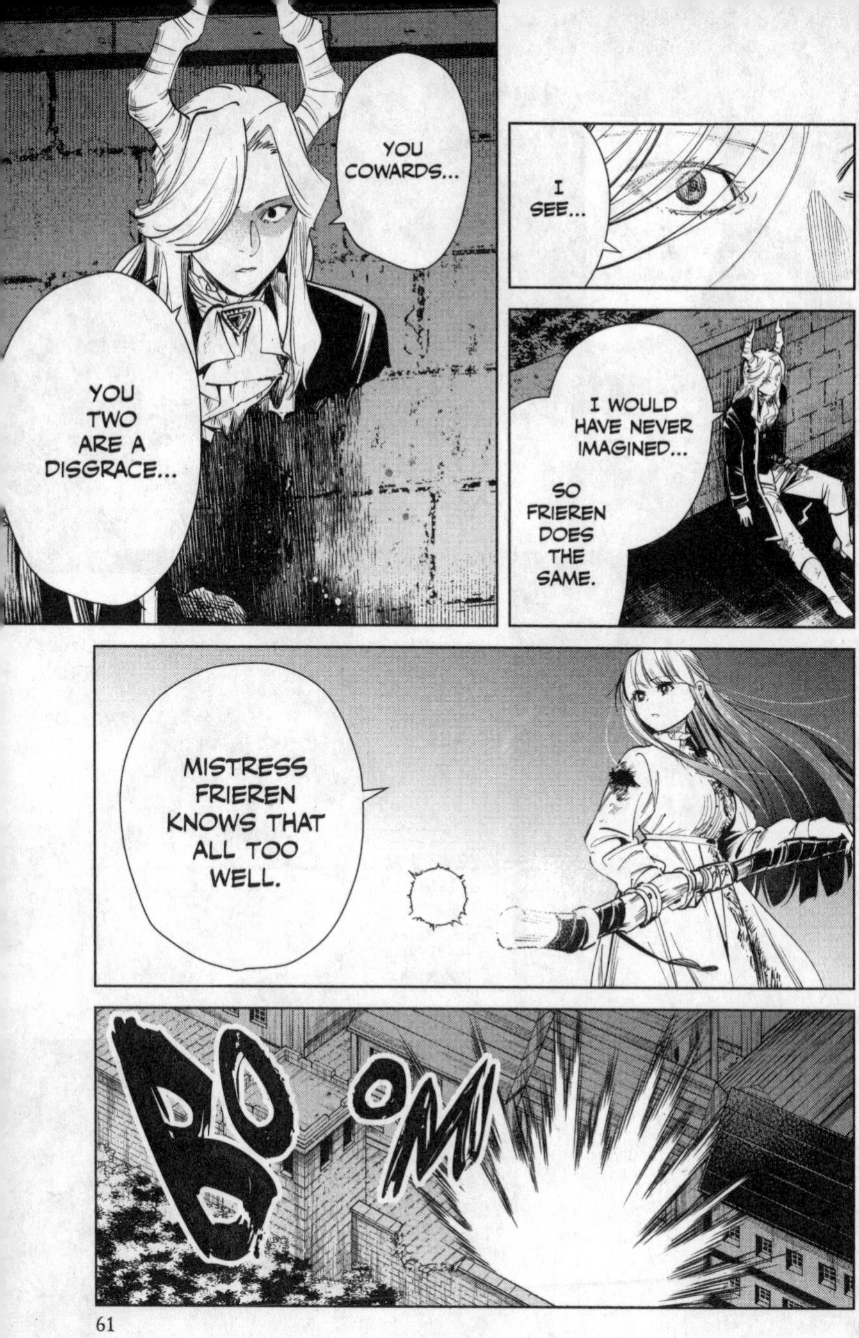
I SEE...
I WOULD HAVE NEVER IMAGINED...
SO FRIEREN DOES THE SAME.
YOU COWARDS...
YOU TWO ARE A DISGRACE...
MISTRESS FRIEREN KNOWS THAT ALL TOO WELL.
BOOM

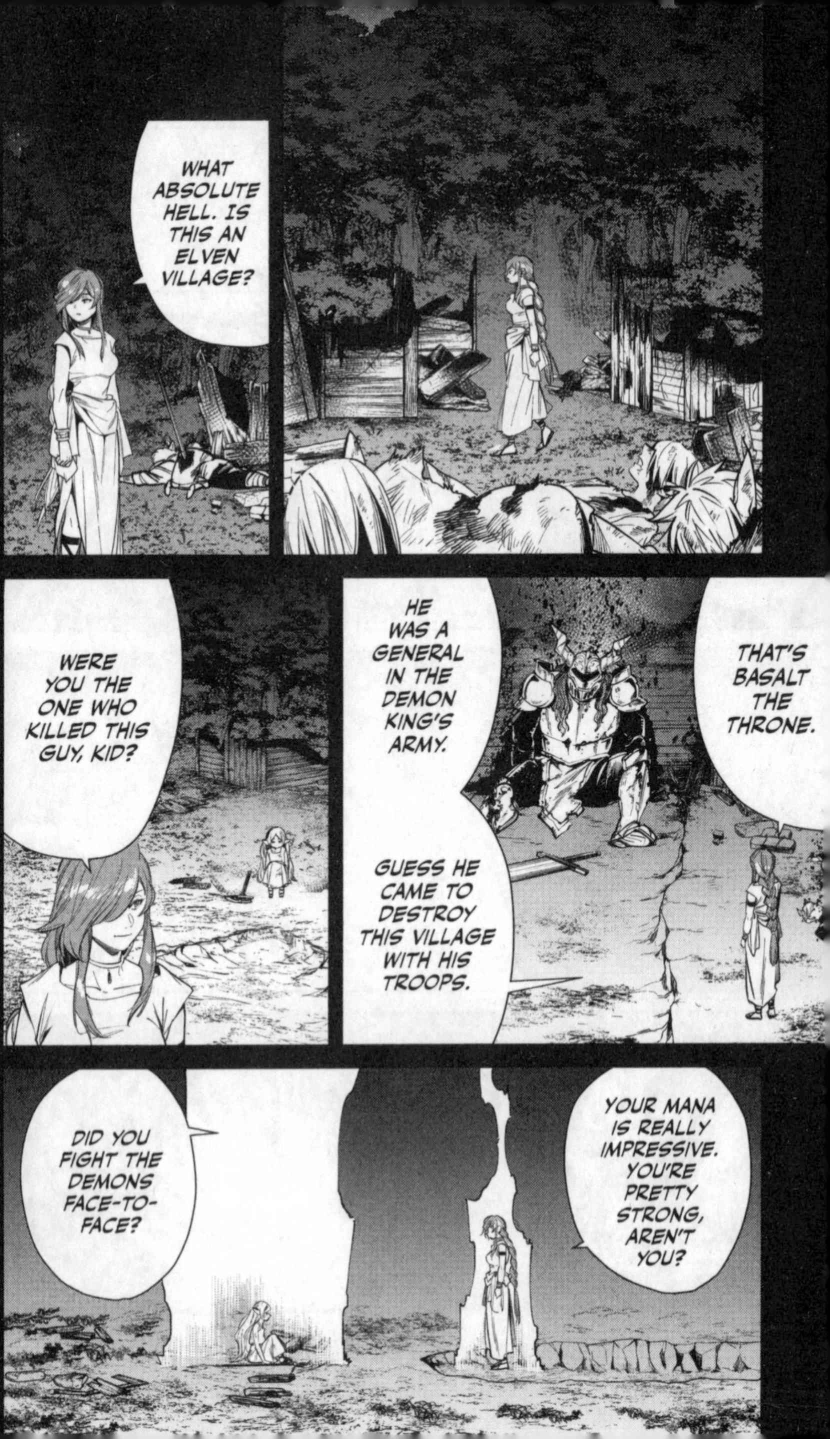
WHAT ABSOLUTE HELL. IS THIS AN ELVEN VILLAGE?
THAT'S BASALT THE THRONE.
HE WAS A GENERAL IN THE DEMON KING'S ARMY.
GUESS HE CAME TO DESTROY THIS VILLAGE WITH HIS TROOPS.
WERE YOU THE ONE WHO KILLED THIS GUY, KID?
YOUR MANA IS REALLY IMPRESSIVE. YOU'RE PRETTY STRONG, AREN'T YOU?
DID YOU FIGHT THE DEMONS FACE-TO-FACE?

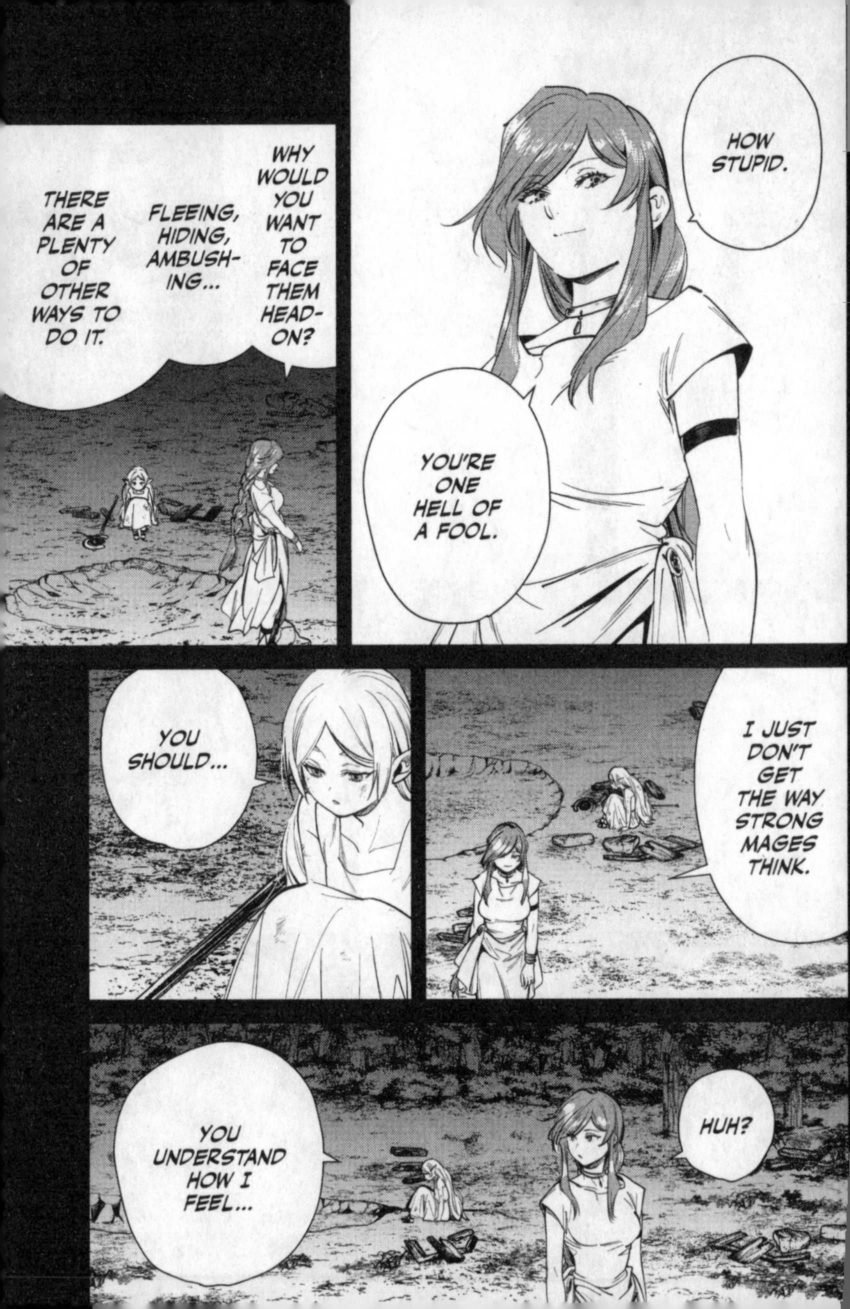
HOW STUPID.
YOU'RE ONE HELL OF A FOOL.
WHY WOULD YOU WANT TO FACE THEM HEAD-ON?
FLEEING, HIDING, AMBUSH-ING...
THERE ARE A PLENTY OF OTHER WAYS TO DO IT.
I JUST DON'T GET THE WAY STRONG MAGES THINK.
YOU SHOULD...
YOU UNDERSTAND HOW I FEEL...
HUH?

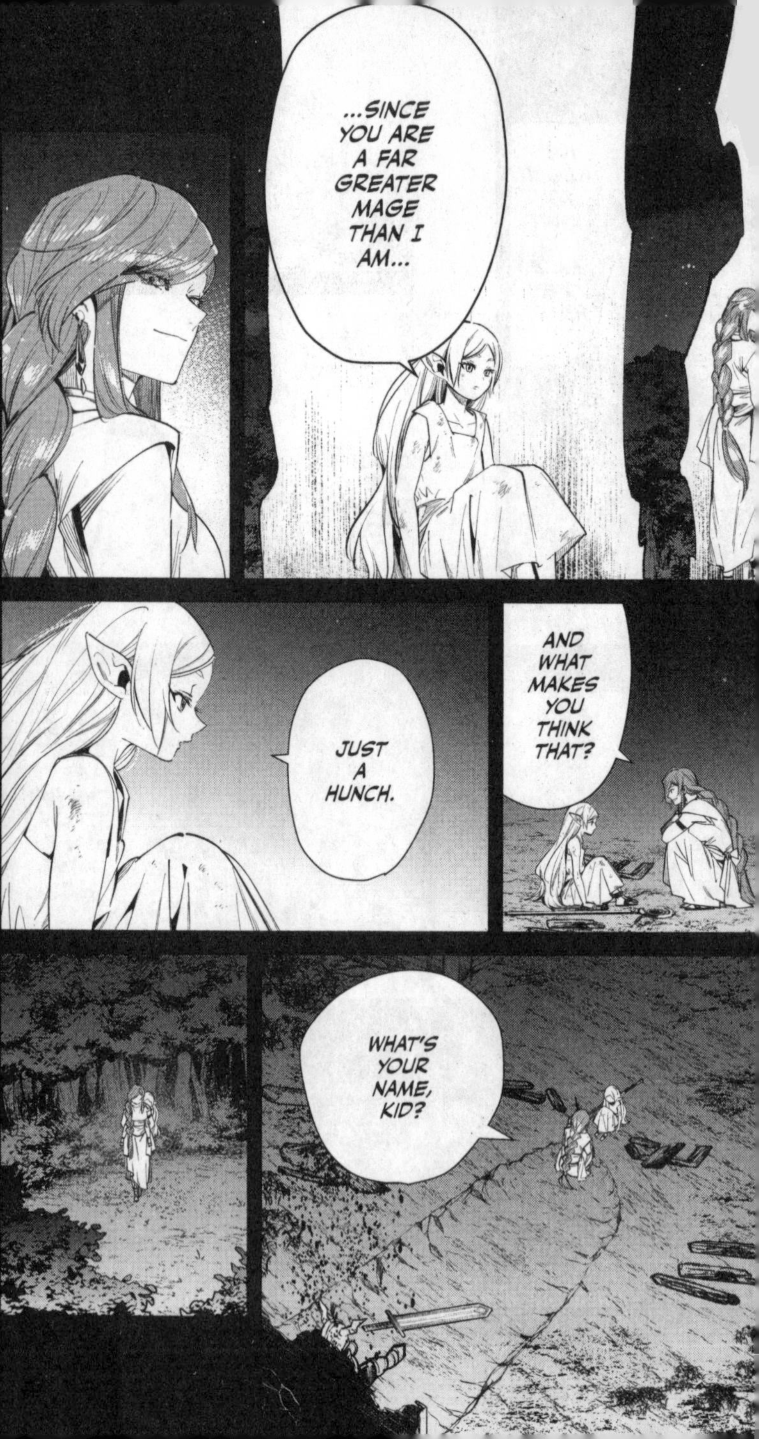
...SINCE YOU ARE A FAR GREATER MAGE THAN I AM...
AND WHAT MAKES YOU THINK THAT?
JUST A HUNCH.
WHAT'S YOUR NAME, KID?

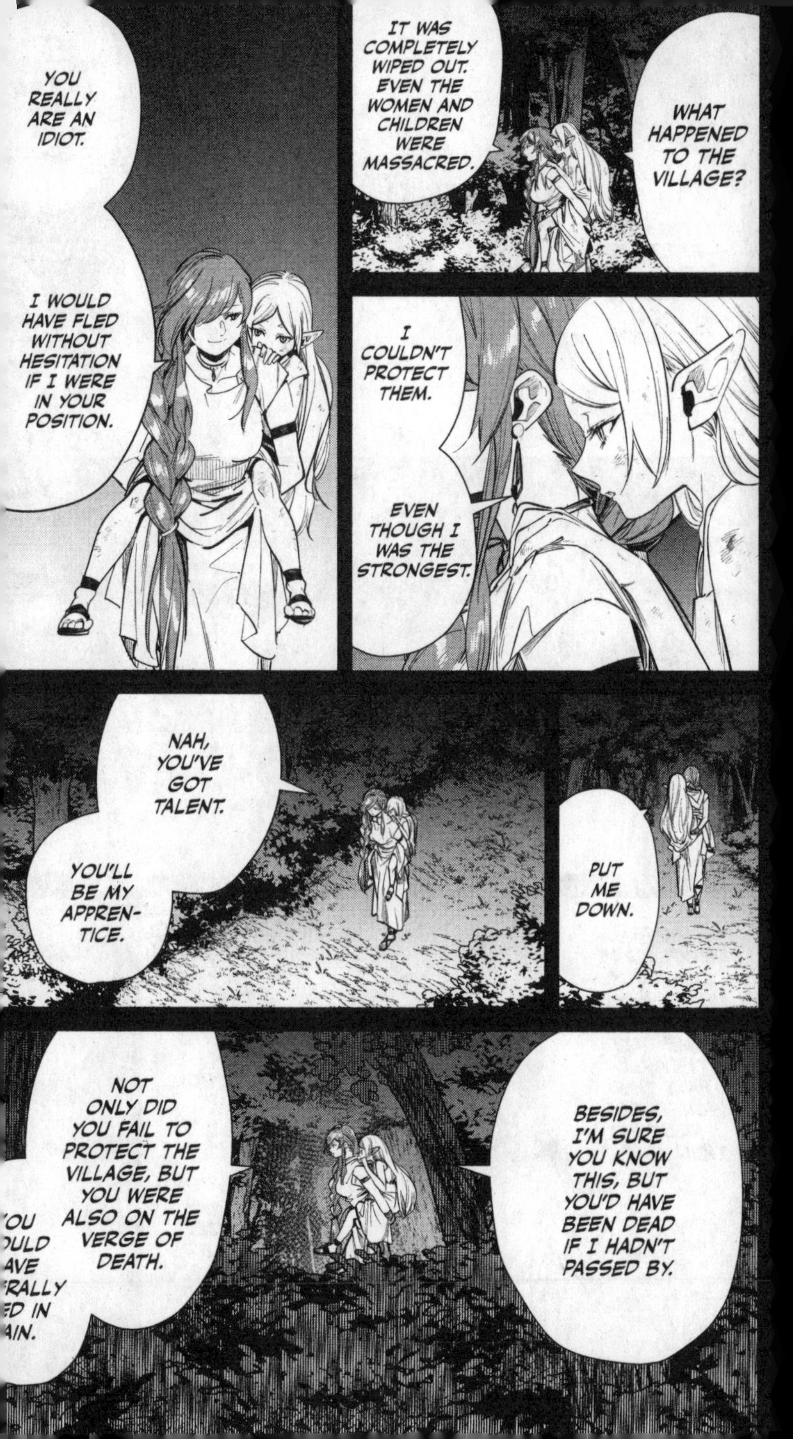
WHAT HAPPENED TO THE VILLAGE?
IT WAS COMPLETELY WIPED OUT. EVEN THE WOMEN AND CHILDREN WERE MASSACRED.
I COULDN'T PROTECT THEM.
EVEN THOUGH I WAS THE STRONGEST.
YOU REALLY ARE AN IDIOT.
I WOULD HAVE FLED WITHOUT HESITATION IF I WERE IN YOUR POSITION.
PUT ME DOWN.
NAH, YOU'VE GOT TALENT.
YOU'LL BE MY APPRENTICE.
BESIDES, I'M SURE YOU KNOW THIS, BUT YOU'D HAVE BEEN DEAD IF I HADN'T PASSED BY.
NOT ONLY DID YOU FAIL TO PROTECT THE VILLAGE, BUT YOU WERE ALSO ON THE VERGE OF DEATH.

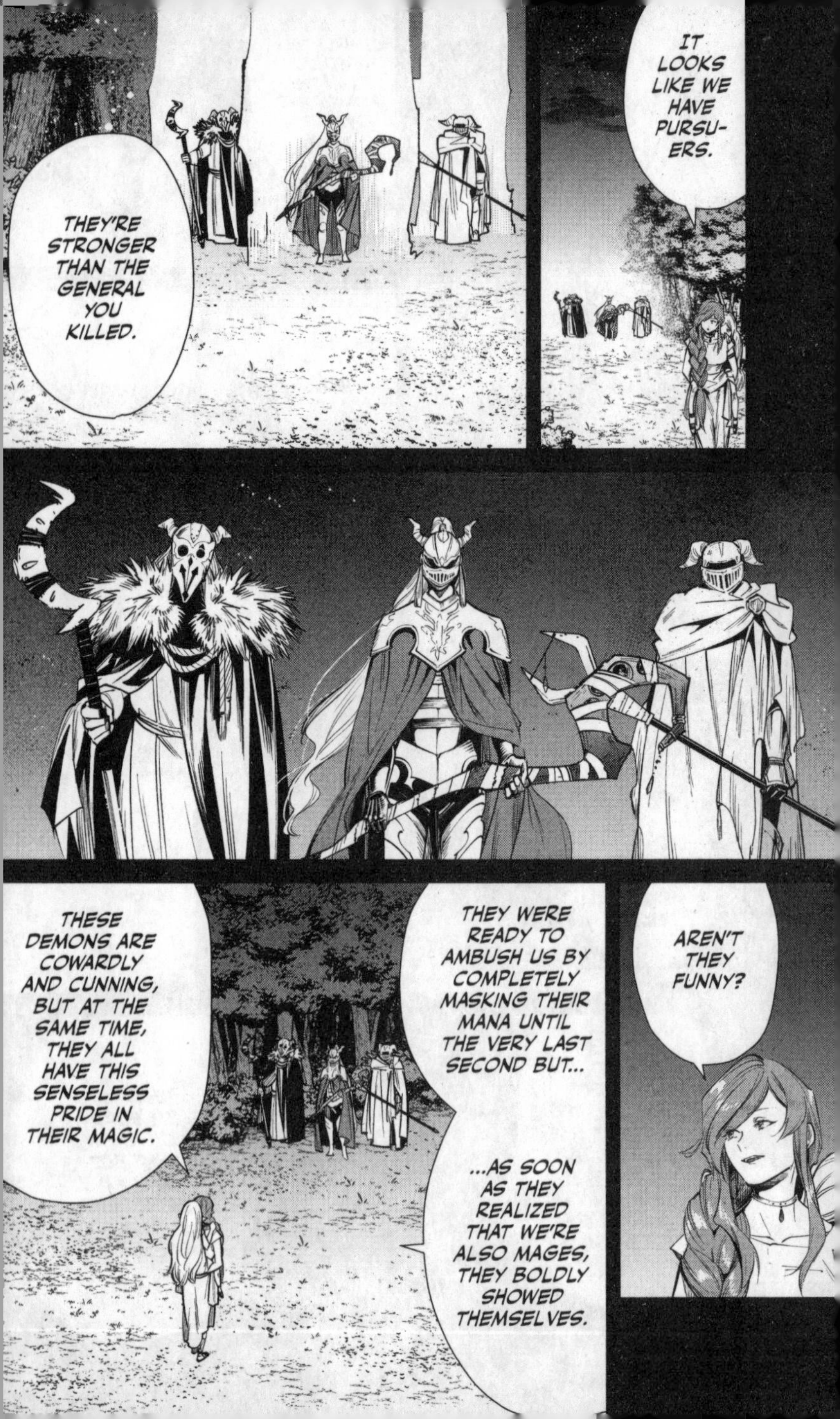
IT LOOKS LIKE WE HAVE PURSU-ERS.
THEY'RE STRONGER THAN THE GENERAL YOU KILLED.
AREN'T THEY FUNNY?
THEY WERE READY TO AMBUSH US BY COMPLETELY MASKING THEIR MANA UNTIL THE VERY LAST SECOND BUT...
...AS SOON AS THEY REALIZED THAT WE'RE ALSO MAGES, THEY BOLDLY SHOWED THEMSELVES.
THESE DEMONS ARE COWARDLY AND CUNNING, BUT AT THE SAME TIME, THEY ALL HAVE THIS SENSELESS PRIDE IN THEIR MAGIC.

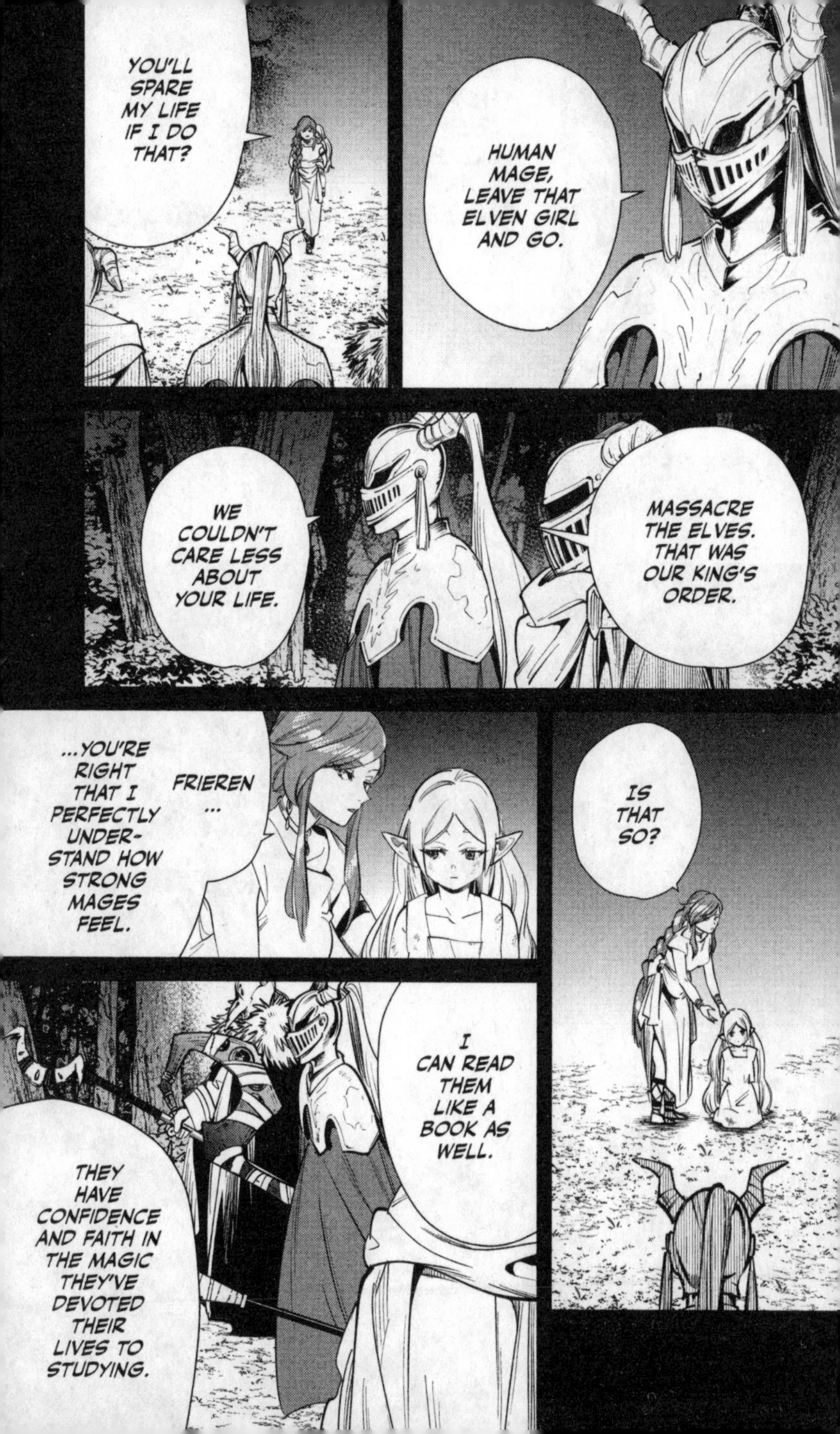
HUMAN MAGE, LEAVE THAT ELVEN GIRL AND GO.
YOU'LL SPARE MY LIFE IF I DO THAT?
MASSACRE THE ELVES. THAT WAS OUR KING'S ORDER.
WE COULDN'T CARE LESS ABOUT YOUR LIFE.
IS THAT SO?
FRIEREN...
...YOU'RE RIGHT THAT I PERFECTLY UNDER-STAND HOW STRONG MAGES FEEL.
I CAN READ THEM LIKE A BOOK AS WELL.
THEY HAVE CONFIDENCE AND FAITH IN THE MAGIC THEY'VE DEVOTED THEIR LIVES TO STUDYING.

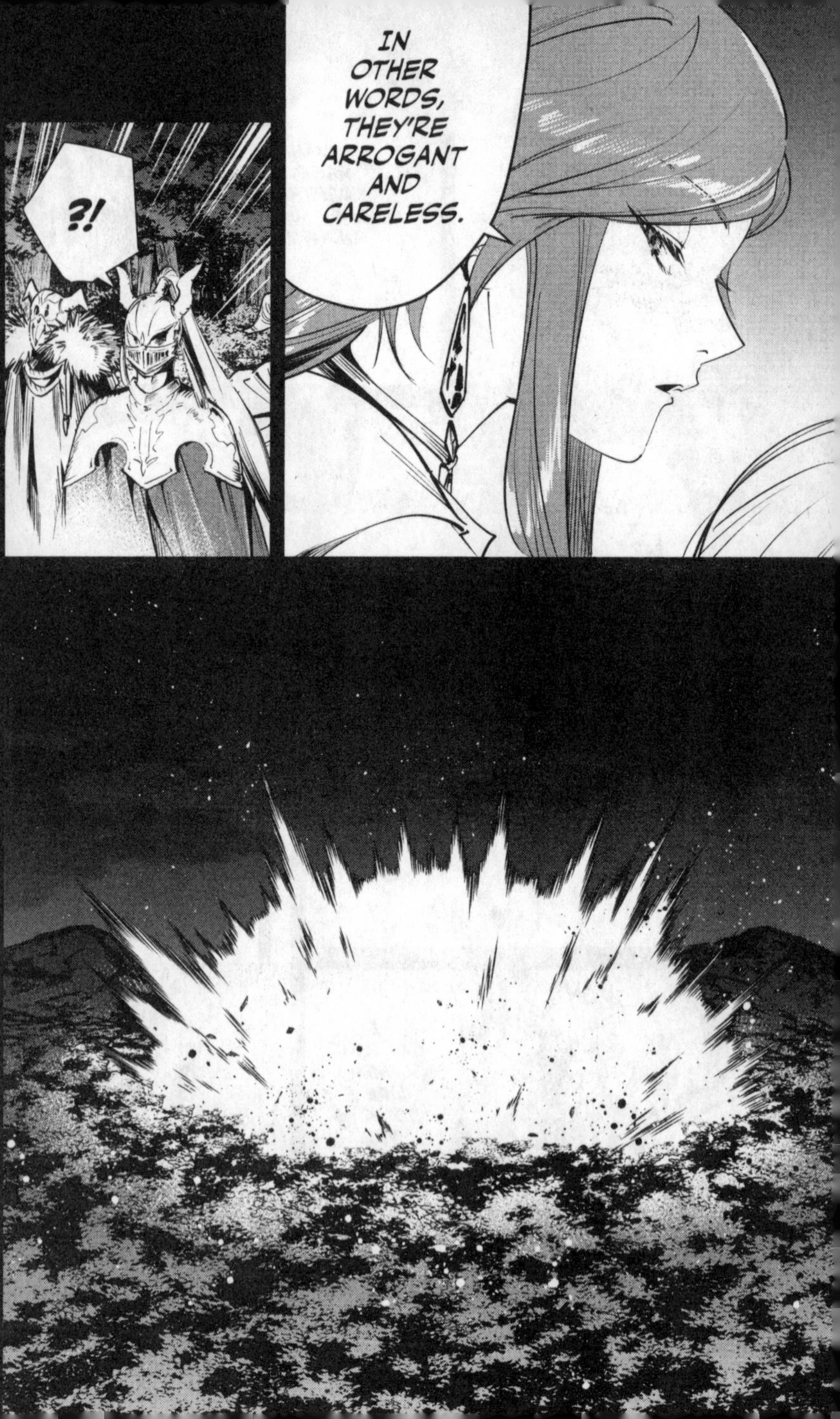
IN OTHER WORDS, THEY'RE ARROGANT AND CARELESS.
?!

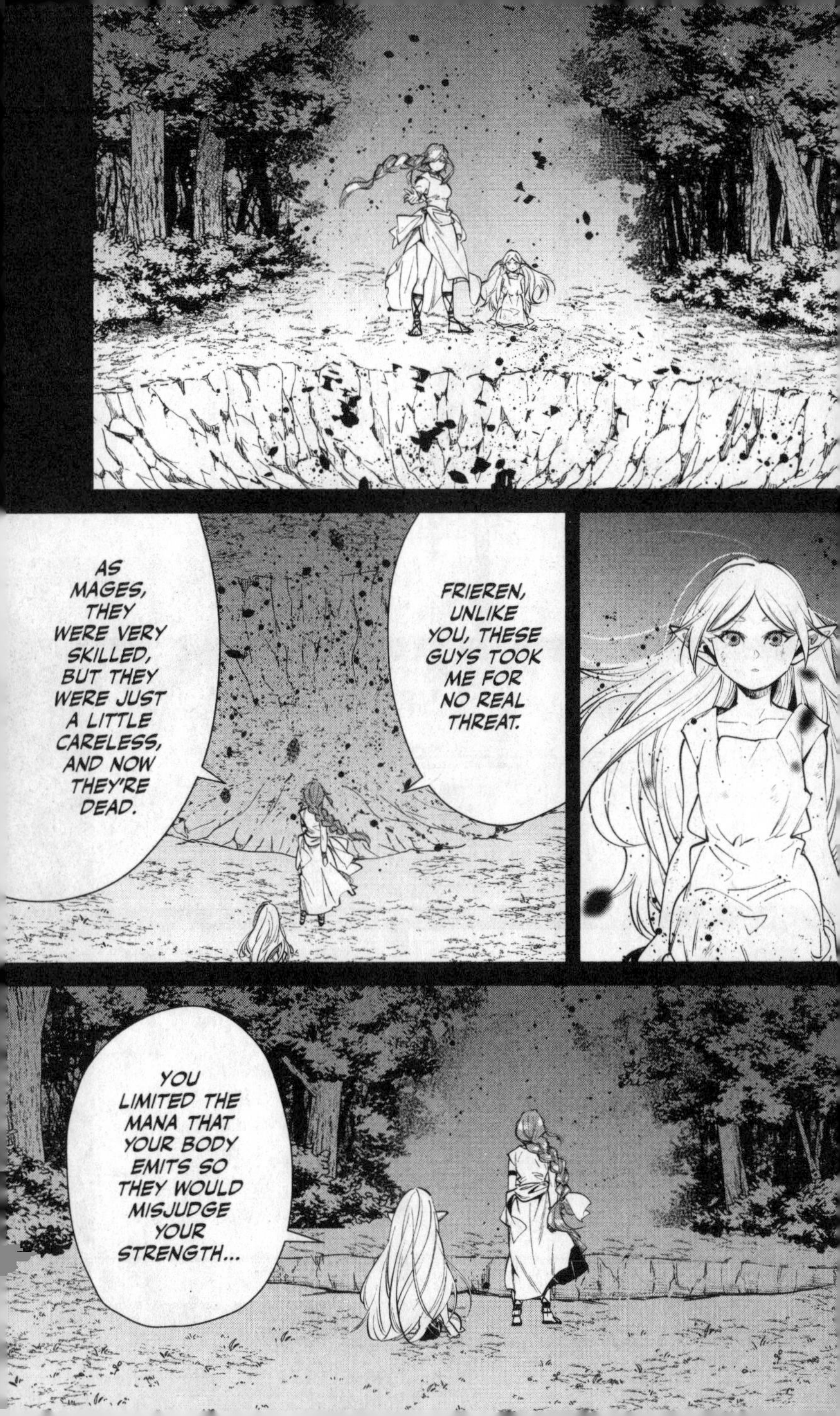
FRIEREN, UNLIKE YOU, THESE GUYS TOOK ME FOR NO REAL THREAT.
AS MAGES, THEY WERE VERY SKILLED, BUT THEY WERE JUST A LITTLE CARELESS, AND NOW THEY'RE DEAD.
YOU LIMITED THE MANA THAT YOUR BODY EMITS SO THEY WOULD MISJUDGE YOUR STRENGTH...

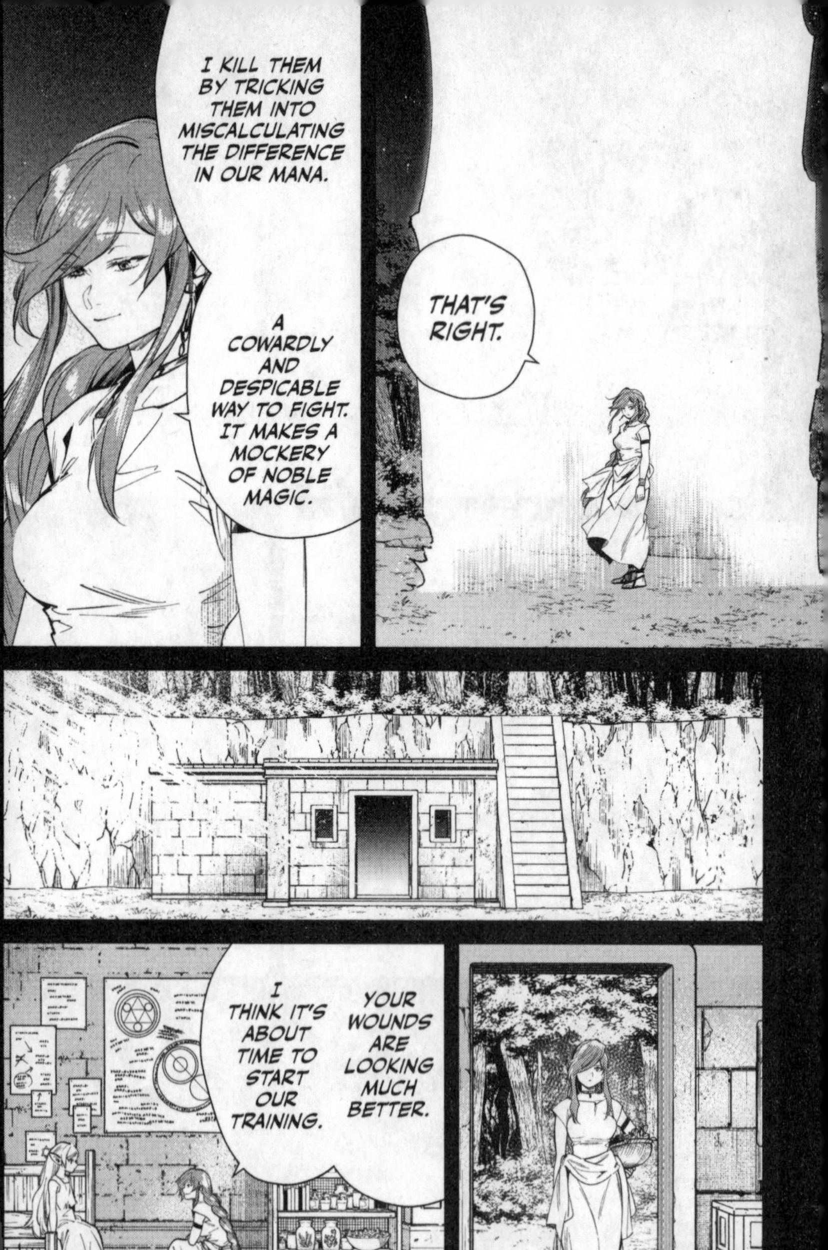
THAT'S RIGHT.
I KILL THEM BY TRICKING THEM INTO MISCALCULATING THE DIFFERENCE IN OUR MANA.
A COWARDLY AND DESPICABLE WAY TO FIGHT. IT MAKES A MOCKERY OF NOBLE MAGIC.
YOUR WOUNDS ARE LOOKING MUCH BETTER.
I THINK IT'S ABOUT TIME TO START OUR TRAINING.

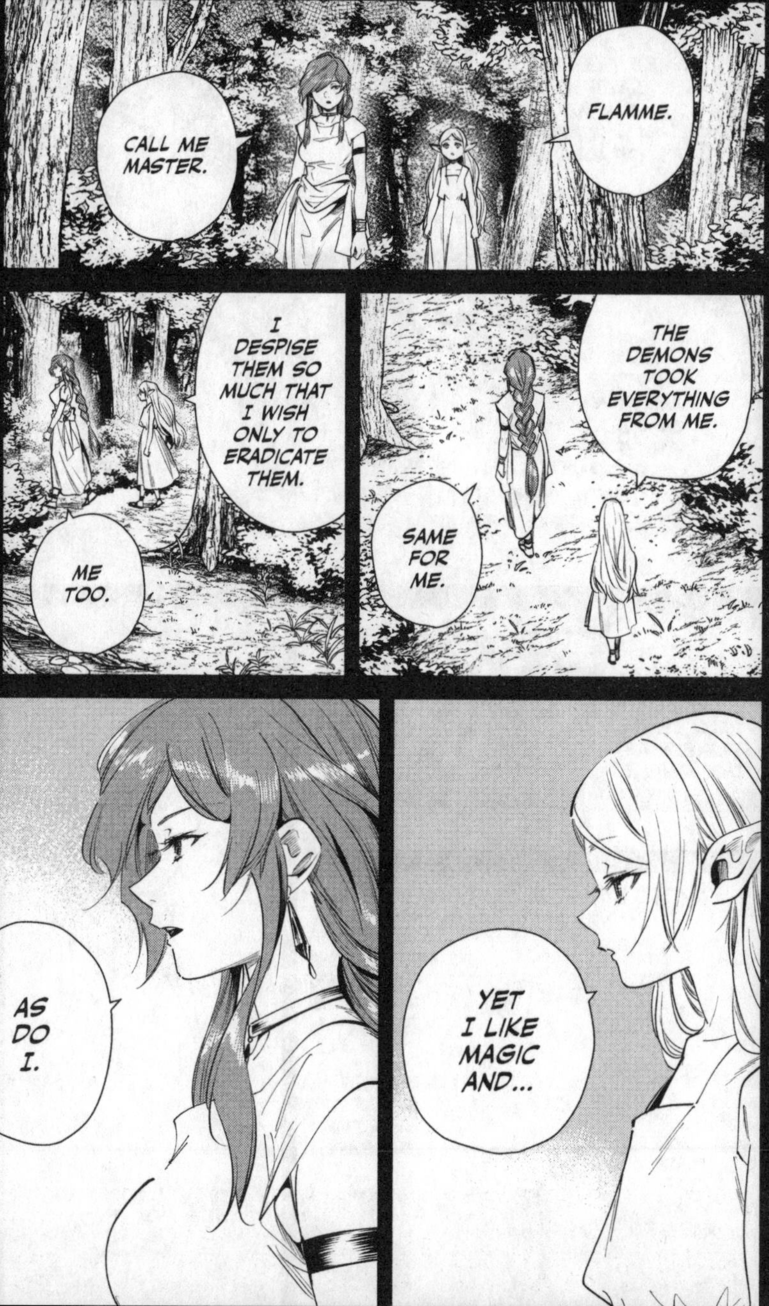
FLAMME.
CALL ME MASTER.
THE DEMONS TOOK EVERYTHING FROM ME.
SAME FOR ME.
I DESPISE THEM SO MUCH THAT I WISH ONLY TO ERADICATE THEM.
ME TOO.
YET I LIKE MAGIC AND...
AS DO I.

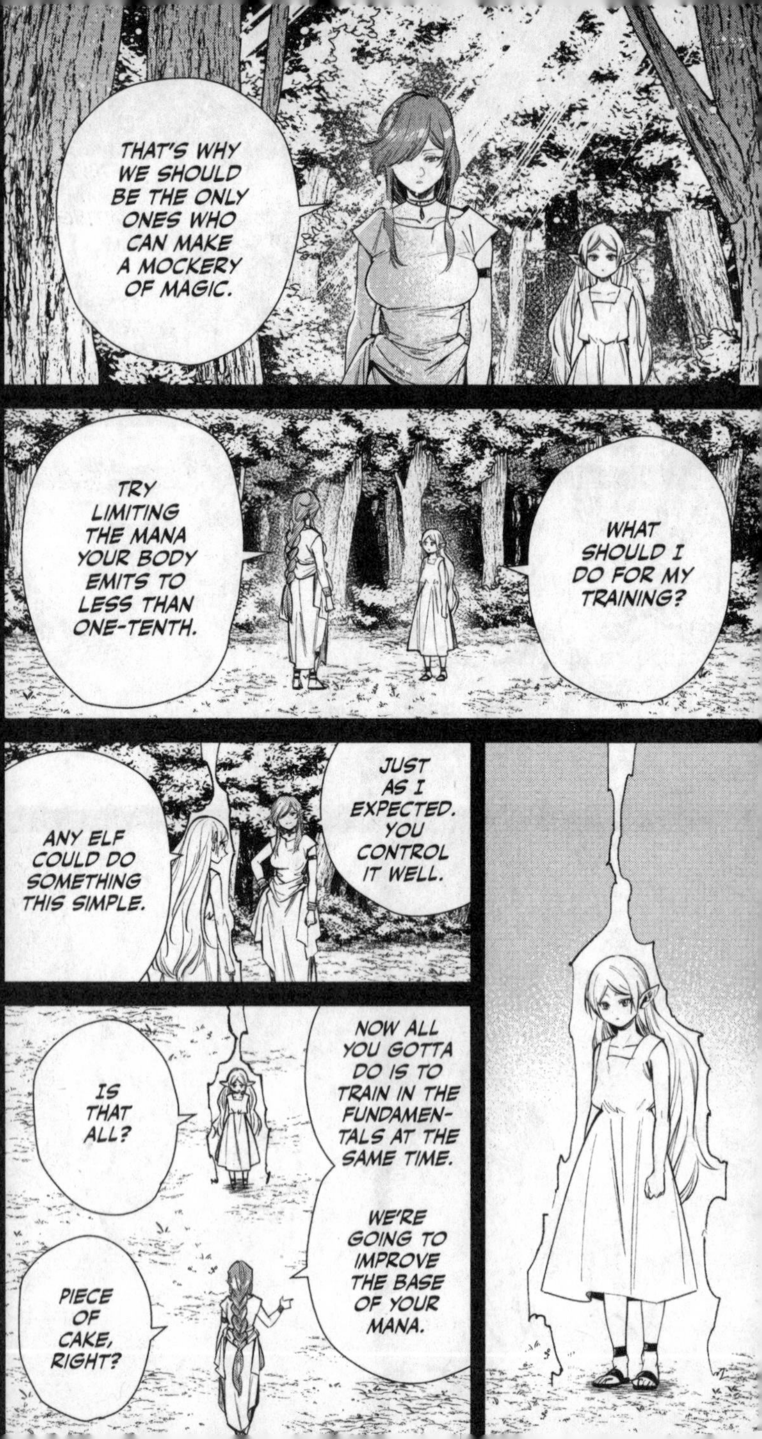
THAT'S WHY WE SHOULD BE THE ONLY ONES WHO CAN MAKE A MOCKERY OF MAGIC.
WHAT SHOULD I DO FOR MY TRAINING?
TRY LIMITING THE MANA YOUR BODY EMITS TO LESS THAN ONE-TENTH.
JUST AS I EXPECTED. YOU CONTROL IT WELL.
ANY ELF COULD DO SOMETHING THIS SIMPLE.
NOW ALL YOU GOTTA DO IS TO TRAIN IN THE FUNDAMEN-TALS AT THE SAME TIME.
WE'RE GOING TO IMPROVE THE BASE OF YOUR MANA.
IS THAT ALL?
PIECE OF CAKE, RIGHT?

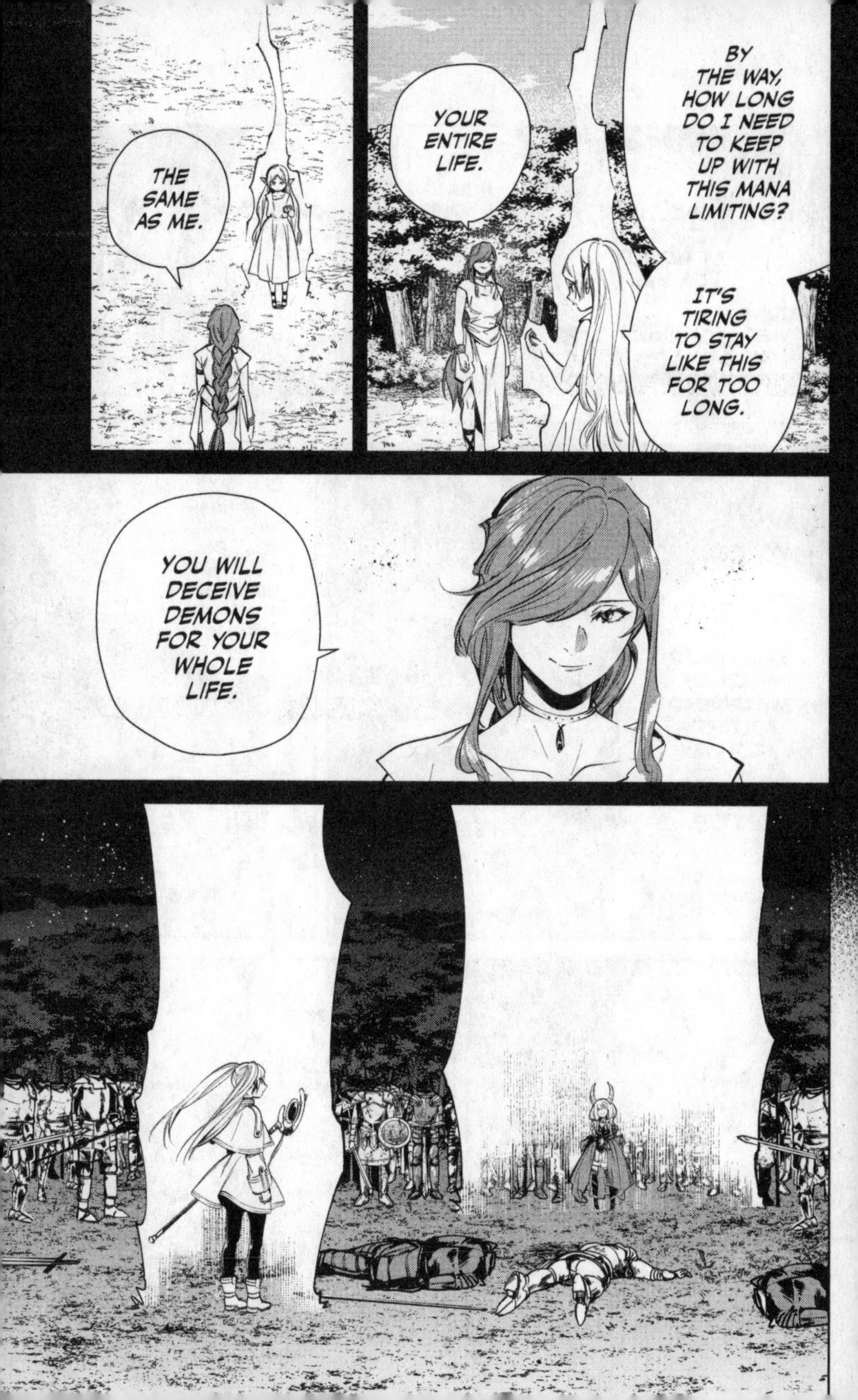
BY THE WAY, HOW LONG DO I NEED TO KEEP UP WITH THIS MANA LIMITING?
IT'S TIRING TO STAY LIKE THIS FOR TOO LONG.
YOUR ENTIRE LIFE.
THE SAME AS ME.
YOU WILL DECEIVE DEMONS FOR YOUR WHOLE LIFE.

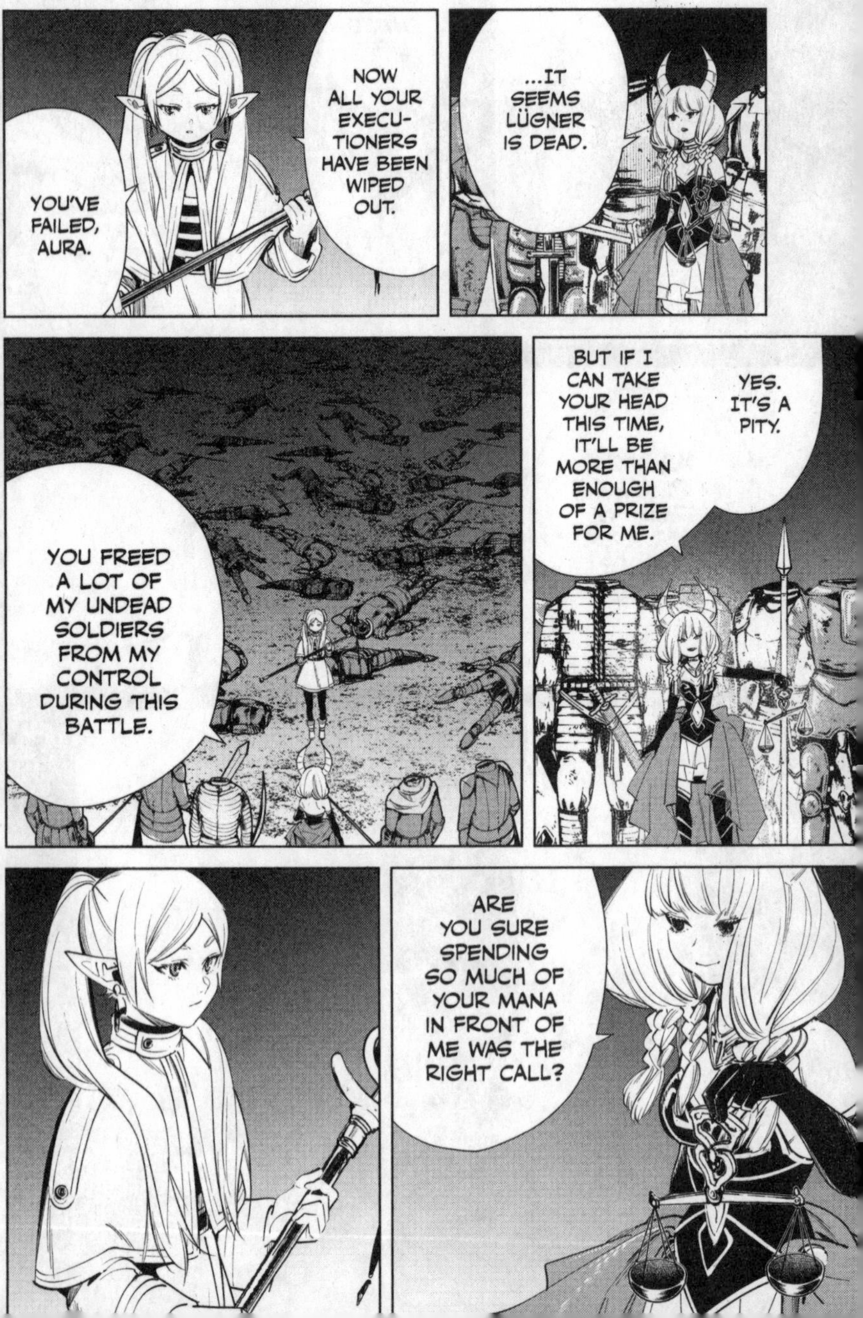
...IT SEEMS LÜGNER IS DEAD.
NOW ALL YOUR EXECU-TIONERS HAVE BEEN WIPED OUT.
YOU'VE FAILED, AURA.
YES. IT'S A PITY.
BUT IF I CAN TAKE YOUR HEAD THIS TIME, IT'LL BE MORE THAN ENOUGH OF A PRIZE FOR ME.
YOU FREED A LOT OF MY UNDEAD SOLDIERS FROM MY CONTROL DURING THIS BATTLE.
ARE YOU SURE SPENDING SO MUCH OF YOUR MANA IN FRONT OF ME WAS THE RIGHT CALL?

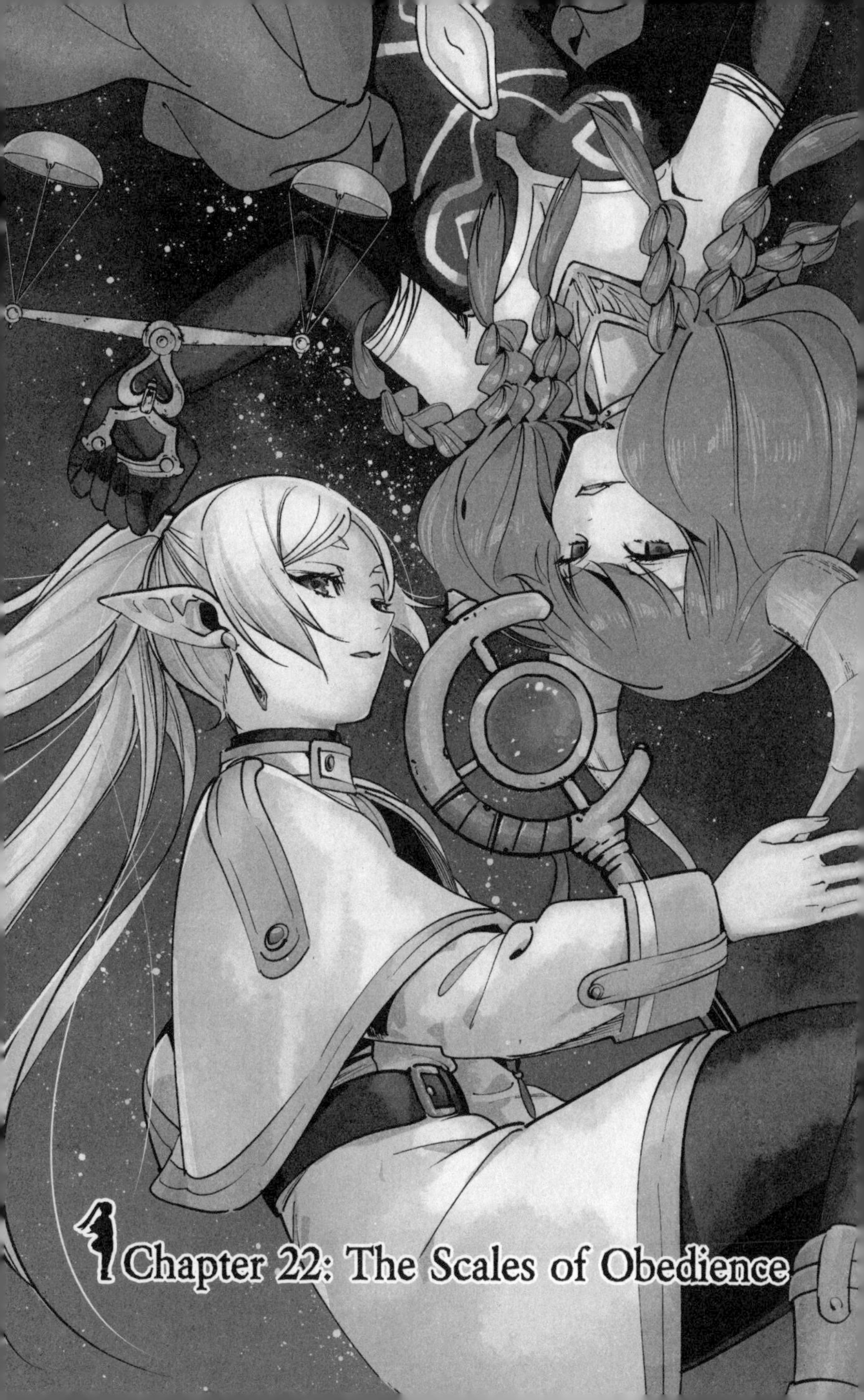

# Chapter 22: The Scales of Obedience

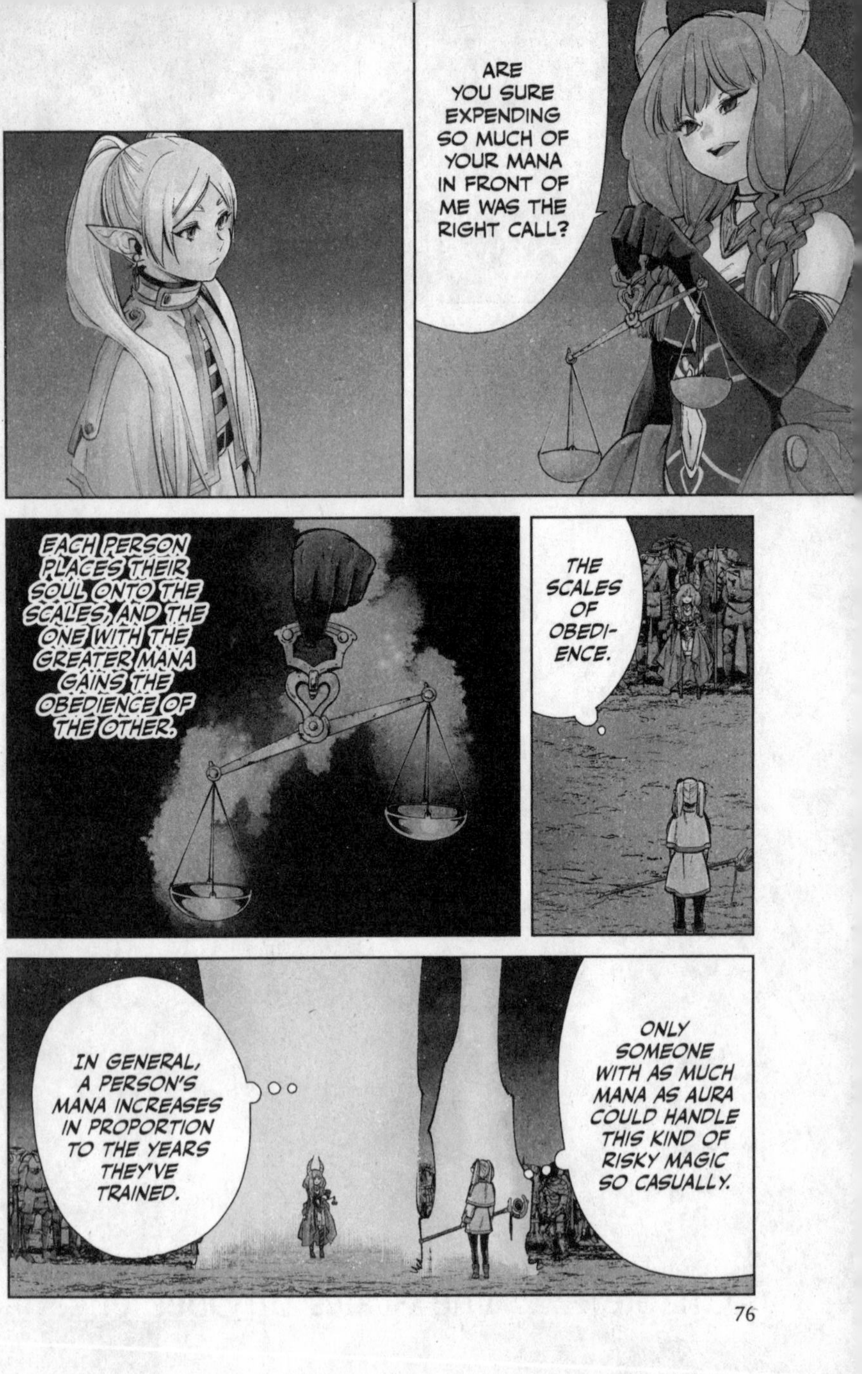
ARE YOU SURE EXPENDING SO MUCH OF YOUR MANA IN FRONT OF ME WAS THE RIGHT CALL?
THE SCALES OF OBEDIENCE.
EACH PERSON PLACES THEIR SOUL ONTO THE SCALES, AND THE ONE WITH THE GREATER MANA GAINS THE OBEDIENCE OF THE OTHER.
ONLY SOMEONE WITH AS MUCH MANA AS AURA COULD HANDLE THIS KIND OF RISKY MAGIC SO CASUALLY.
IN GENERAL, A PERSON'S MANA INCREASES IN PROPORTION TO THE YEARS THEY'VE TRAINED.

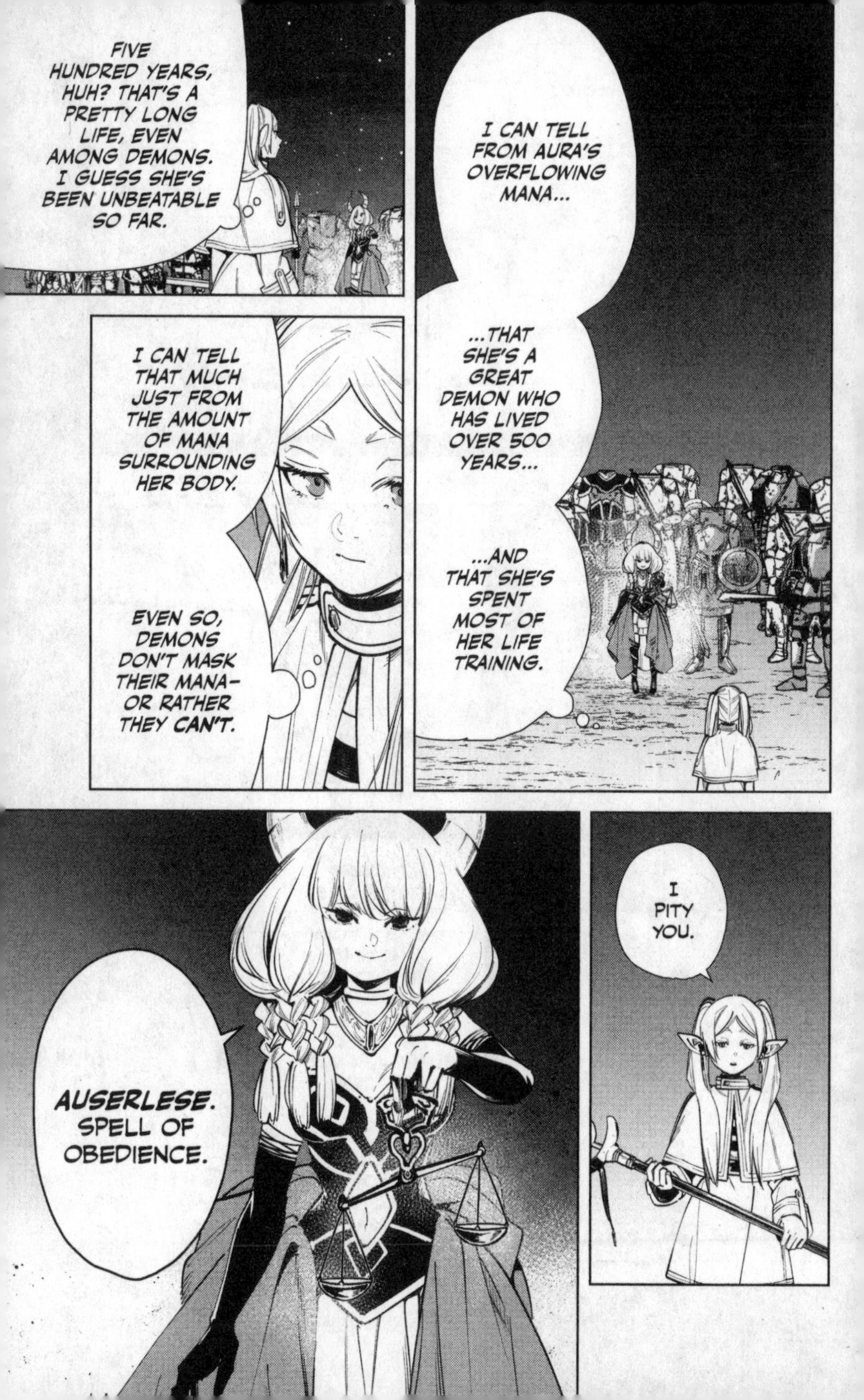
I CAN TELL FROM AURA'S OVERFLOWING MANA...
...THAT SHE'S A GREAT DEMON WHO HAS LIVED OVER 500 YEARS...
...AND THAT SHE'S SPENT MOST OF HER LIFE TRAINING.
FIVE HUNDRED YEARS, HUH? THAT'S A PRETTY LONG LIFE, EVEN AMONG DEMONS. I GUESS SHE'S BEEN UNBEATABLE SO FAR.
I CAN TELL THAT MUCH JUST FROM THE AMOUNT OF MANA SURROUNDING HER BODY.
EVEN SO, DEMONS DON'T MASK THEIR MANA— OR RATHER THEY *CAN'T*.
I PITY YOU.
**AUSERLESE.** SPELL OF OBEDIENCE.

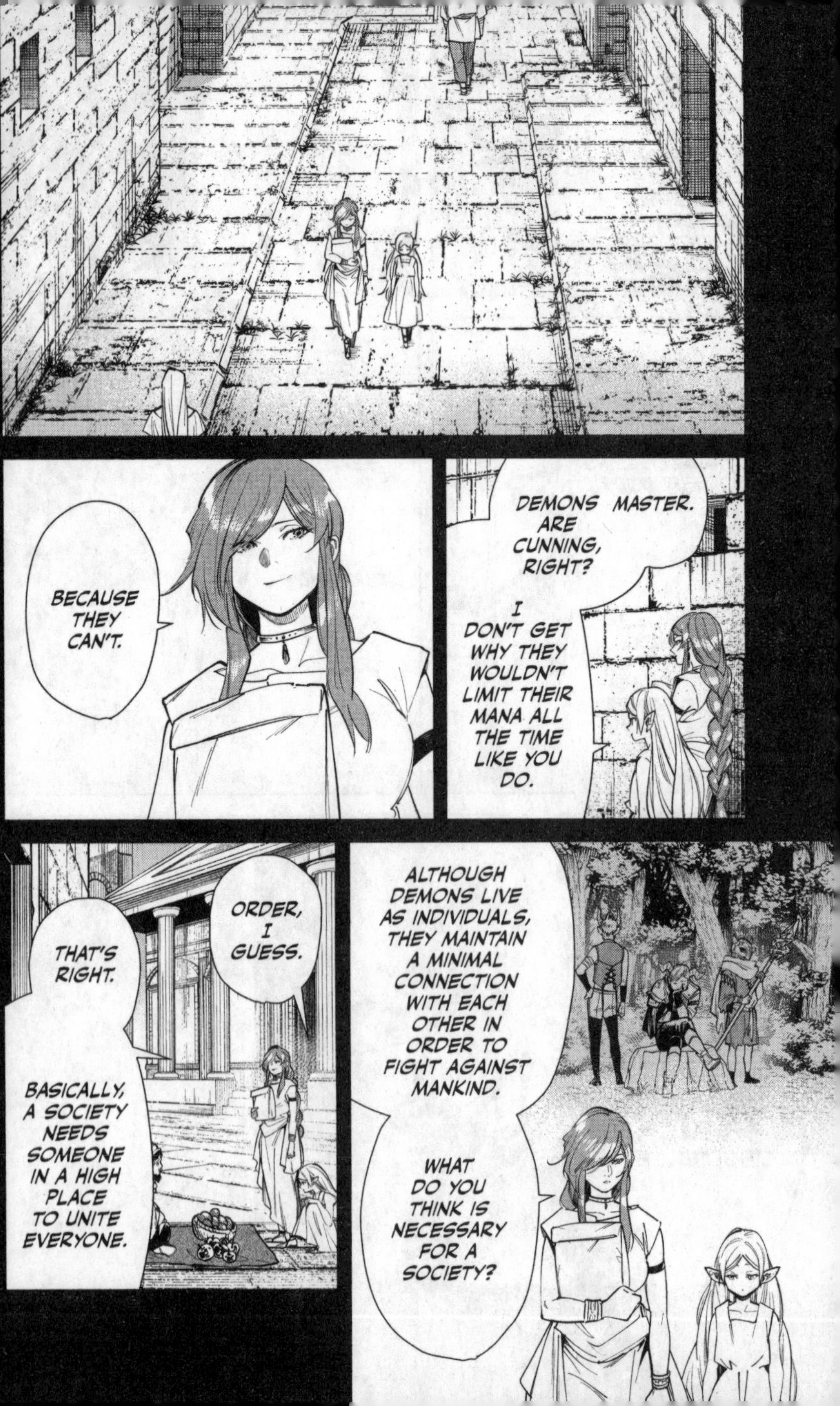
MASTER.
DEMONS ARE CUNNING, RIGHT?
I DON'T GET WHY THEY WOULDN'T LIMIT THEIR MANA ALL THE TIME LIKE YOU DO.
BECAUSE THEY CAN'T.
ALTHOUGH DEMONS LIVE AS INDIVIDUALS, THEY MAINTAIN A MINIMAL CONNECTION WITH EACH OTHER IN ORDER TO FIGHT AGAINST MANKIND.
WHAT DO YOU THINK IS NECESSARY FOR A SOCIETY?
ORDER, I GUESS.
THAT'S RIGHT.
BASICALLY, A SOCIETY NEEDS SOMEONE IN A HIGH PLACE TO UNITE EVERYONE.

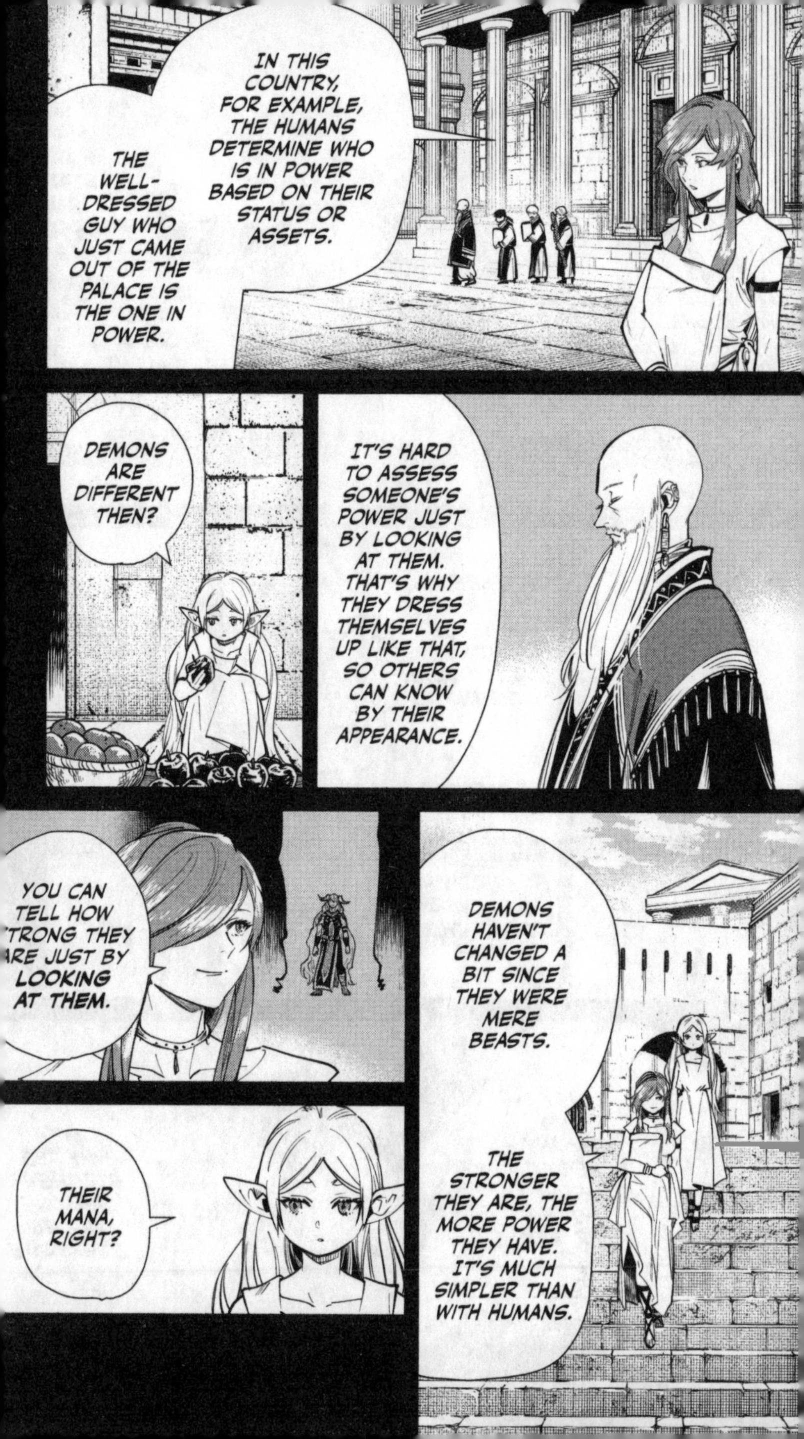
IN THIS COUNTRY, FOR EXAMPLE, THE HUMANS DETERMINE WHO IS IN POWER BASED ON THEIR STATUS OR ASSETS.
THE WELL-DRESSED GUY WHO JUST CAME OUT OF THE PALACE IS THE ONE IN POWER.
IT'S HARD TO ASSESS SOMEONE'S POWER JUST BY LOOKING AT THEM. THAT'S WHY THEY DRESS THEMSELVES UP LIKE THAT, SO OTHERS CAN KNOW BY THEIR APPEARANCE.
DEMONS ARE DIFFERENT THEN?
DEMONS HAVEN'T CHANGED A BIT SINCE THEY WERE MERE BEASTS.
THE STRONGER THEY ARE, THE MORE POWER THEY HAVE. IT'S MUCH SIMPLER THAN WITH HUMANS.
YOU CAN TELL HOW TRONG THEY RE JUST BY LOOKING AT THEM.
THEIR MANA, RIGHT?

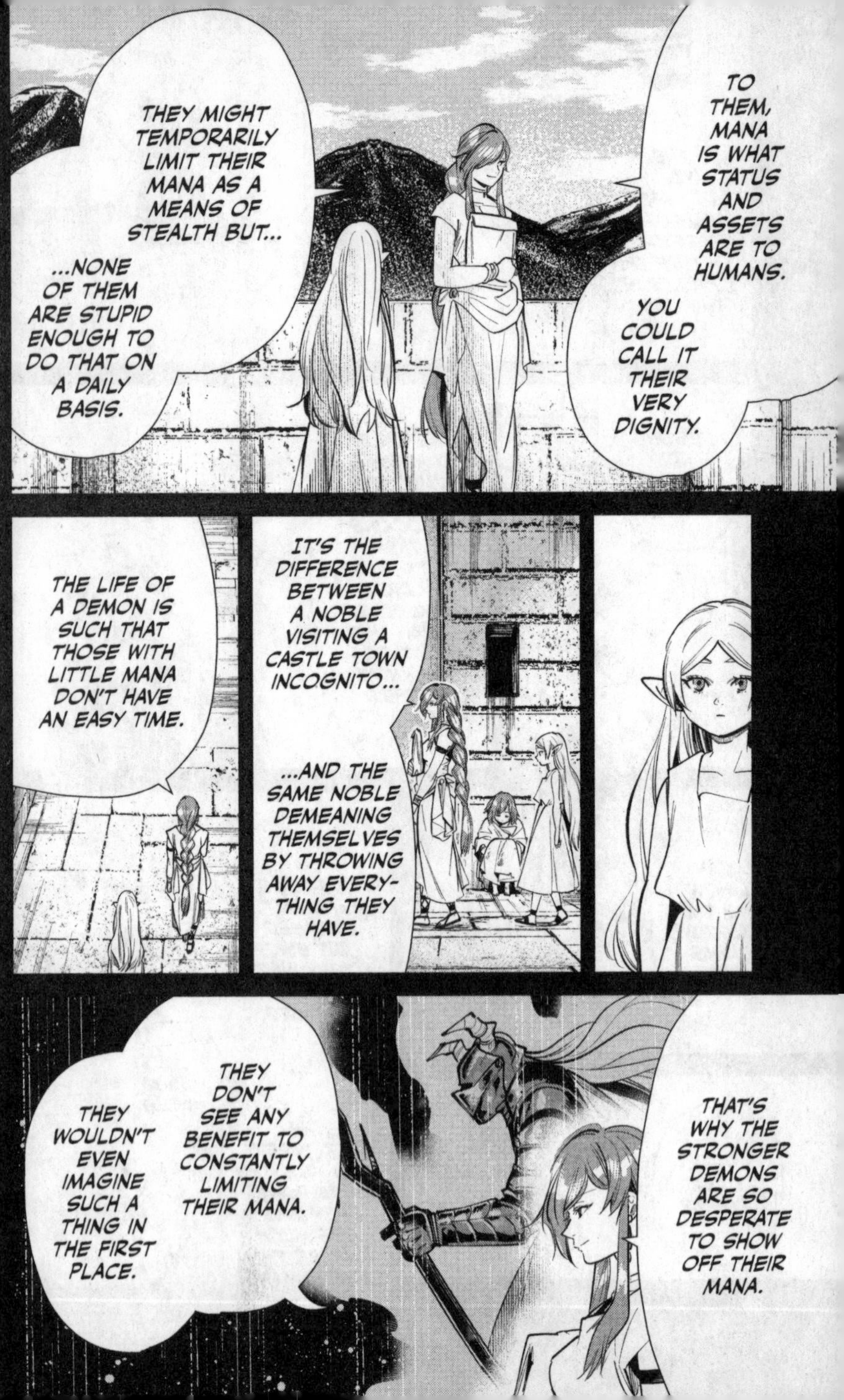
TO THEM, MANA IS WHAT STATUS AND ASSETS ARE TO HUMANS.
YOU COULD CALL IT THEIR VERY DIGNITY.
THEY MIGHT TEMPORARILY LIMIT THEIR MANA AS A MEANS OF STEALTH BUT...
...NONE OF THEM ARE STUPID ENOUGH TO DO THAT ON A DAILY BASIS.
IT'S THE DIFFERENCE BETWEEN A NOBLE VISITING A CASTLE TOWN INCOGNITO...
...AND THE SAME NOBLE DEMEANING THEMSELVES BY THROWING AWAY EVERY-THING THEY HAVE.
THE LIFE OF A DEMON IS SUCH THAT THOSE WITH LITTLE MANA DON'T HAVE AN EASY TIME.
THAT'S WHY THE STRONGER DEMONS ARE SO DESPERATE TO SHOW OFF THEIR MANA.
THEY DON'T SEE ANY BENEFIT TO CONSTANTLY LIMITING THEIR MANA.
THEY WOULDN'T EVEN IMAGINE SUCH A THING IN THE FIRST PLACE.

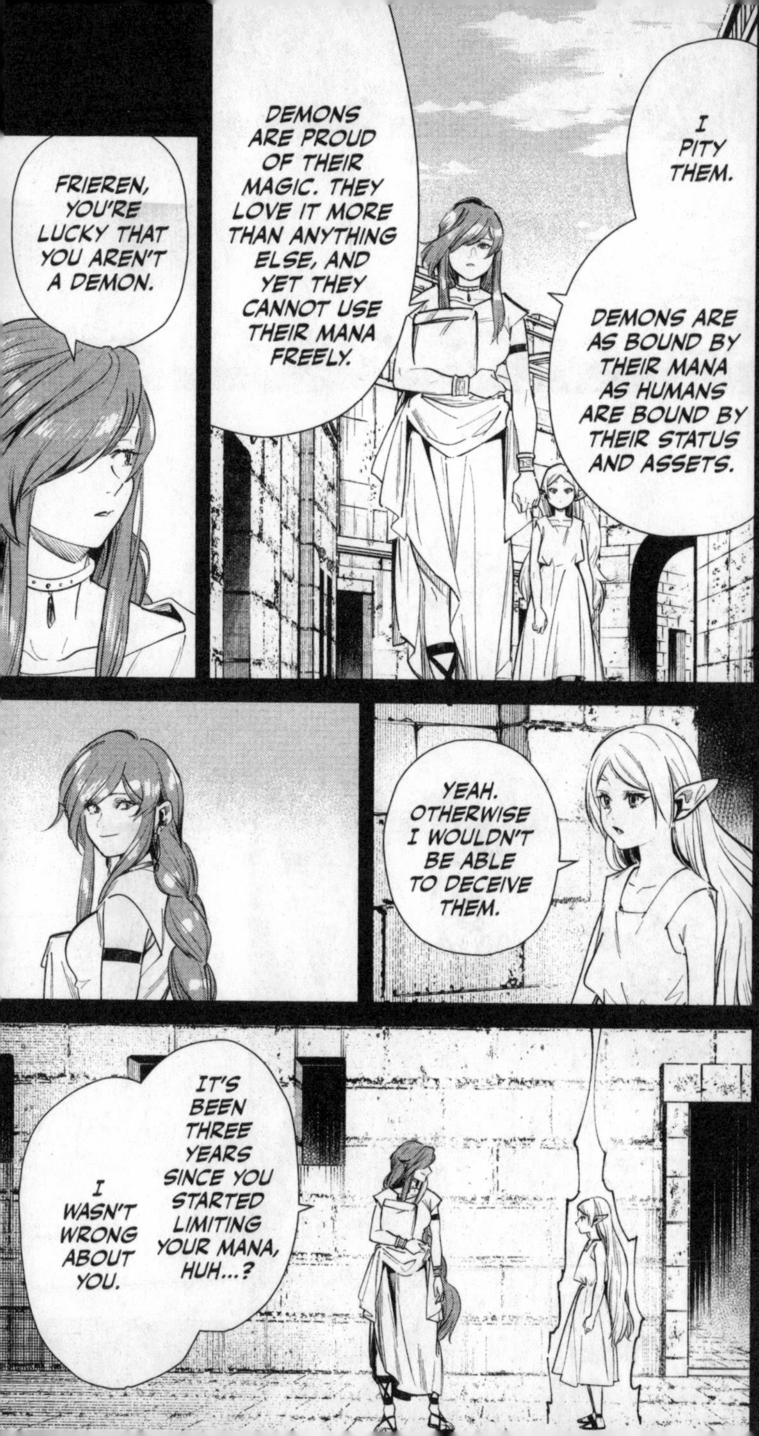
I PITY THEM.
DEMONS ARE AS BOUND BY THEIR MANA AS HUMANS ARE BOUND BY THEIR STATUS AND ASSETS.
DEMONS ARE PROUD OF THEIR MAGIC. THEY LOVE IT MORE THAN ANYTHING ELSE, AND YET THEY CANNOT USE THEIR MANA FREELY.
FRIEREN, YOU'RE LUCKY THAT YOU AREN'T A DEMON.
YEAH. OTHERWISE I WOULDN'T BE ABLE TO DECEIVE THEM.
IT'S BEEN THREE YEARS SINCE YOU STARTED LIMITING YOUR MANA, HUH...?
I WASN'T WRONG ABOUT YOU.

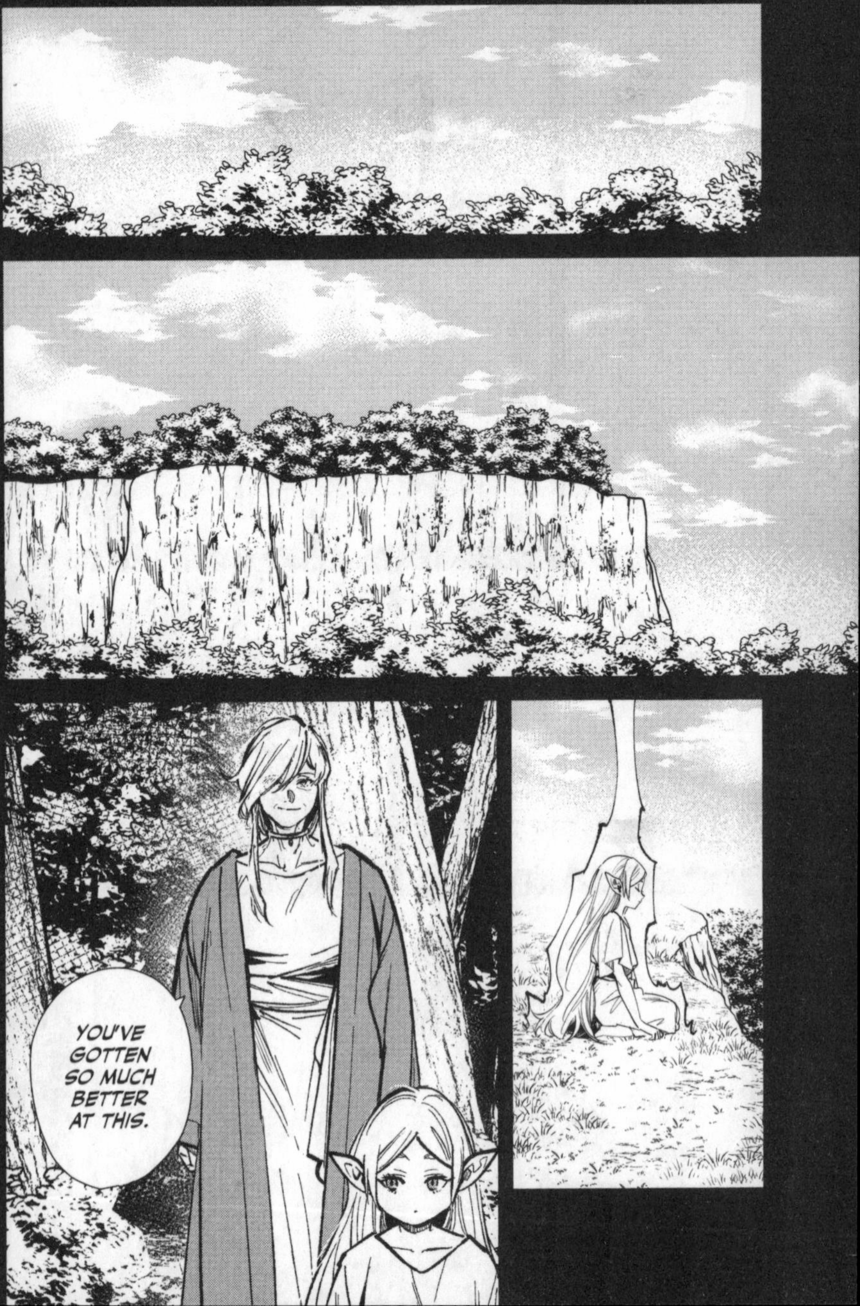
YOU'VE GOTTEN SO MUCH BETTER AT THIS.

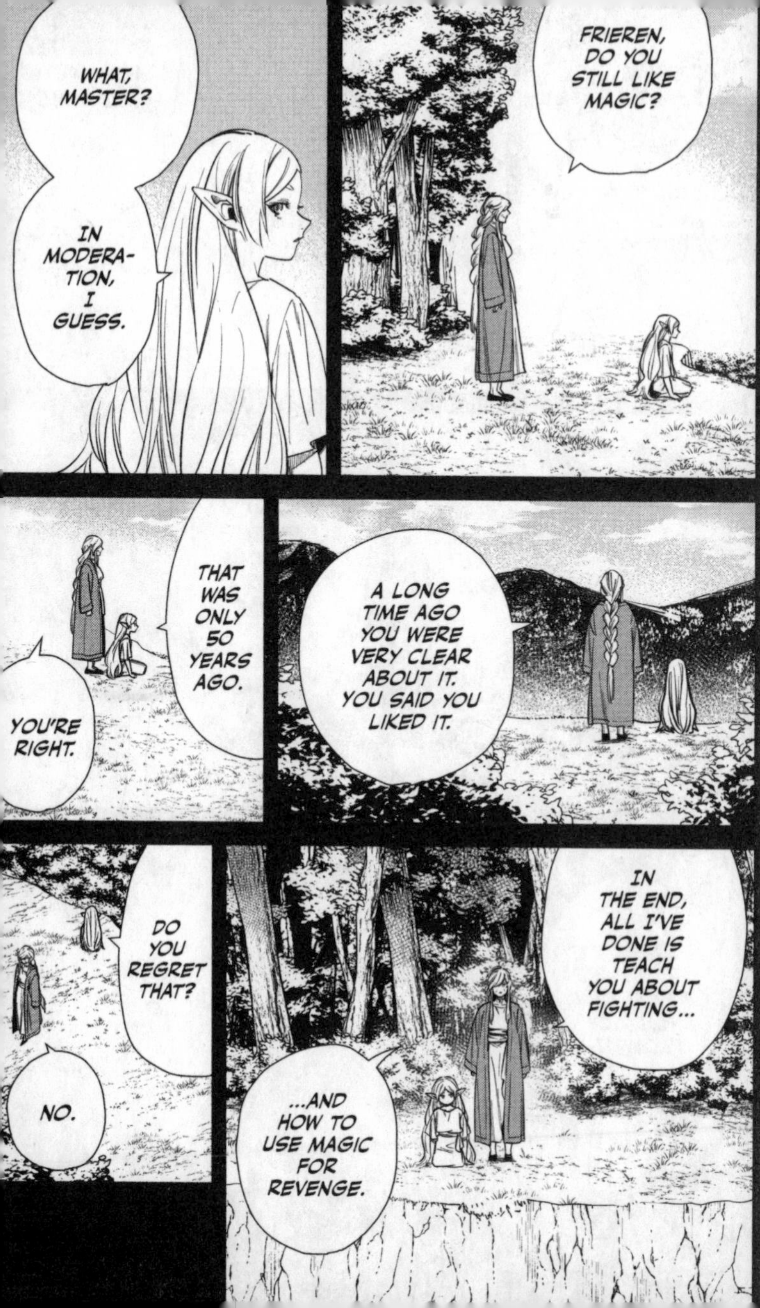
FRIEREN, DO YOU STILL LIKE MAGIC?
WHAT, MASTER?
IN MODERATION, I GUESS.
A LONG TIME AGO YOU WERE VERY CLEAR ABOUT IT. YOU SAID YOU LIKED IT.
THAT WAS ONLY 50 YEARS AGO.
YOU'RE RIGHT.
IN THE END, ALL I'VE DONE IS TEACH YOU ABOUT FIGHTING...
...AND HOW TO USE MAGIC FOR REVENGE.
DO YOU REGRET THAT?
NO.

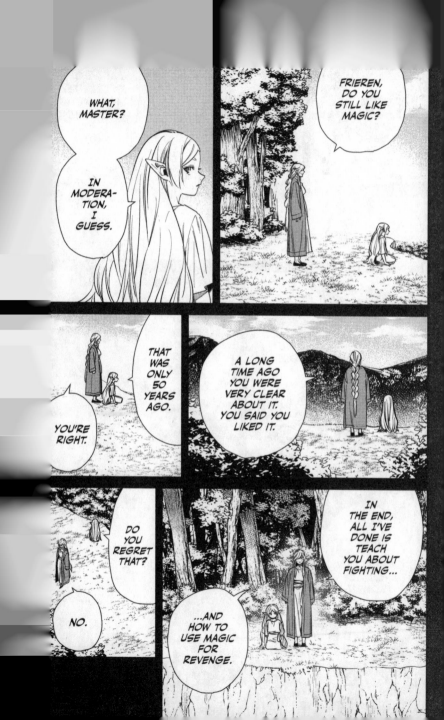

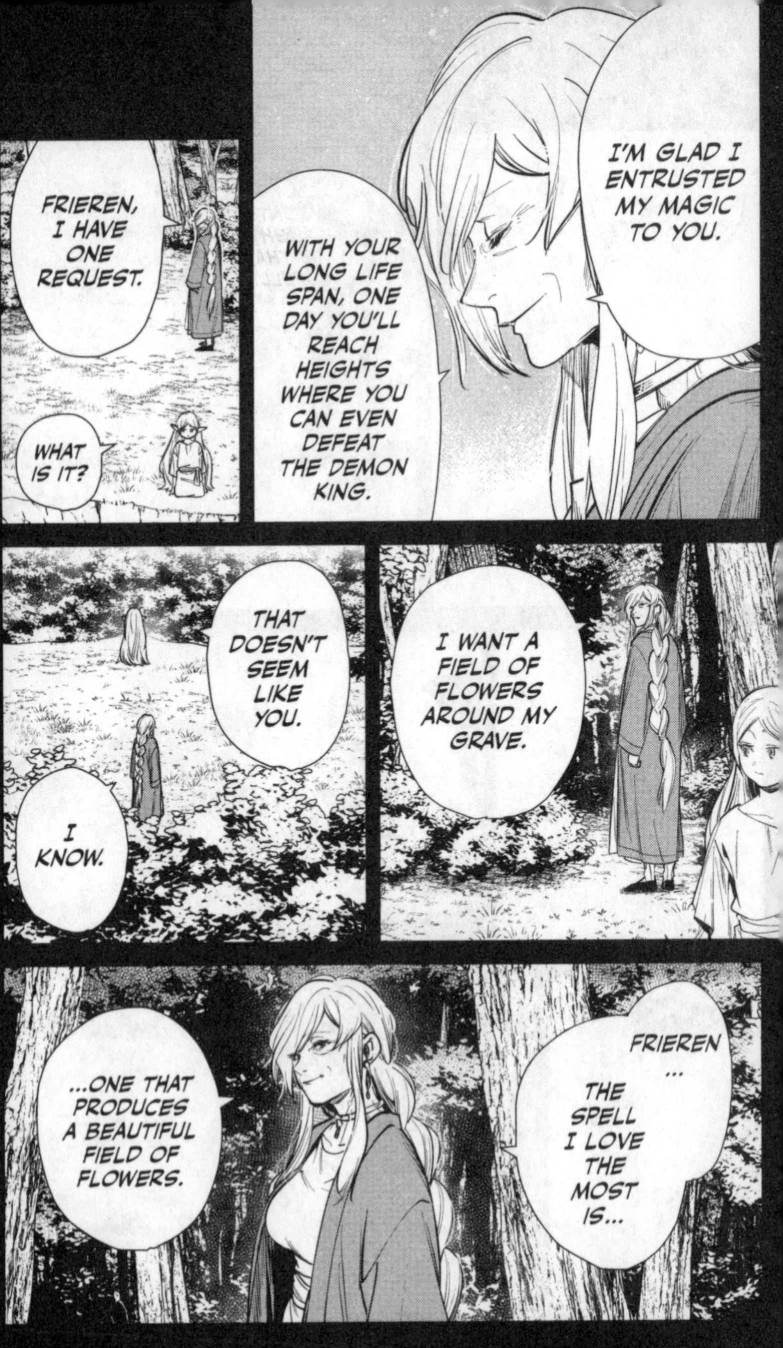
I'M GLAD I ENTRUSTED MY MAGIC TO YOU.
WITH YOUR LONG LIFE SPAN, ONE DAY YOU'LL REACH HEIGHTS WHERE YOU CAN EVEN DEFEAT THE DEMON KING.
FRIEREN, I HAVE ONE REQUEST.
WHAT IS IT?
I WANT A FIELD OF FLOWERS AROUND MY GRAVE.
THAT DOESN'T SEEM LIKE YOU.
I KNOW.
FRIEREN... THE SPELL I LOVE THE MOST IS...
...ONE THAT PRODUCES A BEAUTIFUL FIELD OF FLOWERS.

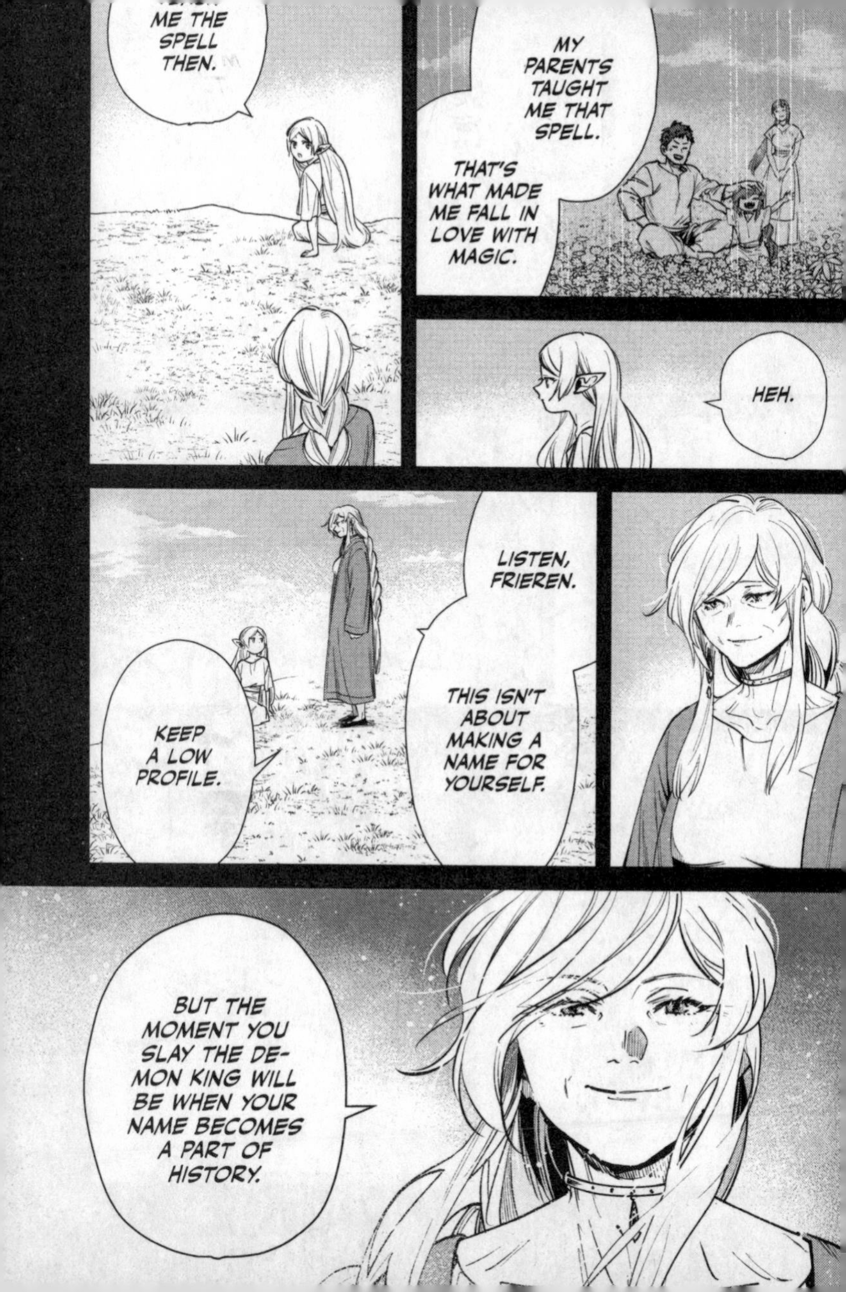
MY PARENTS TAUGHT ME THAT SPELL.
THAT'S WHAT MADE ME FALL IN LOVE WITH MAGIC.
HEH.
ME THE SPELL THEN.
LISTEN, FRIEREN.
THIS ISN'T ABOUT MAKING A NAME FOR YOURSELF.
KEEP A LOW PROFILE.
BUT THE MOMENT YOU SLAY THE DE-MON KING WILL BE WHEN YOUR NAME BECOMES A PART OF HISTORY.

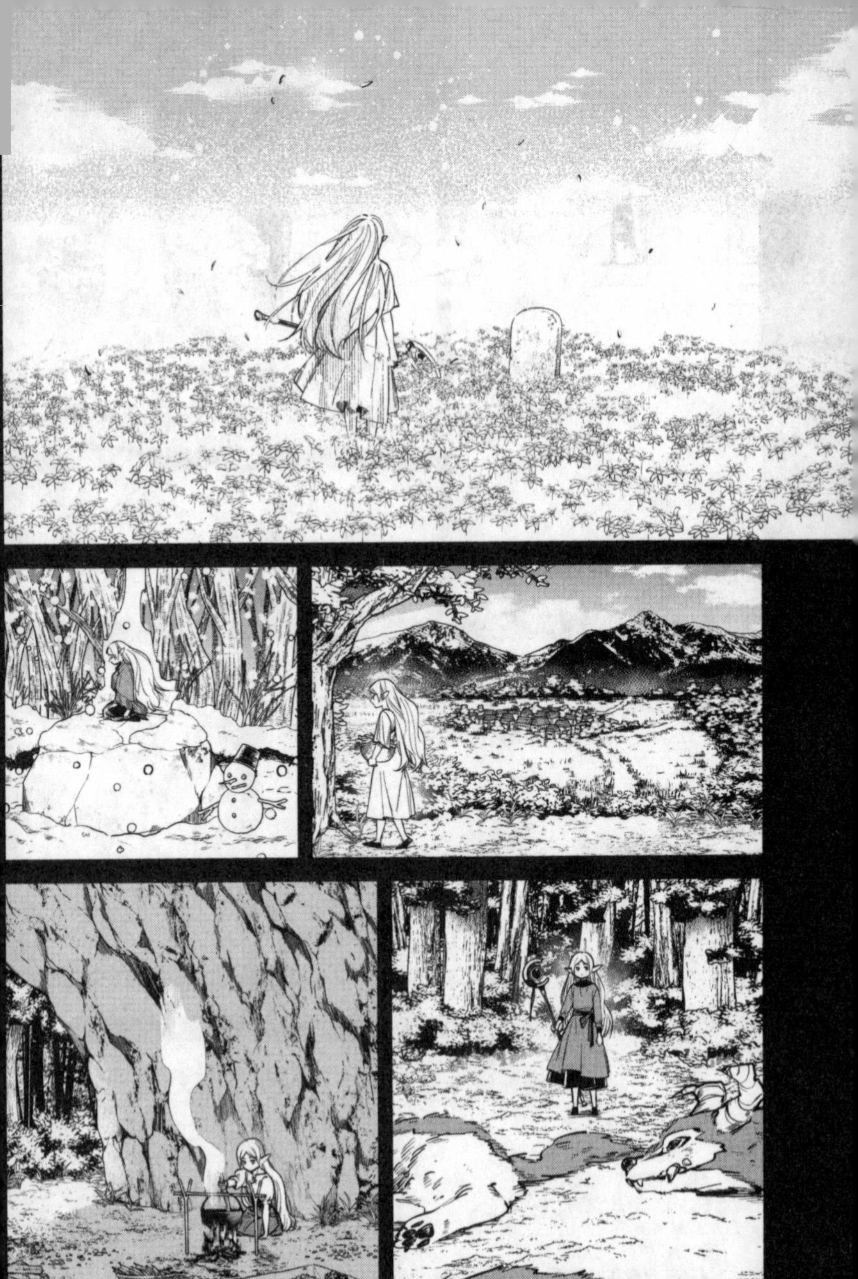

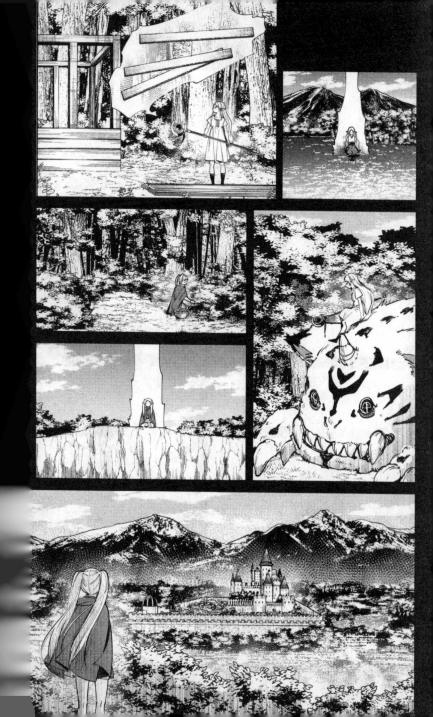

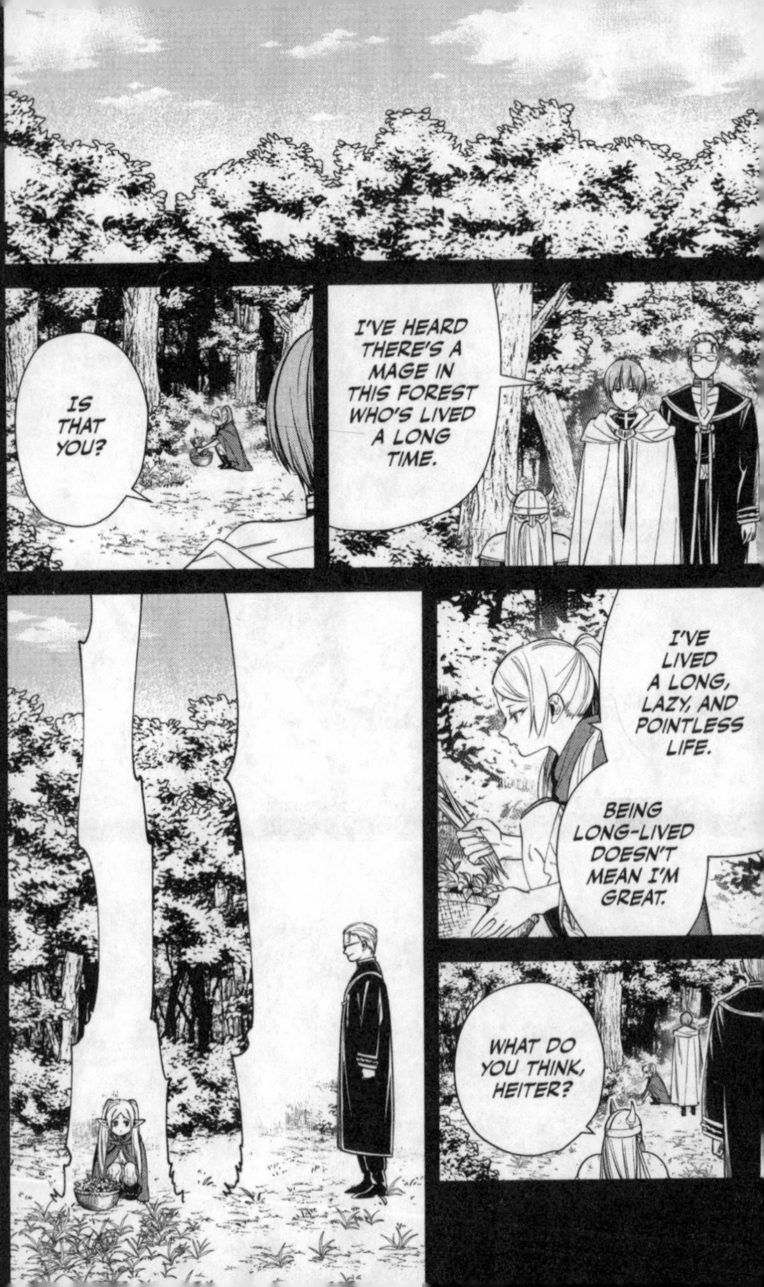
I'VE HEARD THERE'S A MAGE IN THIS FOREST WHO'S LIVED A LONG TIME.
IS THAT YOU?
I'VE LIVED A LONG, LAZY, AND POINTLESS LIFE.
BEING LONG-LIVED DOESN'T MEAN I'M GREAT.
WHAT DO YOU THINK, HEITER?

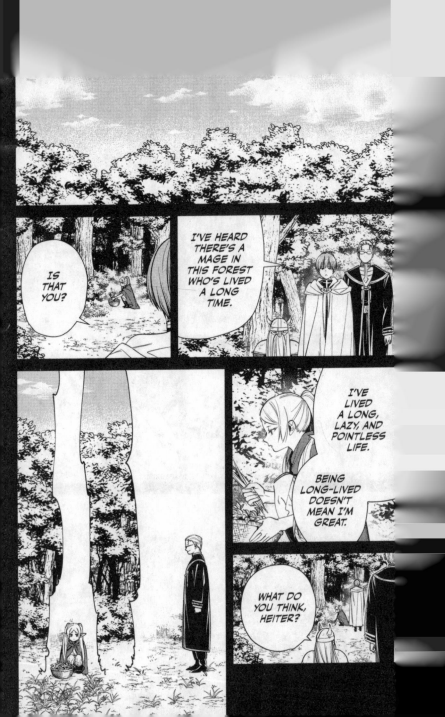

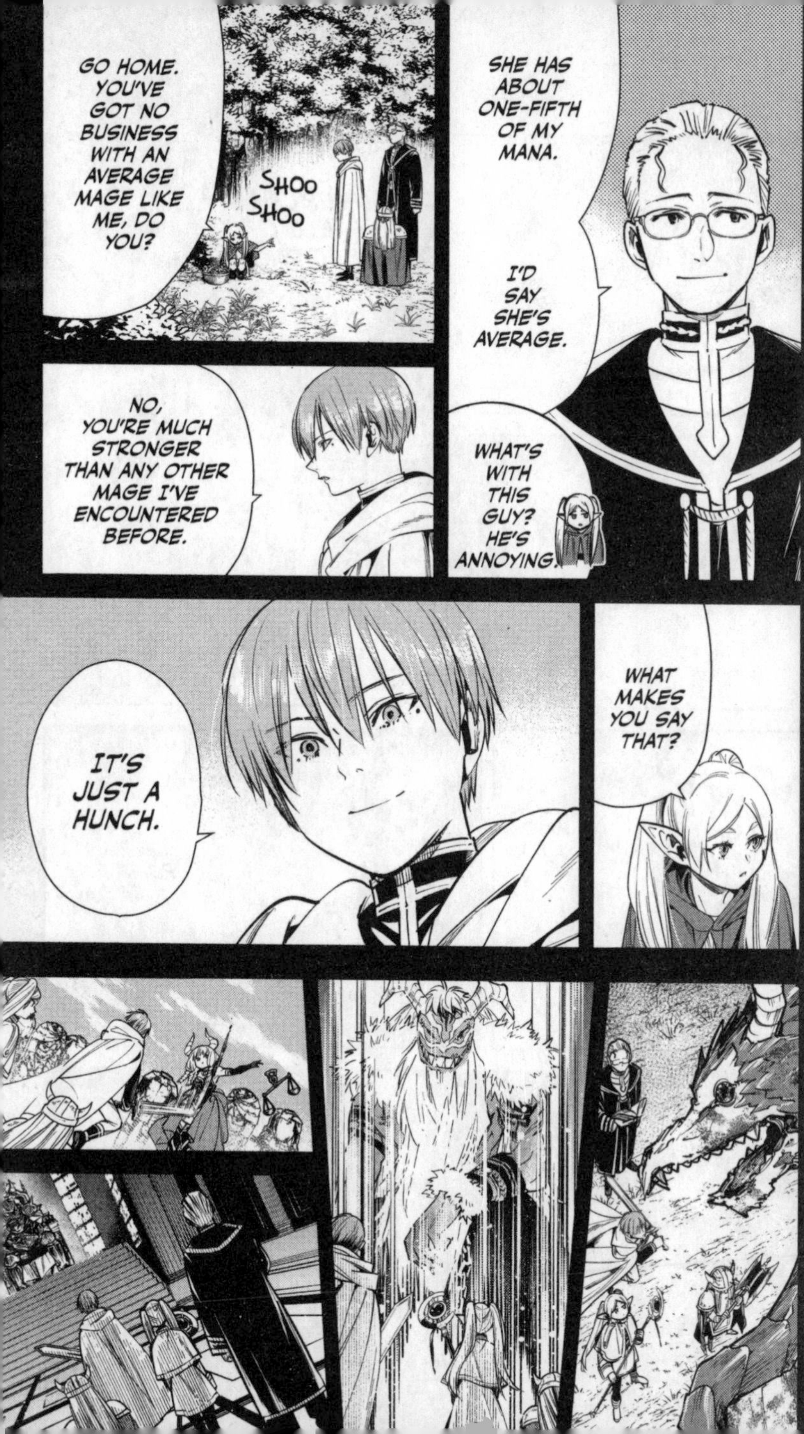
SHE HAS ABOUT ONE-FIFTH OF MY MANA.
I'D SAY SHE'S AVERAGE.
WHAT'S WITH THIS GUY? HE'S ANNOYING.
GO HOME. YOU'VE GOT NO BUSINESS WITH AN AVERAGE MAGE LIKE ME, DO YOU?
SHOO SHOO
NO, YOU'RE MUCH STRONGER THAN ANY OTHER MAGE I'VE ENCOUNTERED BEFORE.
WHAT MAKES YOU SAY THAT?
IT'S JUST A HUNCH.

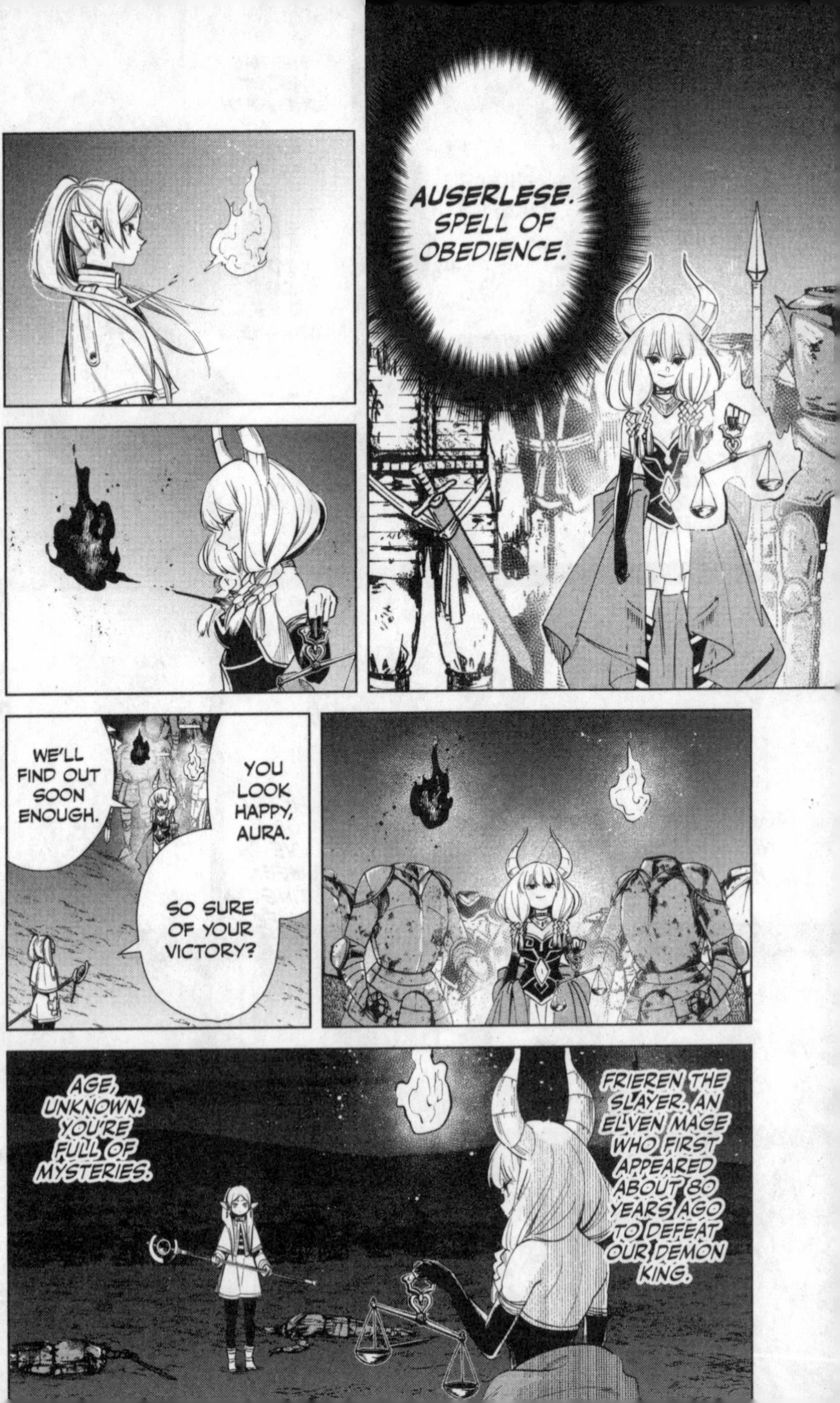
AUSERLESE. SPELL OF OBEDIENCE.
YOU LOOK HAPPY, AURA.
SO SURE OF YOUR VICTORY?
WE'LL FIND OUT SOON ENOUGH.
FRIEREN THE SLAYER. AN ELVEN MAGE WHO FIRST APPEARED ABOUT 80 YEARS AGO TO DEFEAT OUR DEMON KING.
AGE, UNKNOWN. YOU'RE FULL OF MYSTERIES.

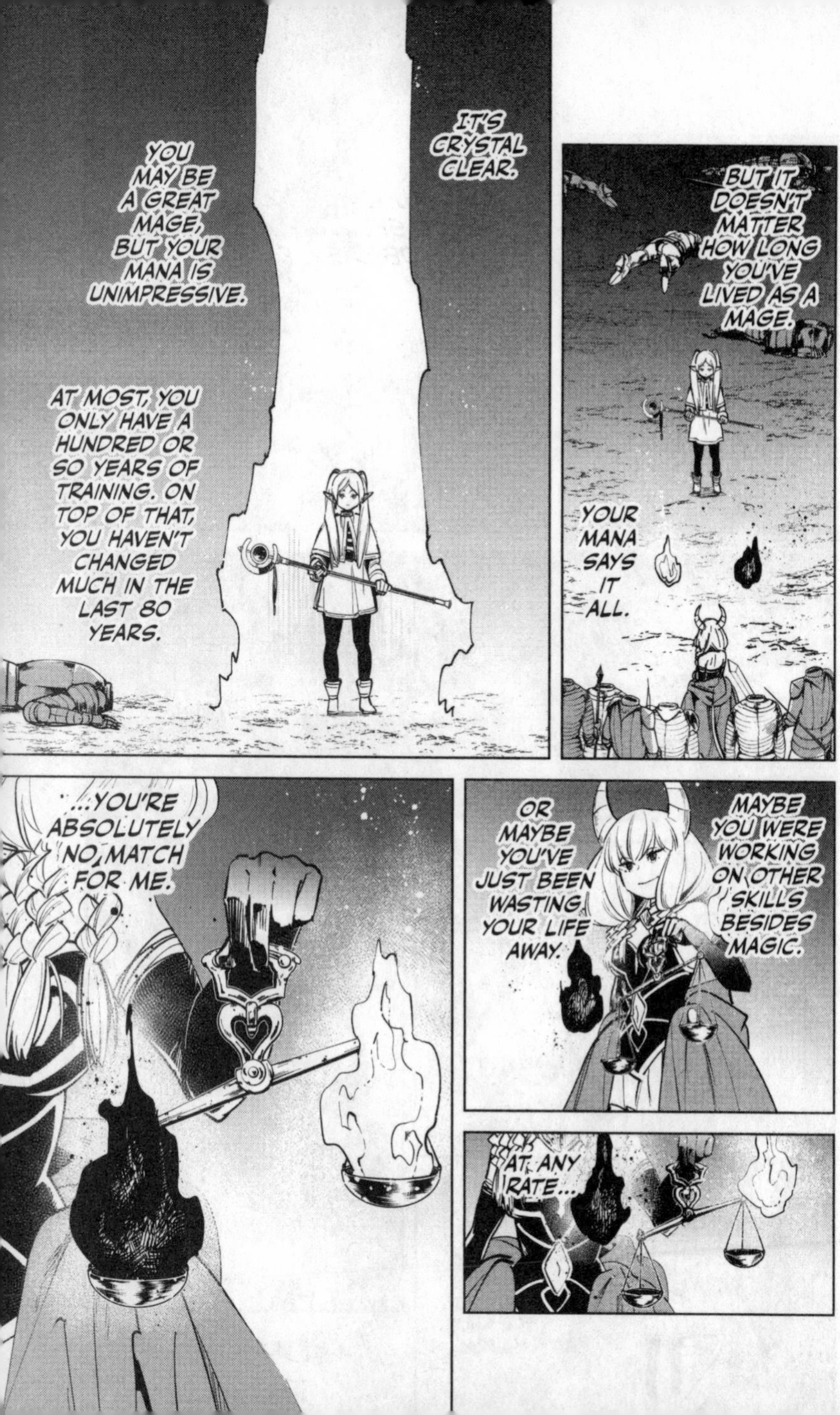
BUT IT DOESN'T MATTER HOW LONG YOU'VE LIVED AS A MAGE.
YOUR MANA SAYS IT ALL.
IT'S CRYSTAL CLEAR.
YOU MAY BE A GREAT MAGE, BUT YOUR MANA IS UNIMPRESSIVE.
AT MOST, YOU ONLY HAVE A HUNDRED OR SO YEARS OF TRAINING. ON TOP OF THAT, YOU HAVEN'T CHANGED MUCH IN THE LAST 80 YEARS.
MAYBE YOU WERE WORKING ON OTHER SKILLS BESIDES MAGIC.
OR MAYBE YOU'VE JUST BEEN WASTING YOUR LIFE AWAY.
AT ANY RATE...
...YOU'RE ABSOLUTELY NO MATCH FOR ME.

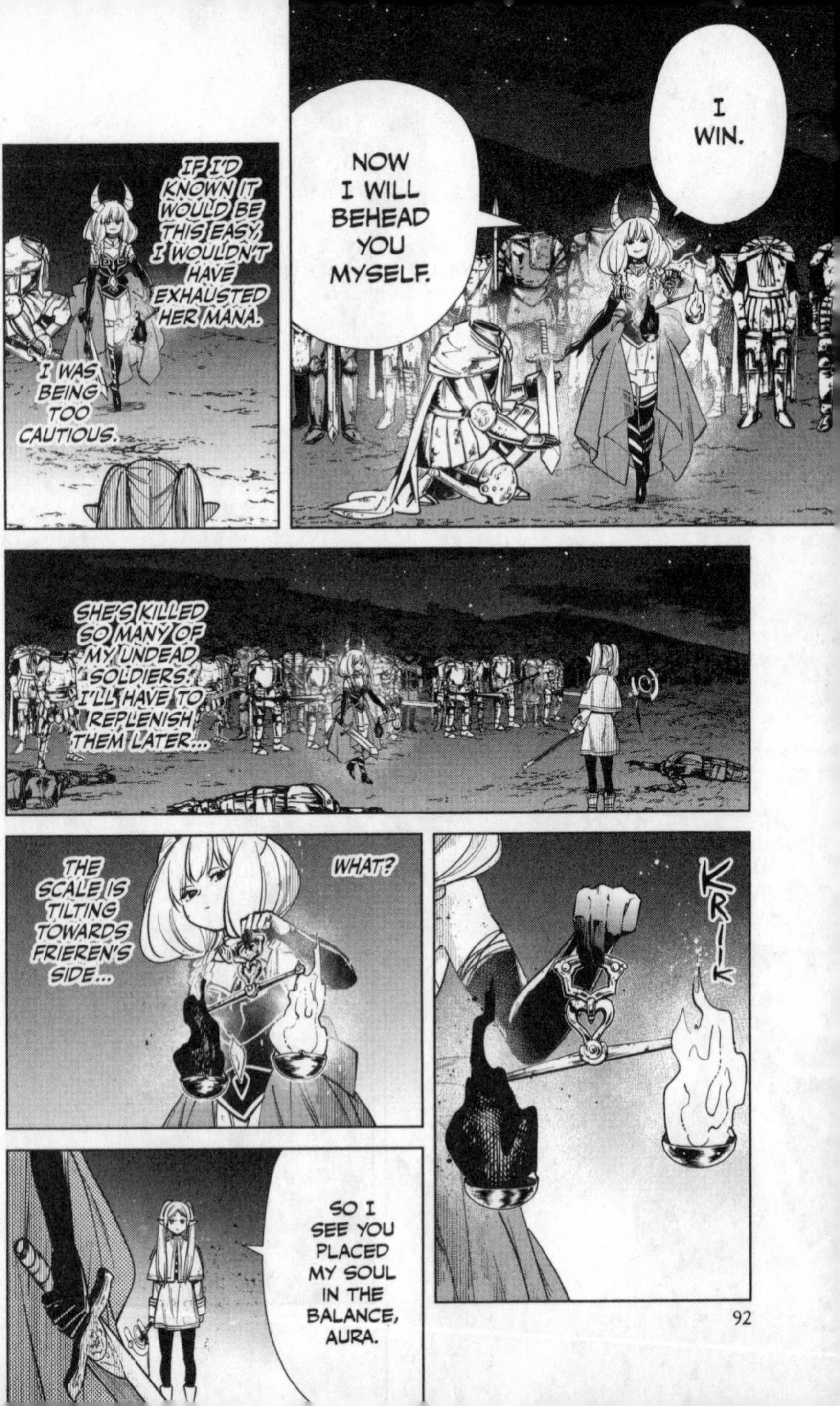

I WIN.
NOW I WILL BEHEAD YOU MYSELF.
IF I'D KNOWN IT WOULD BE THIS EASY, I WOULDN'T HAVE EXHAUSTED HER MANA.
I WAS BEING TOO CAUTIOUS.
SHE'S KILLED SO MANY OF MY UNDEAD SOLDIERS. I'LL HAVE TO REPLENISH THEM LATER...
KRIK
WHAT?
THE SCALE IS TILTING TOWARDS FRIEREN'S SIDE...
SO I SEE YOU PLACED MY SOUL IN THE BALANCE, AURA.

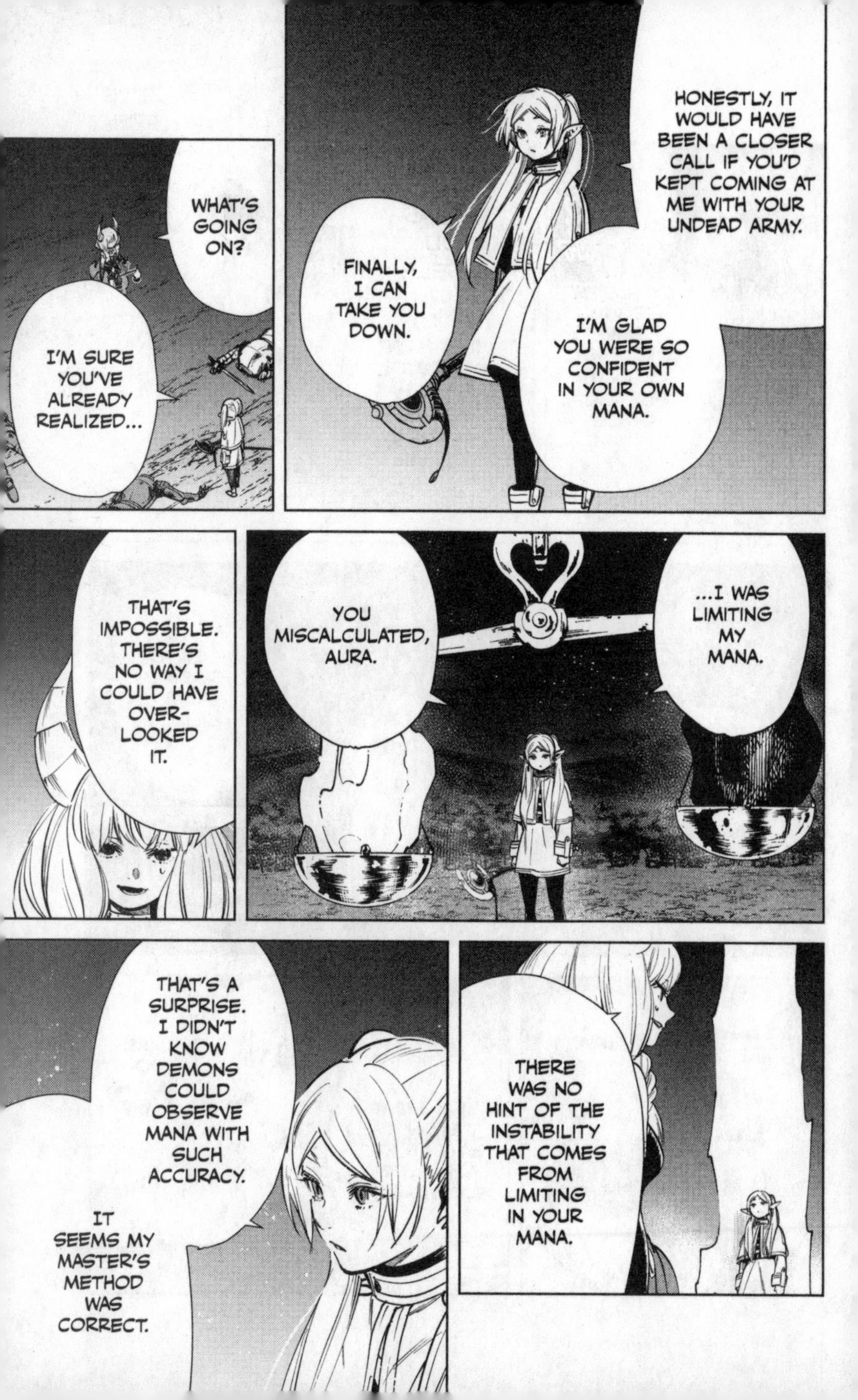
HONESTLY, IT WOULD HAVE BEEN A CLOSER CALL IF YOU'D KEPT COMING AT ME WITH YOUR UNDEAD ARMY.
I'M GLAD YOU WERE SO CONFIDENT IN YOUR OWN MANA.
FINALLY, I CAN TAKE YOU DOWN.
WHAT'S GOING ON?
I'M SURE YOU'VE ALREADY REALIZED...
...I WAS LIMITING MY MANA.
YOU MISCALCULATED, AURA.
THAT'S IMPOSSIBLE. THERE'S NO WAY I COULD HAVE OVER-LOOKED IT.
THERE WAS NO HINT OF THE INSTABILITY THAT COMES FROM LIMITING IN YOUR MANA.
THAT'S A SURPRISE. I DIDN'T KNOW DEMONS COULD OBSERVE MANA WITH SUCH ACCURACY.
IT SEEMS MY MASTER'S METHOD WAS CORRECT.

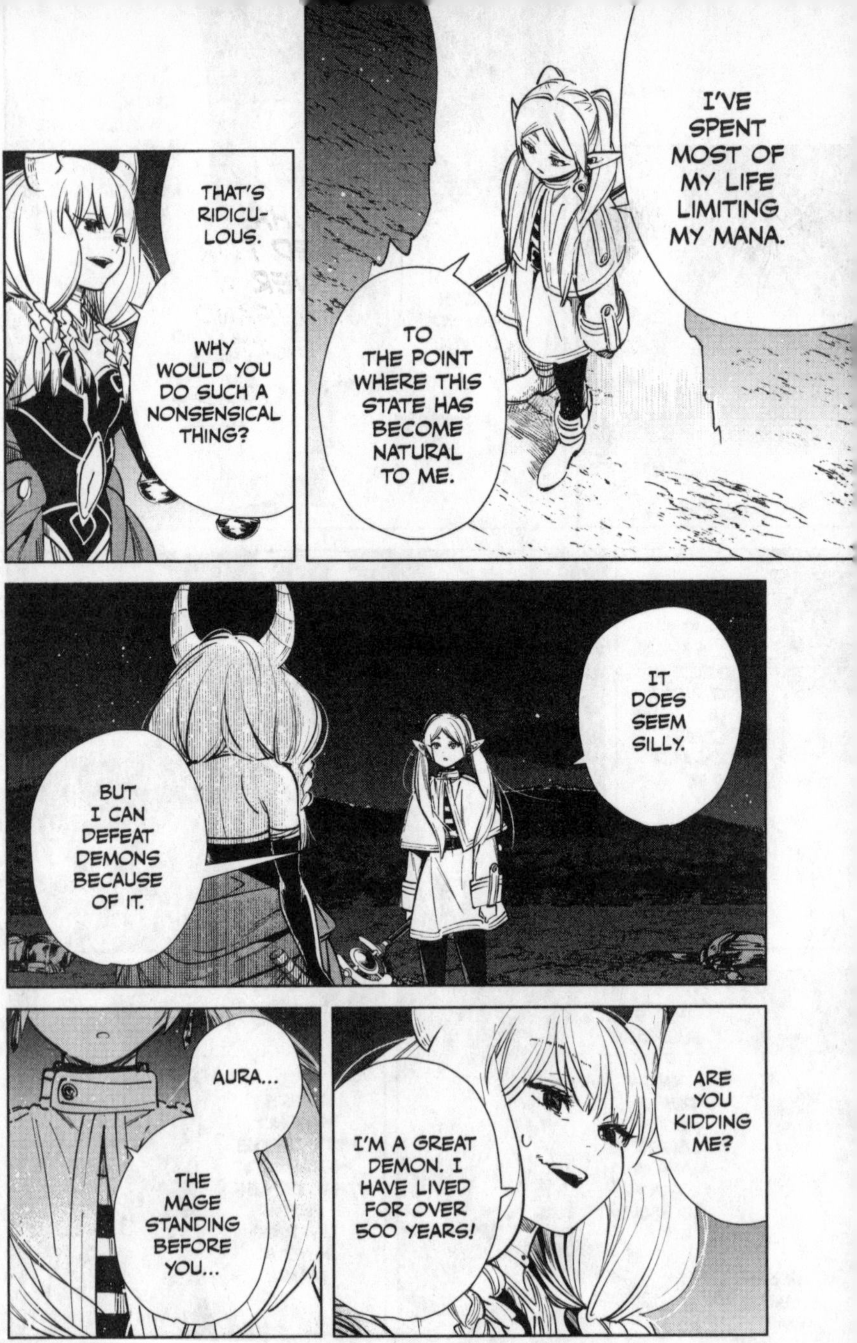
I'VE SPENT MOST OF MY LIFE LIMITING MY MANA.
TO THE POINT WHERE THIS STATE HAS BECOME NATURAL TO ME.
THAT'S RIDICULOUS.
WHY WOULD YOU DO SUCH A NONSENSICAL THING?
IT DOES SEEM SILLY.
BUT I CAN DEFEAT DEMONS BECAUSE OF IT.
ARE YOU KIDDING ME?
I'M A GREAT DEMON. I HAVE LIVED FOR OVER 500 YEARS!
AURA...
THE MAGE STANDING BEFORE YOU...

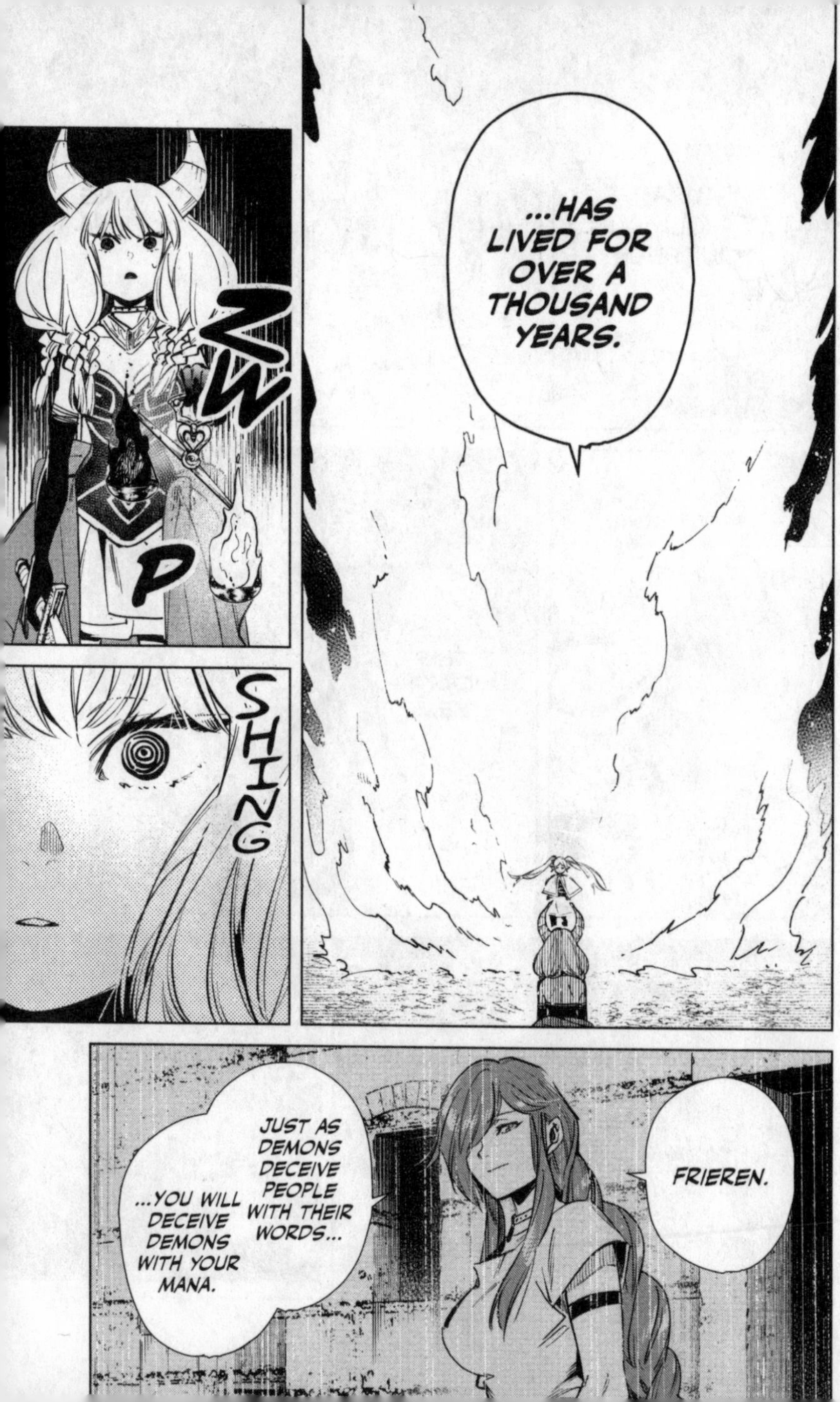
...HAS LIVED FOR OVER A THOUSAND YEARS.
ZW
P
SHING
FRIEREN.
JUST AS DEMONS DECEIVE PEOPLE WITH THEIR WORDS...
...YOU WILL DECEIVE DEMONS WITH YOUR MANA.

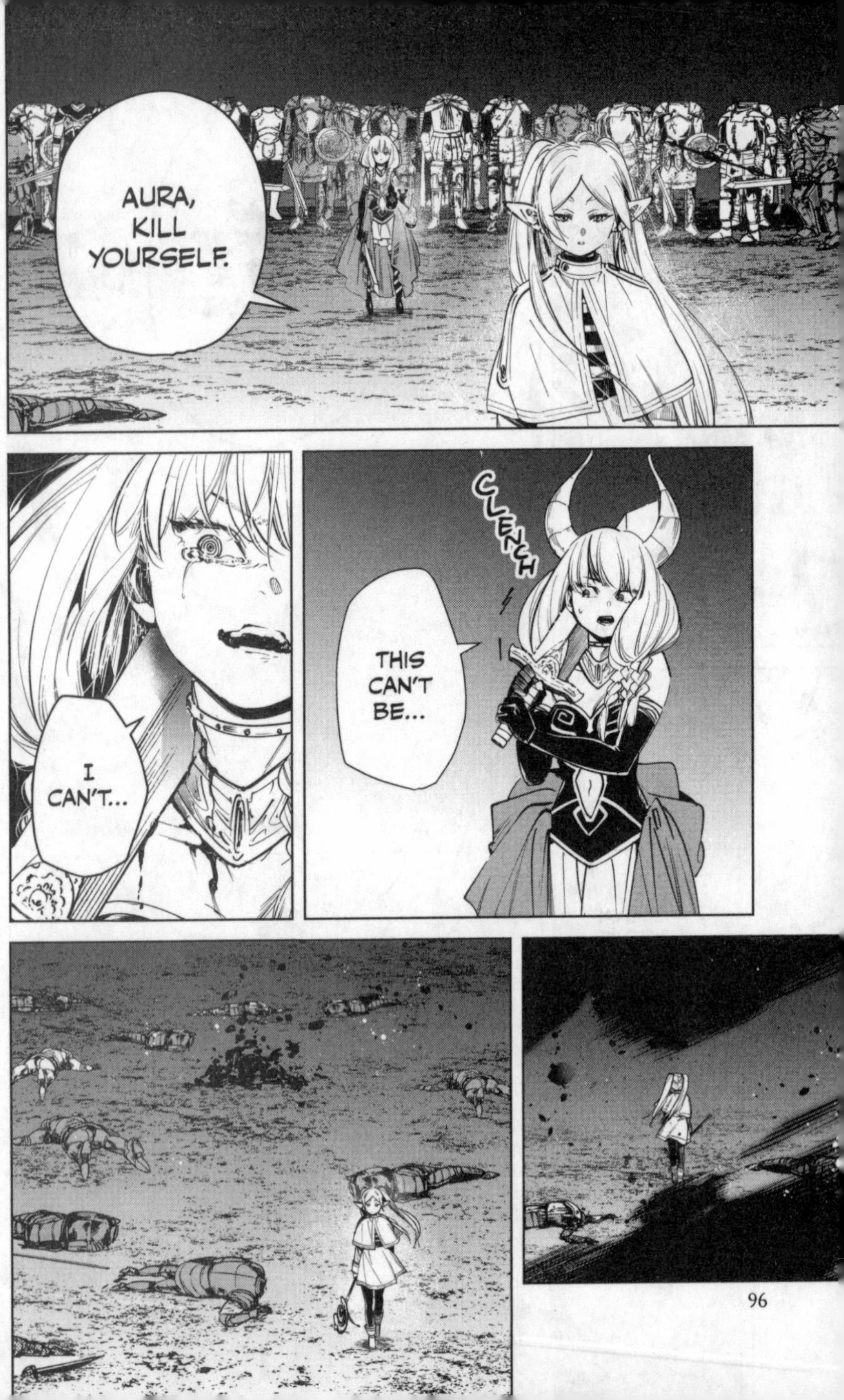
AURA, KILL YOURSELF.
CLENCH
THIS CAN'T BE...
I CAN'T...

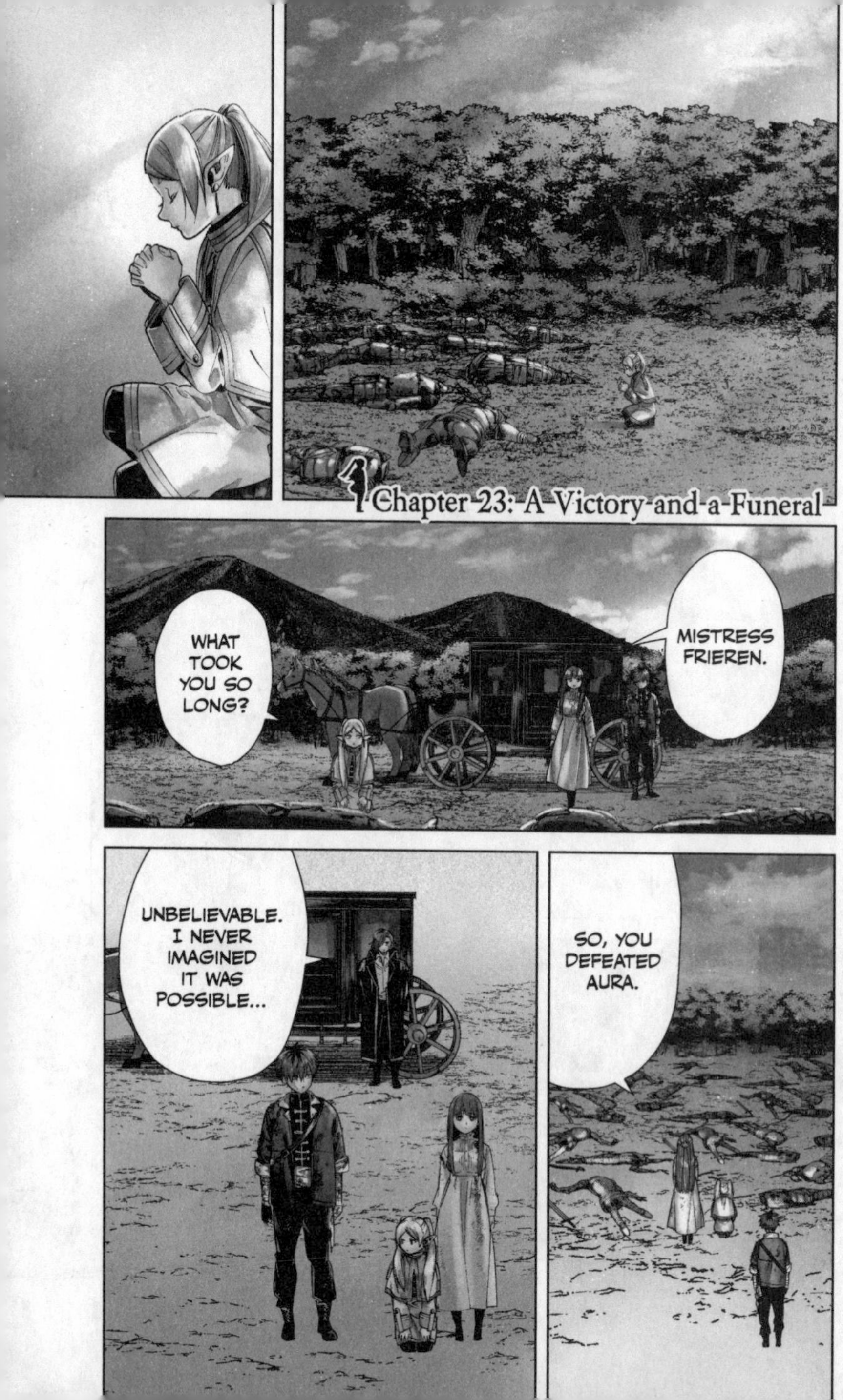
Chapter 23: A Victory and a Funeral
MISTRESS FRIEREN.
WHAT TOOK YOU SO LONG?
SO, YOU DEFEATED AURA.
UNBELIEVABLE. I NEVER IMAGINED IT WAS POSSIBLE...

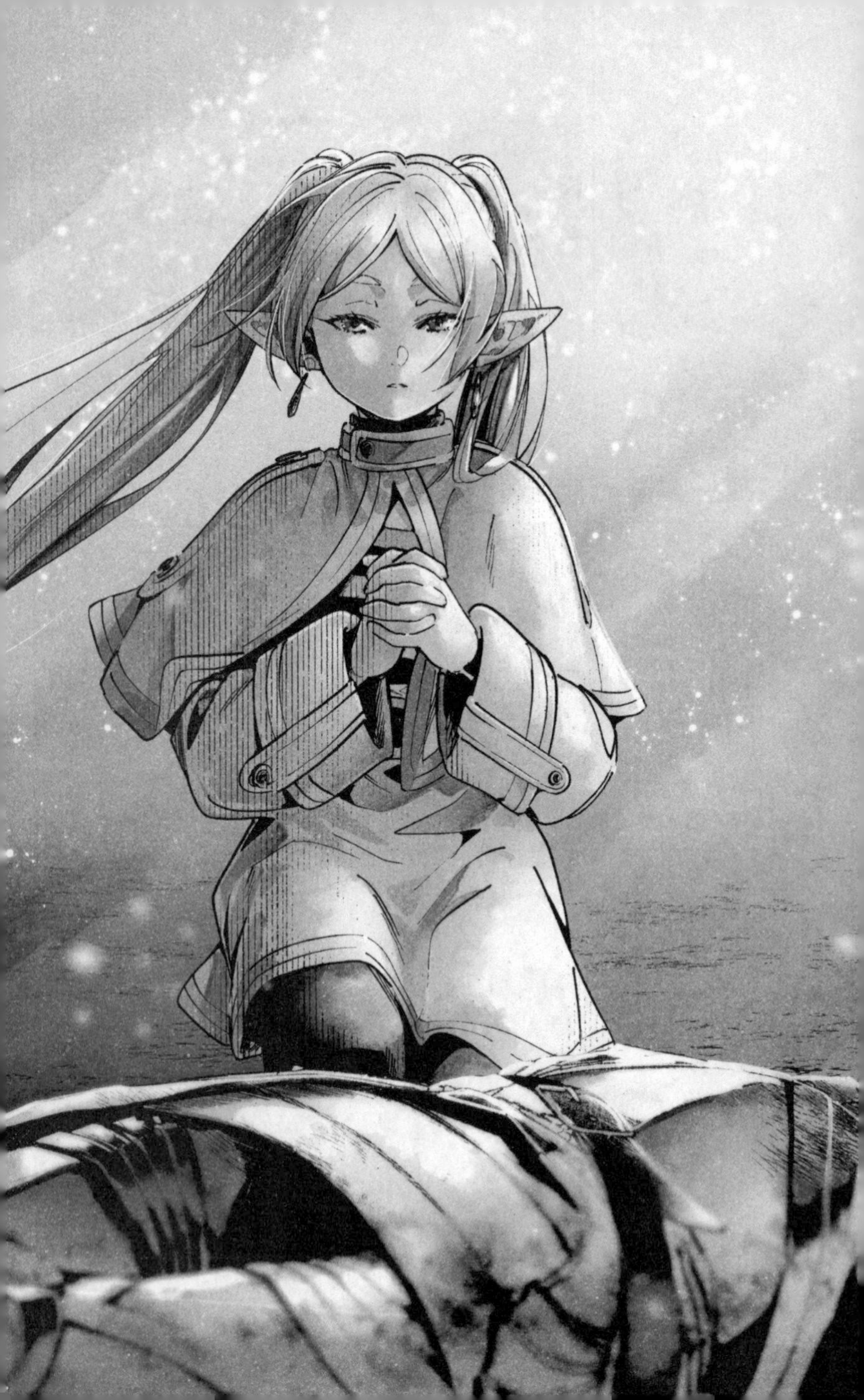

# Chapter 23: A Victory and a Funeral

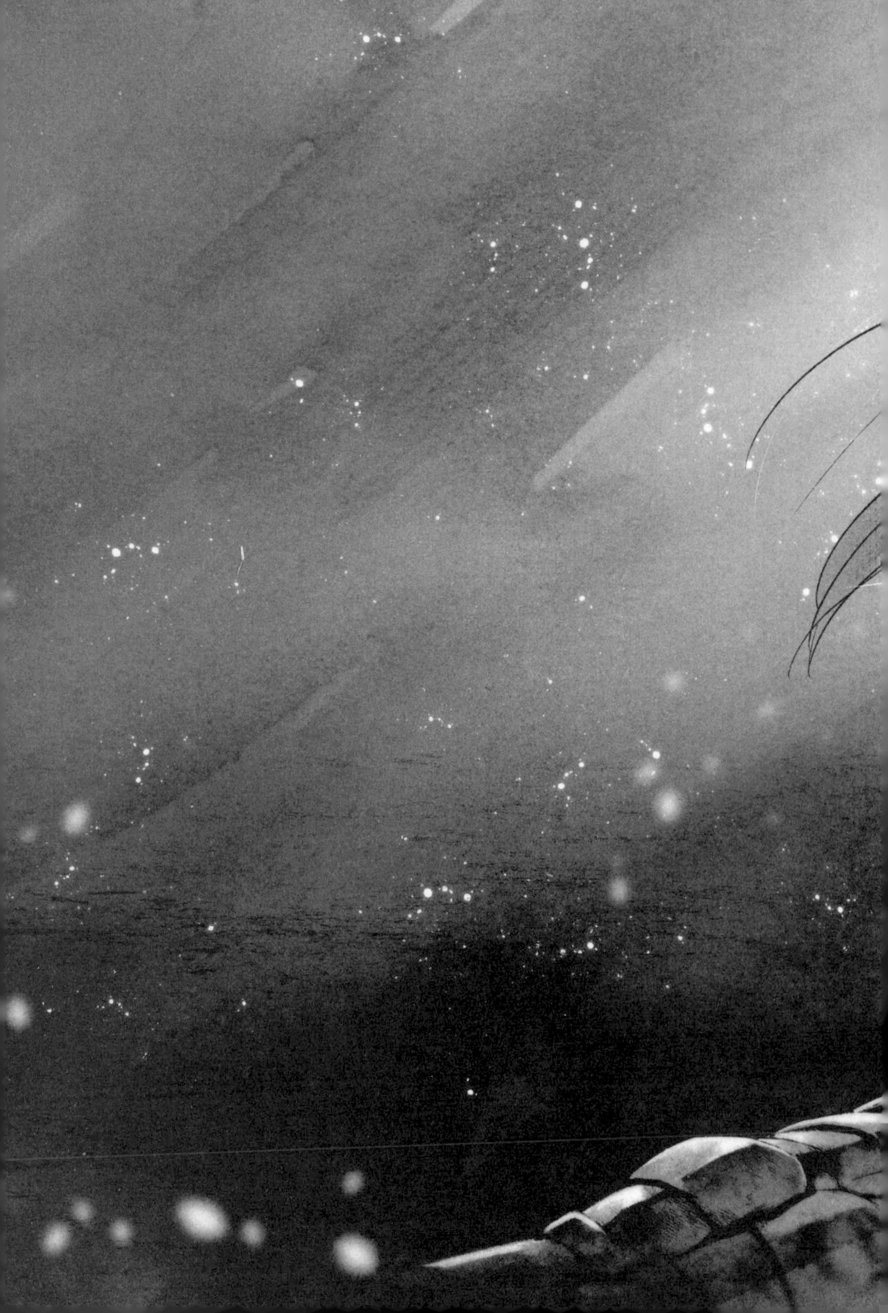

Frieren

Beyond Journey's End

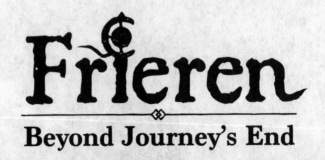

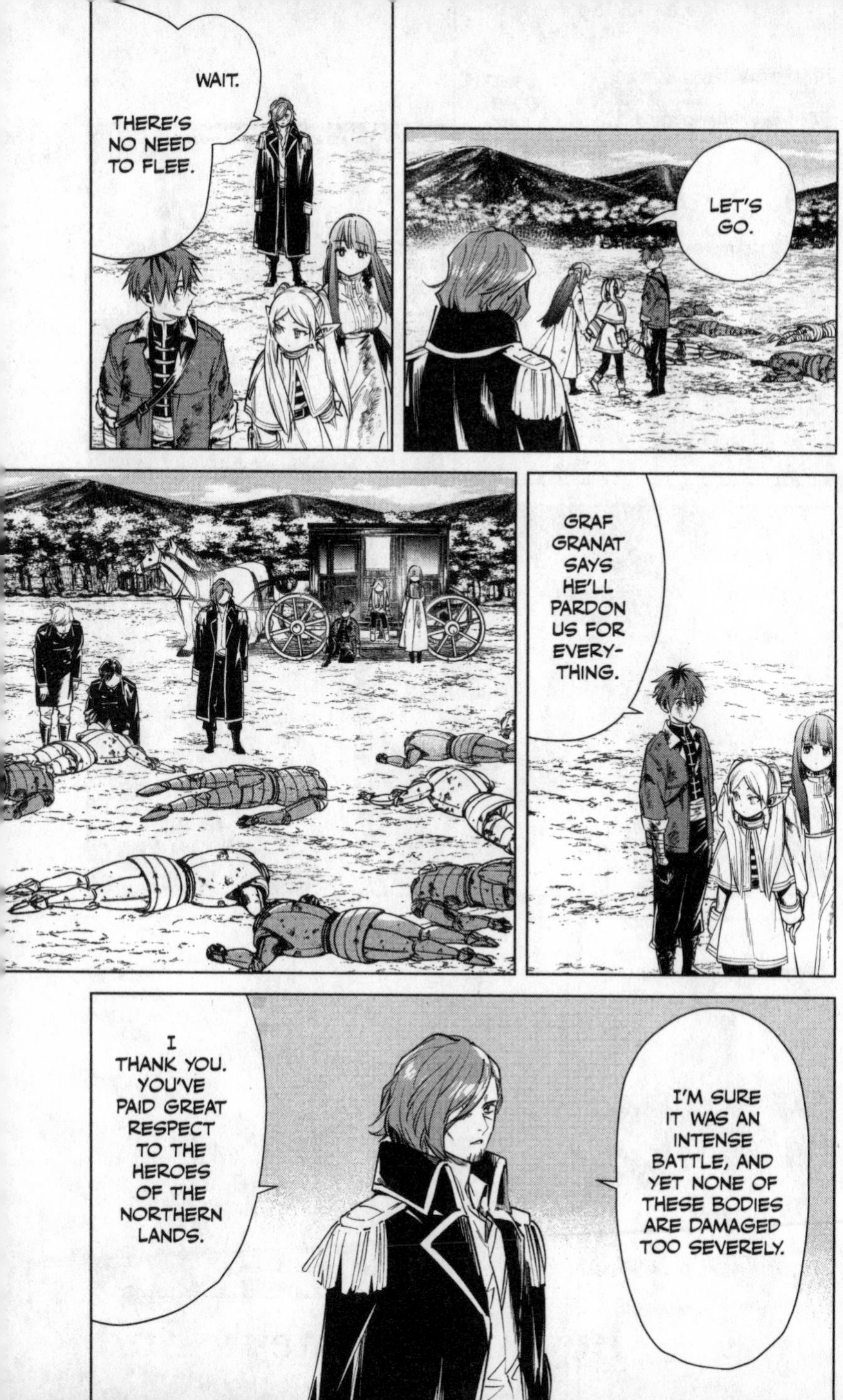
LET'S GO.
WAIT. THERE'S NO NEED TO FLEE.
GRAF GRANAT SAYS HE'LL PARDON US FOR EVERY-THING.
I'M SURE IT WAS AN INTENSE BATTLE, AND YET NONE OF THESE BODIES ARE DAMAGED TOO SEVERELY.
I THANK YOU. YOU'VE PAID GREAT RESPECT TO THE HEROES OF THE NORTHERN LANDS.

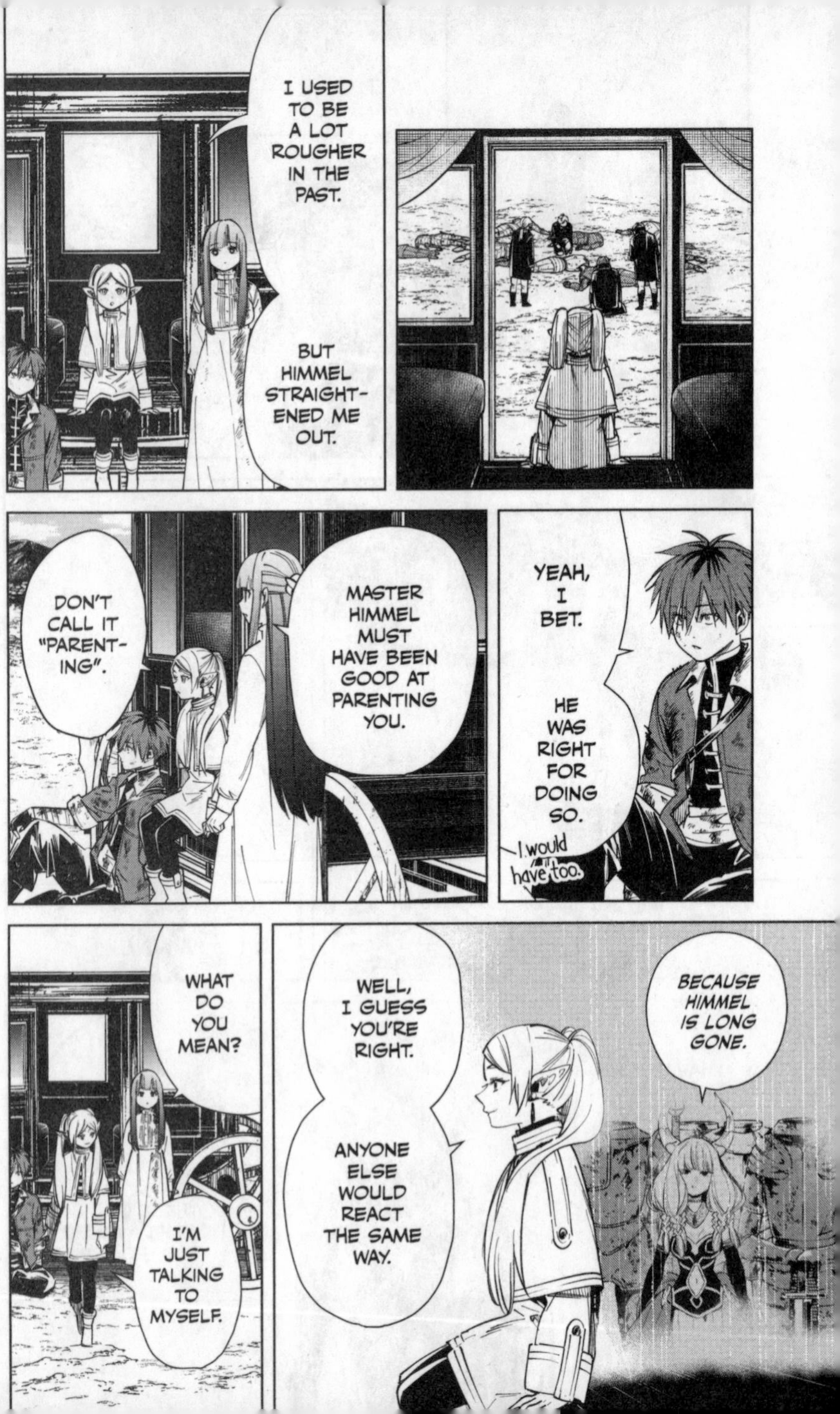
I USED TO BE A LOT ROUGHER IN THE PAST.
BUT HIMMEL STRAIGHTENED ME OUT.
YEAH, I BET.
HE WAS RIGHT FOR DOING SO.
I would have too.
MASTER HIMMEL MUST HAVE BEEN GOOD AT PARENTING YOU.
DON'T CALL IT "PARENTING".
WELL, I GUESS YOU'RE RIGHT.
ANYONE ELSE WOULD REACT THE SAME WAY.
BECAUSE HIMMEL IS LONG GONE.
WHAT DO YOU MEAN?
I'M JUST TALKING TO MYSELF.

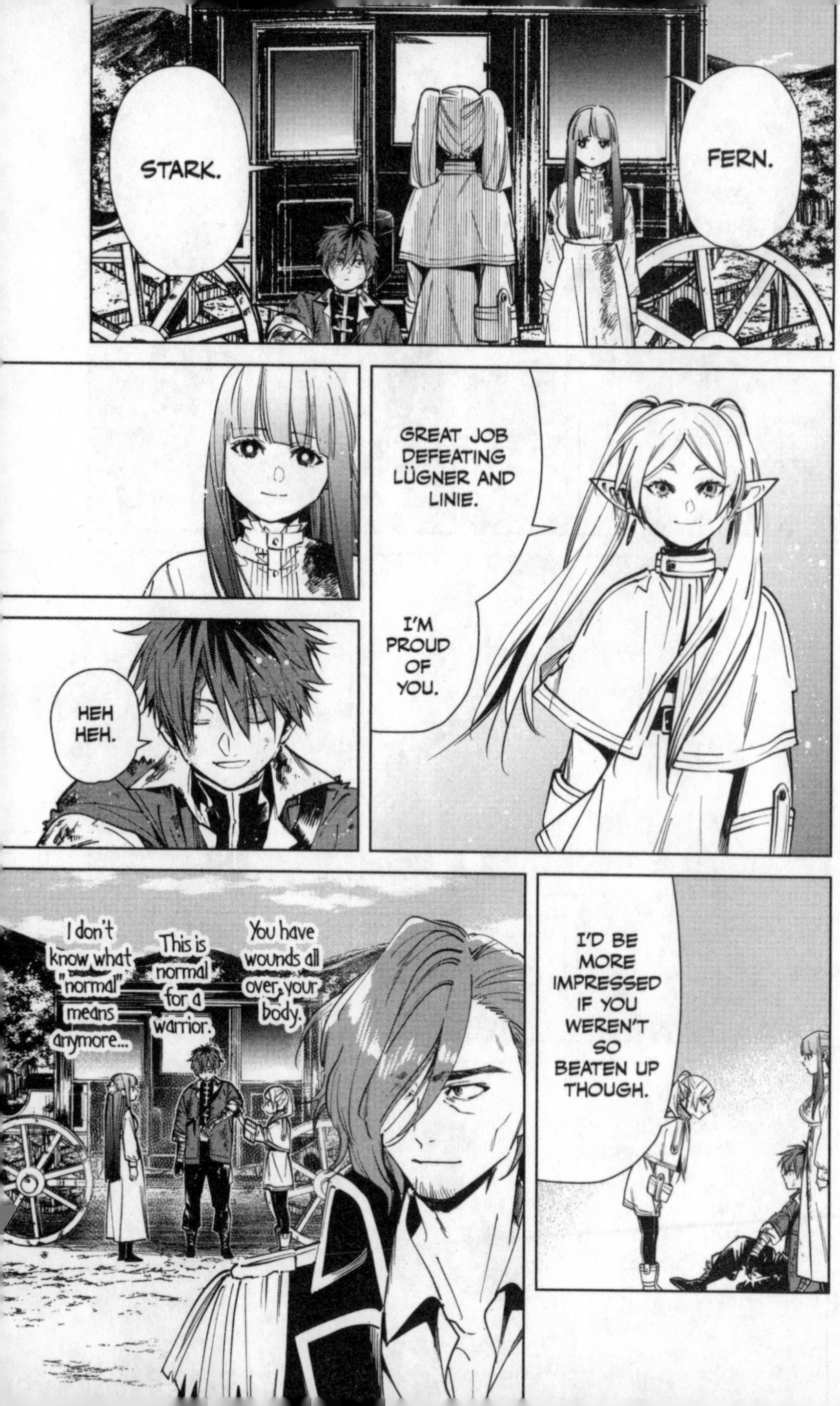
FERN.
STARK.
GREAT JOB DEFEATING LÜGNER AND LINIE.
I'M PROUD OF YOU.
HEH HEH.
I'D BE MORE IMPRESSED IF YOU WEREN'T SO BEATEN UP THOUGH.
You have wounds all over your body.
This is normal for a warrior.
I don't know what "normal" means anymore...

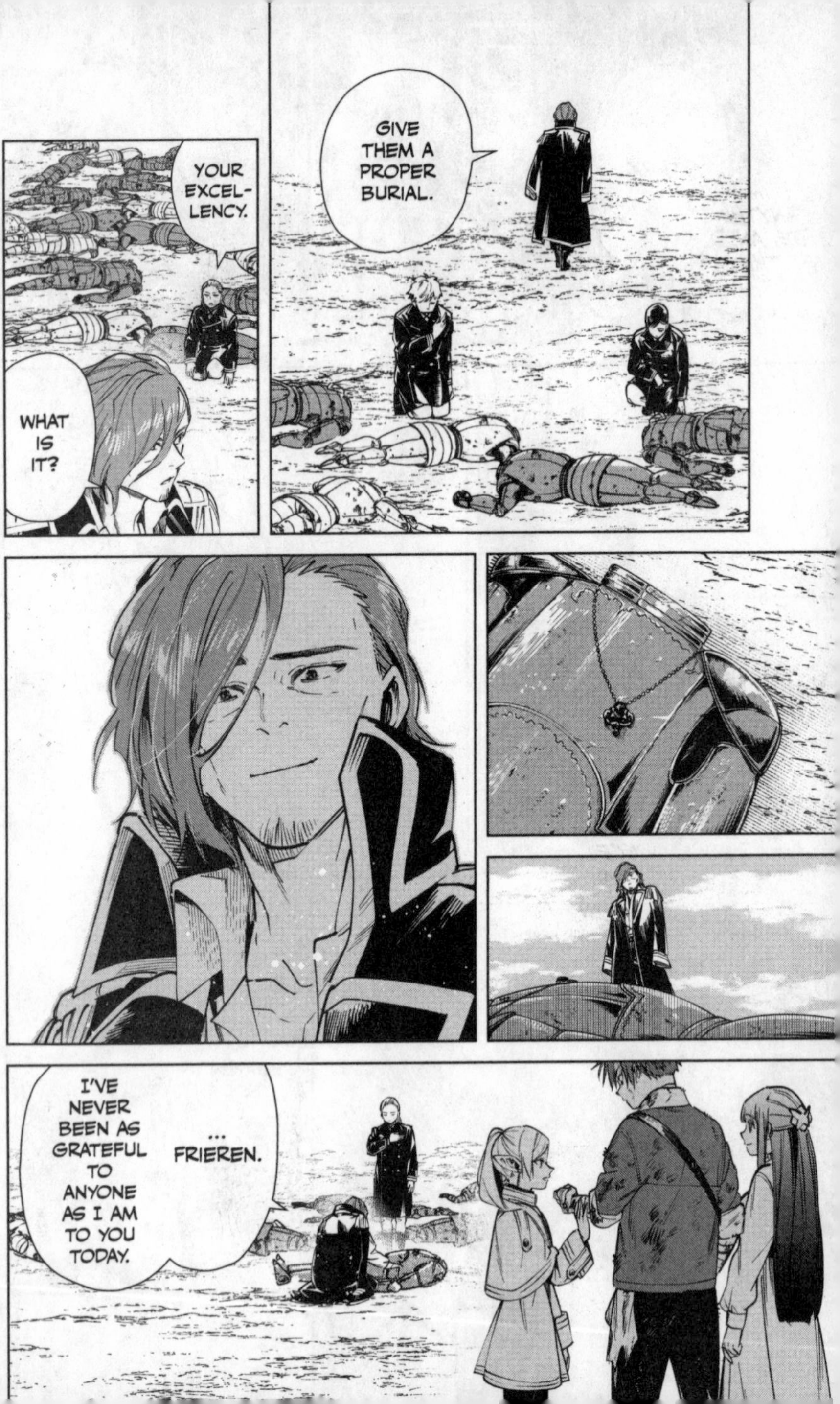
GIVE THEM A PROPER BURIAL.
YOUR EXCEL-LENCY.
WHAT IS IT?
... FRIEREN.
I'VE NEVER BEEN AS GRATEFUL TO ANYONE AS I AM TO YOU TODAY.

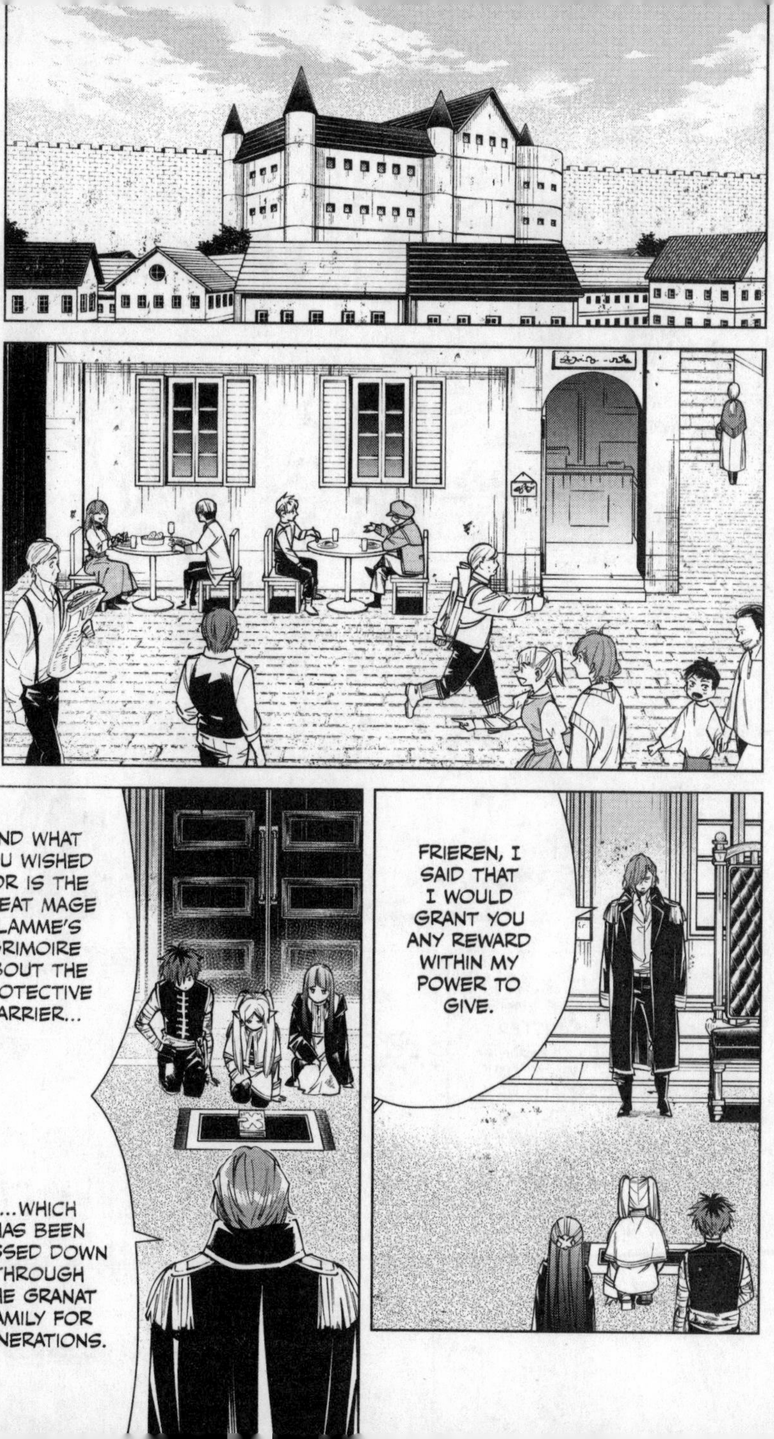
FRIEREN, I SAID THAT I WOULD GRANT YOU ANY REWARD WITHIN MY POWER TO GIVE.
AND WHAT YOU WISHED FOR IS THE GREAT MAGE FLAMME'S GRIMOIRE ABOUT THE PROTECTIVE BARRIER...
...WHICH HAS BEEN PASSED DOWN THROUGH THE GRANAT FAMILY FOR GENERATIONS.

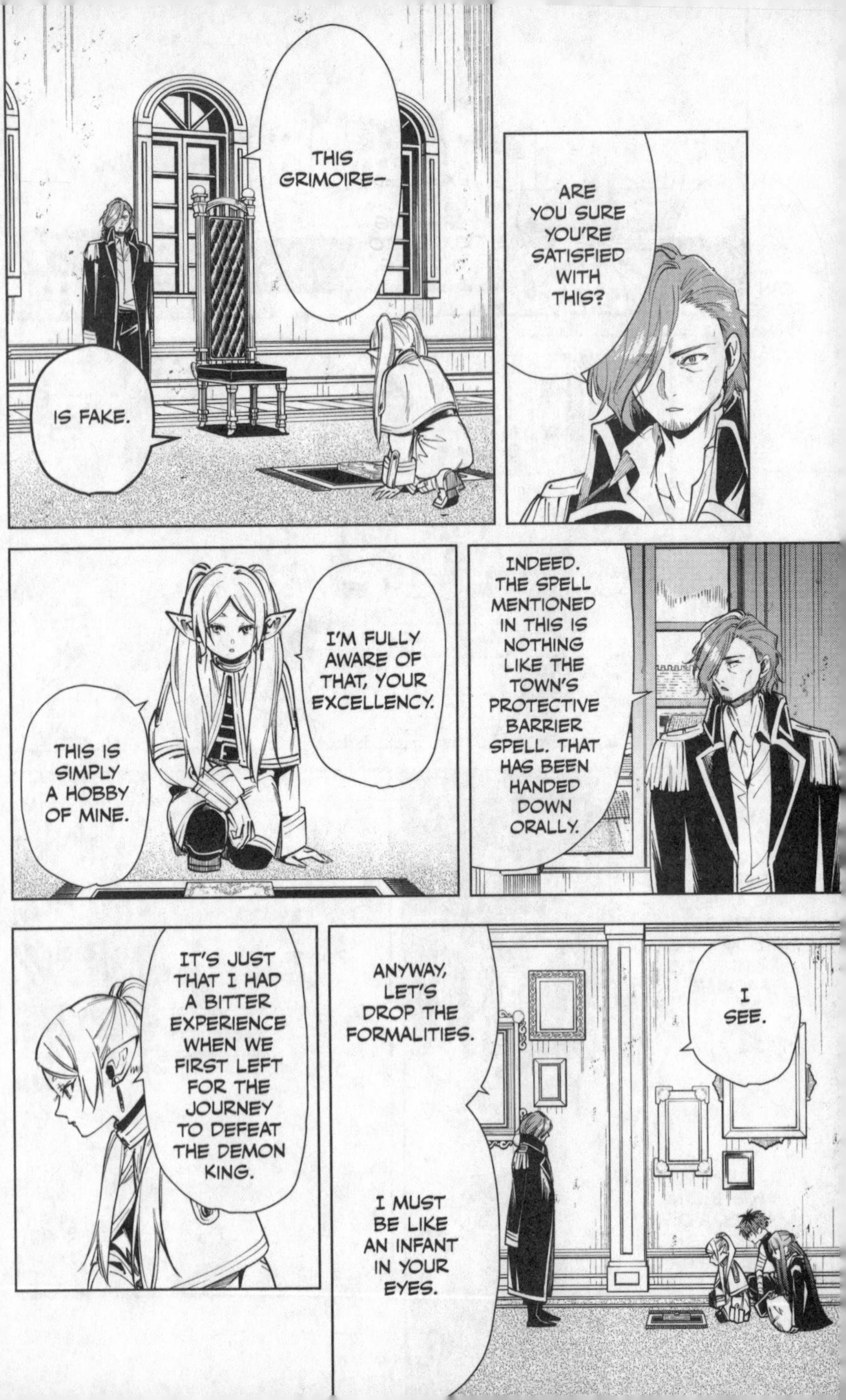
ARE YOU SURE YOU'RE SATISFIED WITH THIS?
THIS GRIMOIRE—
IS FAKE.
INDEED. THE SPELL MENTIONED IN THIS IS NOTHING LIKE THE TOWN'S PROTECTIVE BARRIER SPELL. THAT HAS BEEN HANDED DOWN ORALLY.
I'M FULLY AWARE OF THAT, YOUR EXCELLENCY.
THIS IS SIMPLY A HOBBY OF MINE.
I SEE.
ANYWAY, LET'S DROP THE FORMALITIES.
I MUST BE LIKE AN INFANT IN YOUR EYES.
IT'S JUST THAT I HAD A BITTER EXPERIENCE WHEN WE FIRST LEFT FOR THE JOURNEY TO DEFEAT THE DEMON KING.

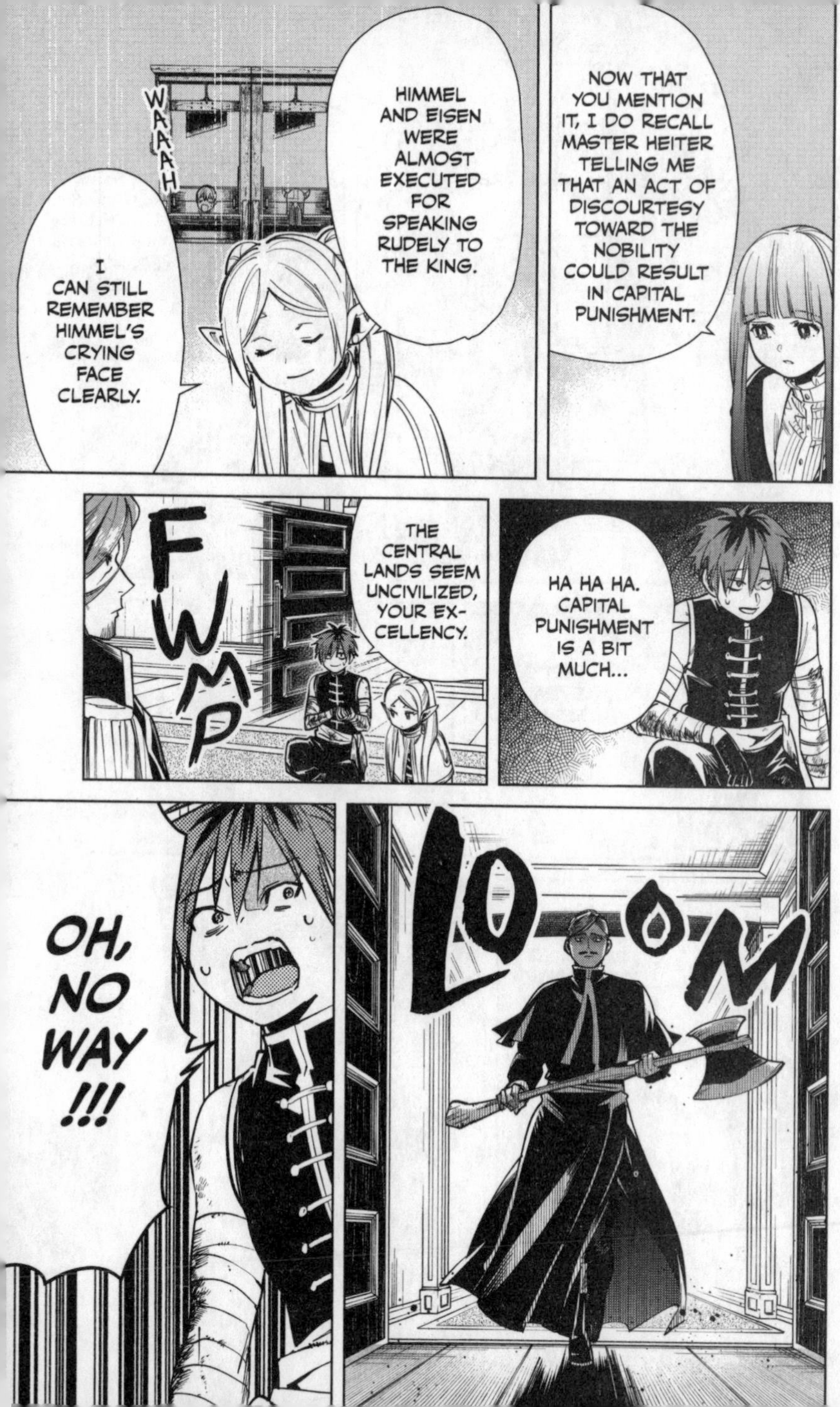
NOW THAT YOU MENTION IT, I DO RECALL MASTER HEITER TELLING ME THAT AN ACT OF DISCOURTESY TOWARD THE NOBILITY COULD RESULT IN CAPITAL PUNISHMENT.
HIMMEL AND EISEN WERE ALMOST EXECUTED FOR SPEAKING RUDELY TO THE KING.
WAAAH
I CAN STILL REMEMBER HIMMEL'S CRYING FACE CLEARLY.
HA HA HA. CAPITAL PUNISHMENT IS A BIT MUCH...
THE CENTRAL LANDS SEEM UNCIVILIZED, YOUR EX-CELLENCY.
FWMP
LOOM
OH, NO WAY!!!

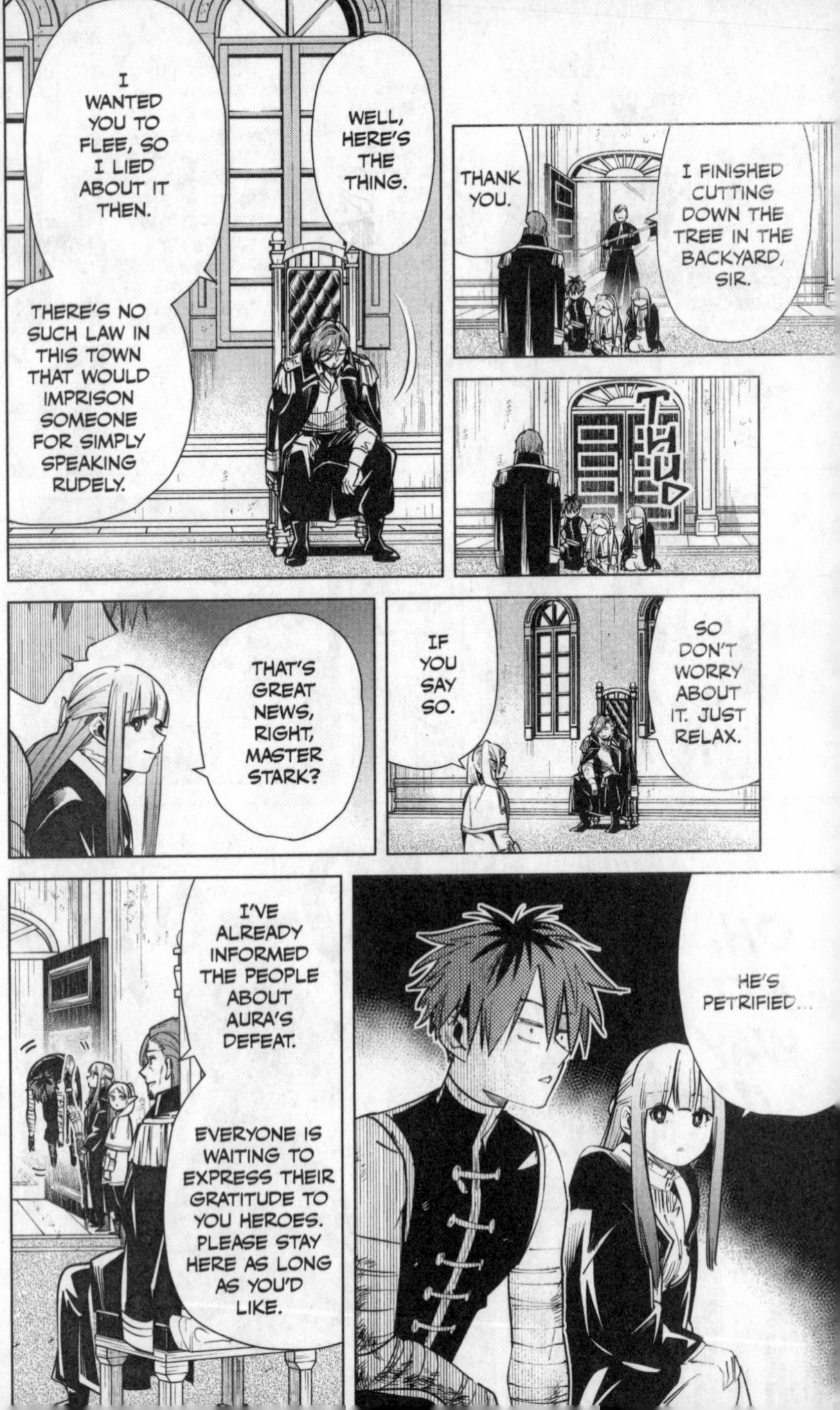
I FINISHED CUTTING DOWN THE TREE IN THE BACKYARD, SIR.
THANK YOU.
THUD
WELL, HERE'S THE THING.
I WANTED YOU TO FLEE, SO I LIED ABOUT IT THEN.
THERE'S NO SUCH LAW IN THIS TOWN THAT WOULD IMPRISON SOMEONE FOR SIMPLY SPEAKING RUDELY.
SO DON'T WORRY ABOUT IT. JUST RELAX.
IF YOU SAY SO.
THAT'S GREAT NEWS, RIGHT, MASTER STARK?
HE'S PETRIFIED...
I'VE ALREADY INFORMED THE PEOPLE ABOUT AURA'S DEFEAT.
EVERYONE IS WAITING TO EXPRESS THEIR GRATITUDE TO YOU HEROES. PLEASE STAY HERE AS LONG AS YOU'D LIKE.

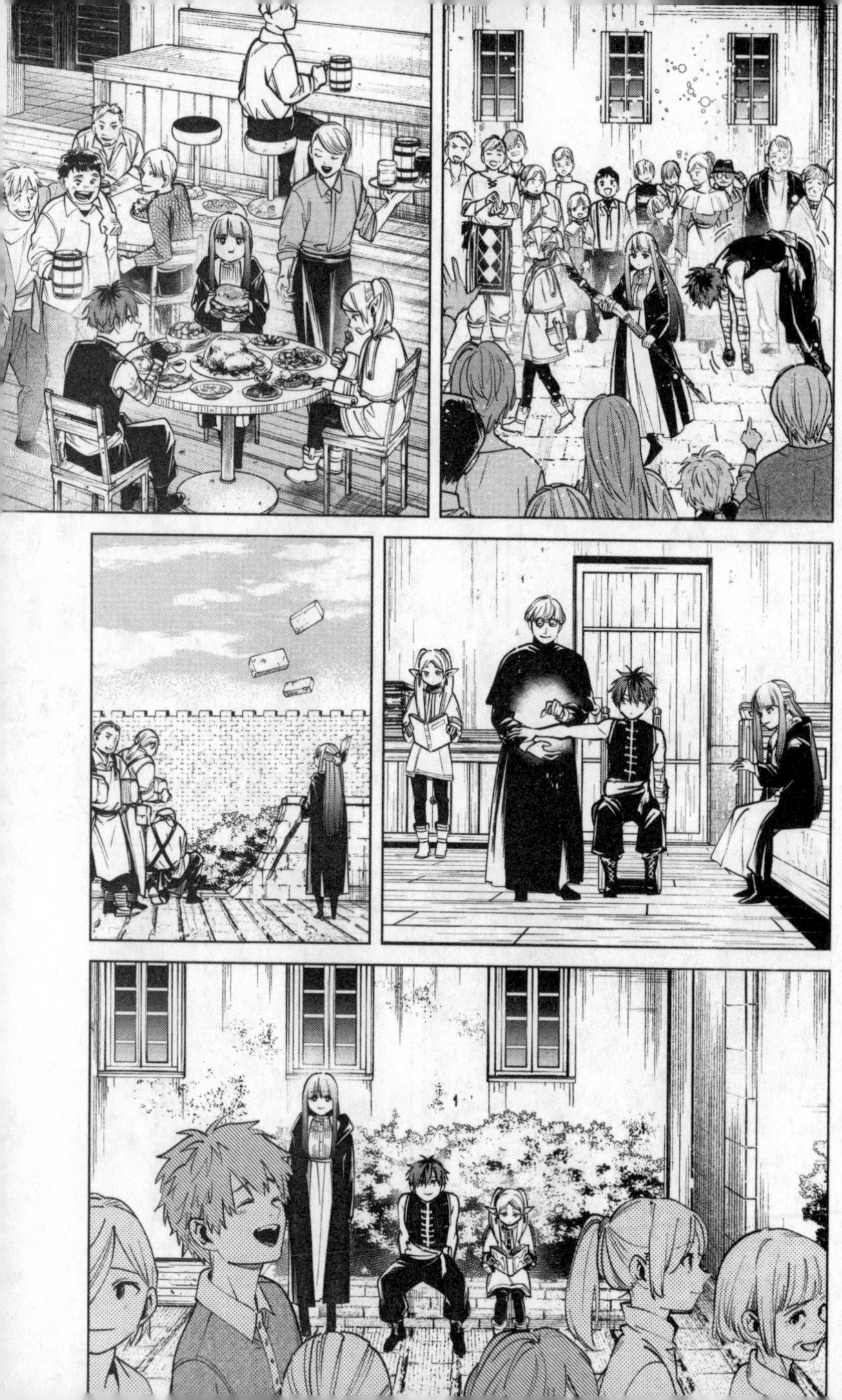

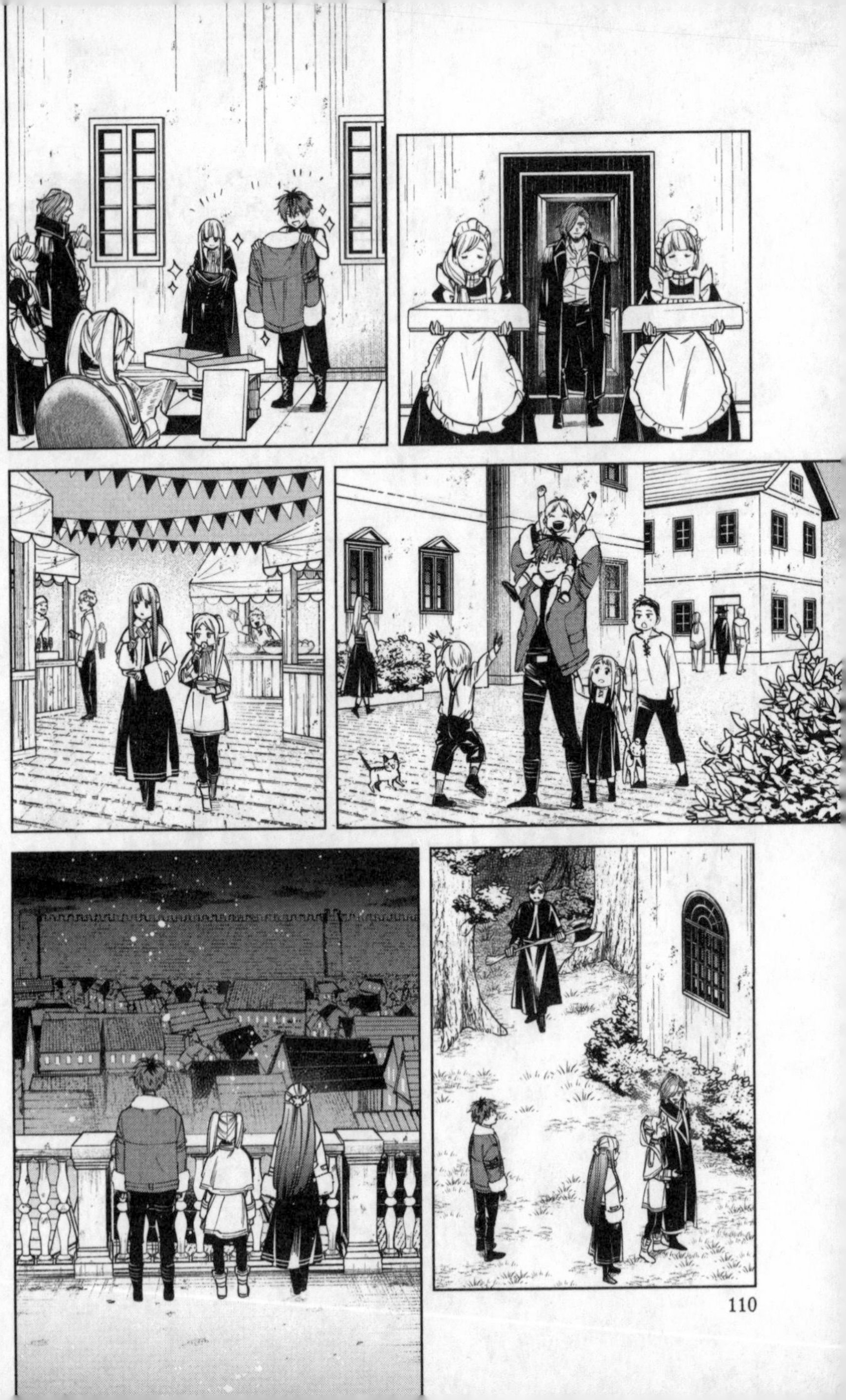

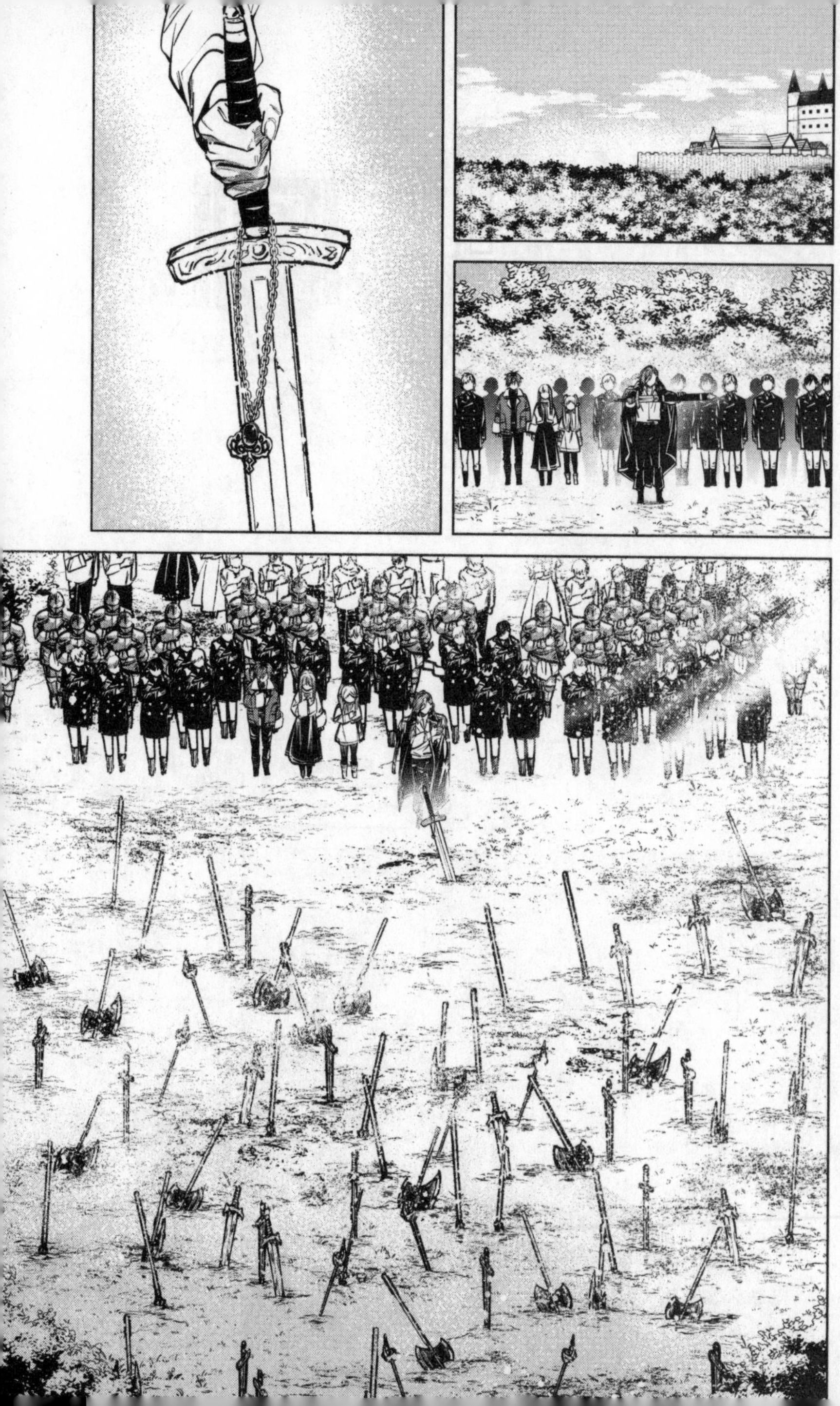

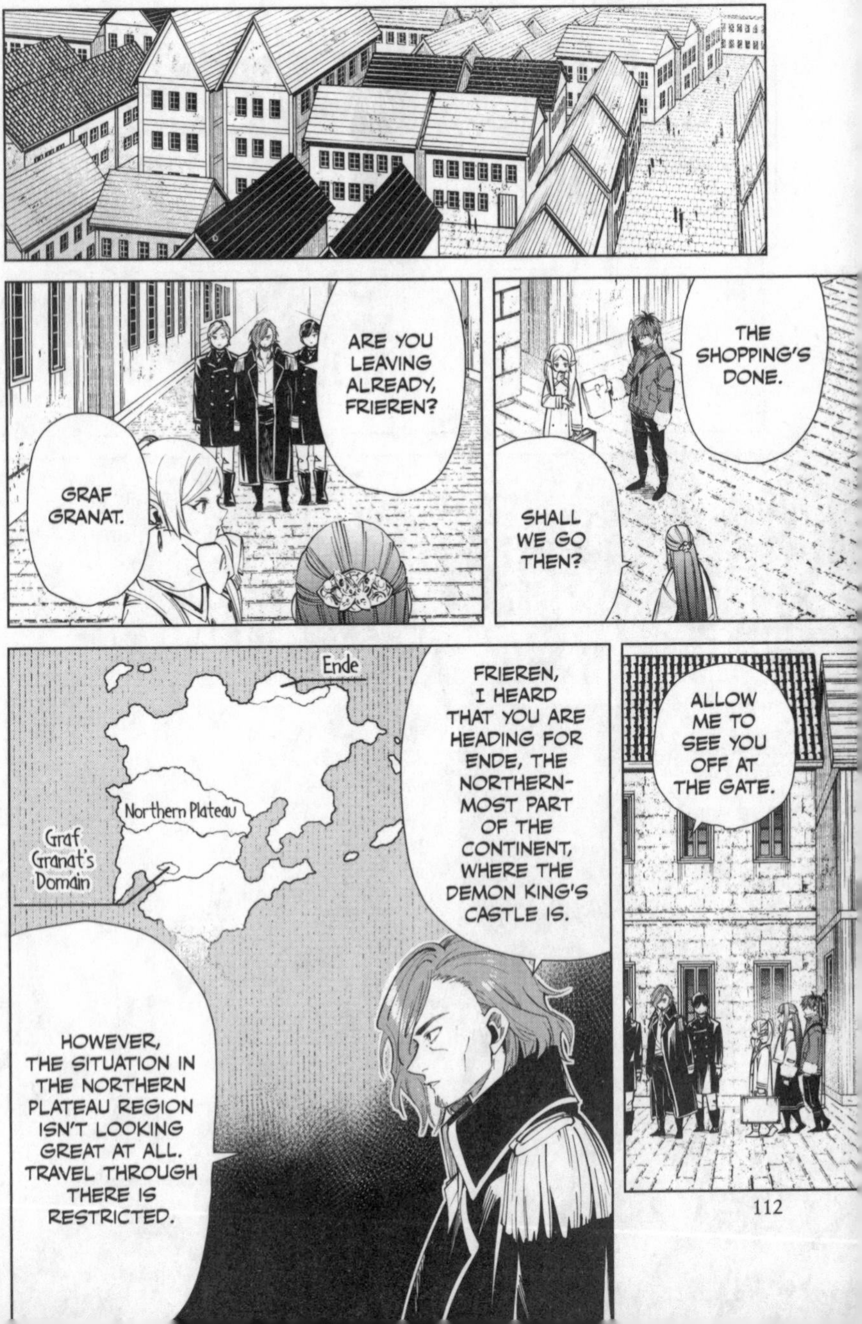
THE SHOPPING'S DONE.
SHALL WE GO THEN?
ARE YOU LEAVING ALREADY, FRIEREN?
GRAF GRANAT.
ALLOW ME TO SEE YOU OFF AT THE GATE.
FRIEREN, I HEARD THAT YOU ARE HEADING FOR ENDE, THE NORTHERN-MOST PART OF THE CONTINENT, WHERE THE DEMON KING'S CASTLE IS.
Ende
Northern Plateau
Graf Granat's Domain
HOWEVER, THE SITUATION IN THE NORTHERN PLATEAU REGION ISN'T LOOKING GREAT AT ALL. TRAVEL THROUGH THERE IS RESTRICTED.

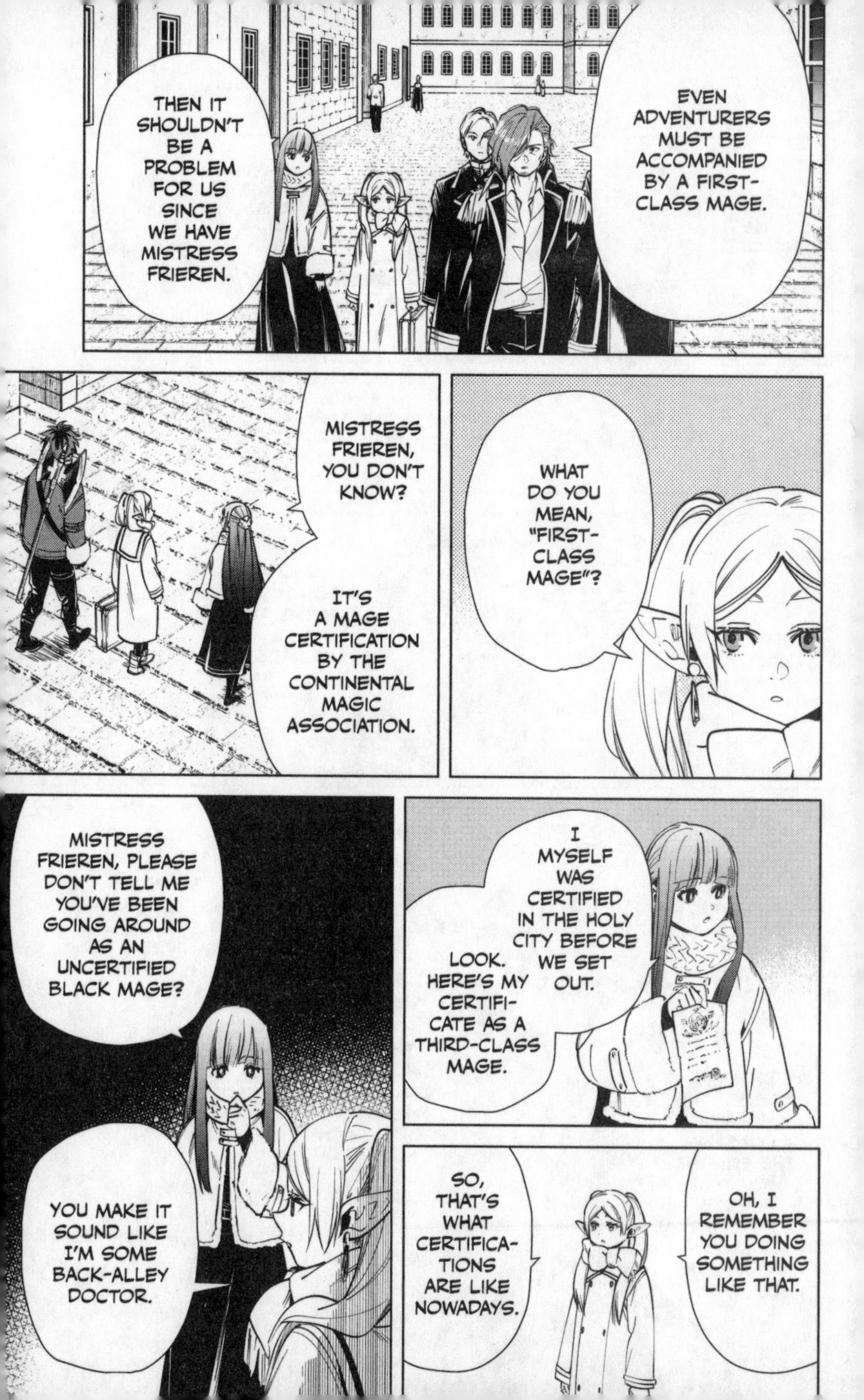
EVEN ADVENTURERS MUST BE ACCOMPANIED BY A FIRST-CLASS MAGE.
THEN IT SHOULDN'T BE A PROBLEM FOR US SINCE WE HAVE MISTRESS FRIEREN.
WHAT DO YOU MEAN, "FIRST-CLASS MAGE"?
MISTRESS FRIEREN, YOU DON'T KNOW?
IT'S A MAGE CERTIFICATION BY THE CONTINENTAL MAGIC ASSOCIATION.
I MYSELF WAS CERTIFIED IN THE HOLY CITY BEFORE WE SET OUT.
LOOK. HERE'S MY CERTIFICATE AS A THIRD-CLASS MAGE.
OH, I REMEMBER YOU DOING SOMETHING LIKE THAT.
SO, THAT'S WHAT CERTIFICATIONS ARE LIKE NOWADAYS.
MISTRESS FRIEREN, PLEASE DON'T TELL ME YOU'VE BEEN GOING AROUND AS AN UNCERTIFIED BLACK MAGE?
YOU MAKE IT SOUND LIKE I'M SOME BACK-ALLEY DOCTOR.

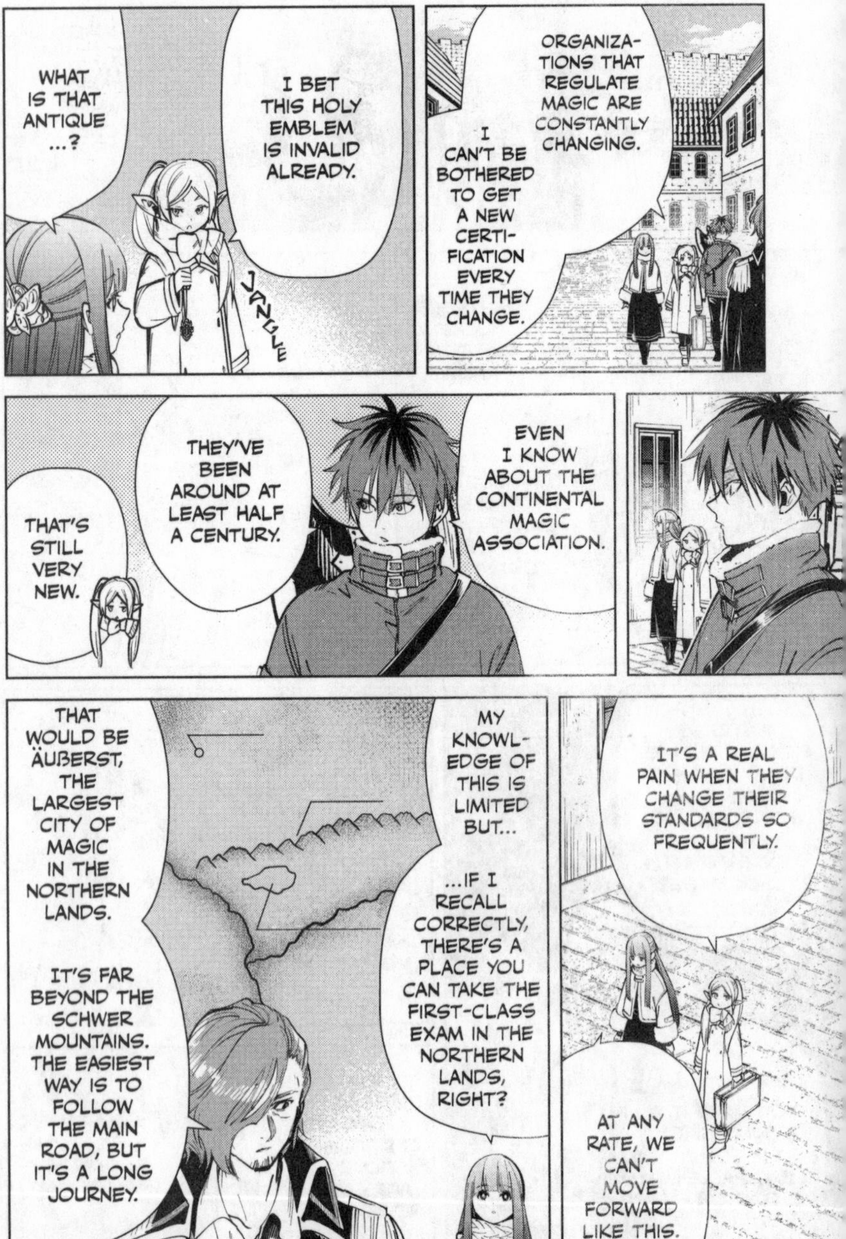
ORGANIZATIONS THAT REGULATE MAGIC ARE CONSTANTLY CHANGING.
I CAN'T BE BOTHERED TO GET A NEW CERTIFICATION EVERY TIME THEY CHANGE.
I BET THIS HOLY EMBLEM IS INVALID ALREADY.
JANGLE
WHAT IS THAT ANTIQUE ...?
EVEN I KNOW ABOUT THE CONTINENTAL MAGIC ASSOCIATION.
THEY'VE BEEN AROUND AT LEAST HALF A CENTURY.
THAT'S STILL VERY NEW.
IT'S A REAL PAIN WHEN THEY CHANGE THEIR STANDARDS SO FREQUENTLY.
AT ANY RATE, WE CAN'T MOVE FORWARD LIKE THIS.
MY KNOWLEDGE OF THIS IS LIMITED BUT...
...IF I RECALL CORRECTLY, THERE'S A PLACE YOU CAN TAKE THE FIRST-CLASS EXAM IN THE NORTHERN LANDS, RIGHT?
THAT WOULD BE ÄUßERST, THE LARGEST CITY OF MAGIC IN THE NORTHERN LANDS.
IT'S FAR BEYOND THE SCHWER MOUNTAINS. THE EASIEST WAY IS TO FOLLOW THE MAIN ROAD, BUT IT'S A LONG JOURNEY.

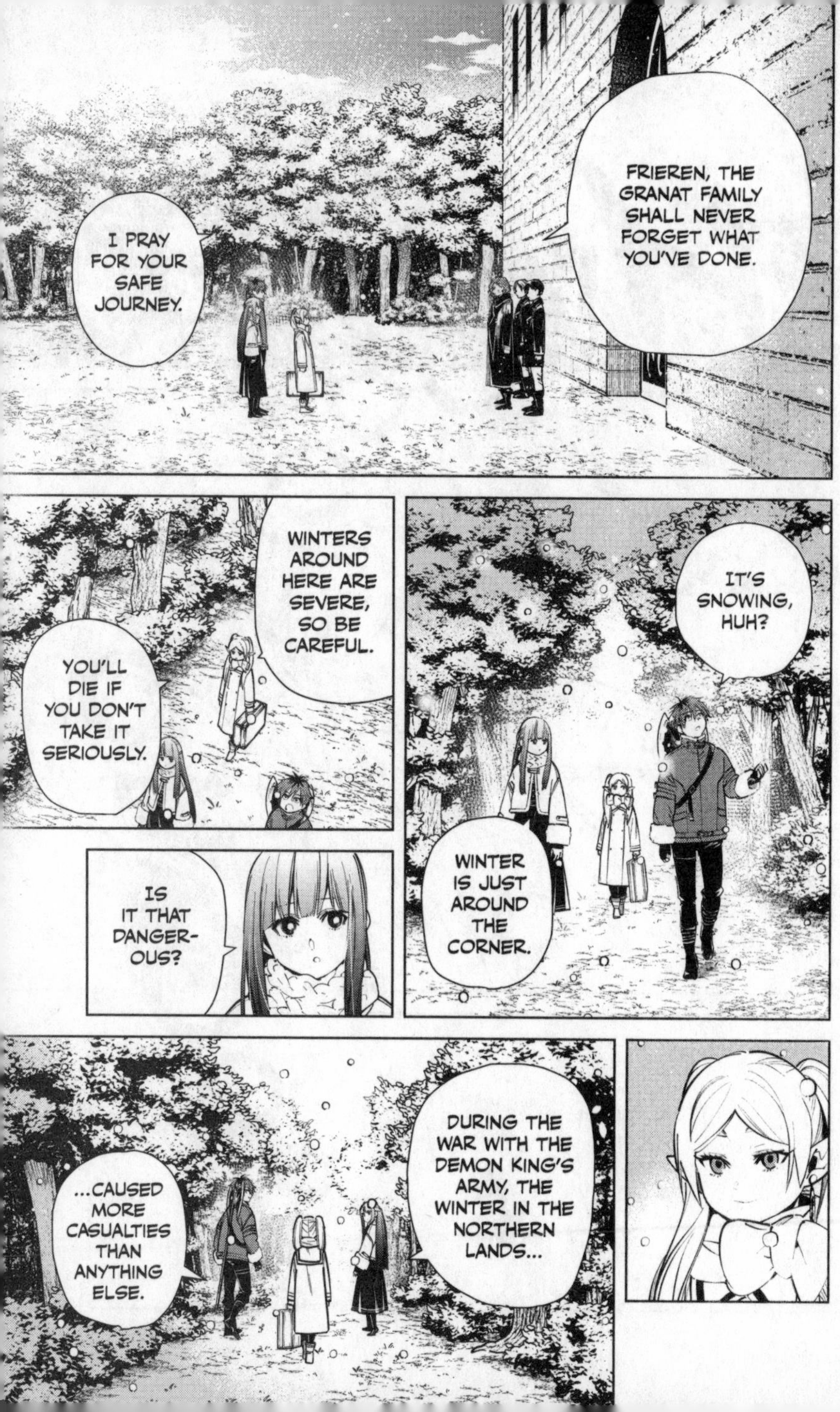
FRIEREN, THE GRANAT FAMILY SHALL NEVER FORGET WHAT YOU'VE DONE.
I PRAY FOR YOUR SAFE JOURNEY.
IT'S SNOWING, HUH?
WINTER IS JUST AROUND THE CORNER.
WINTERS AROUND HERE ARE SEVERE, SO BE CAREFUL.
YOU'LL DIE IF YOU DON'T TAKE IT SERIOUSLY.
IS IT THAT DANGER-OUS?
DURING THE WAR WITH THE DEMON KING'S ARMY, THE WINTER IN THE NORTHERN LANDS...
...CAUSED MORE CASUALTIES THAN ANYTHING ELSE.

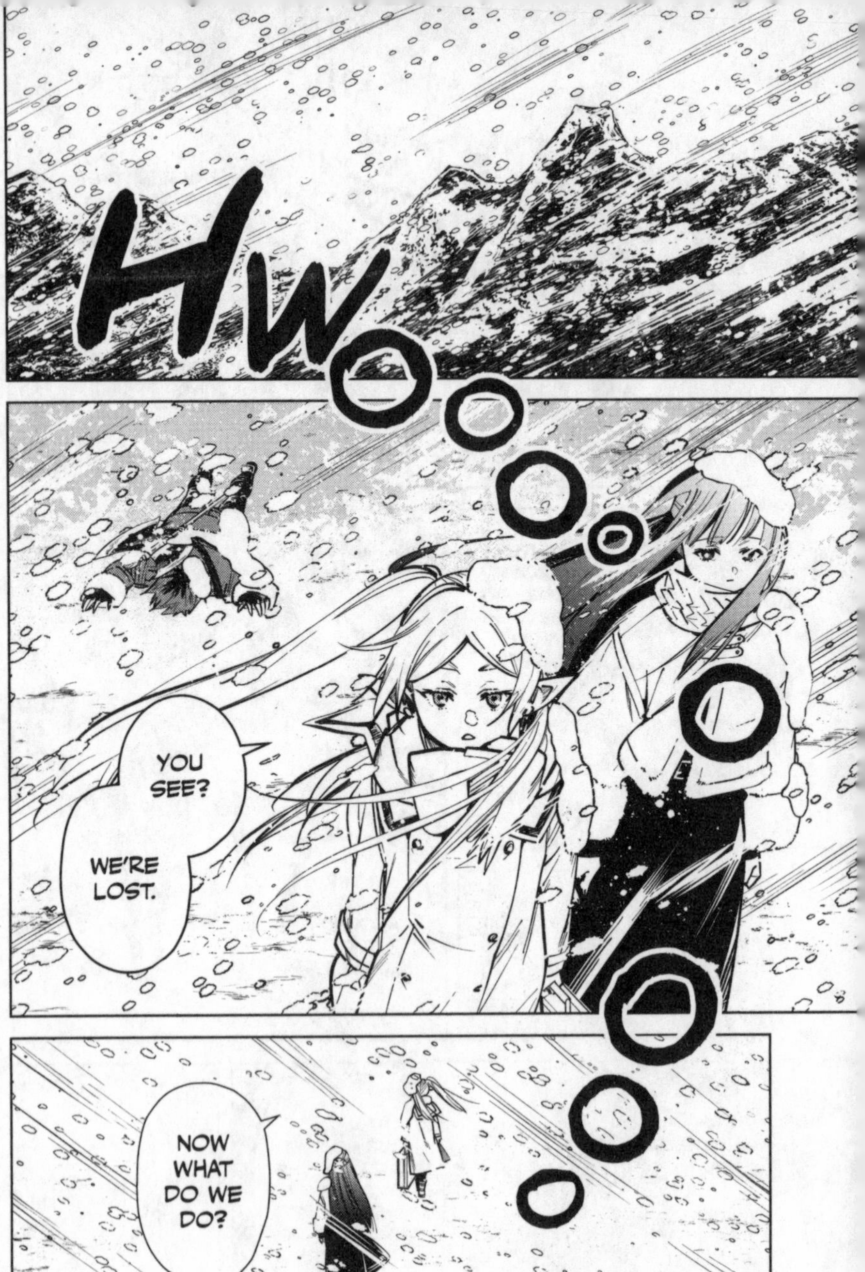
HWOOOOOOOOO
YOU SEE?
WE'RE LOST.
NOW WHAT DO WE DO?

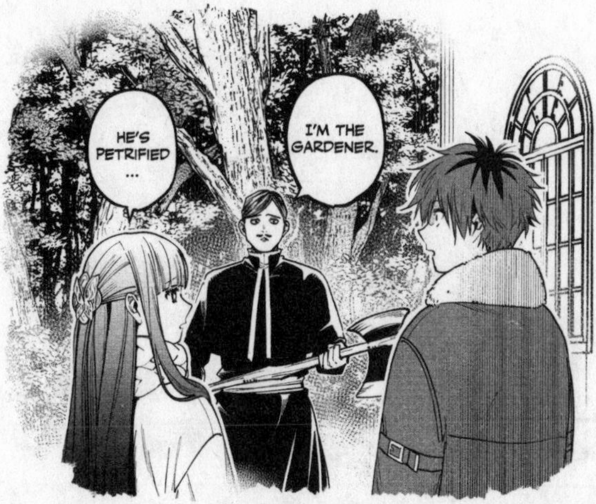
I'M THE GARDENER.
HE'S PETRIFIED ...

# Frieren

## Beyond Journey's End

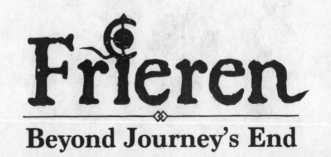

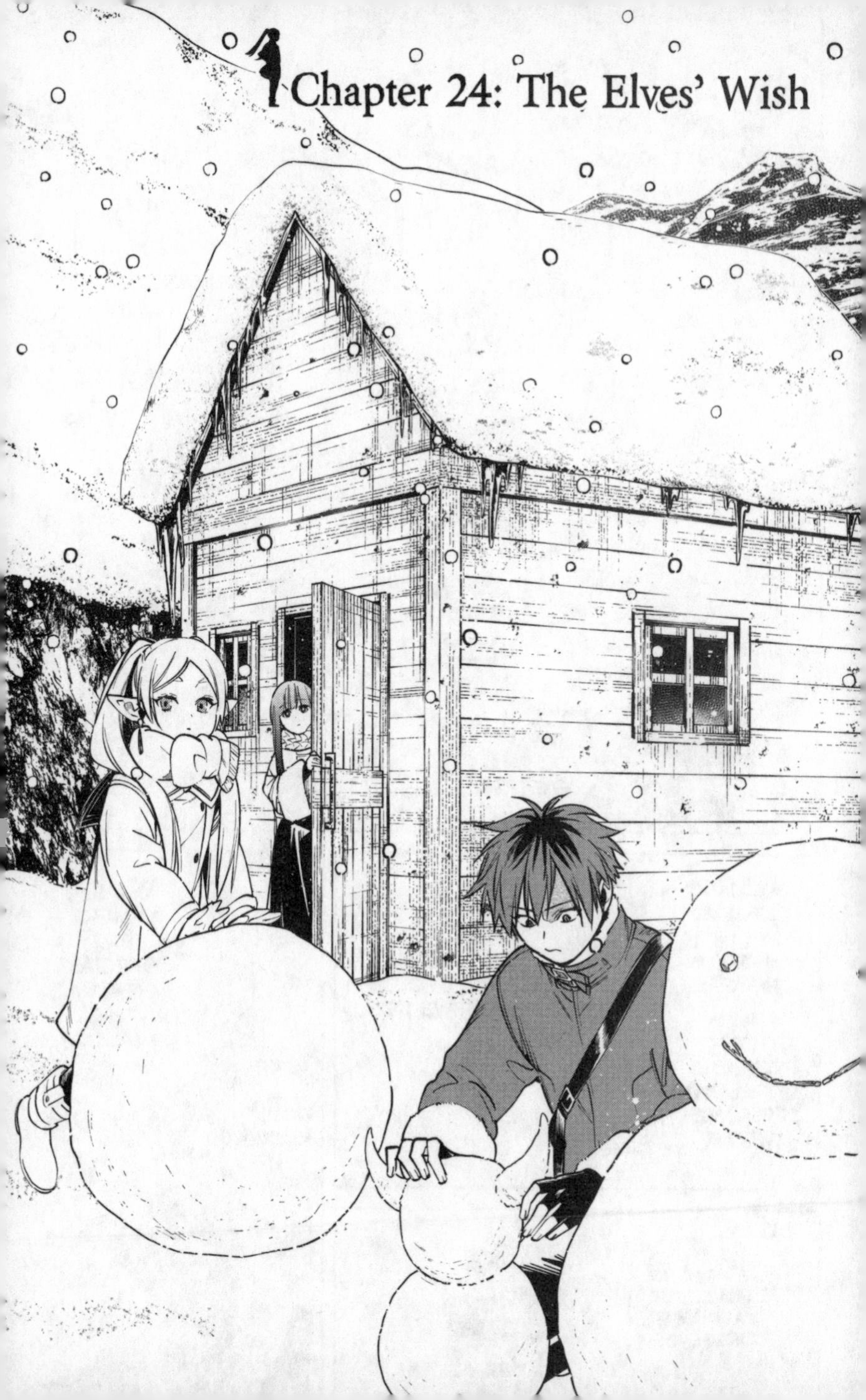
Chapter 24: The Elves' Wish

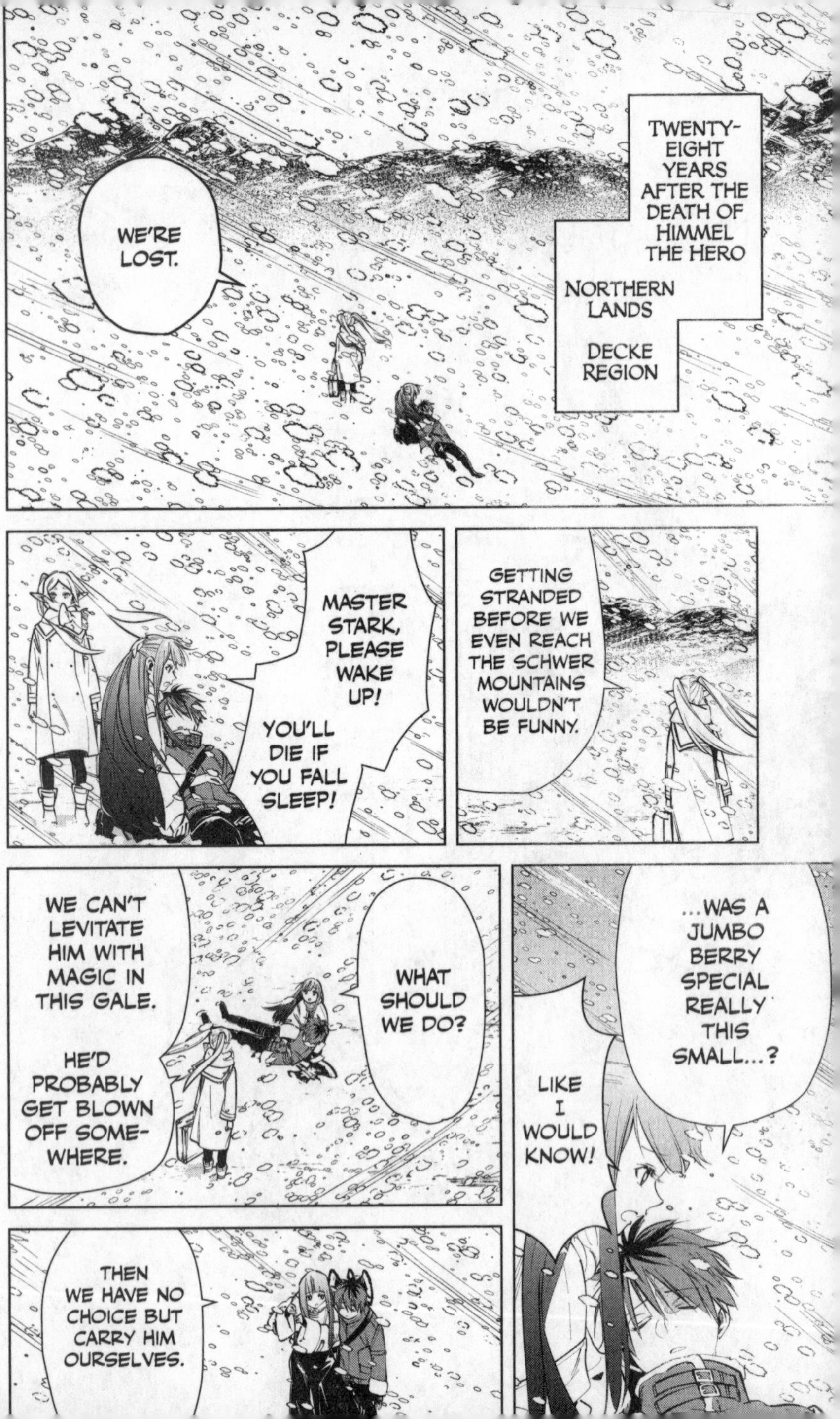
TWENTY-EIGHT YEARS AFTER THE DEATH OF HIMMEL THE HERO
NORTHERN LANDS
DECKE REGION
WE'RE LOST.
GETTING STRANDED BEFORE WE EVEN REACH THE SCHWER MOUNTAINS WOULDN'T BE FUNNY.
MASTER STARK, PLEASE WAKE UP!
YOU'LL DIE IF YOU FALL SLEEP!
...WAS A JUMBO BERRY SPECIAL REALLY THIS SMALL...?
LIKE I WOULD KNOW!
WHAT SHOULD WE DO?
WE CAN'T LEVITATE HIM WITH MAGIC IN THIS GALE.
HE'D PROBABLY GET BLOWN OFF SOME-WHERE.
THEN WE HAVE NO CHOICE BUT CARRY HIM OURSELVES.

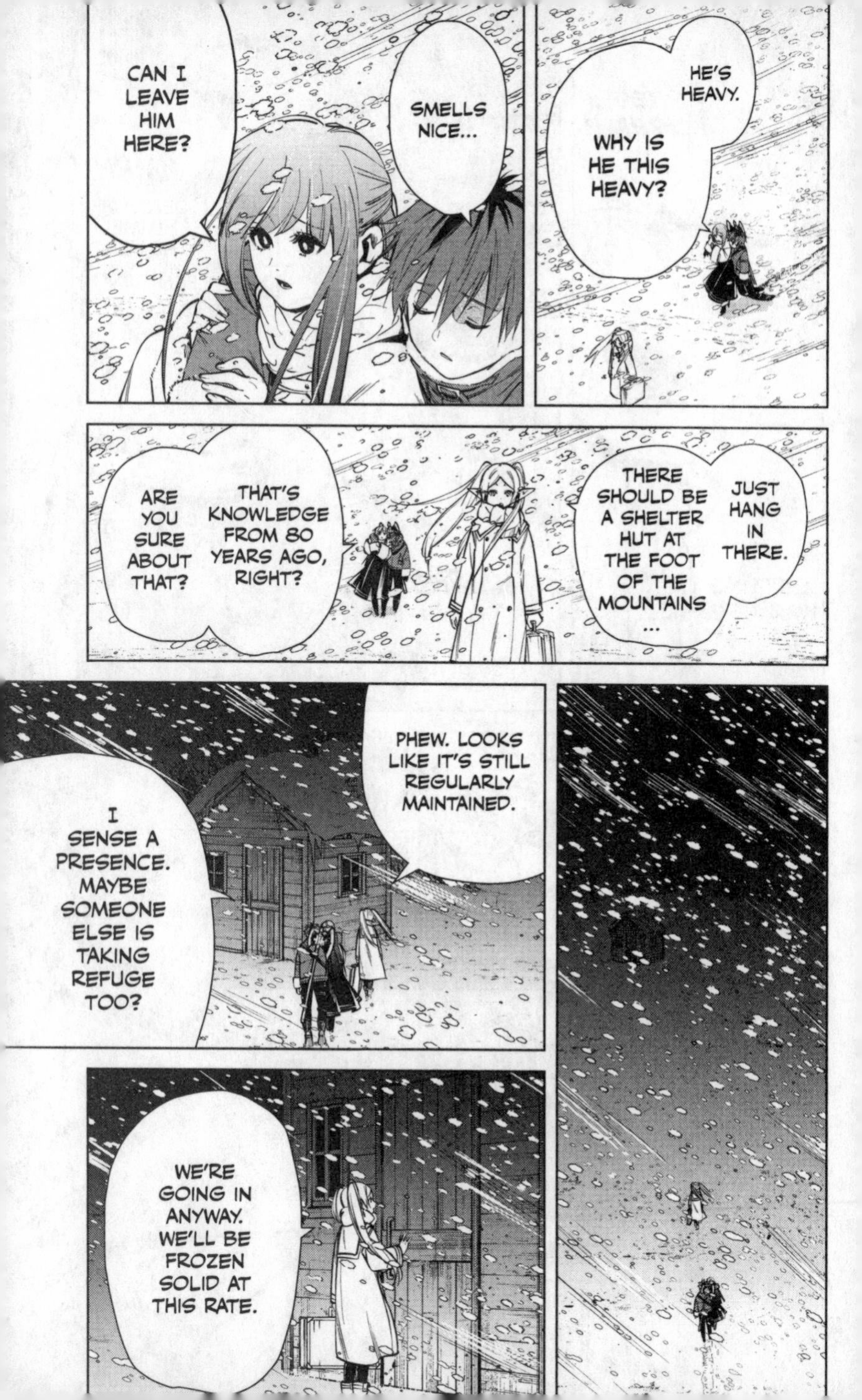
HE'S HEAVY.
WHY IS HE THIS HEAVY?
SMELLS NICE...
CAN I LEAVE HIM HERE?
JUST HANG IN THERE.
THERE SHOULD BE A SHELTER HUT AT THE FOOT OF THE MOUNTAINS ...
THAT'S KNOWLEDGE FROM 80 YEARS AGO, RIGHT?
ARE YOU SURE ABOUT THAT?
PHEW. LOOKS LIKE IT'S STILL REGULARLY MAINTAINED.
I SENSE A PRESENCE. MAYBE SOMEONE ELSE IS TAKING REFUGE TOO?
WE'RE GOING IN ANYWAY. WE'LL BE FROZEN SOLID AT THIS RATE.

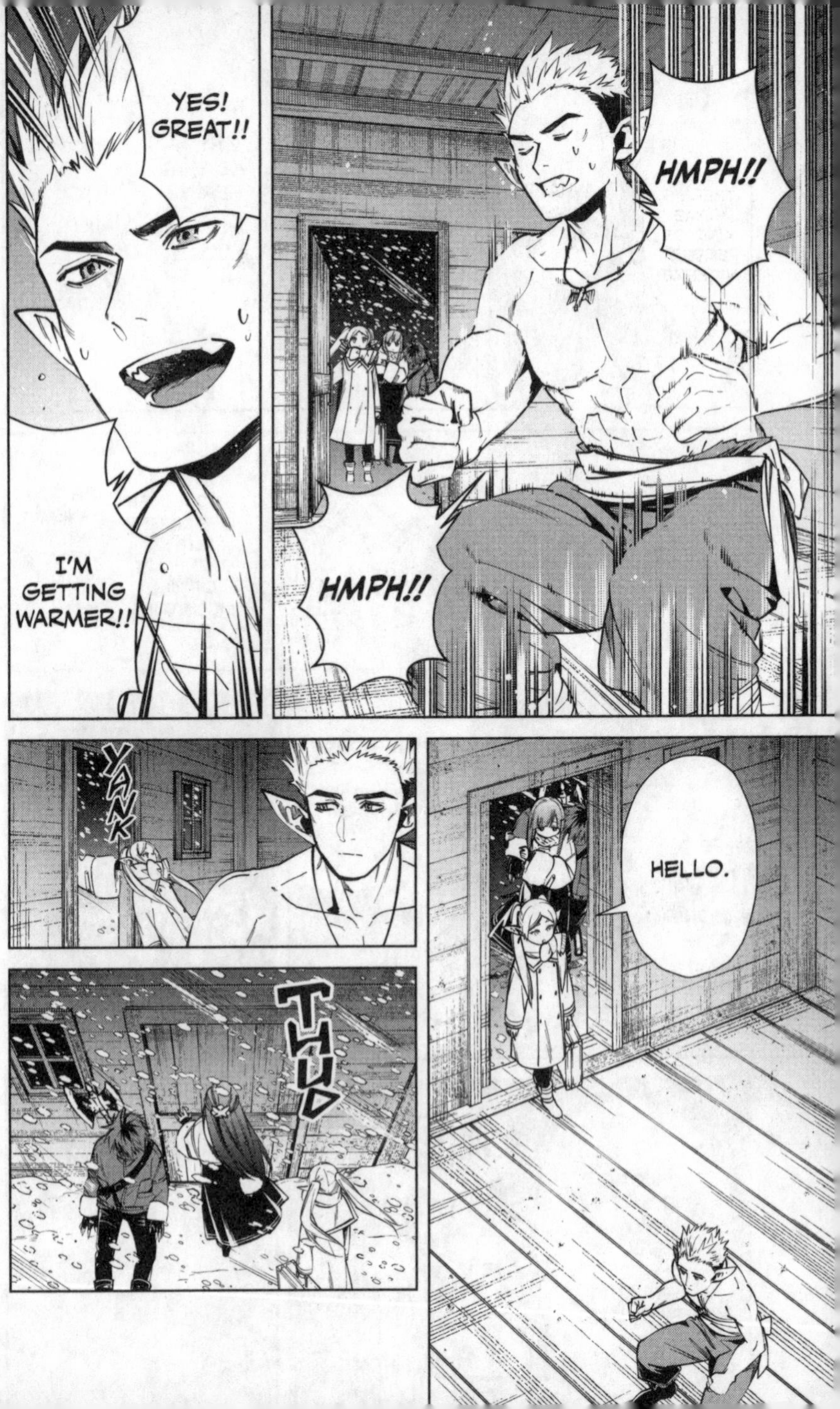
HMPH!!
HMPH!!
YES! GREAT!!
I'M GETTING WARMER!!
HELLO.
YANK
THUD

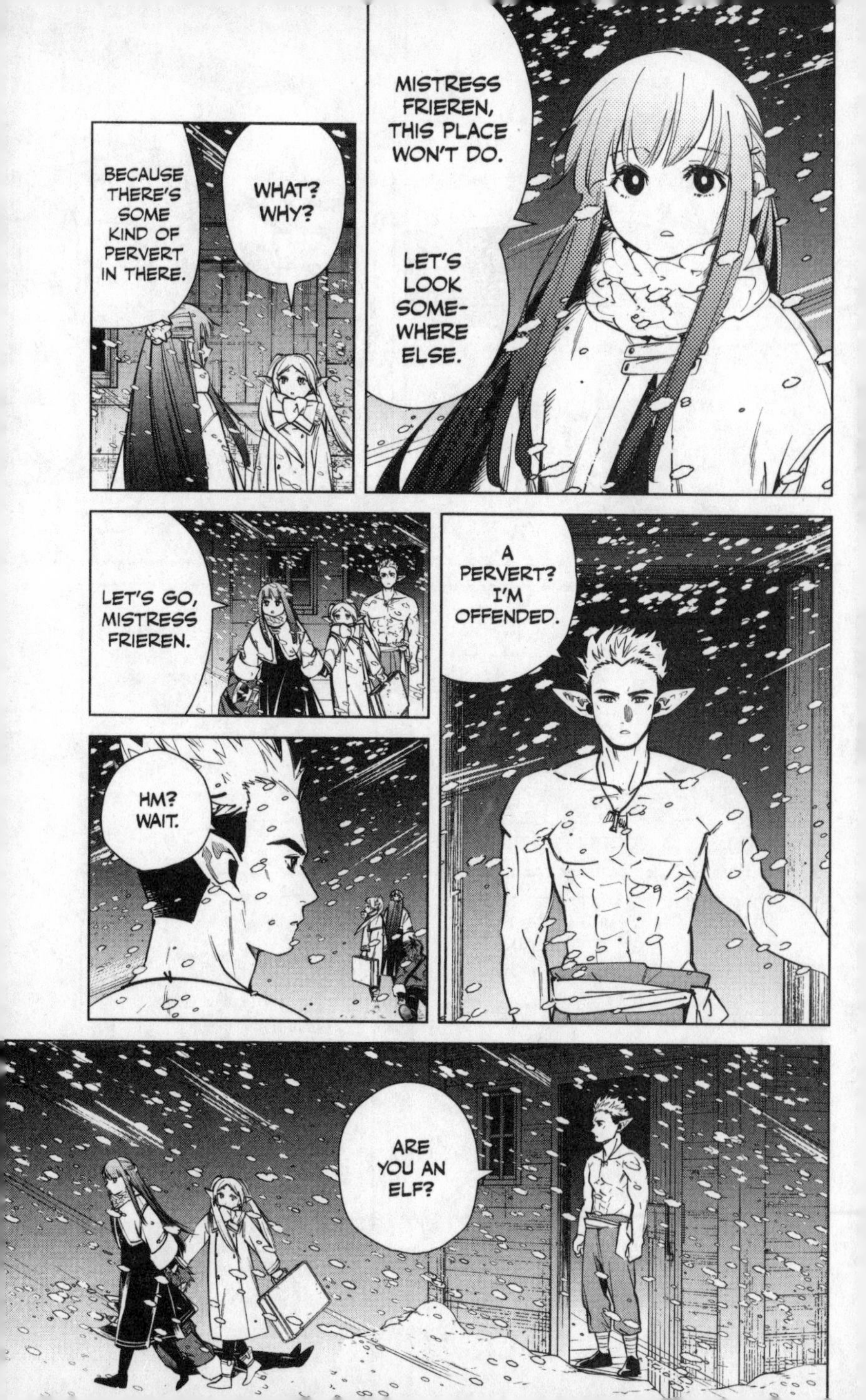
MISTRESS FRIEREN, THIS PLACE WON'T DO.
LET'S LOOK SOME-WHERE ELSE.
WHAT? WHY?
BECAUSE THERE'S SOME KIND OF PERVERT IN THERE.
A PERVERT? I'M OFFENDED.
LET'S GO, MISTRESS FRIEREN.
HM? WAIT.
ARE YOU AN ELF?

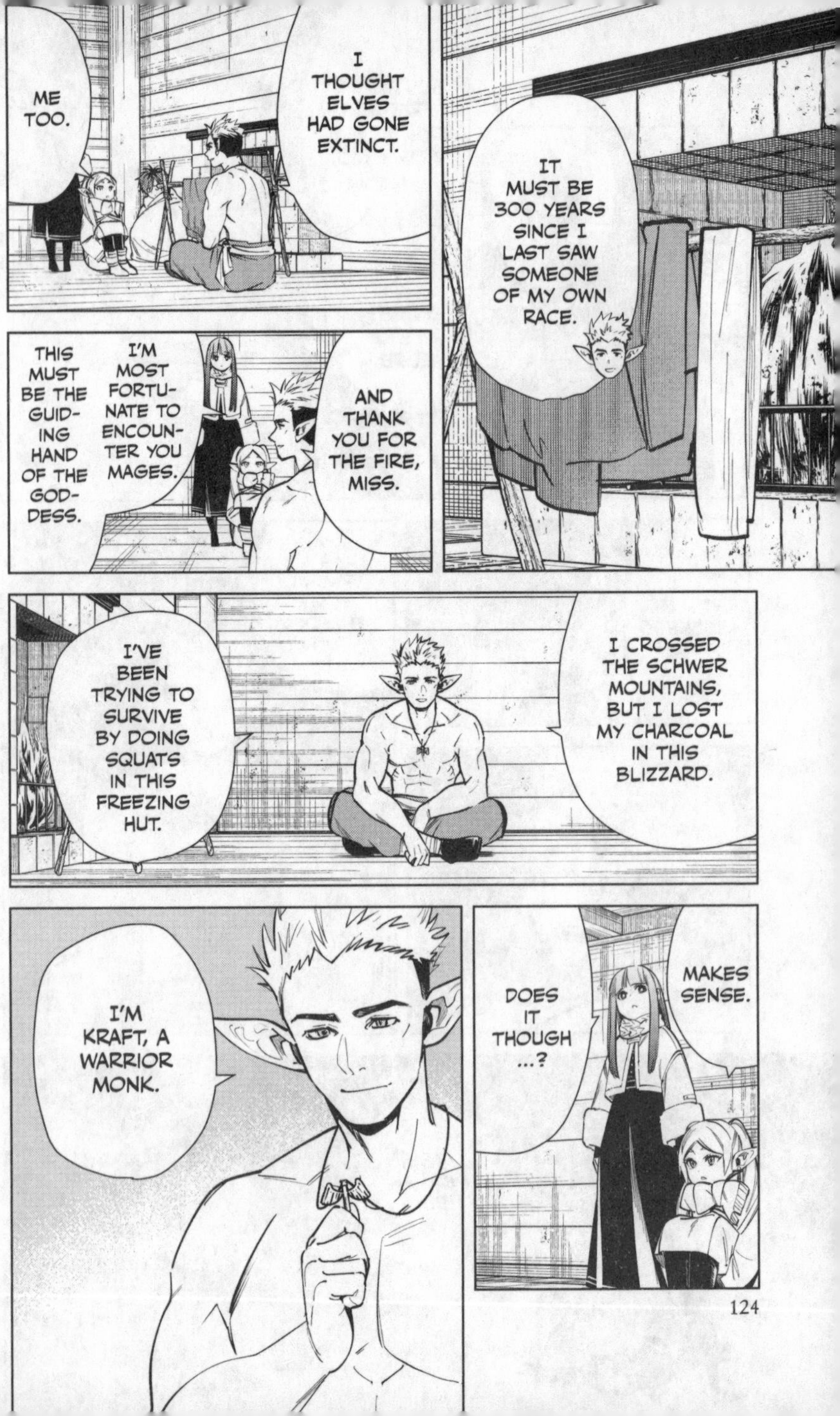
IT MUST BE 300 YEARS SINCE I LAST SAW SOMEONE OF MY OWN RACE.
I THOUGHT ELVES HAD GONE EXTINCT.
ME TOO.
AND THANK YOU FOR THE FIRE, MISS.
I'M MOST FORTUNATE TO ENCOUNTER YOU MAGES.
THIS MUST BE THE GUIDING HAND OF THE GODDESS.
I CROSSED THE SCHWER MOUNTAINS, BUT I LOST MY CHARCOAL IN THIS BLIZZARD.
I'VE BEEN TRYING TO SURVIVE BY DOING SQUATS IN THIS FREEZING HUT.
MAKES SENSE.
DOES IT THOUGH ...?
I'M KRAFT, A WARRIOR MONK.

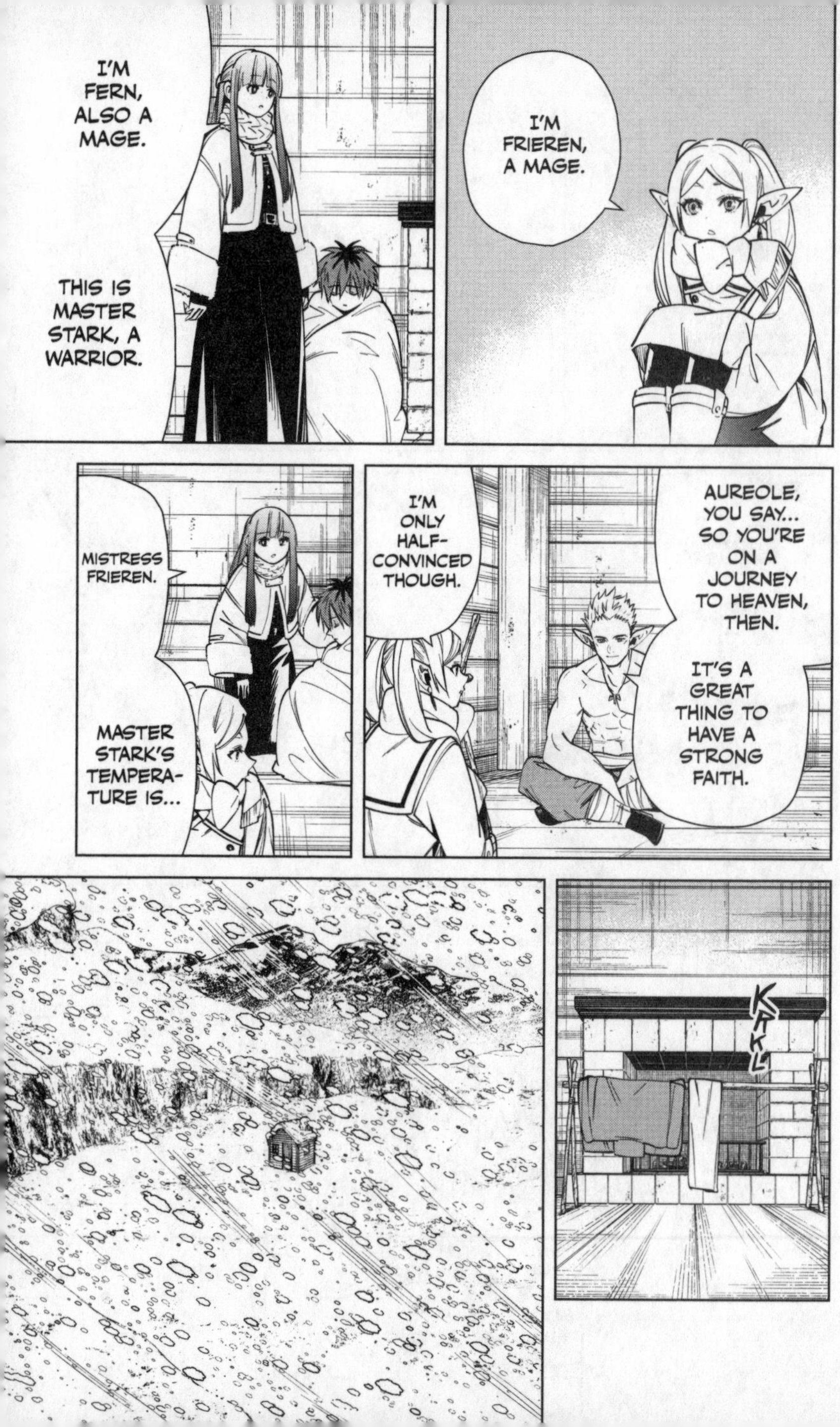
I'M FRIEREN, A MAGE.
I'M FERN, ALSO A MAGE.
THIS IS MASTER STARK, A WARRIOR.
AUREOLE, YOU SAY... SO YOU'RE ON A JOURNEY TO HEAVEN, THEN.
IT'S A GREAT THING TO HAVE A STRONG FAITH.
I'M ONLY HALF-CONVINCED THOUGH.
MISTRESS FRIEREN.
MASTER STARK'S TEMPERATURE IS...
KRKL

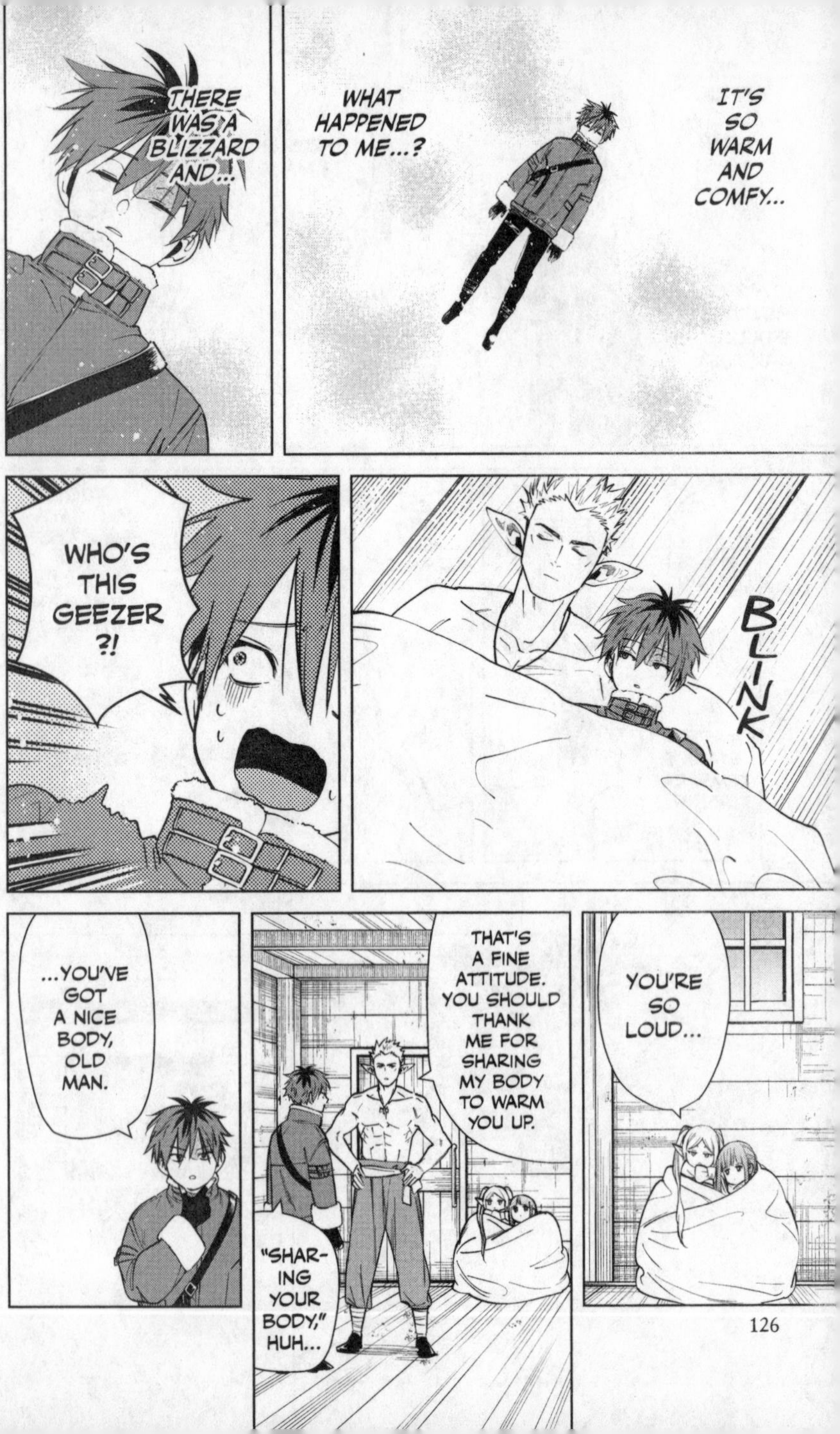
IT'S SO WARM AND COMFY...
WHAT HAPPENED TO ME...?
THERE WAS A BLIZZARD AND...
BLINK
WHO'S THIS GEEZER ?!
YOU'RE SO LOUD...
THAT'S A FINE ATTITUDE. YOU SHOULD THANK ME FOR SHARING MY BODY TO WARM YOU UP.
"SHARING YOUR BODY," HUH...
...YOU'VE GOT A NICE BODY, OLD MAN.

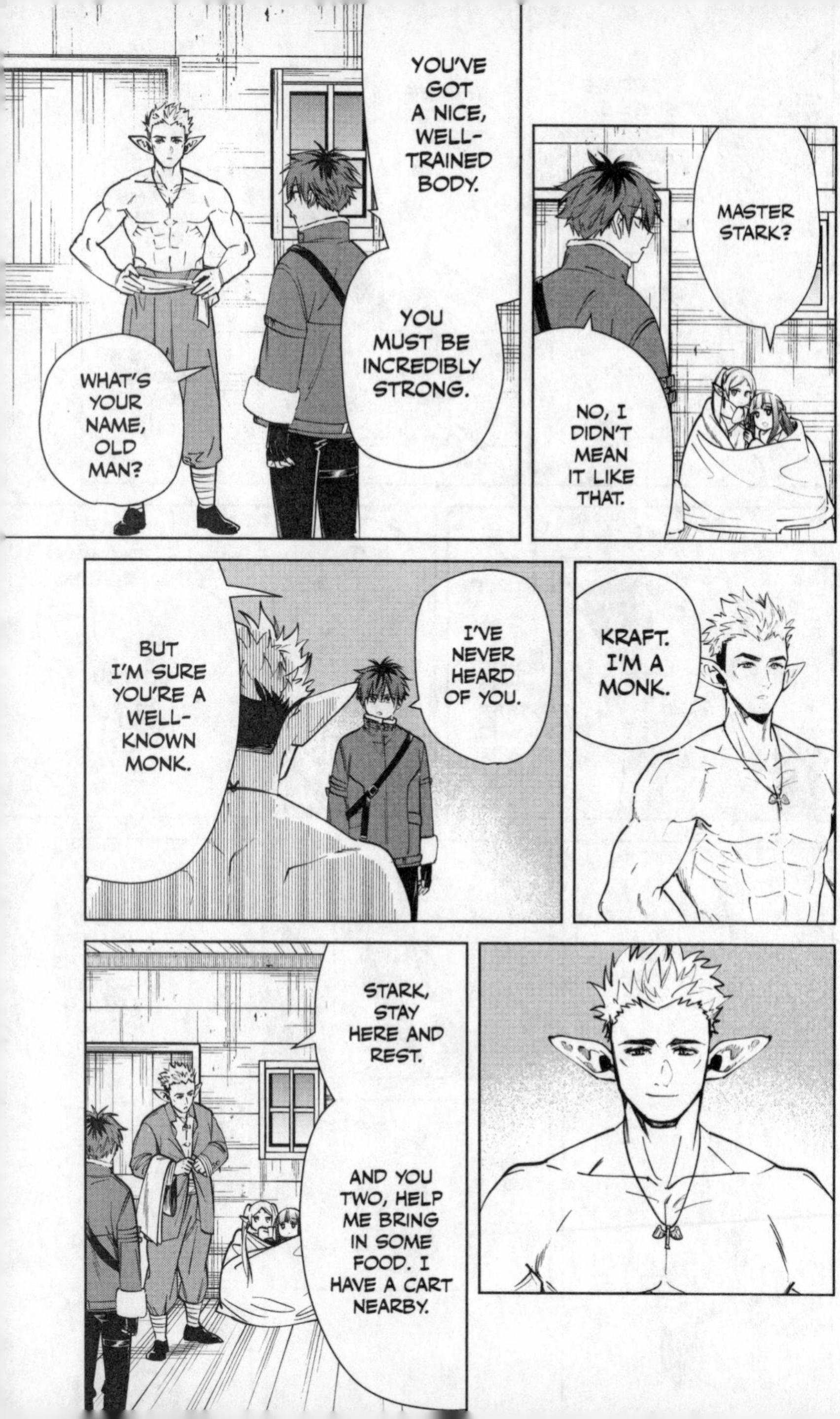
MASTER STARK?
NO, I DIDN'T MEAN IT LIKE THAT.
YOU'VE GOT A NICE, WELL-TRAINED BODY.
YOU MUST BE INCREDIBLY STRONG.
WHAT'S YOUR NAME, OLD MAN?
KRAFT. I'M A MONK.
I'VE NEVER HEARD OF YOU.
BUT I'M SURE YOU'RE A WELL-KNOWN MONK.
STARK, STAY HERE AND REST.
AND YOU TWO, HELP ME BRING IN SOME FOOD. I HAVE A CART NEARBY.

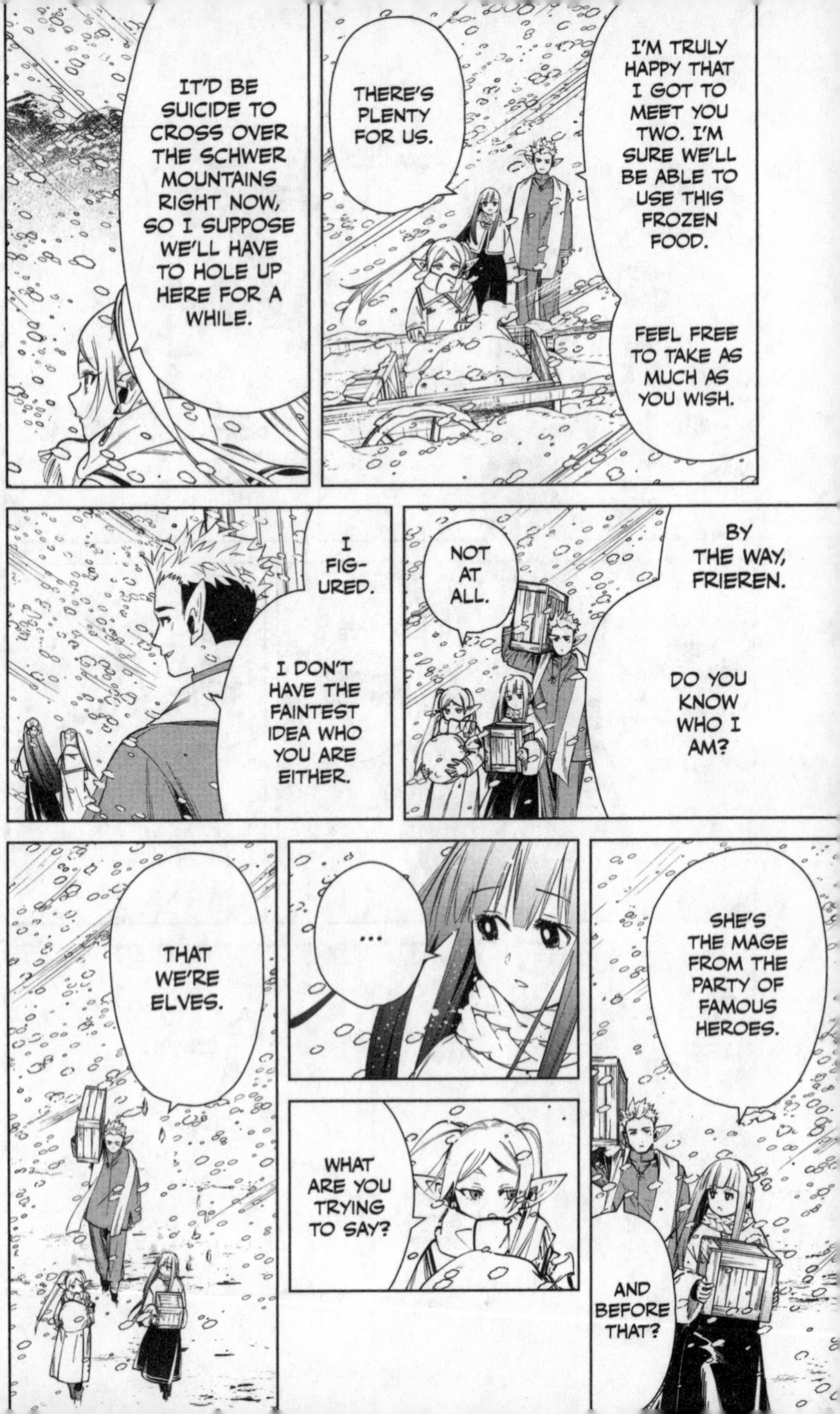
I'M TRULY HAPPY THAT I GOT TO MEET YOU TWO. I'M SURE WE'LL BE ABLE TO USE THIS FROZEN FOOD.
FEEL FREE TO TAKE AS MUCH AS YOU WISH.
THERE'S PLENTY FOR US.
IT'D BE SUICIDE TO CROSS OVER THE SCHWER MOUNTAINS RIGHT NOW, SO I SUPPOSE WE'LL HAVE TO HOLE UP HERE FOR A WHILE.
BY THE WAY, FRIEREN.
DO YOU KNOW WHO I AM?
NOT AT ALL.
I FIG- URED.
I DON'T HAVE THE FAINTEST IDEA WHO YOU ARE EITHER.
SHE'S THE MAGE FROM THE PARTY OF FAMOUS HEROES.
AND BEFORE THAT?
...
WHAT ARE YOU TRYING TO SAY?
THAT WE'RE ELVES.

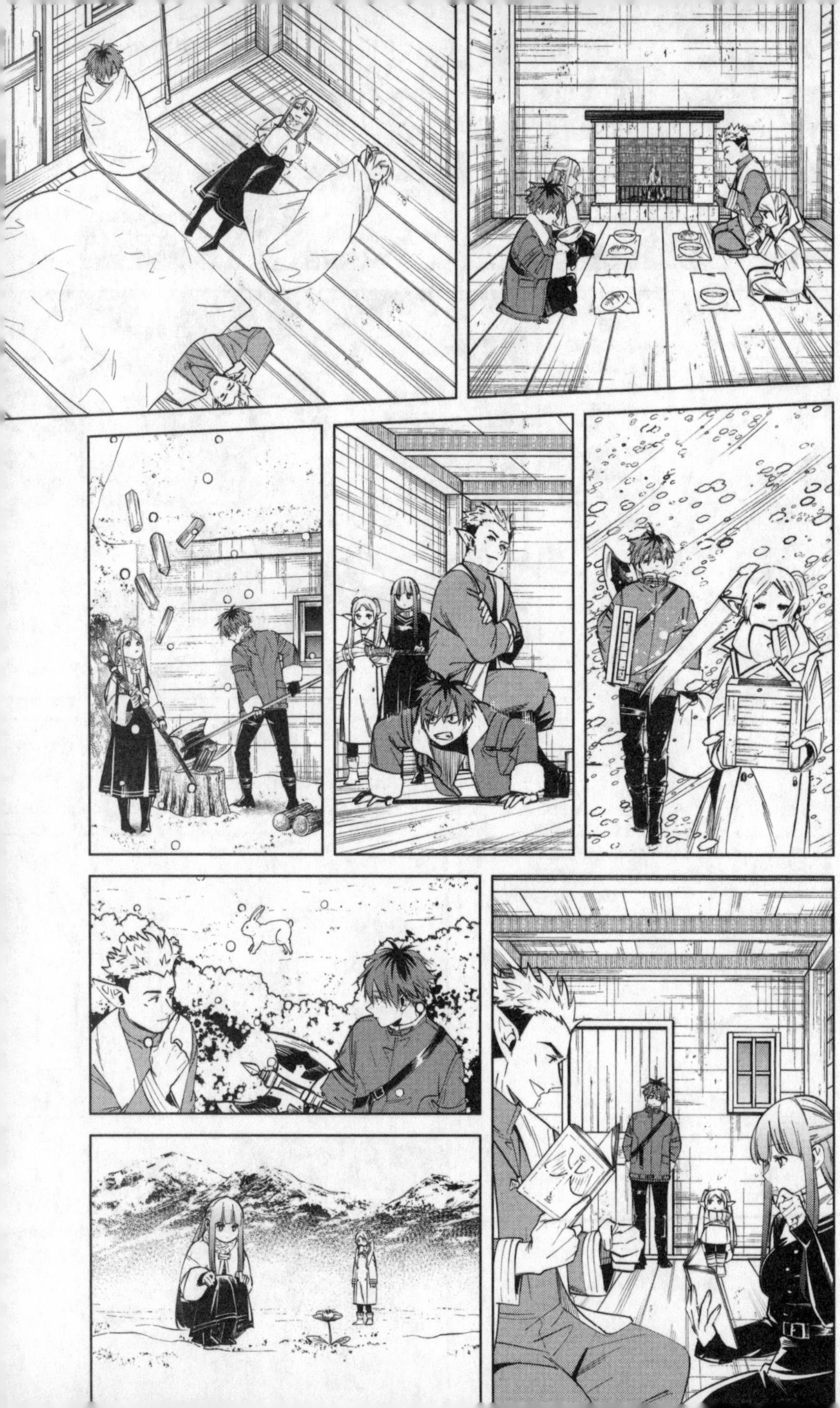

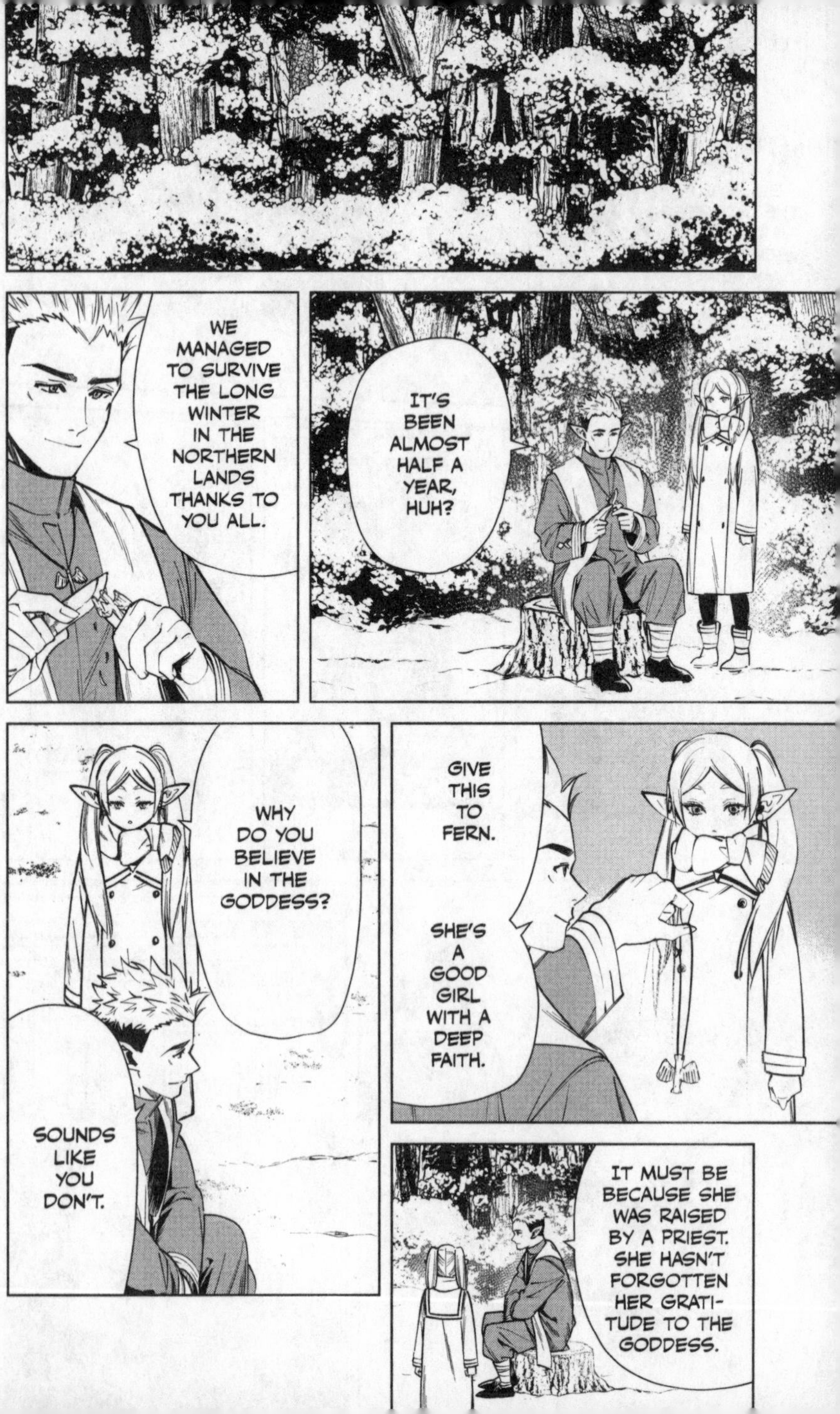
IT'S BEEN ALMOST HALF A YEAR, HUH?
WE MANAGED TO SURVIVE THE LONG WINTER IN THE NORTHERN LANDS THANKS TO YOU ALL.
GIVE THIS TO FERN.
SHE'S A GOOD GIRL WITH A DEEP FAITH.
IT MUST BE BECAUSE SHE WAS RAISED BY A PRIEST. SHE HASN'T FORGOTTEN HER GRATI-TUDE TO THE GODDESS.
WHY DO YOU BELIEVE IN THE GODDESS?
SOUNDS LIKE YOU DON'T.

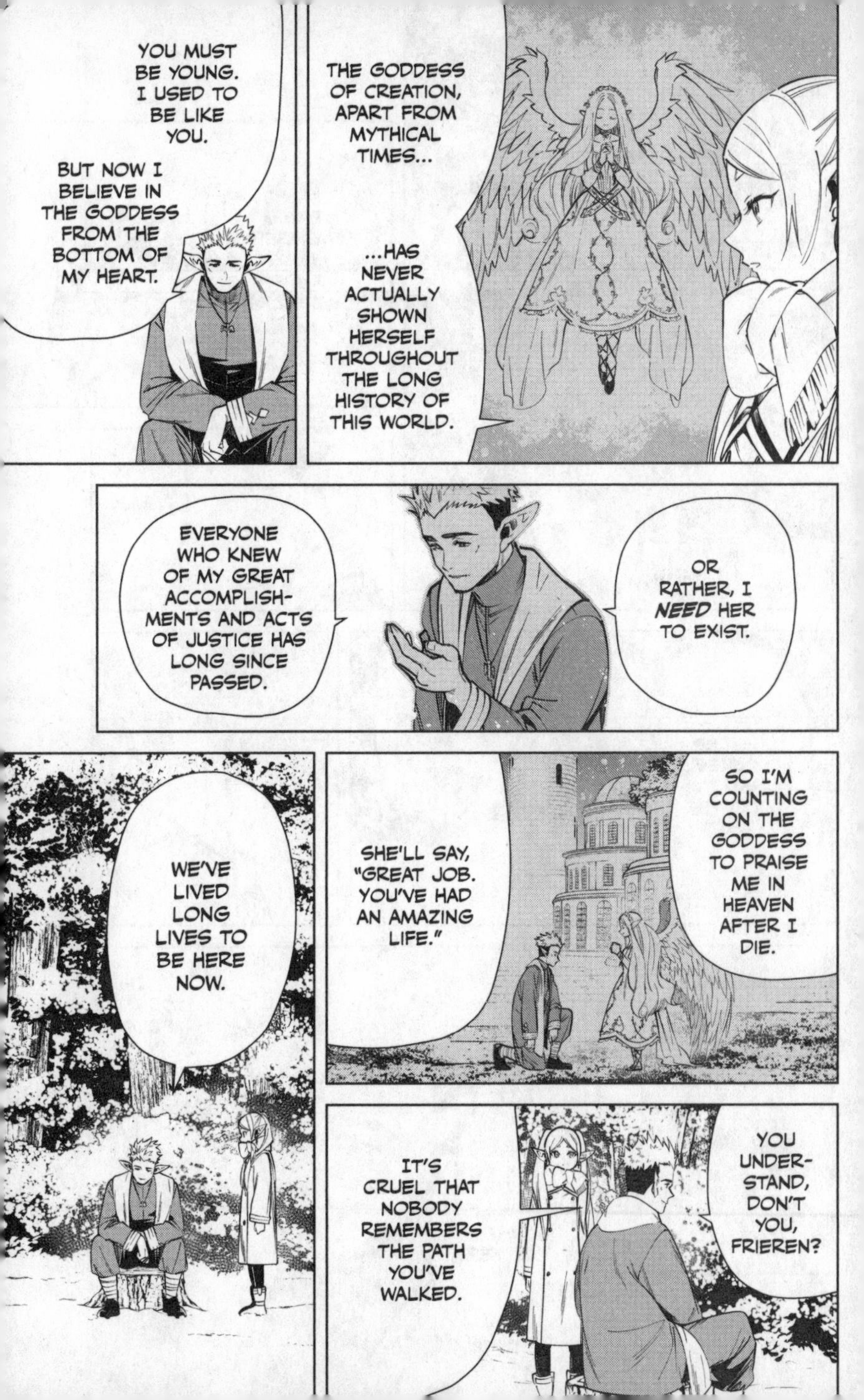
THE GODDESS OF CREATION, APART FROM MYTHICAL TIMES...
...HAS NEVER ACTUALLY SHOWN HERSELF THROUGHOUT THE LONG HISTORY OF THIS WORLD.
YOU MUST BE YOUNG. I USED TO BE LIKE YOU.
BUT NOW I BELIEVE IN THE GODDESS FROM THE BOTTOM OF MY HEART.
OR RATHER, I ***NEED*** HER TO EXIST.
EVERYONE WHO KNEW OF MY GREAT ACCOMPLISH-MENTS AND ACTS OF JUSTICE HAS LONG SINCE PASSED.
SO I'M COUNTING ON THE GODDESS TO PRAISE ME IN HEAVEN AFTER I DIE.
SHE'LL SAY, "GREAT JOB. YOU'VE HAD AN AMAZING LIFE."
YOU UNDER-STAND, DON'T YOU, FRIEREN?
IT'S CRUEL THAT NOBODY REMEMBERS THE PATH YOU'VE WALKED.
WE'VE LIVED LONG LIVES TO BE HERE NOW.

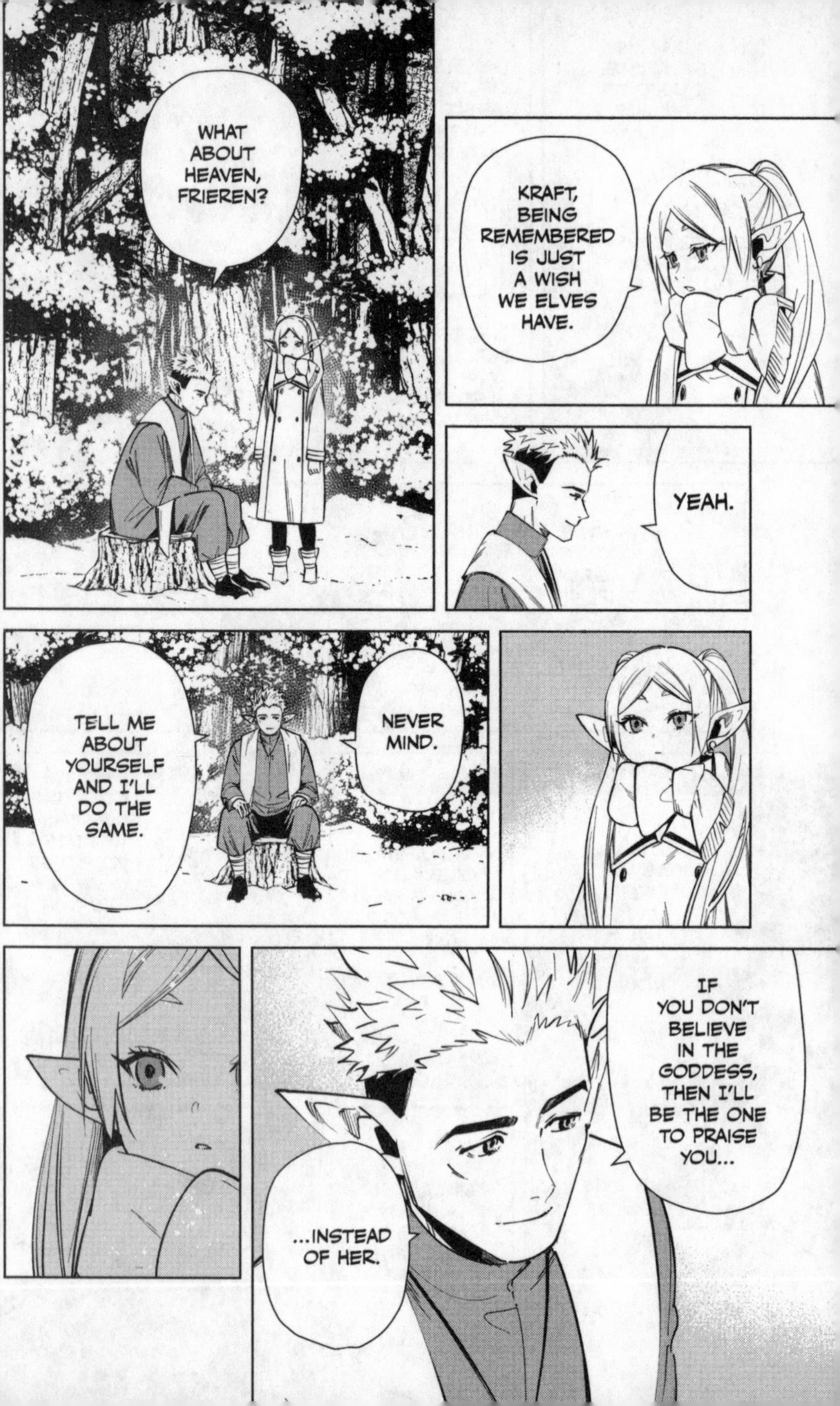
KRAFT, BEING REMEMBERED IS JUST A WISH WE ELVES HAVE.
YEAH.
WHAT ABOUT HEAVEN, FRIEREN?
NEVER MIND.
TELL ME ABOUT YOURSELF AND I'LL DO THE SAME.
IF YOU DON'T BELIEVE IN THE GODDESS, THEN I'LL BE THE ONE TO PRAISE YOU...
...INSTEAD OF HER.

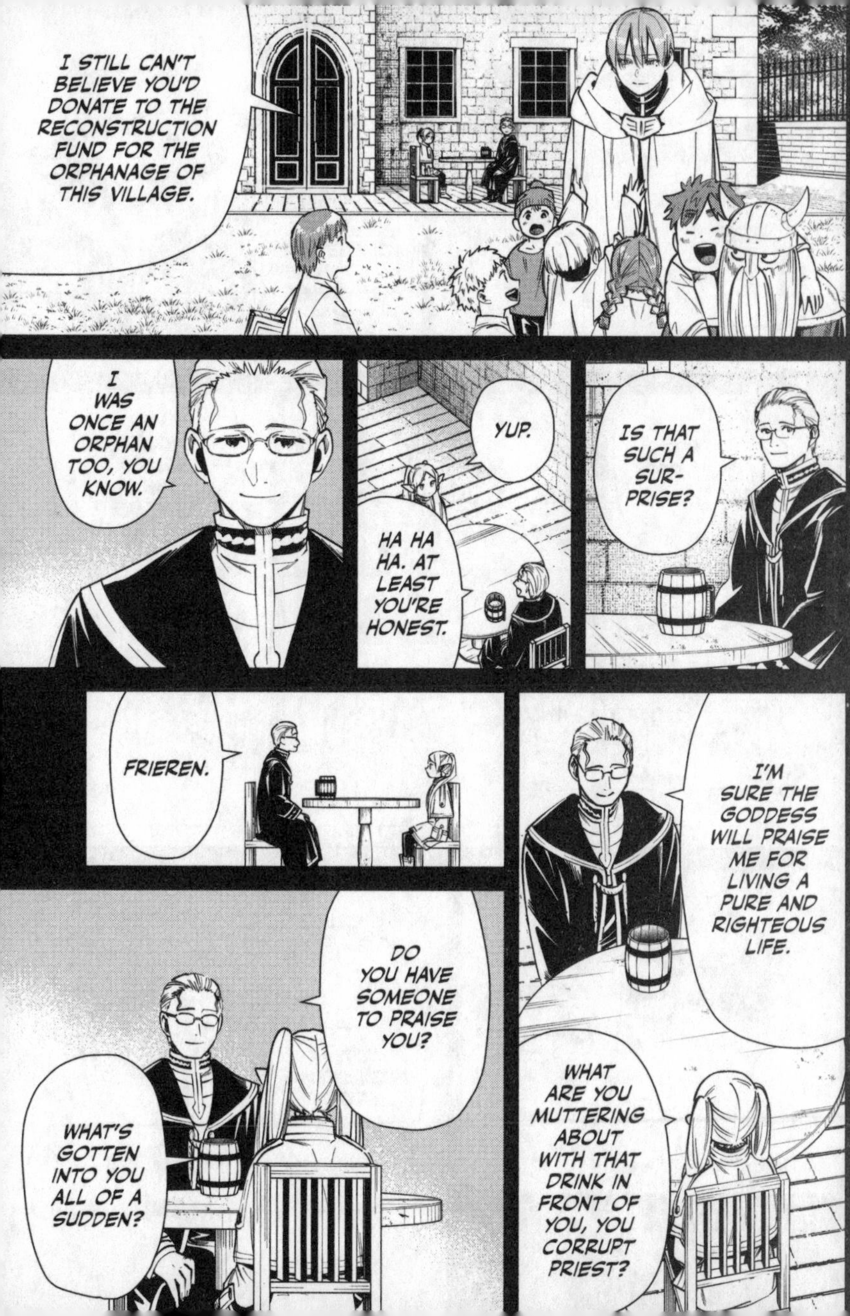
I STILL CAN'T BELIEVE YOU'D DONATE TO THE RECONSTRUCTION FUND FOR THE ORPHANAGE OF THIS VILLAGE.
IS THAT SUCH A SUR-PRISE?
YUP.
HA HA HA. AT LEAST YOU'RE HONEST.
I WAS ONCE AN ORPHAN TOO, YOU KNOW.
I'M SURE THE GODDESS WILL PRAISE ME FOR LIVING A PURE AND RIGHTEOUS LIFE.
WHAT ARE YOU MUTTERING ABOUT WITH THAT DRINK IN FRONT OF YOU, YOU CORRUPT PRIEST?
FRIEREN.
DO YOU HAVE SOMEONE TO PRAISE YOU?
WHAT'S GOTTEN INTO YOU ALL OF A SUDDEN?

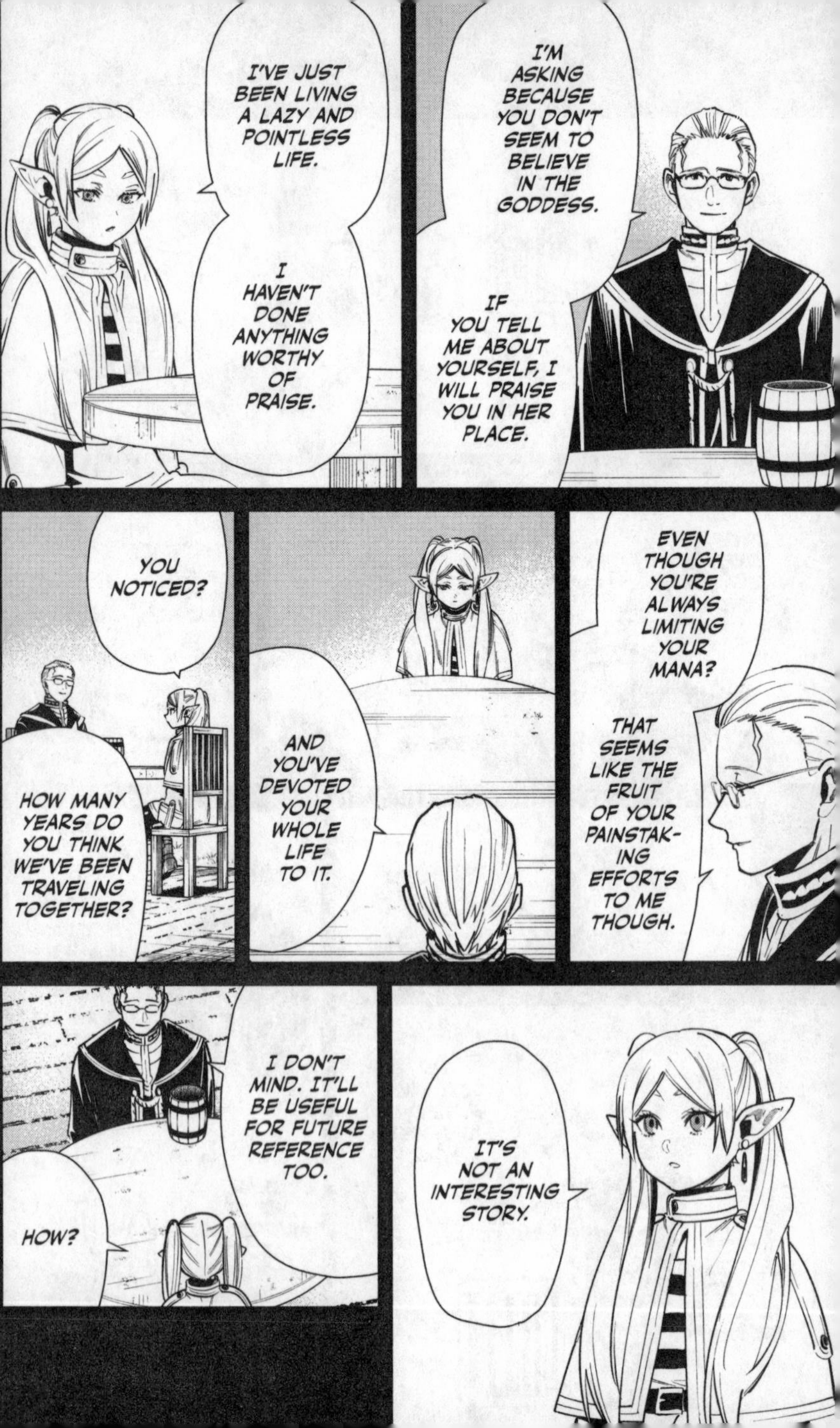
I'M ASKING BECAUSE YOU DON'T SEEM TO BELIEVE IN THE GODDESS.
IF YOU TELL ME ABOUT YOURSELF, I WILL PRAISE YOU IN HER PLACE.
I'VE JUST BEEN LIVING A LAZY AND POINTLESS LIFE.
I HAVEN'T DONE ANYTHING WORTHY OF PRAISE.
EVEN THOUGH YOU'RE ALWAYS LIMITING YOUR MANA?
THAT SEEMS LIKE THE FRUIT OF YOUR PAINSTAKING EFFORTS TO ME THOUGH.
AND YOU'VE DEVOTED YOUR WHOLE LIFE TO IT.
YOU NOTICED?
HOW MANY YEARS DO YOU THINK WE'VE BEEN TRAVELING TOGETHER?
IT'S NOT AN INTERESTING STORY.
I DON'T MIND. IT'LL BE USEFUL FOR FUTURE REFERENCE TOO.
HOW?

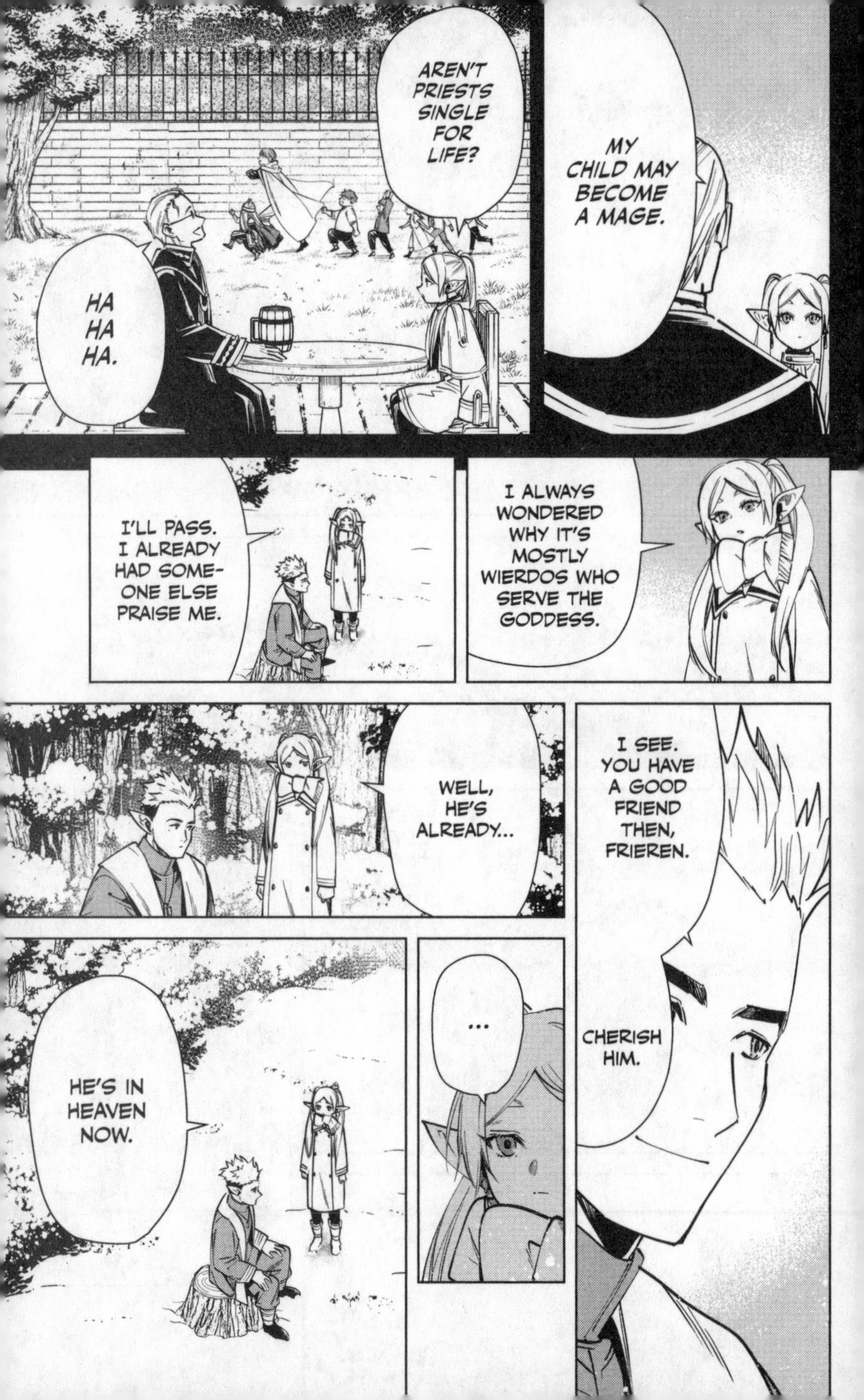
MY CHILD MAY BECOME A MAGE.
AREN'T PRIESTS SINGLE FOR LIFE?
HA HA HA.
I ALWAYS WONDERED WHY IT'S MOSTLY WIERDOS WHO SERVE THE GODDESS.
I'LL PASS. I ALREADY HAD SOME-ONE ELSE PRAISE ME.
I SEE. YOU HAVE A GOOD FRIEND THEN, FRIEREN.
CHERISH HIM.
WELL, HE'S ALREADY...
...
HE'S IN HEAVEN NOW.

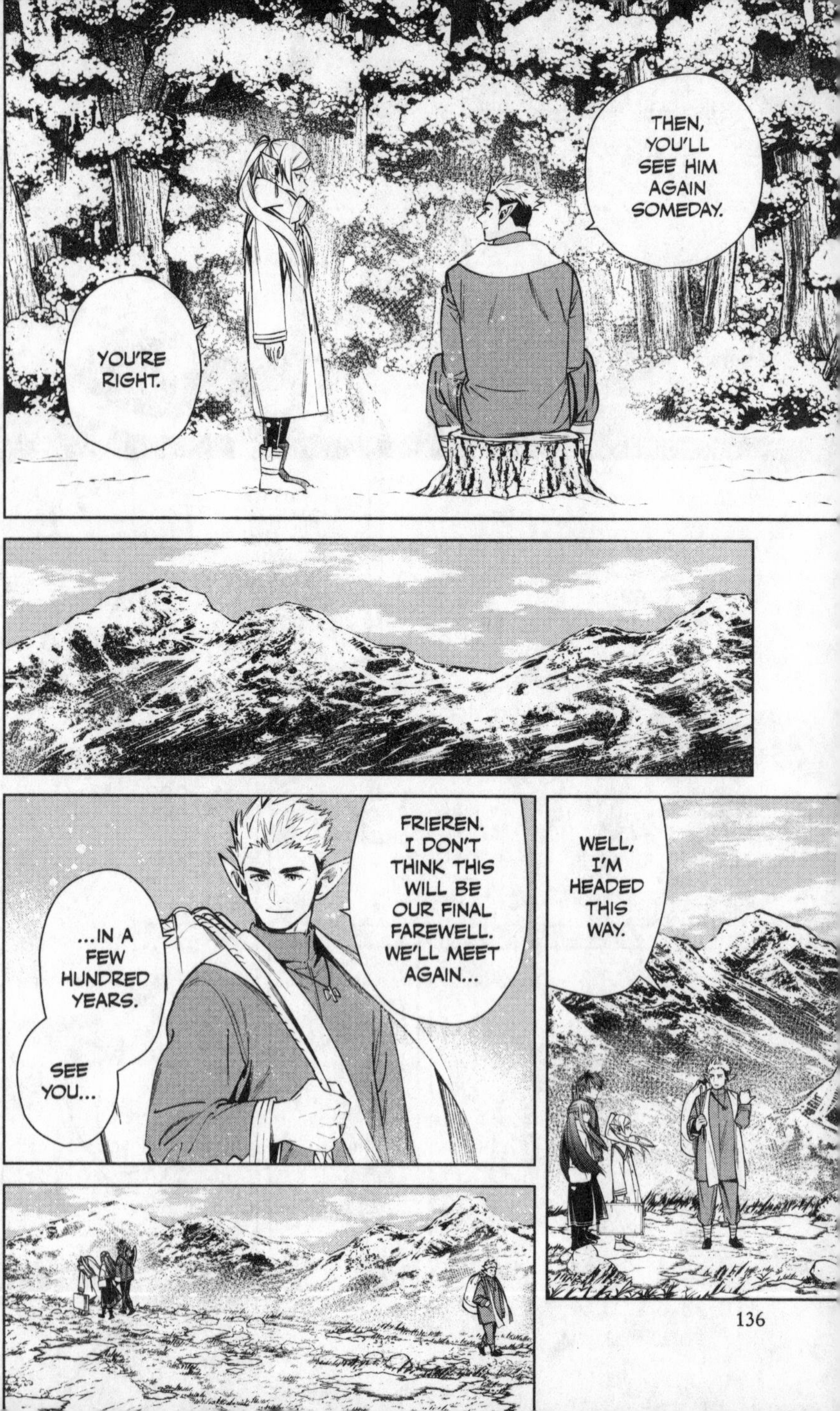
THEN, YOU'LL SEE HIM AGAIN SOMEDAY.
YOU'RE RIGHT.
WELL, I'M HEADED THIS WAY.
FRIEREN. I DON'T THINK THIS WILL BE OUR FINAL FAREWELL. WE'LL MEET AGAIN...
...IN A FEW HUNDRED YEARS.
SEE YOU...

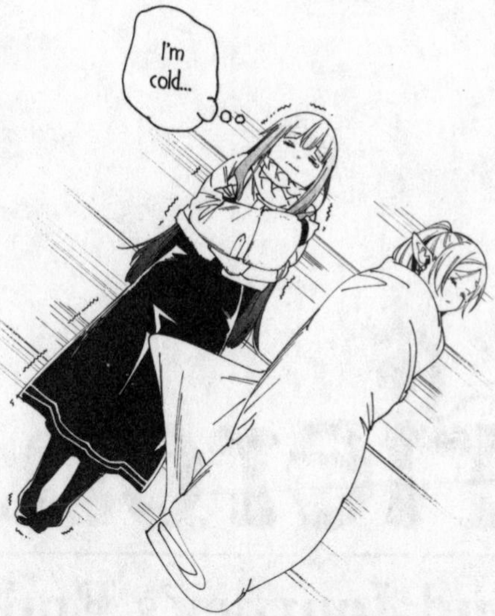
I'm cold...

Frieren

Beyond Journey's End

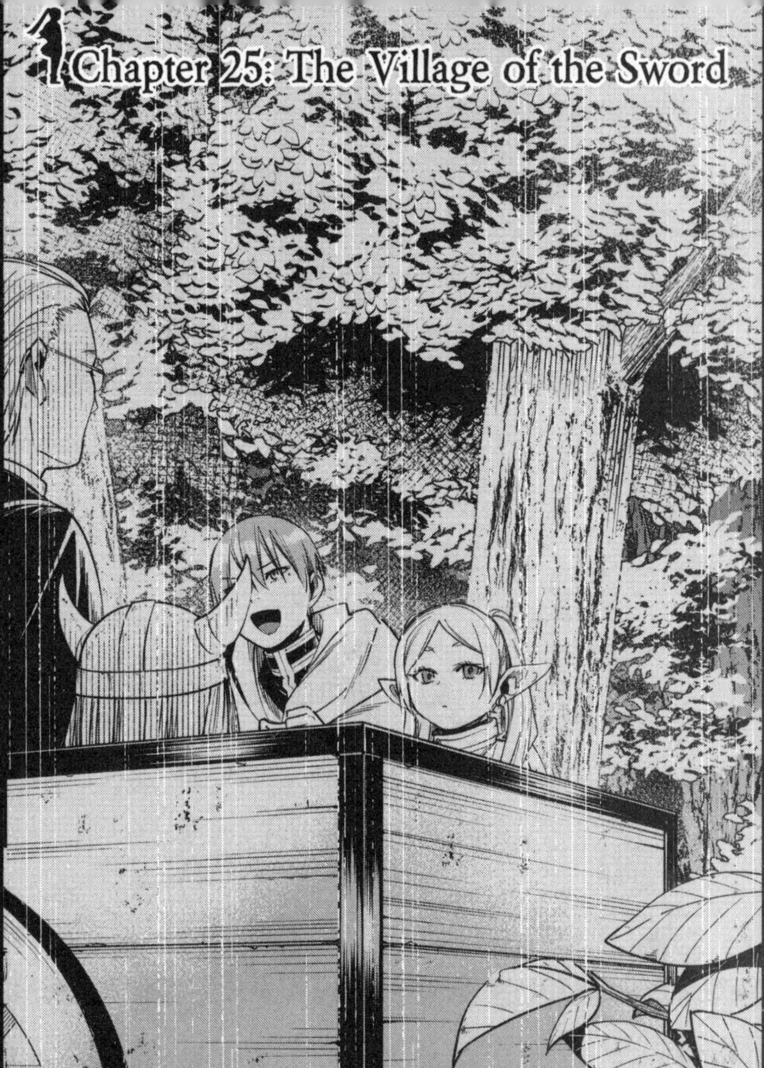
Chapter 25: The Village of the Sword

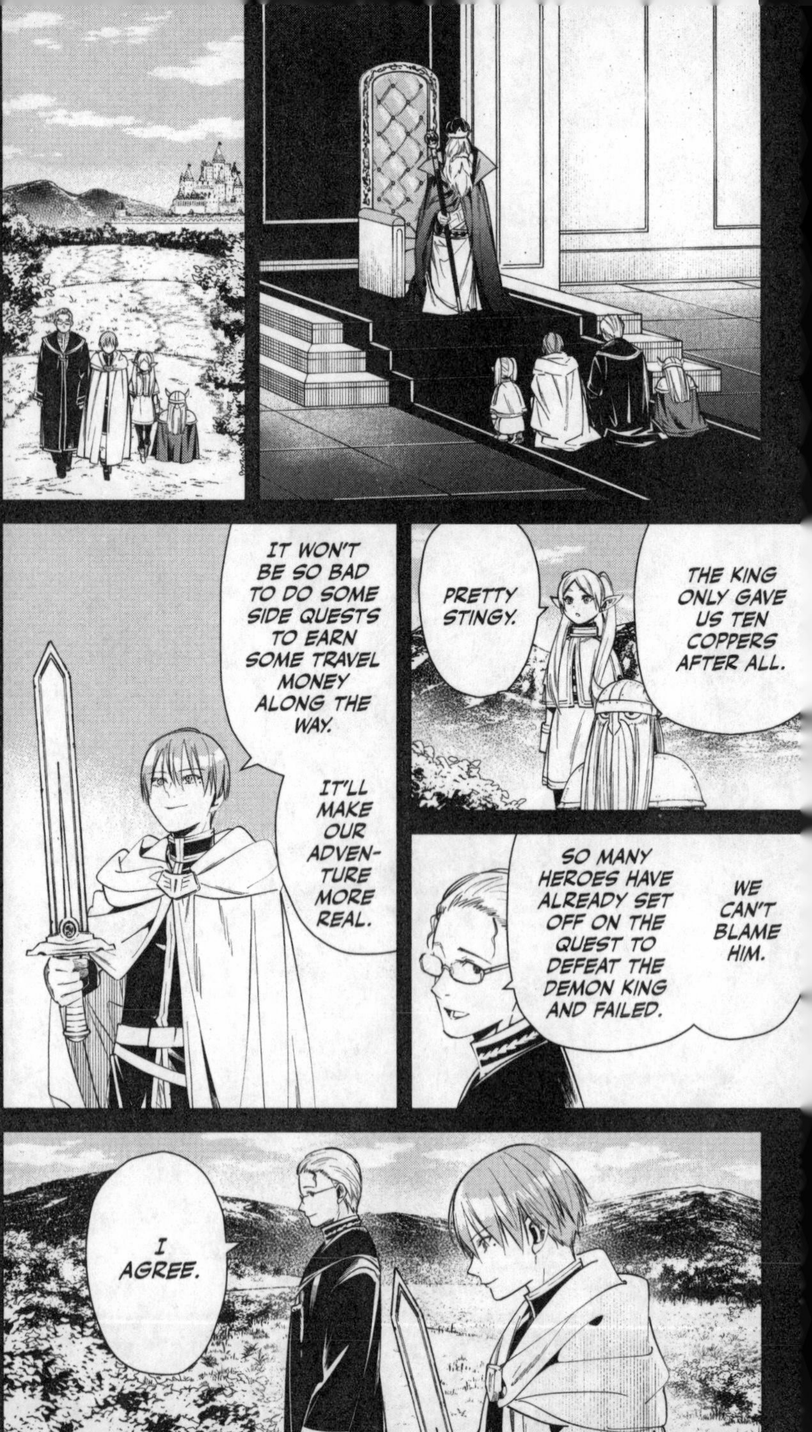
THE KING ONLY GAVE US TEN COPPERS AFTER ALL.
PRETTY STINGY.
WE CAN'T BLAME HIM.
SO MANY HEROES HAVE ALREADY SET OFF ON THE QUEST TO DEFEAT THE DEMON KING AND FAILED.
IT WON'T BE SO BAD TO DO SOME SIDE QUESTS TO EARN SOME TRAVEL MONEY ALONG THE WAY.
IT'LL MAKE OUR ADVENTURE MORE REAL.
I AGREE.

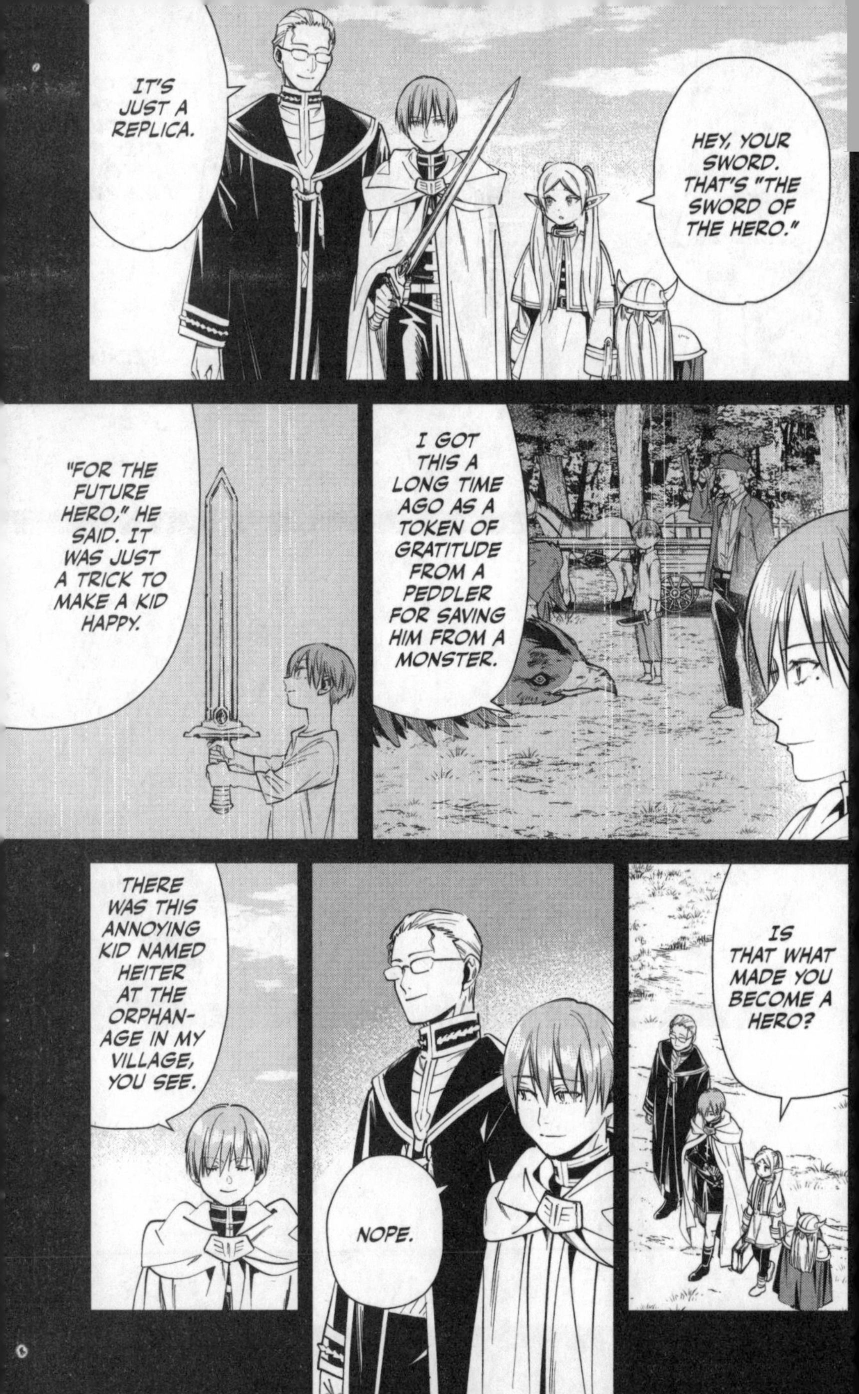
HEY, YOUR SWORD. THAT'S "THE SWORD OF THE HERO."
IT'S JUST A REPLICA.
I GOT THIS A LONG TIME AGO AS A TOKEN OF GRATITUDE FROM A PEDDLER FOR SAVING HIM FROM A MONSTER.
"FOR THE FUTURE HERO," HE SAID. IT WAS JUST A TRICK TO MAKE A KID HAPPY.
IS THAT WHAT MADE YOU BECOME A HERO?
NOPE.
THERE WAS THIS ANNOYING KID NAMED HEITER AT THE ORPHAN-AGE IN MY VILLAGE, YOU SEE.

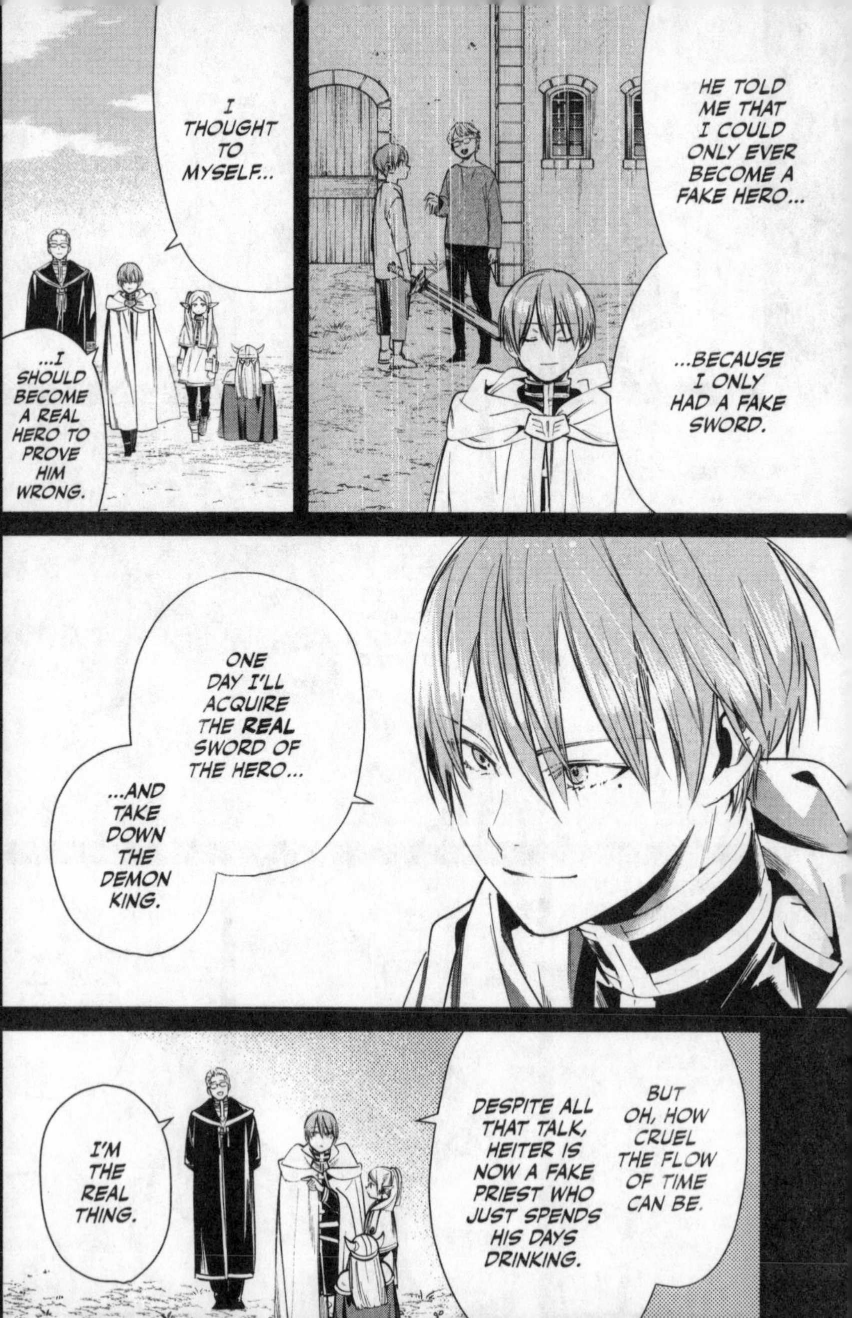
HE TOLD ME THAT I COULD ONLY EVER BECOME A FAKE HERO...
...BECAUSE I ONLY HAD A FAKE SWORD.
I THOUGHT TO MYSELF...
...I SHOULD BECOME A REAL HERO TO PROVE HIM WRONG.
ONE DAY I'LL ACQUIRE THE **REAL** SWORD OF THE HERO...
...AND TAKE DOWN THE DEMON KING.
BUT OH, HOW CRUEL THE FLOW OF TIME CAN BE.
DESPITE ALL THAT TALK, HEITER IS NOW A FAKE PRIEST WHO JUST SPENDS HIS DAYS DRINKING.
I'M THE REAL THING.

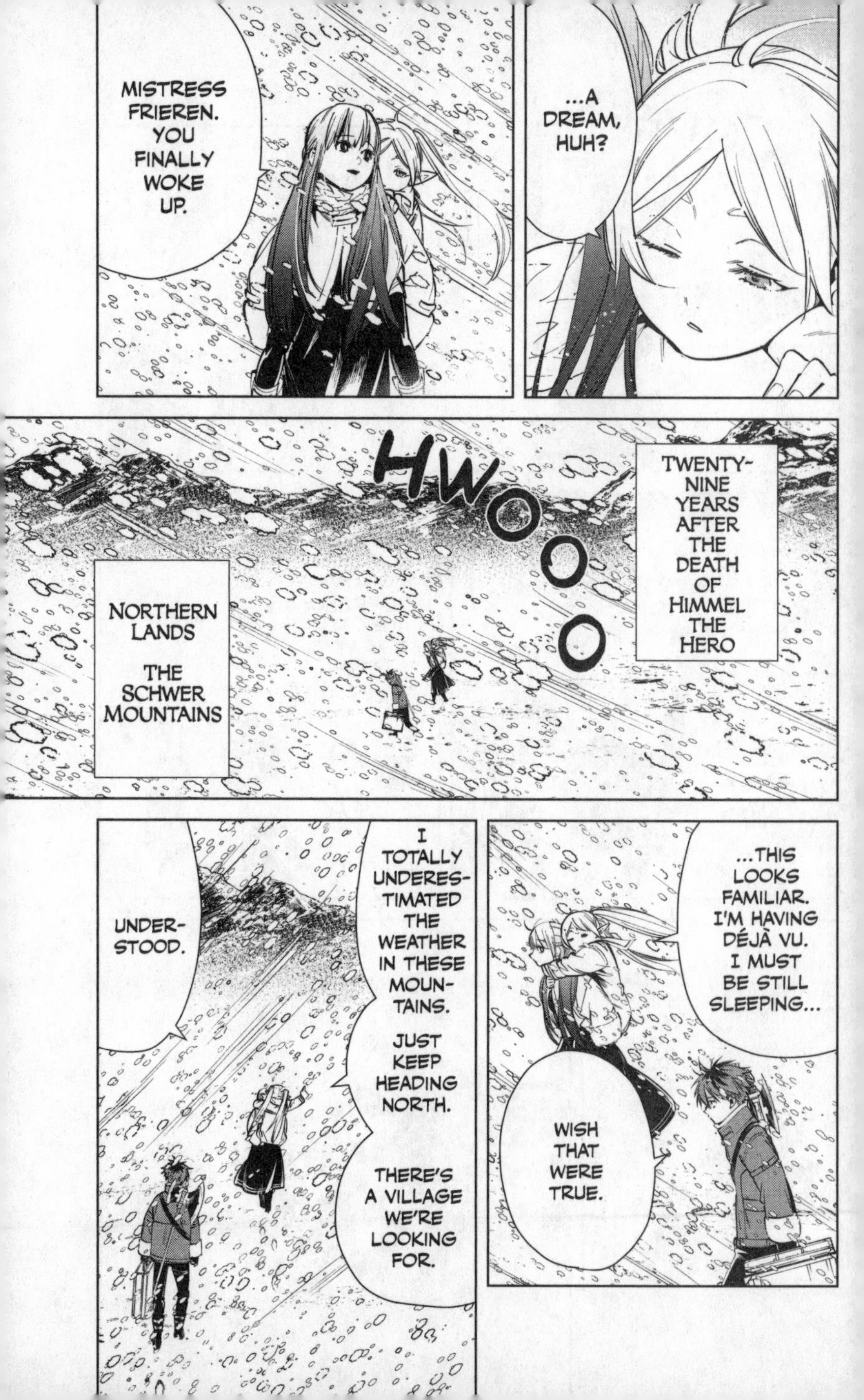
...A DREAM, HUH?
MISTRESS FRIEREN. YOU FINALLY WOKE UP.
TWENTY-NINE YEARS AFTER THE DEATH OF HIMMEL THE HERO
HWOOO
NORTHERN LANDS
THE SCHWER MOUNTAINS
...THIS LOOKS FAMILIAR. I'M HAVING DÉJÀ VU. I MUST BE STILL SLEEPING...
WISH THAT WERE TRUE.
I TOTALLY UNDERESTIMATED THE WEATHER IN THESE MOUNTAINS.
JUST KEEP HEADING NORTH.
THERE'S A VILLAGE WE'RE LOOKING FOR.
UNDERSTOOD.

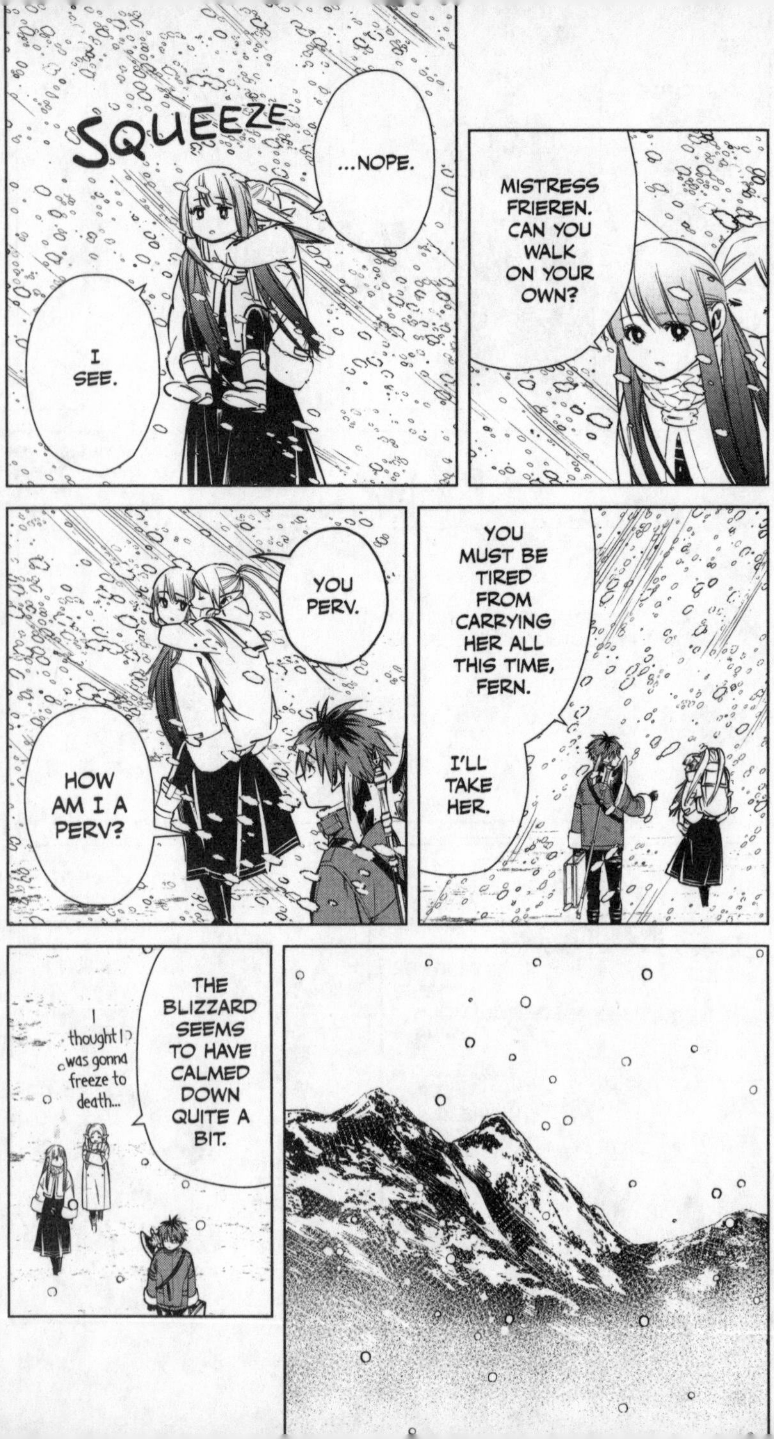
MISTRESS FRIEREN. CAN YOU WALK ON YOUR OWN?
...NOPE.
SQUEEZE
I SEE.
YOU MUST BE TIRED FROM CARRYING HER ALL THIS TIME, FERN.
I'LL TAKE HER.
YOU PERV.
HOW AM I A PERV?
THE BLIZZARD SEEMS TO HAVE CALMED DOWN QUITE A BIT.
I thought I was gonna freeze to death...

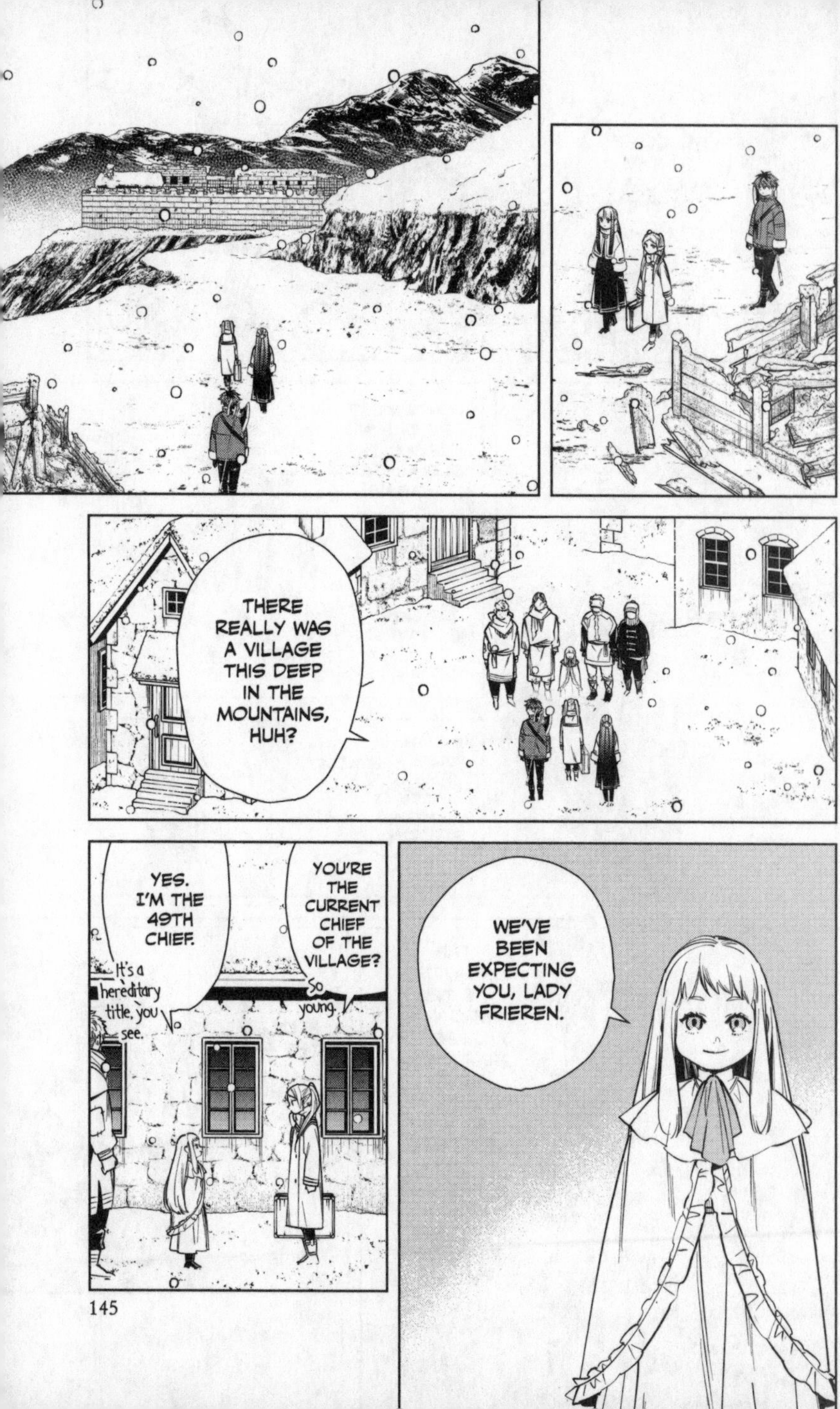
THERE REALLY WAS A VILLAGE THIS DEEP IN THE MOUNTAINS, HUH?
WE'VE BEEN EXPECTING YOU, LADY FRIEREN.
YOU'RE THE CURRENT CHIEF OF THE VILLAGE?
So young.
YES. I'M THE 49TH CHIEF.
It's a hereditary title, you see.

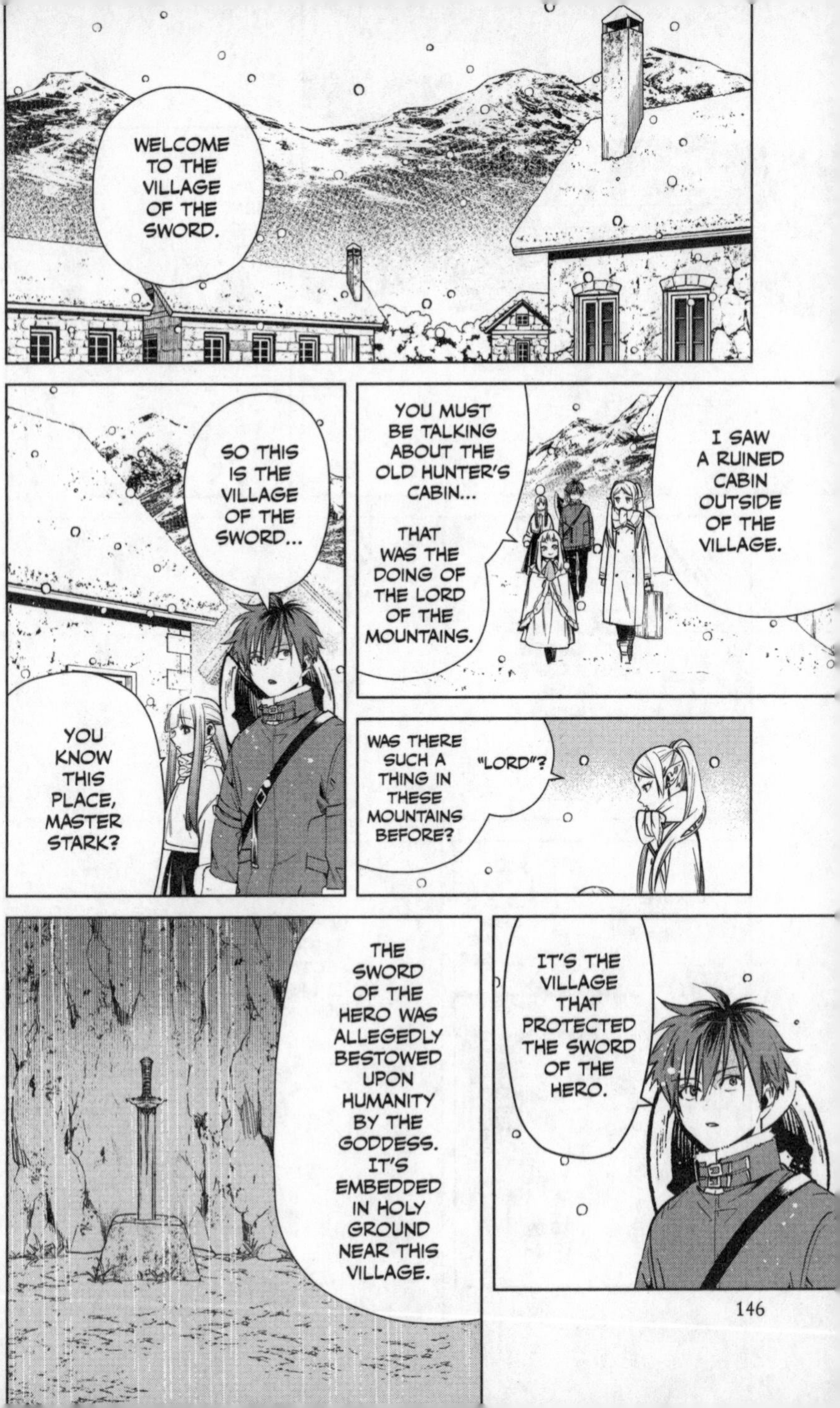
WELCOME TO THE VILLAGE OF THE SWORD.
I SAW A RUINED CABIN OUTSIDE OF THE VILLAGE.
YOU MUST BE TALKING ABOUT THE OLD HUNTER'S CABIN...
THAT WAS THE DOING OF THE LORD OF THE MOUNTAINS.
"LORD"?
WAS THERE SUCH A THING IN THESE MOUNTAINS BEFORE?
SO THIS IS THE VILLAGE OF THE SWORD...
YOU KNOW THIS PLACE, MASTER STARK?
IT'S THE VILLAGE THAT PROTECTED THE SWORD OF THE HERO.
THE SWORD OF THE HERO WAS ALLEGEDLY BESTOWED UPON HUMANITY BY THE GODDESS. IT'S EMBEDDED IN HOLY GROUND NEAR THIS VILLAGE.

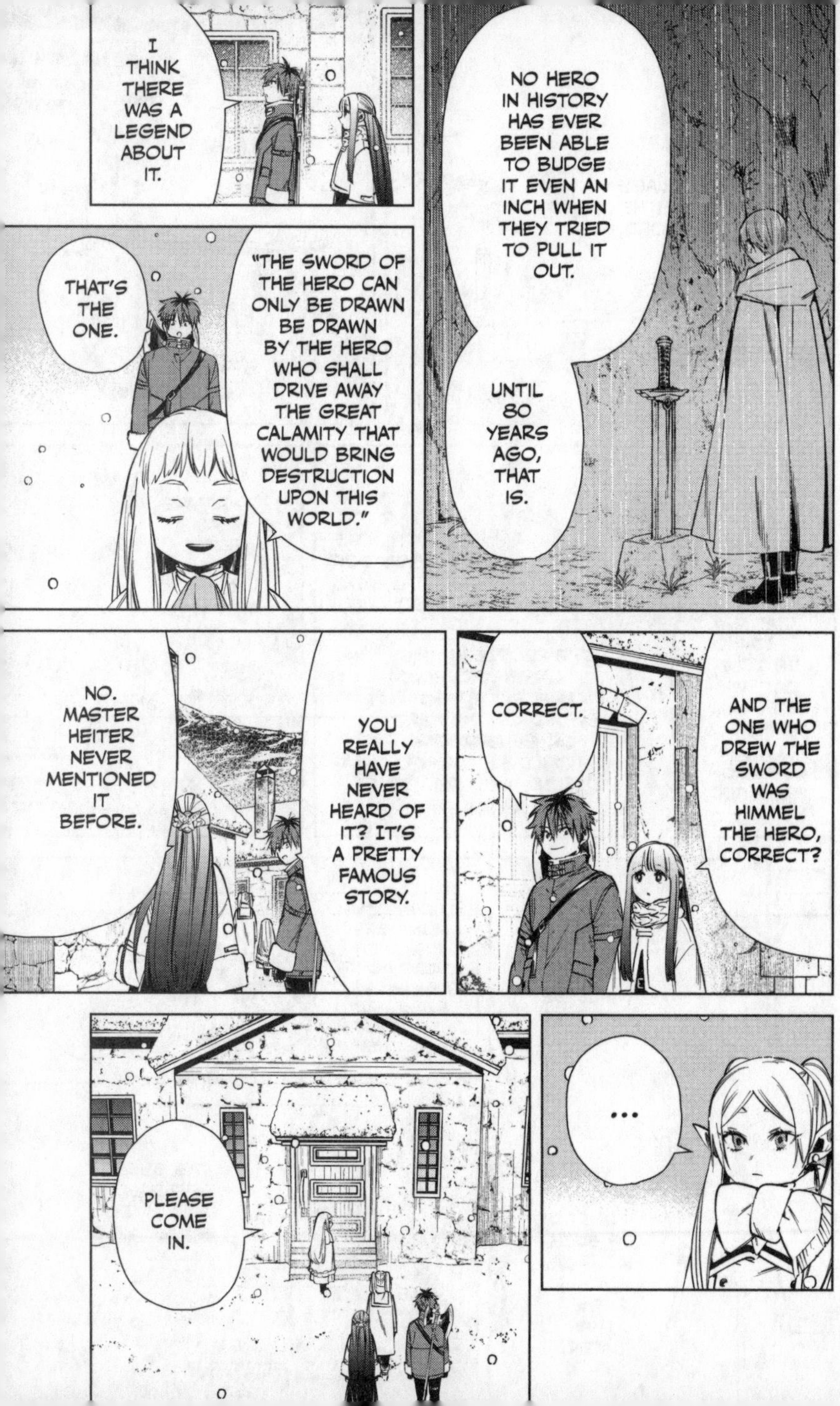
NO HERO IN HISTORY HAS EVER BEEN ABLE TO BUDGE IT EVEN AN INCH WHEN THEY TRIED TO PULL IT OUT.
UNTIL 80 YEARS AGO, THAT IS.
I THINK THERE WAS A LEGEND ABOUT IT.
"THE SWORD OF THE HERO CAN ONLY BE DRAWN BE DRAWN BY THE HERO WHO SHALL DRIVE AWAY THE GREAT CALAMITY THAT WOULD BRING DESTRUCTION UPON THIS WORLD."
THAT'S THE ONE.
AND THE ONE WHO DREW THE SWORD WAS HIMMEL THE HERO, CORRECT?
CORRECT.
YOU REALLY HAVE NEVER HEARD OF IT? IT'S A PRETTY FAMOUS STORY.
NO. MASTER HEITER NEVER MENTIONED IT BEFORE.
...
PLEASE COME IN.

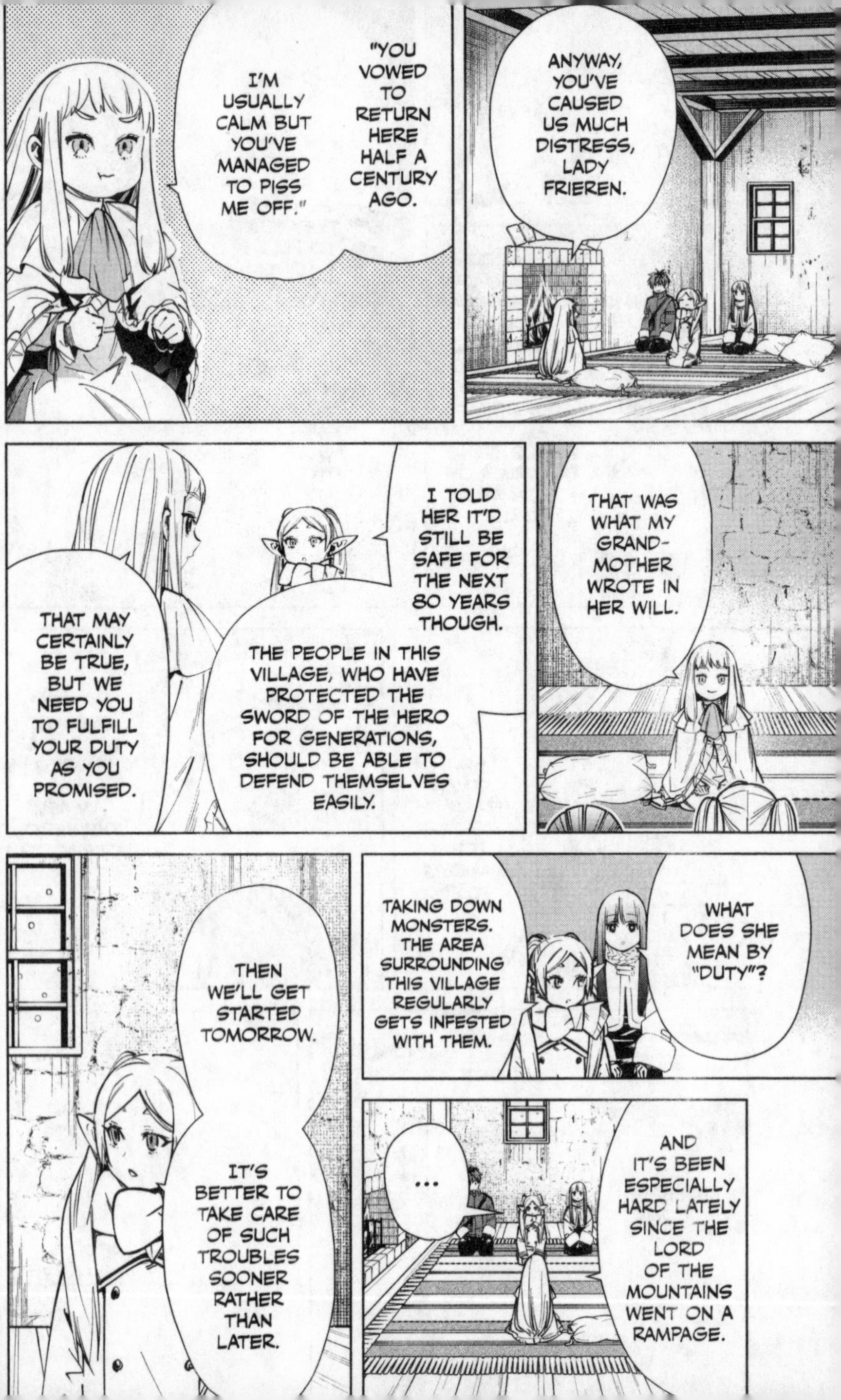
ANYWAY, YOU'VE CAUSED US MUCH DISTRESS, LADY FRIEREN.
"YOU VOWED TO RETURN HERE HALF A CENTURY AGO.
I'M USUALLY CALM BUT YOU'VE MANAGED TO PISS ME OFF."
THAT WAS WHAT MY GRANDMOTHER WROTE IN HER WILL.
I TOLD HER IT'D STILL BE SAFE FOR THE NEXT 80 YEARS THOUGH.
THE PEOPLE IN THIS VILLAGE, WHO HAVE PROTECTED THE SWORD OF THE HERO FOR GENERATIONS, SHOULD BE ABLE TO DEFEND THEMSELVES EASILY.
THAT MAY CERTAINLY BE TRUE, BUT WE NEED YOU TO FULFILL YOUR DUTY AS YOU PROMISED.
WHAT DOES SHE MEAN BY "DUTY"?
TAKING DOWN MONSTERS. THE AREA SURROUNDING THIS VILLAGE REGULARLY GETS INFESTED WITH THEM.
AND IT'S BEEN ESPECIALLY HARD LATELY SINCE THE LORD OF THE MOUNTAINS WENT ON A RAMPAGE.
...
THEN WE'LL GET STARTED TOMORROW.
IT'S BETTER TO TAKE CARE OF SUCH TROUBLES SOONER RATHER THAN LATER.

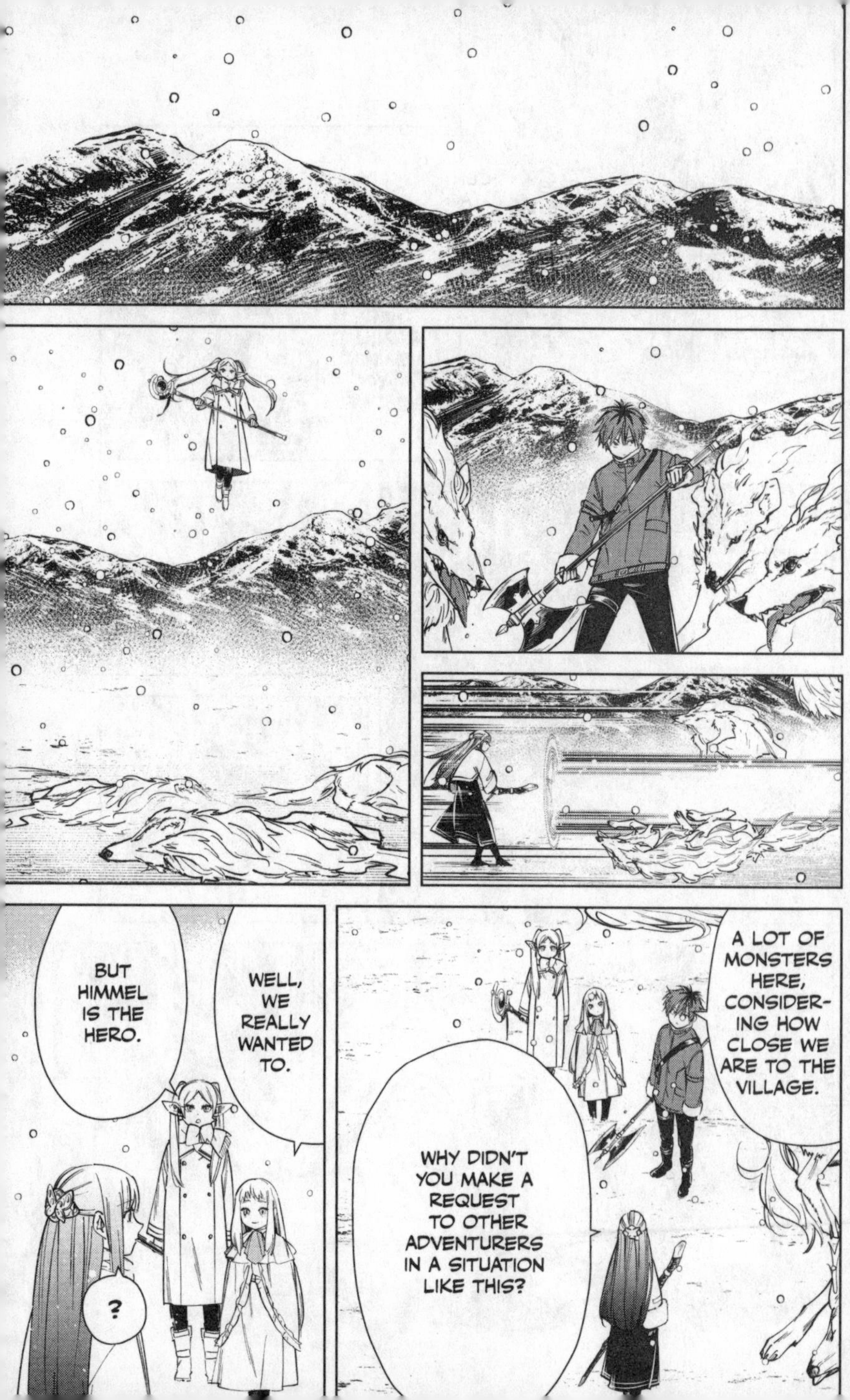

A LOT OF MONSTERS HERE, CONSIDERING HOW CLOSE WE ARE TO THE VILLAGE.
WHY DIDN'T YOU MAKE A REQUEST TO OTHER ADVENTURERS IN A SITUATION LIKE THIS?
WELL, WE REALLY WANTED TO.
BUT HIMMEL IS THE HERO.
?

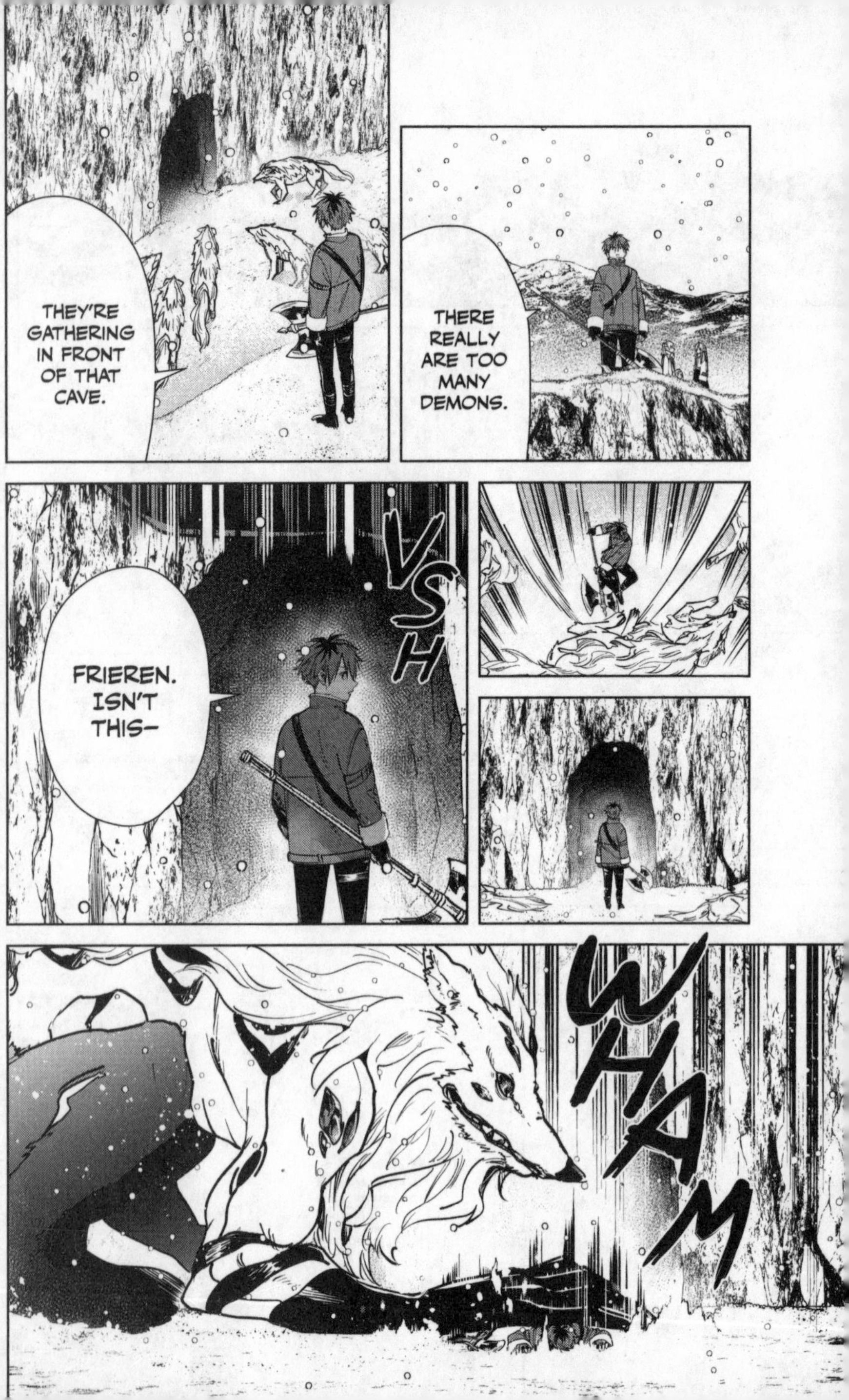
THERE REALLY ARE TOO MANY DEMONS.
THEY'RE GATHERING IN FRONT OF THAT CAVE.
VSH
FRIEREN. ISN'T THIS–
WHAM

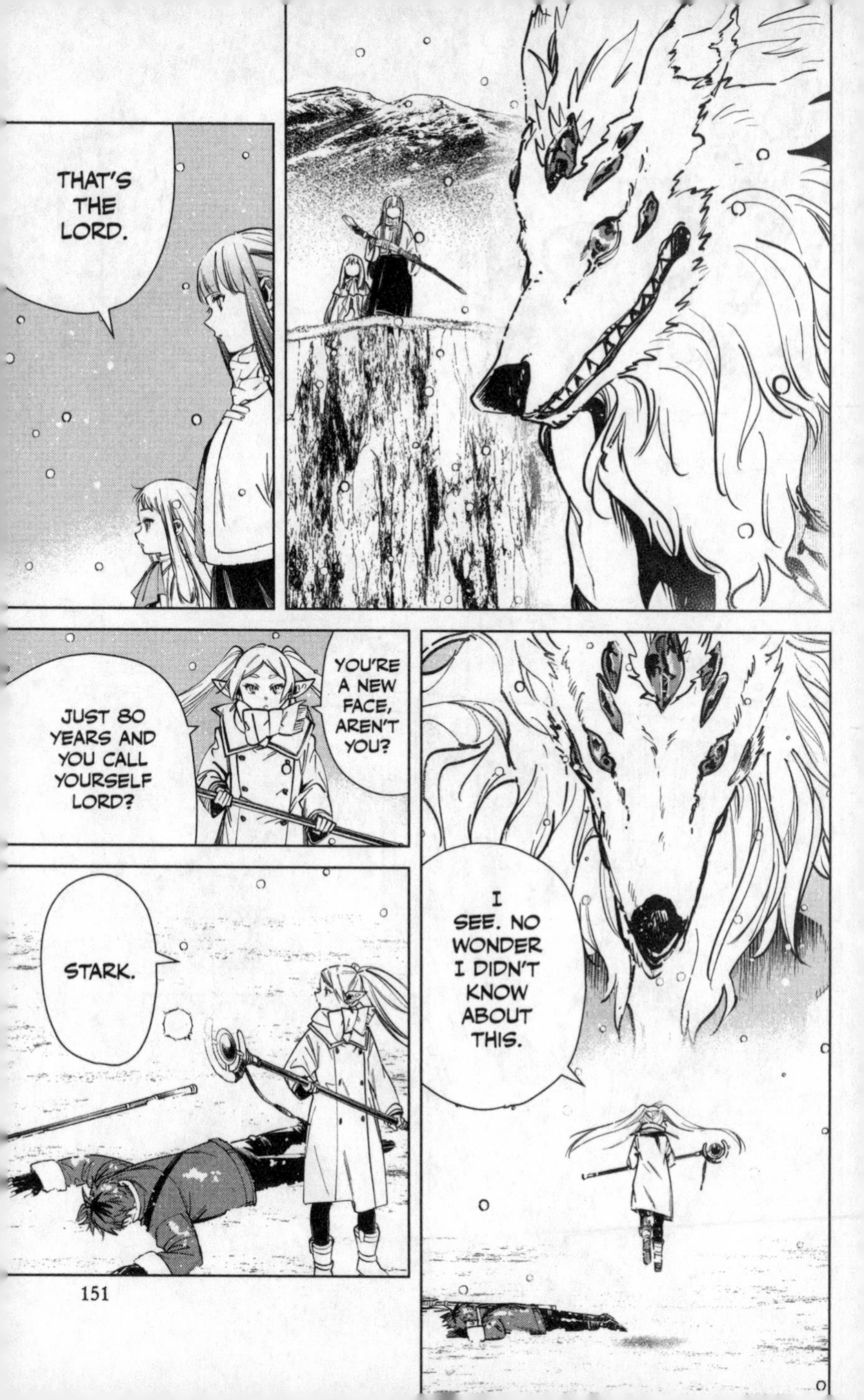
THAT'S THE LORD.
I SEE. NO WONDER I DIDN'T KNOW ABOUT THIS.
YOU'RE A NEW FACE, AREN'T YOU?
JUST 80 YEARS AND YOU CALL YOURSELF LORD?
STARK.

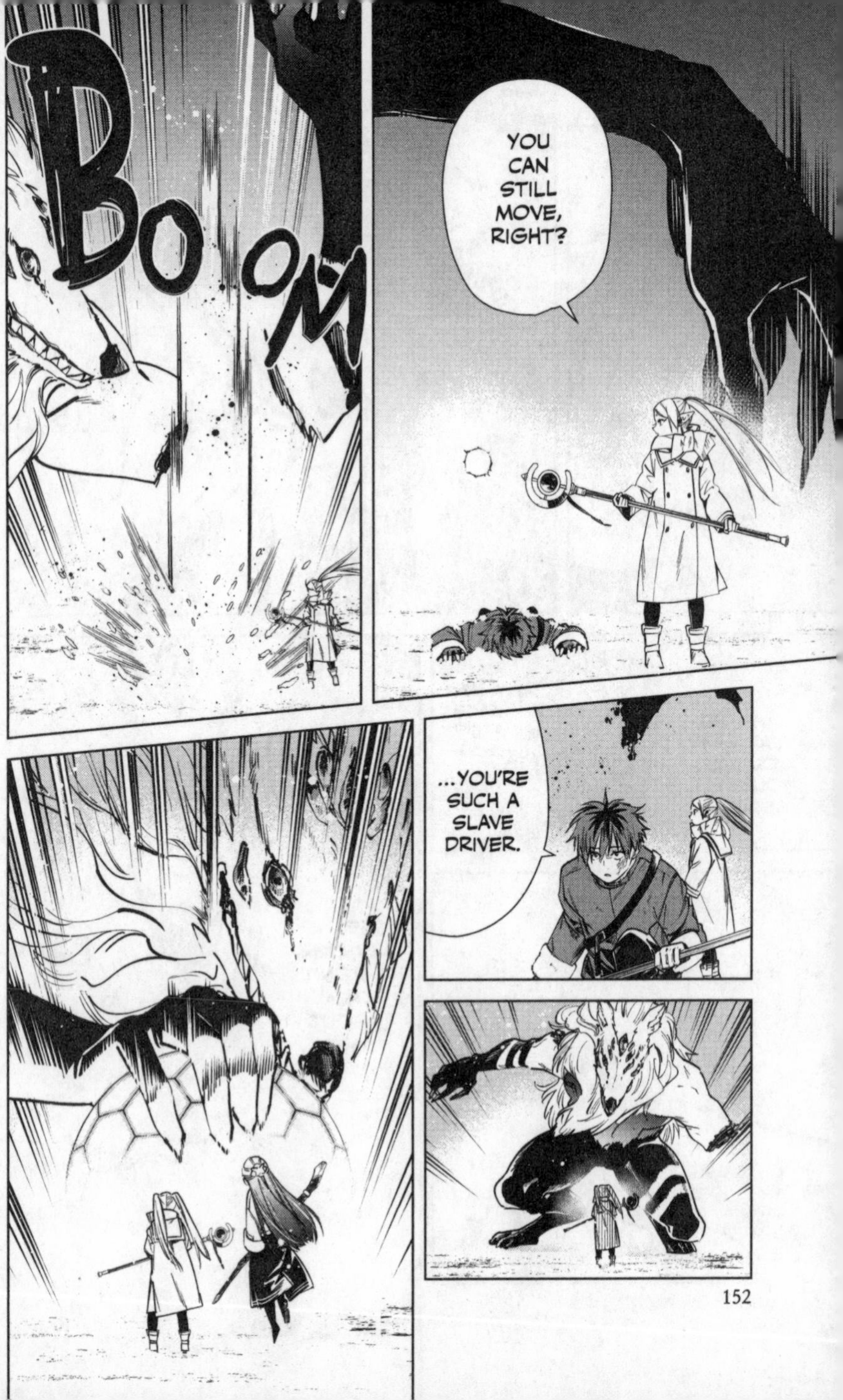
YOU CAN STILL MOVE, RIGHT?
BOOM
...YOU'RE SUCH A SLAVE DRIVER.

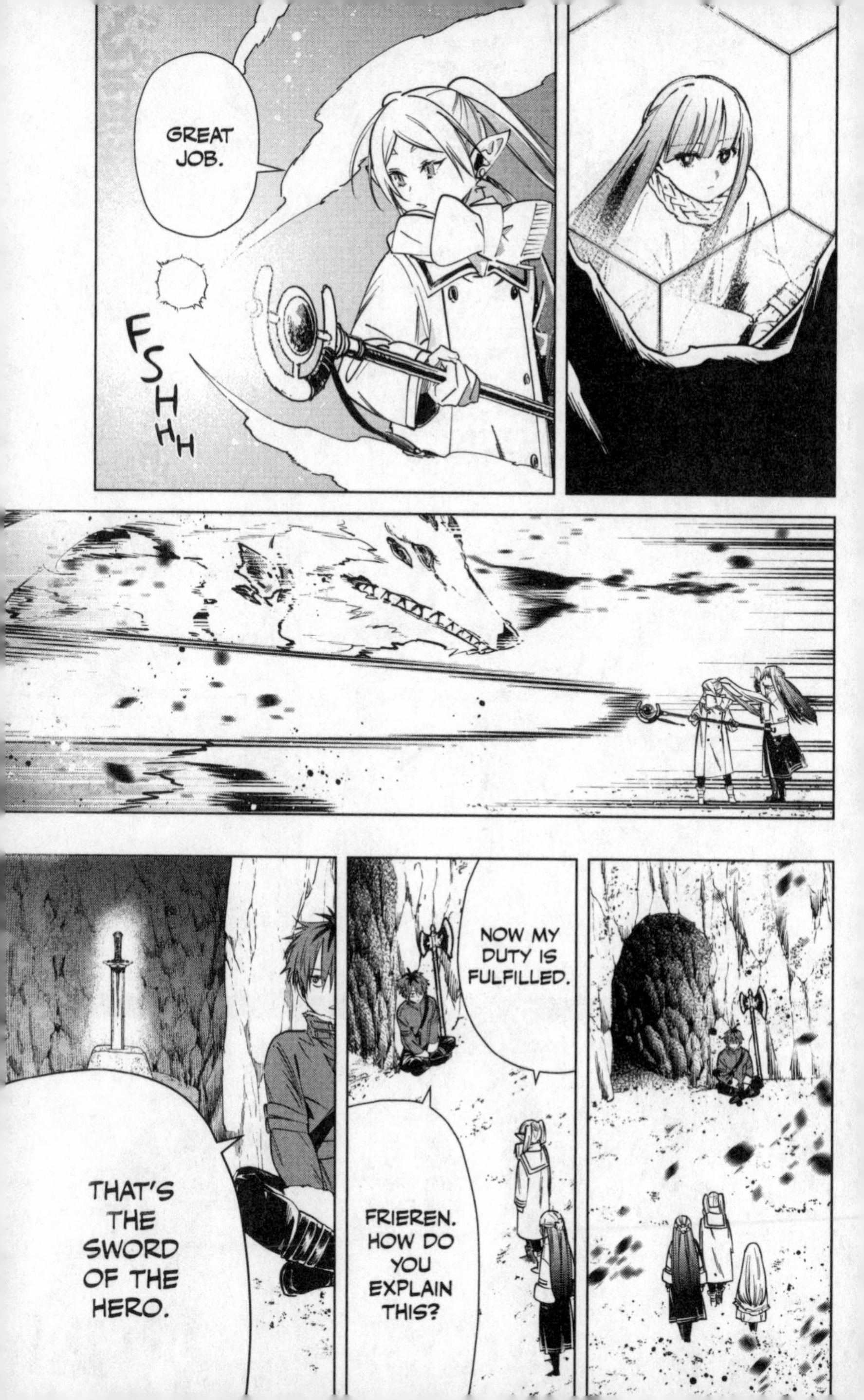
GREAT JOB.
FSHHH
NOW MY DUTY IS FULFILLED.
FRIEREN. HOW DO YOU EXPLAIN THIS?
THAT'S THE SWORD OF THE HERO.

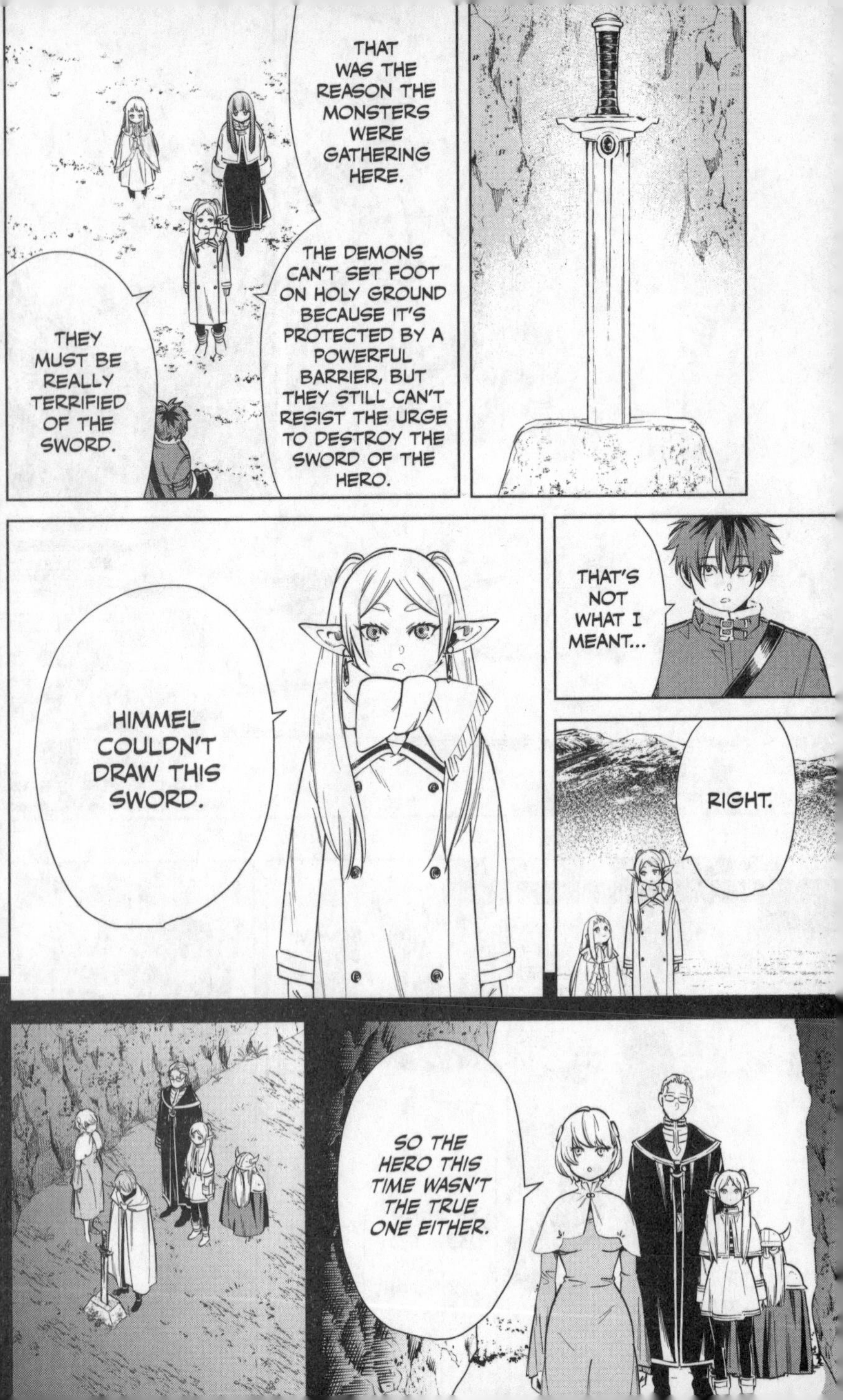
THAT WAS THE REASON THE MONSTERS WERE GATHERING HERE.
THE DEMONS CAN'T SET FOOT ON HOLY GROUND BECAUSE IT'S PROTECTED BY A POWERFUL BARRIER, BUT THEY STILL CAN'T RESIST THE URGE TO DESTROY THE SWORD OF THE HERO.
THEY MUST BE REALLY TERRIFIED OF THE SWORD.
THAT'S NOT WHAT I MEANT...
RIGHT.
HIMMEL COULDN'T DRAW THIS SWORD.
SO THE HERO THIS TIME WASN'T THE TRUE ONE EITHER.

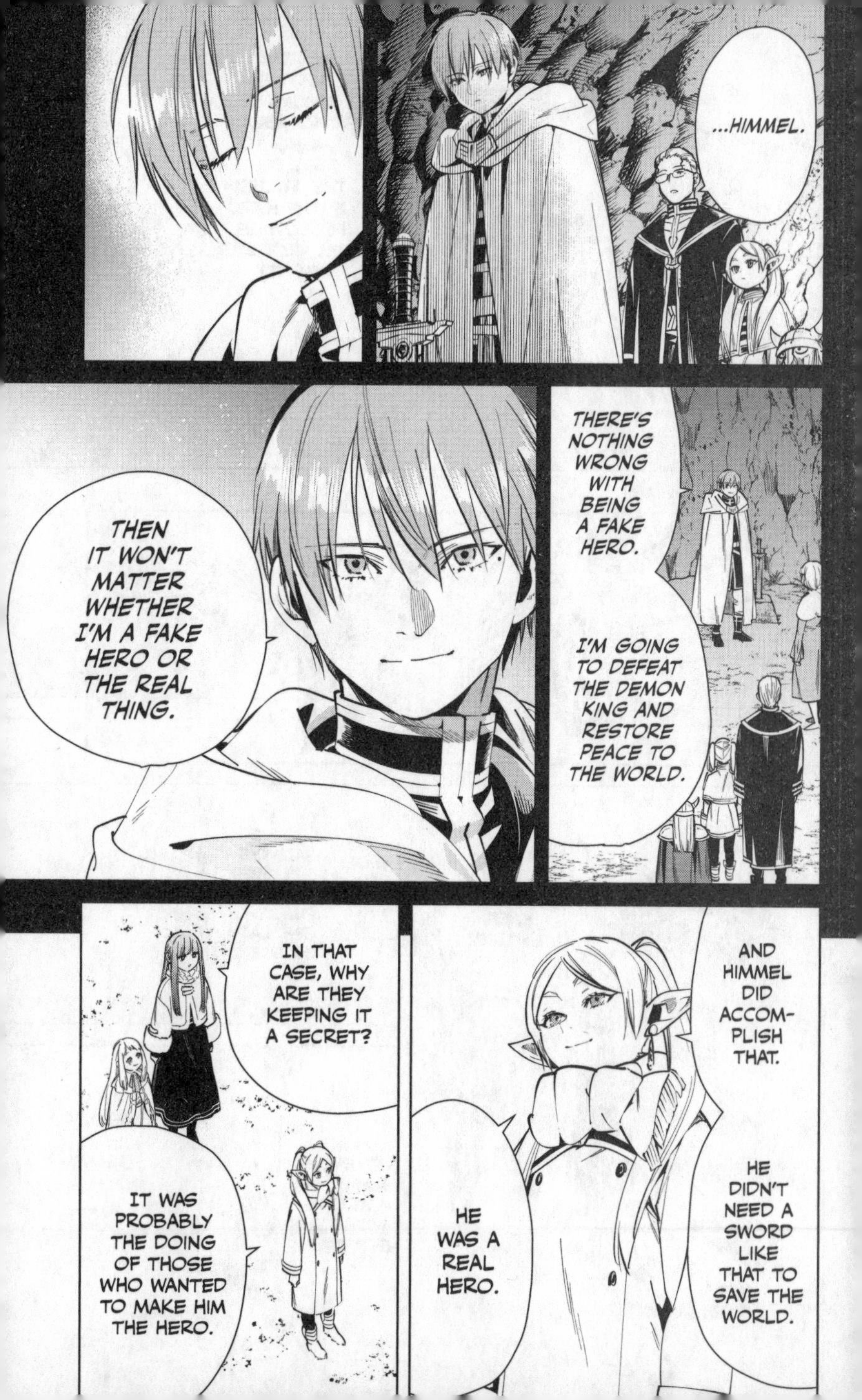
...HIMMEL.
THERE'S NOTHING WRONG WITH BEING A FAKE HERO.
I'M GOING TO DEFEAT THE DEMON KING AND RESTORE PEACE TO THE WORLD.
THEN IT WON'T MATTER WHETHER I'M A FAKE HERO OR THE REAL THING.
AND HIMMEL DID ACCOMPLISH THAT.
HE DIDN'T NEED A SWORD LIKE THAT TO SAVE THE WORLD.
HE WAS A REAL HERO.
IN THAT CASE, WHY ARE THEY KEEPING IT A SECRET?
IT WAS PROBABLY THE DOING OF THOSE WHO WANTED TO MAKE HIM THE HERO.

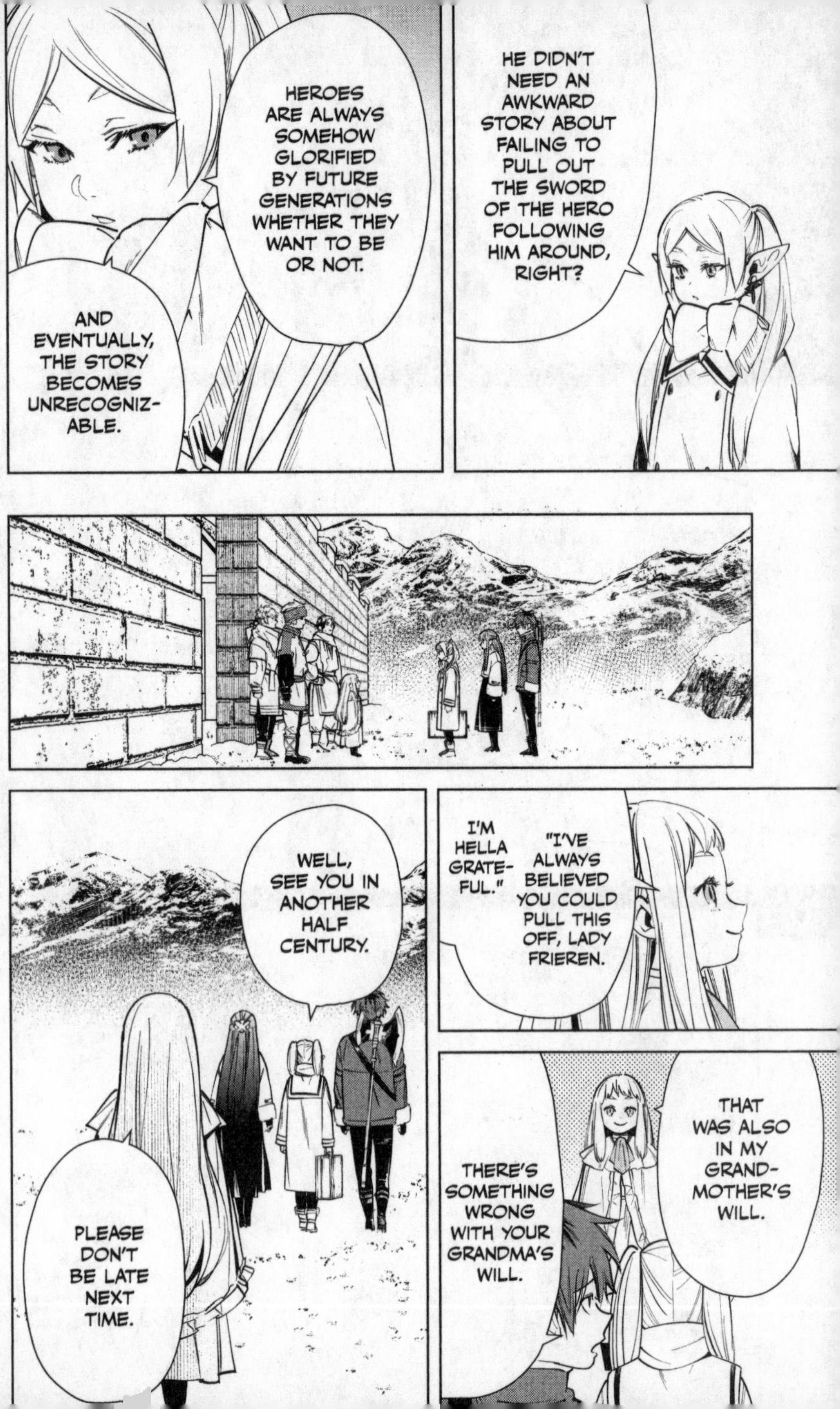
HE DIDN'T NEED AN AWKWARD STORY ABOUT FAILING TO PULL OUT THE SWORD OF THE HERO FOLLOWING HIM AROUND, RIGHT?
HEROES ARE ALWAYS SOMEHOW GLORIFIED BY FUTURE GENERATIONS WHETHER THEY WANT TO BE OR NOT.
AND EVENTUALLY, THE STORY BECOMES UNRECOGNIZ-ABLE.
"I'VE ALWAYS BELIEVED YOU COULD PULL THIS OFF, LADY FRIEREN.
I'M HELLA GRATE-FUL."
THAT WAS ALSO IN MY GRAND-MOTHER'S WILL.
THERE'S SOMETHING WRONG WITH YOUR GRANDMA'S WILL.
WELL, SEE YOU IN ANOTHER HALF CENTURY.
PLEASE DON'T BE LATE NEXT TIME.

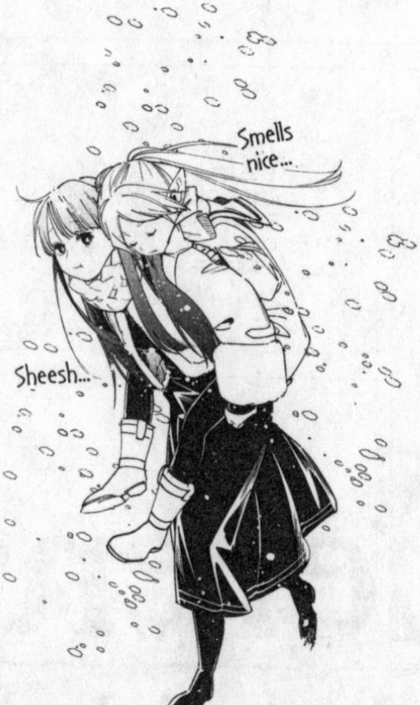
Smells nice...
Sheesh...

# Frieren

## Beyond Journey's End

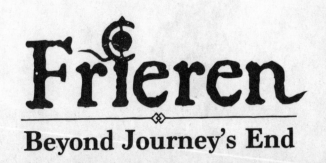

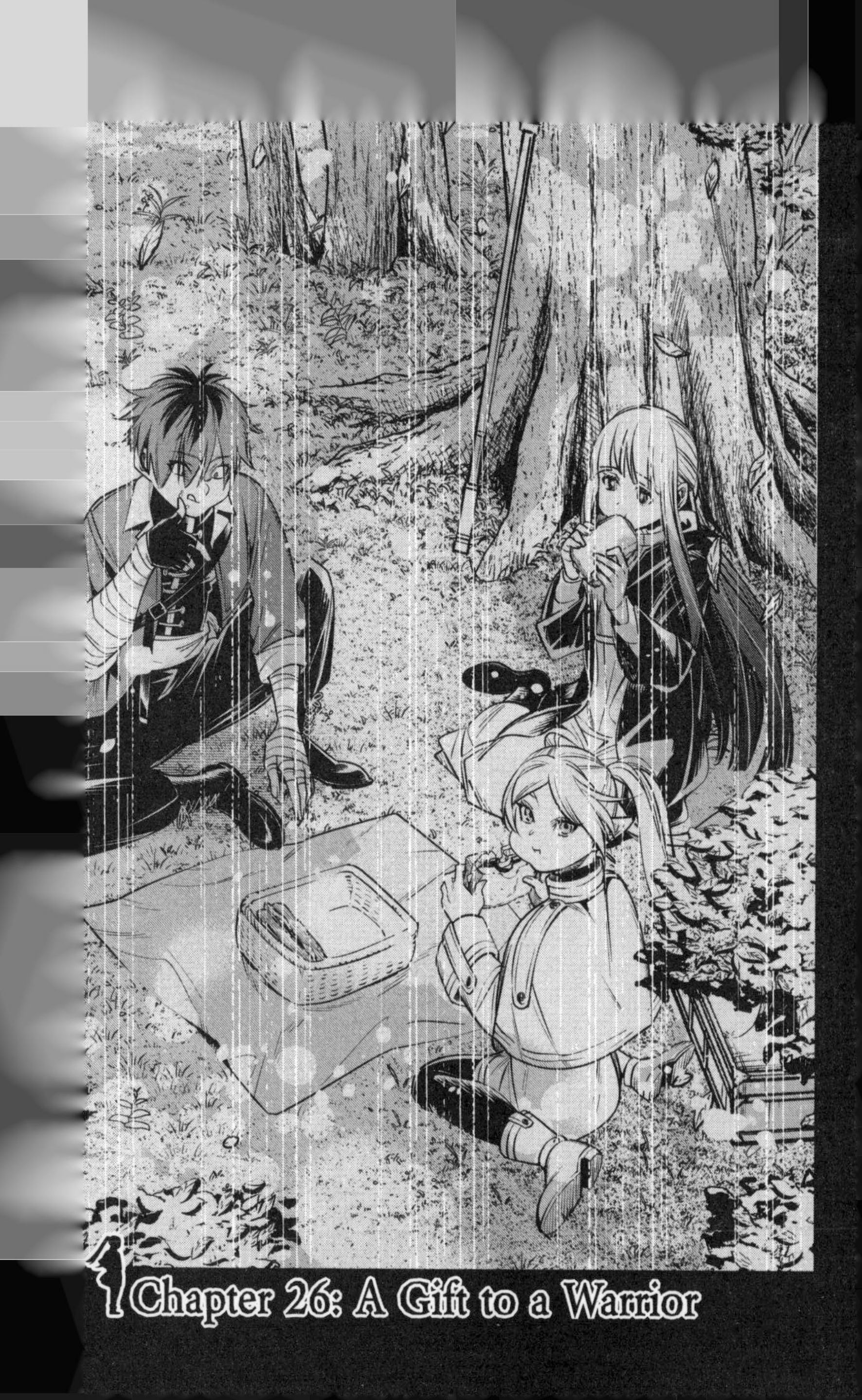

# Chapter 26: A Gift to a Warrior

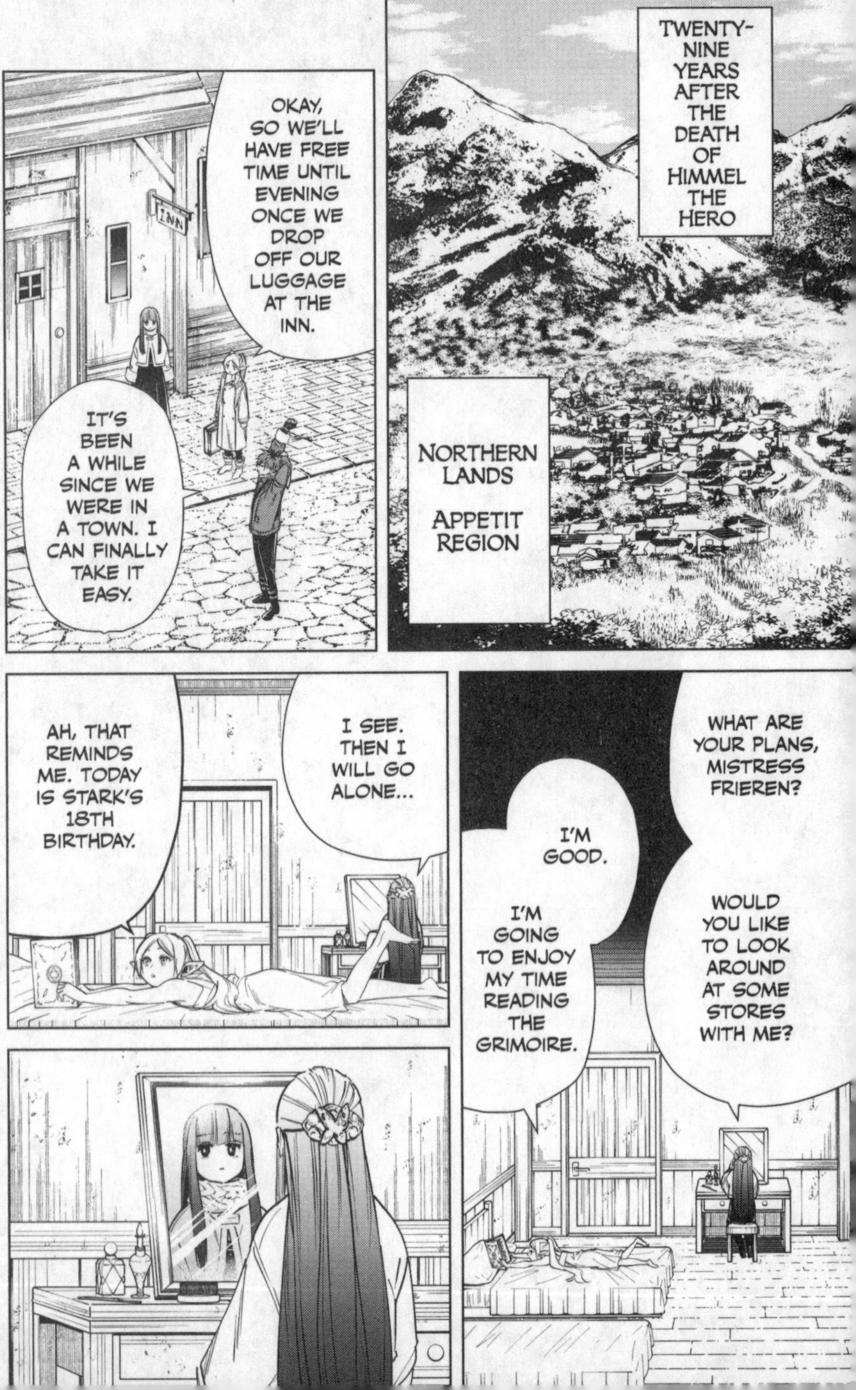
TWENTY-NINE YEARS AFTER THE DEATH OF HIMMEL THE HERO
NORTHERN LANDS
APPETIT REGION
INN
OKAY, SO WE'LL HAVE FREE TIME UNTIL EVENING ONCE WE DROP OFF OUR LUGGAGE AT THE INN.
IT'S BEEN A WHILE SINCE WE WERE IN A TOWN. I CAN FINALLY TAKE IT EASY.
WHAT ARE YOUR PLANS, MISTRESS FRIEREN?
I'M GOOD.
WOULD YOU LIKE TO LOOK AROUND AT SOME STORES WITH ME?
I'M GOING TO ENJOY MY TIME READING THE GRIMOIRE.
I SEE. THEN I WILL GO ALONE...
AH, THAT REMINDS ME. TODAY IS STARK'S 18TH BIRTHDAY.

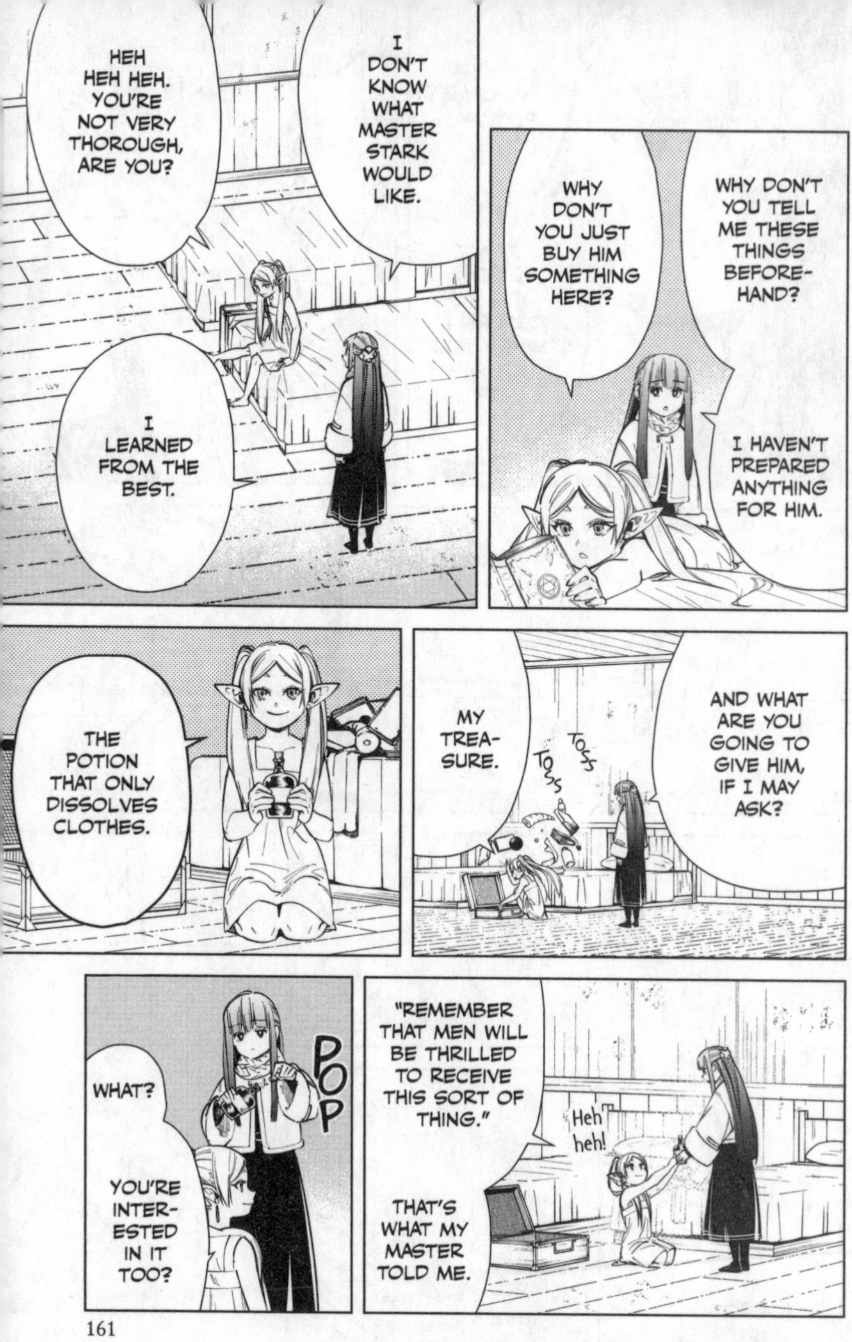
WHY DON'T YOU TELL ME THESE THINGS BEFORE-HAND?
WHY DON'T YOU JUST BUY HIM SOMETHING HERE?
I HAVEN'T PREPARED ANYTHING FOR HIM.
I DON'T KNOW WHAT MASTER STARK WOULD LIKE.
HEH HEH HEH. YOU'RE NOT VERY THOROUGH, ARE YOU?
I LEARNED FROM THE BEST.
AND WHAT ARE YOU GOING TO GIVE HIM, IF I MAY ASK?
TOSS
TOSS
MY TREA-SURE.
THE POTION THAT ONLY DISSOLVES CLOTHES.
"REMEMBER THAT MEN WILL BE THRILLED TO RECEIVE THIS SORT OF THING."
Heh heh!
THAT'S WHAT MY MASTER TOLD ME.
POP
POP
WHAT?
YOU'RE INTER-ESTED IN IT TOO?

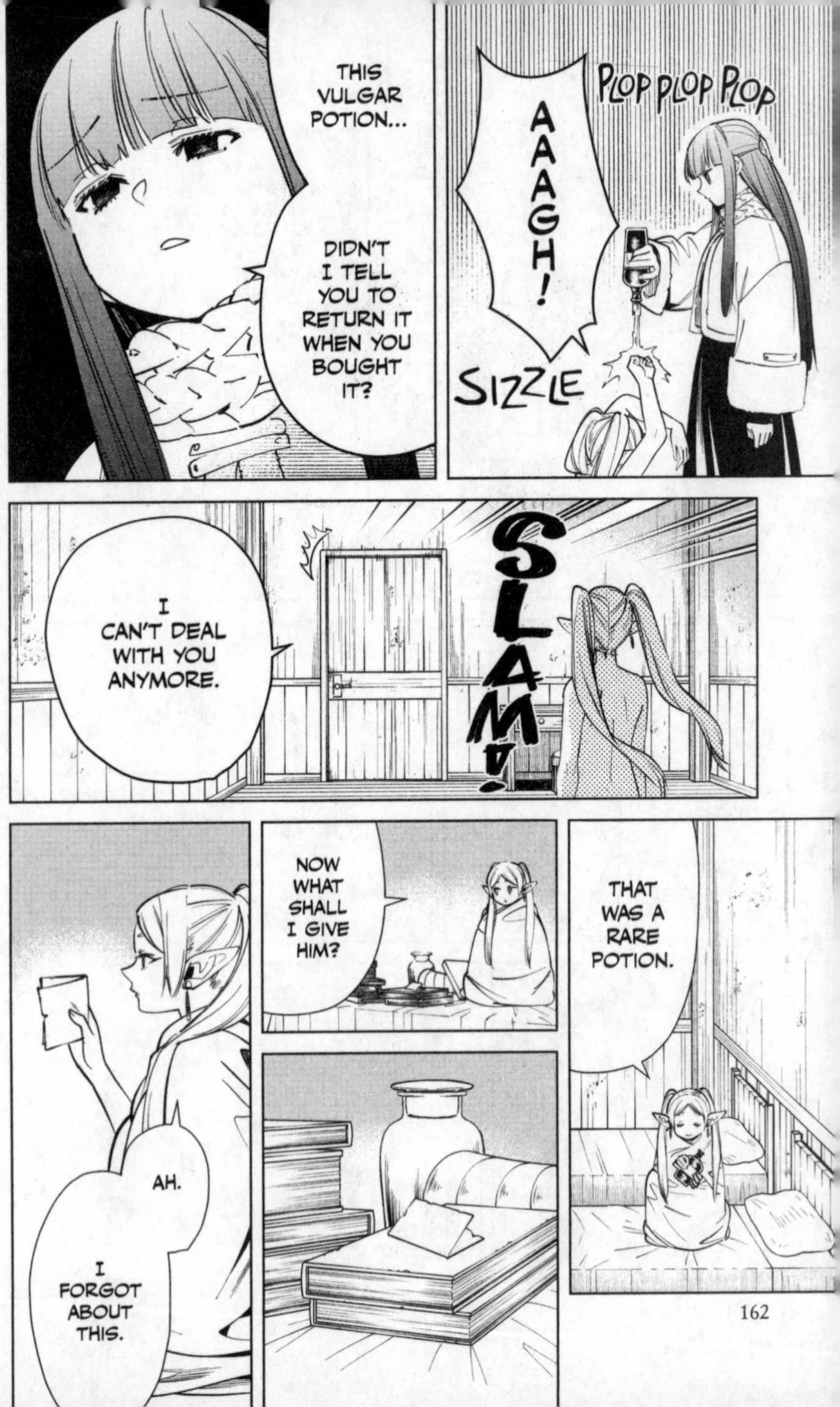

PLOP PLOP PLOP
AAAGH!
SIZZLE
THIS VULGAR POTION...
DIDN'T I TELL YOU TO RETURN IT WHEN YOU BOUGHT IT?
SLAM!
I CAN'T DEAL WITH YOU ANYMORE.
THAT WAS A RARE POTION.
NOW WHAT SHALL I GIVE HIM?
AH.
I FORGOT ABOUT THIS.

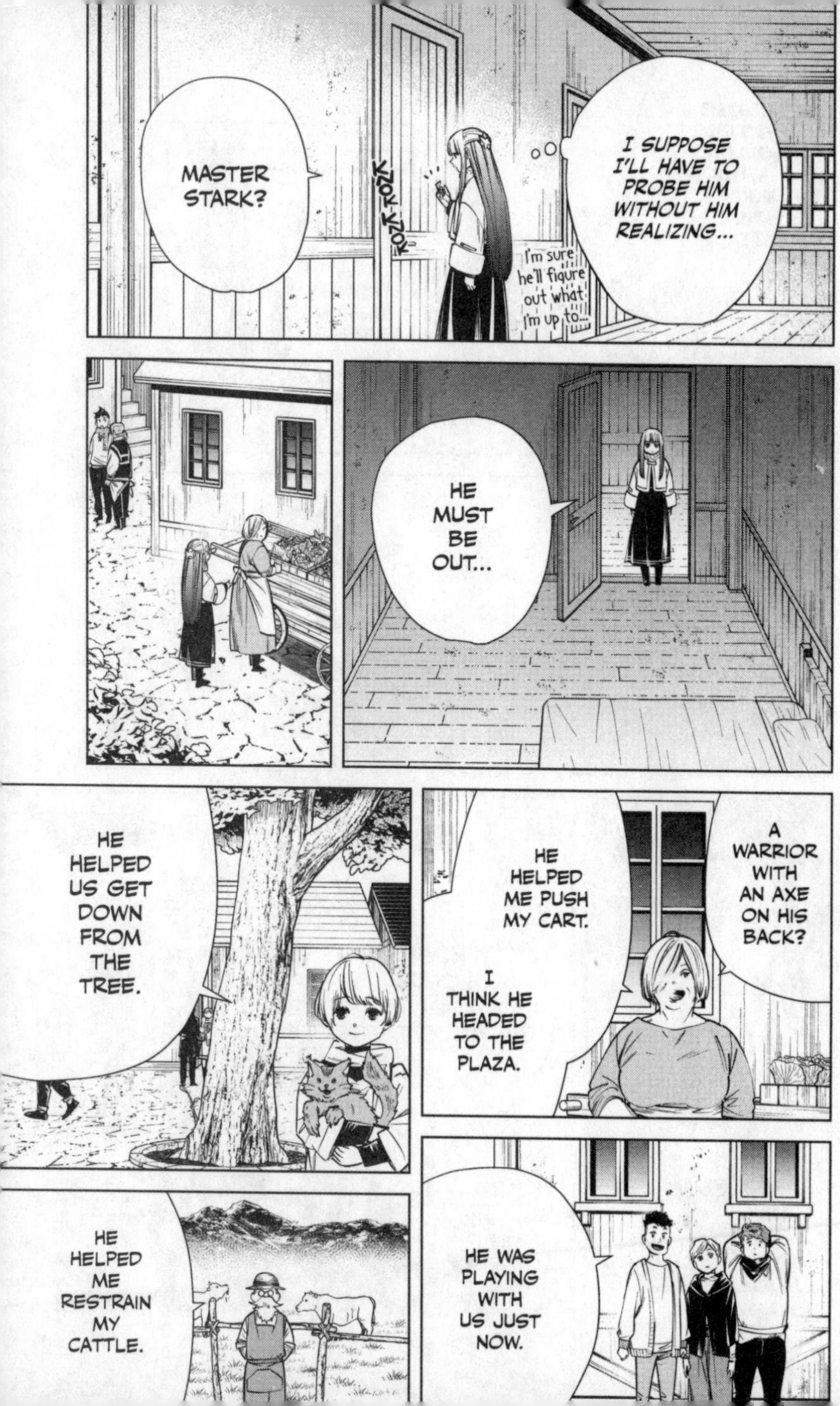
I SUPPOSE I'LL HAVE TO PROBE HIM WITHOUT HIM REALIZING...
I'm sure he'll figure out what I'm up to...
KNOK KNOK
MASTER STARK?
HE MUST BE OUT...
A WARRIOR WITH AN AXE ON HIS BACK?
HE HELPED ME PUSH MY CART.
I THINK HE HEADED TO THE PLAZA.
HE HELPED US GET DOWN FROM THE TREE.
HE WAS PLAYING WITH US JUST NOW.
HE HELPED ME RESTRAIN MY CATTLE.

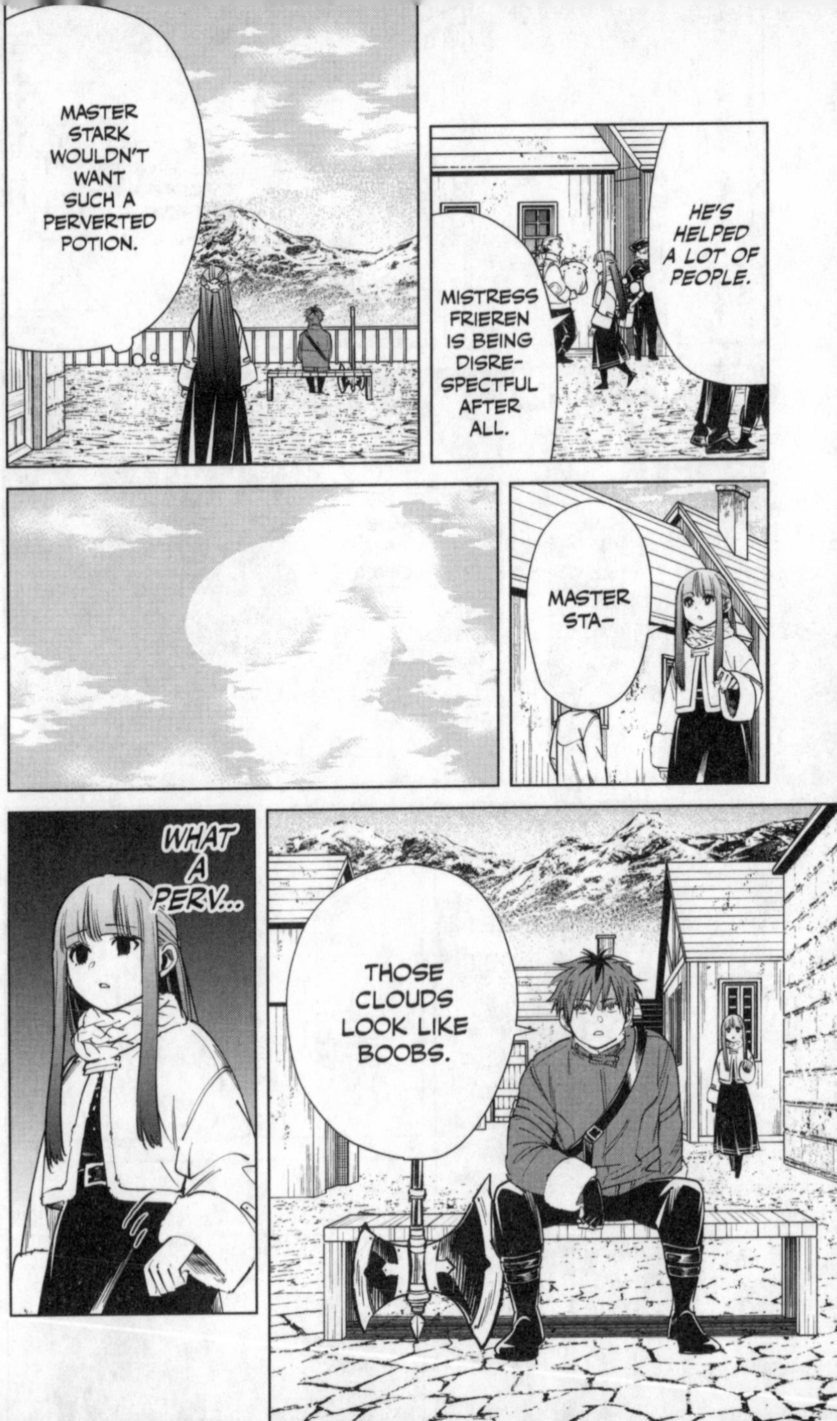
HE'S HELPED A LOT OF PEOPLE.
MISTRESS FRIEREN IS BEING DISRE-SPECTFUL AFTER ALL.
MASTER STARK WOULDN'T WANT SUCH A PERVERTED POTION.
MASTER STA-
THOSE CLOUDS LOOK LIKE BOOBS.
WHAT A PERV...

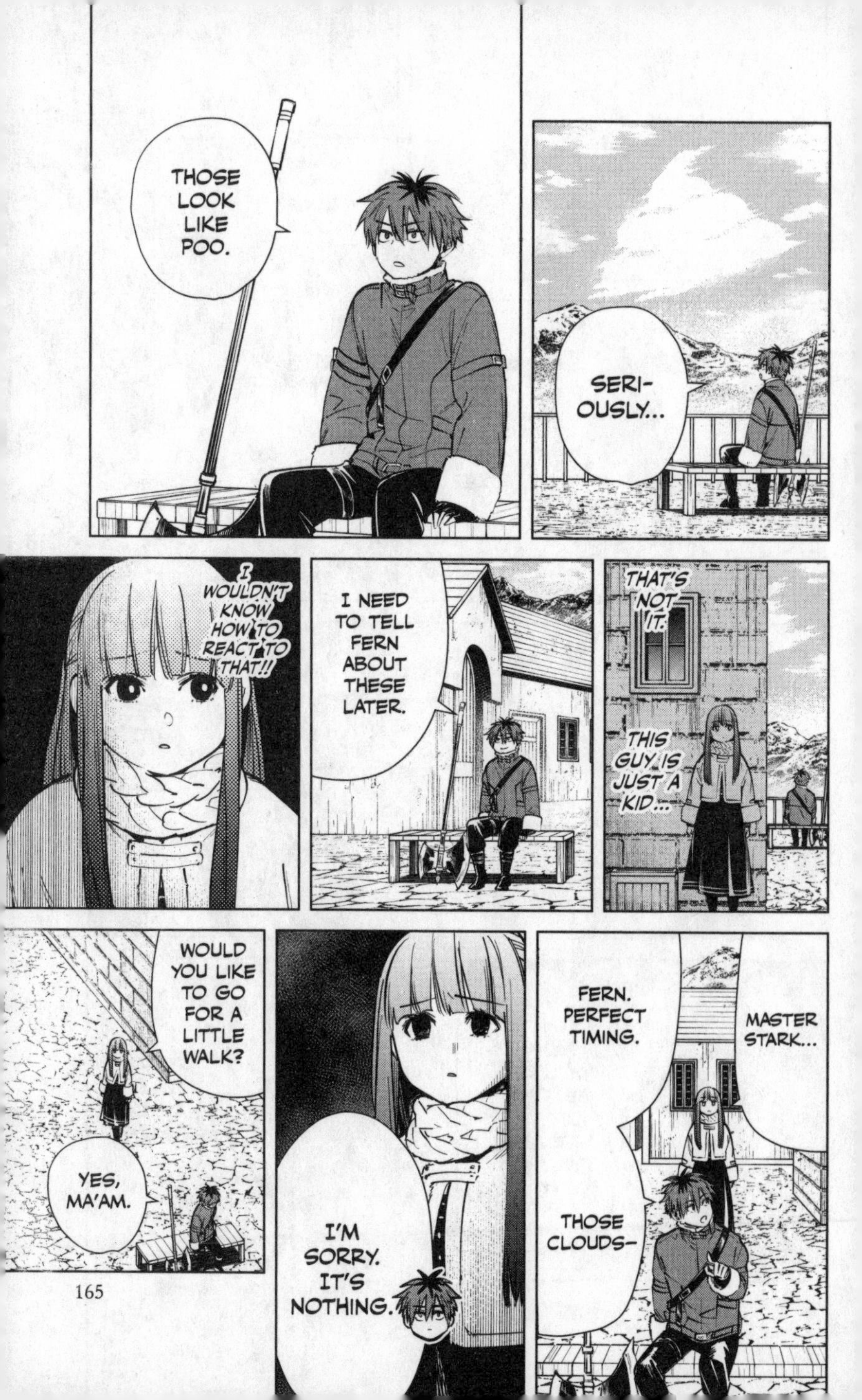
SERI-OUSLY...
THOSE LOOK LIKE POO.
THAT'S NOT IT.
THIS GUY IS JUST A KID...
I NEED TO TELL FERN ABOUT THESE LATER.
I WOULDN'T KNOW HOW TO REACT TO THAT!!
MASTER STARK...
FERN. PERFECT TIMING.
THOSE CLOUDS—
I'M SORRY. IT'S NOTHING.
WOULD YOU LIKE TO GO FOR A LITTLE WALK?
YES, MA'AM.

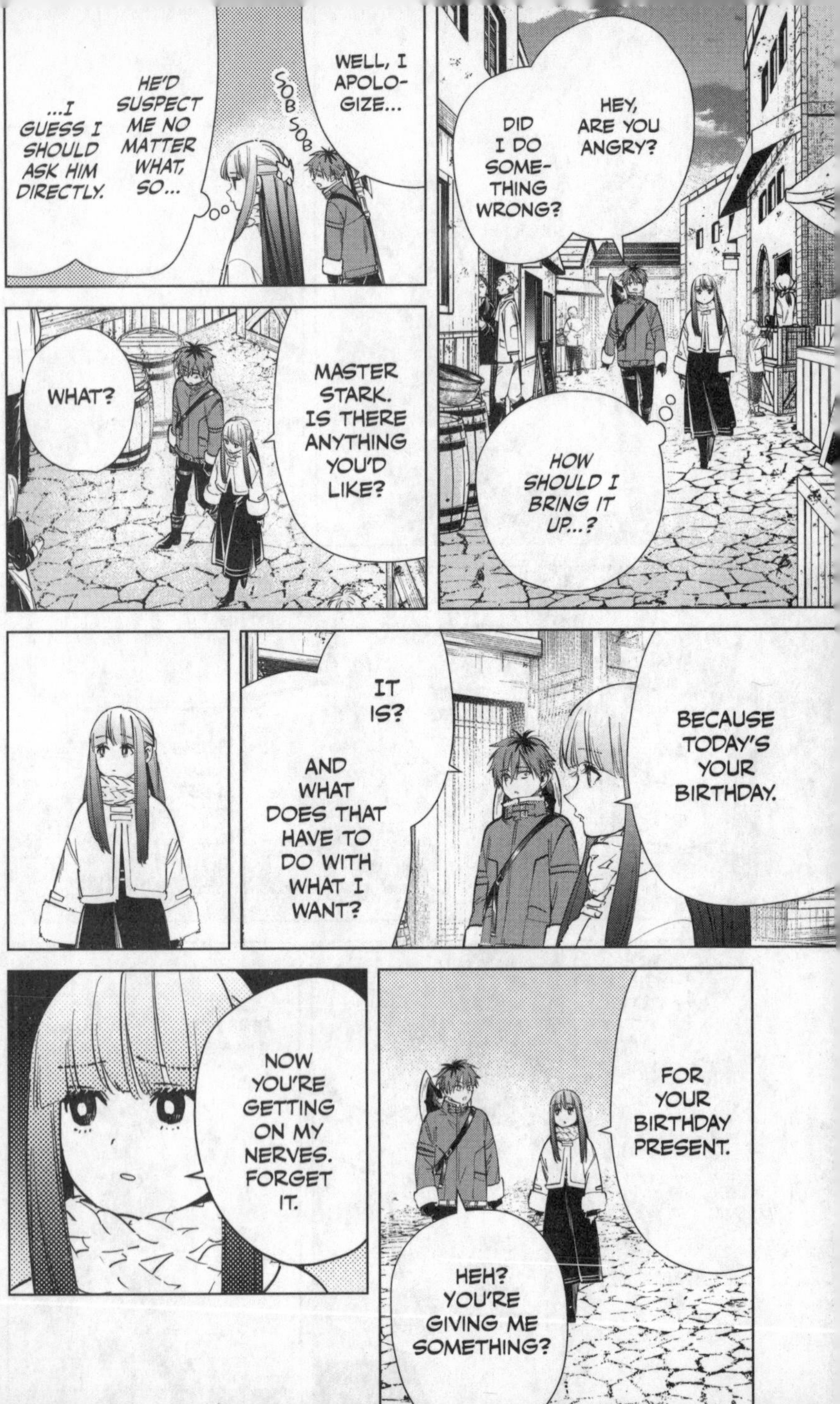
HEY, ARE YOU ANGRY?
DID I DO SOMETHING WRONG?
HOW SHOULD I BRING IT UP...?
WELL, I APOLOGIZE...
SOB SOB
HE'D SUSPECT ME NO MATTER WHAT, SO...
...I GUESS I SHOULD ASK HIM DIRECTLY.
MASTER STARK. IS THERE ANYTHING YOU'D LIKE?
WHAT?
BECAUSE TODAY'S YOUR BIRTHDAY.
IT IS?
AND WHAT DOES THAT HAVE TO DO WITH WHAT I WANT?
FOR YOUR BIRTHDAY PRESENT.
HEH? YOU'RE GIVING ME SOMETHING?
NOW YOU'RE GETTING ON MY NERVES. FORGET IT.

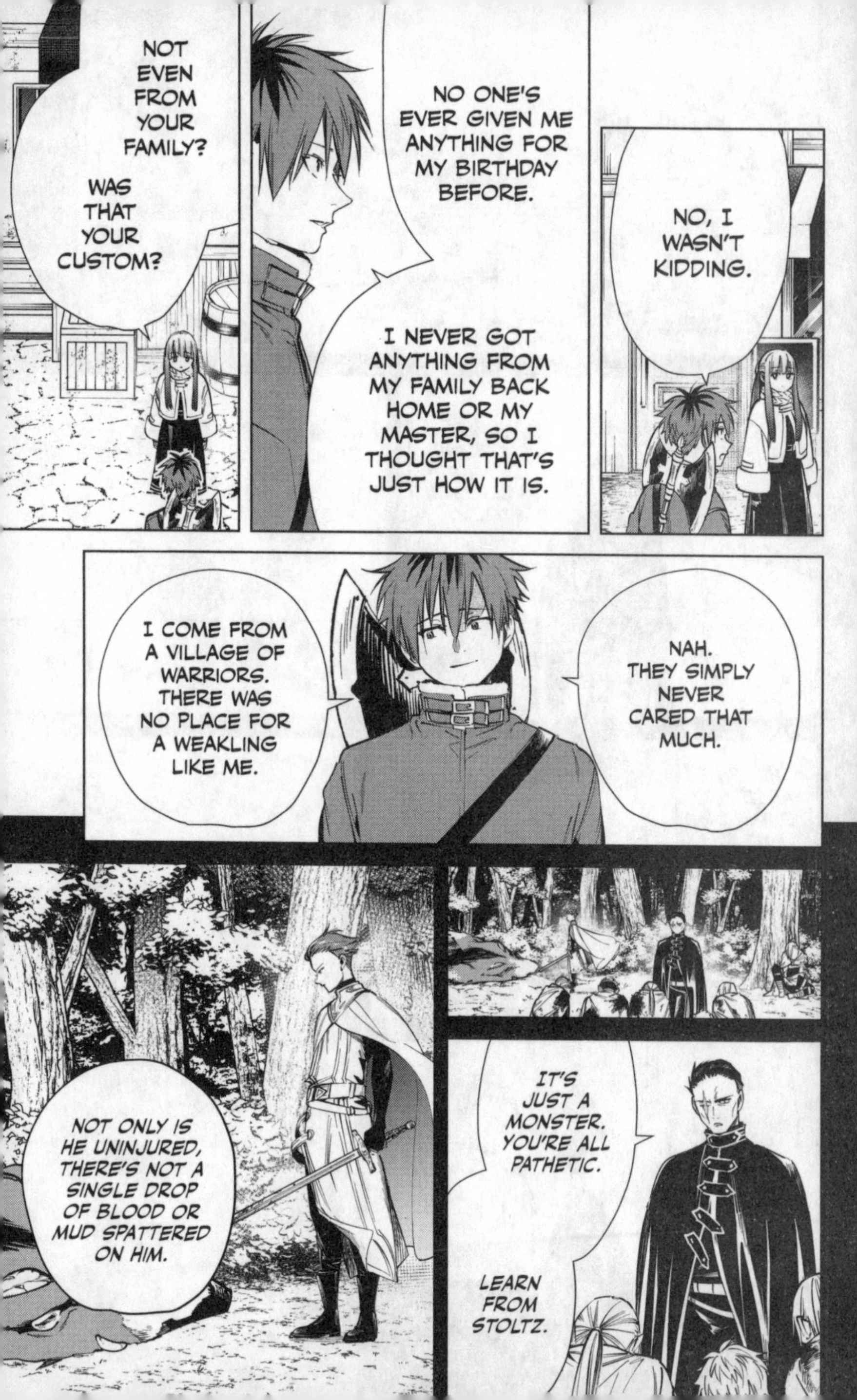
NO, I WASN'T KIDDING.
NO ONE'S EVER GIVEN ME ANYTHING FOR MY BIRTHDAY BEFORE.
I NEVER GOT ANYTHING FROM MY FAMILY BACK HOME OR MY MASTER, SO I THOUGHT THAT'S JUST HOW IT IS.
NOT EVEN FROM YOUR FAMILY?
WAS THAT YOUR CUSTOM?
NAH. THEY SIMPLY NEVER CARED THAT MUCH.
I COME FROM A VILLAGE OF WARRIORS. THERE WAS NO PLACE FOR A WEAKLING LIKE ME.
IT'S JUST A MONSTER. YOU'RE ALL PATHETIC.
LEARN FROM STOLTZ.
NOT ONLY IS HE UNINJURED, THERE'S NOT A SINGLE DROP OF BLOOD OR MUD SPATTERED ON HIM.

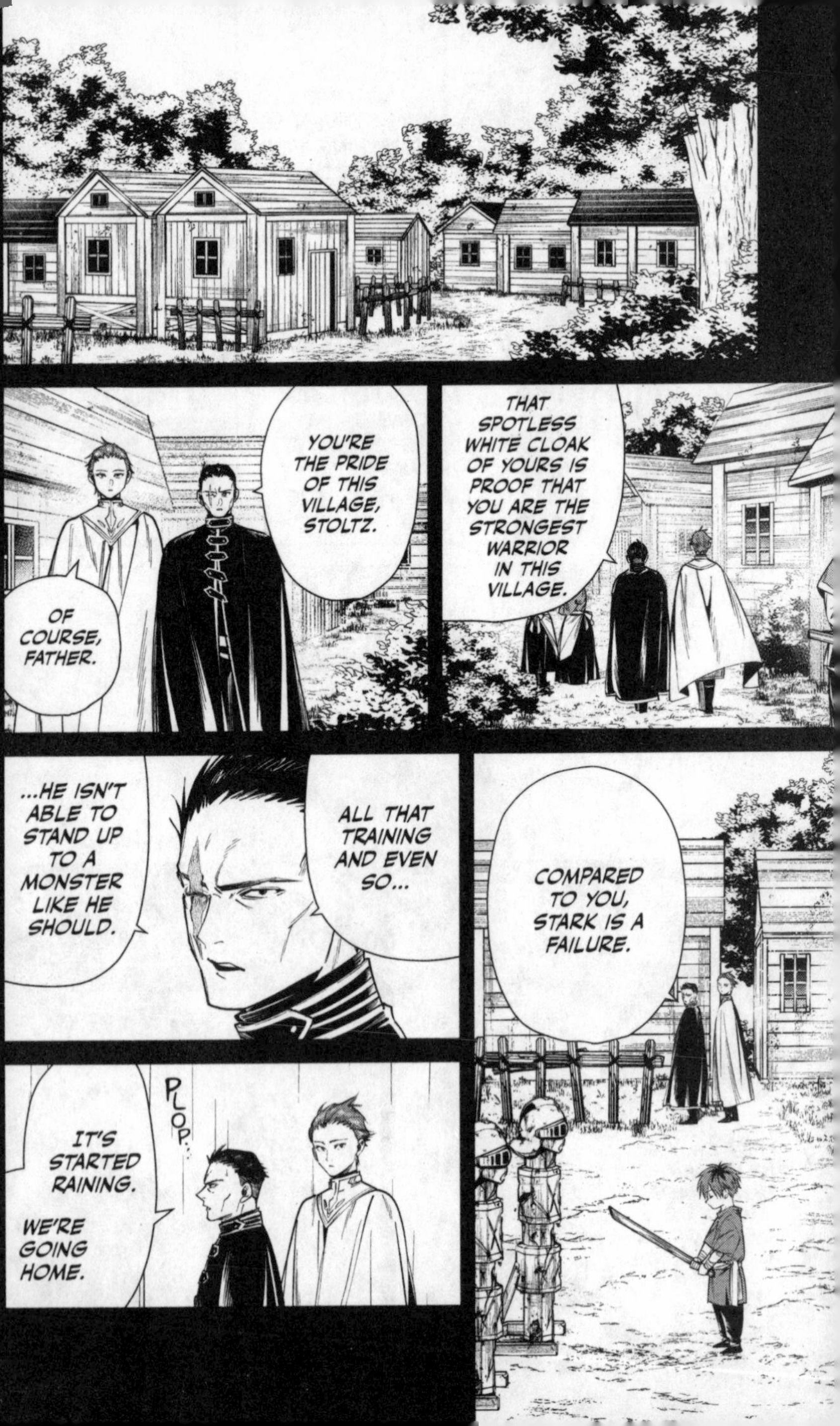
THAT SPOTLESS WHITE CLOAK OF YOURS IS PROOF THAT YOU ARE THE STRONGEST WARRIOR IN THIS VILLAGE.
YOU'RE THE PRIDE OF THIS VILLAGE, STOLTZ.
OF COURSE, FATHER.
COMPARED TO YOU, STARK IS A FAILURE.
ALL THAT TRAINING AND EVEN SO...
...HE ISN'T ABLE TO STAND UP TO A MONSTER LIKE HE SHOULD.
PLOP...
IT'S STARTED RAINING.
WE'RE GOING HOME.

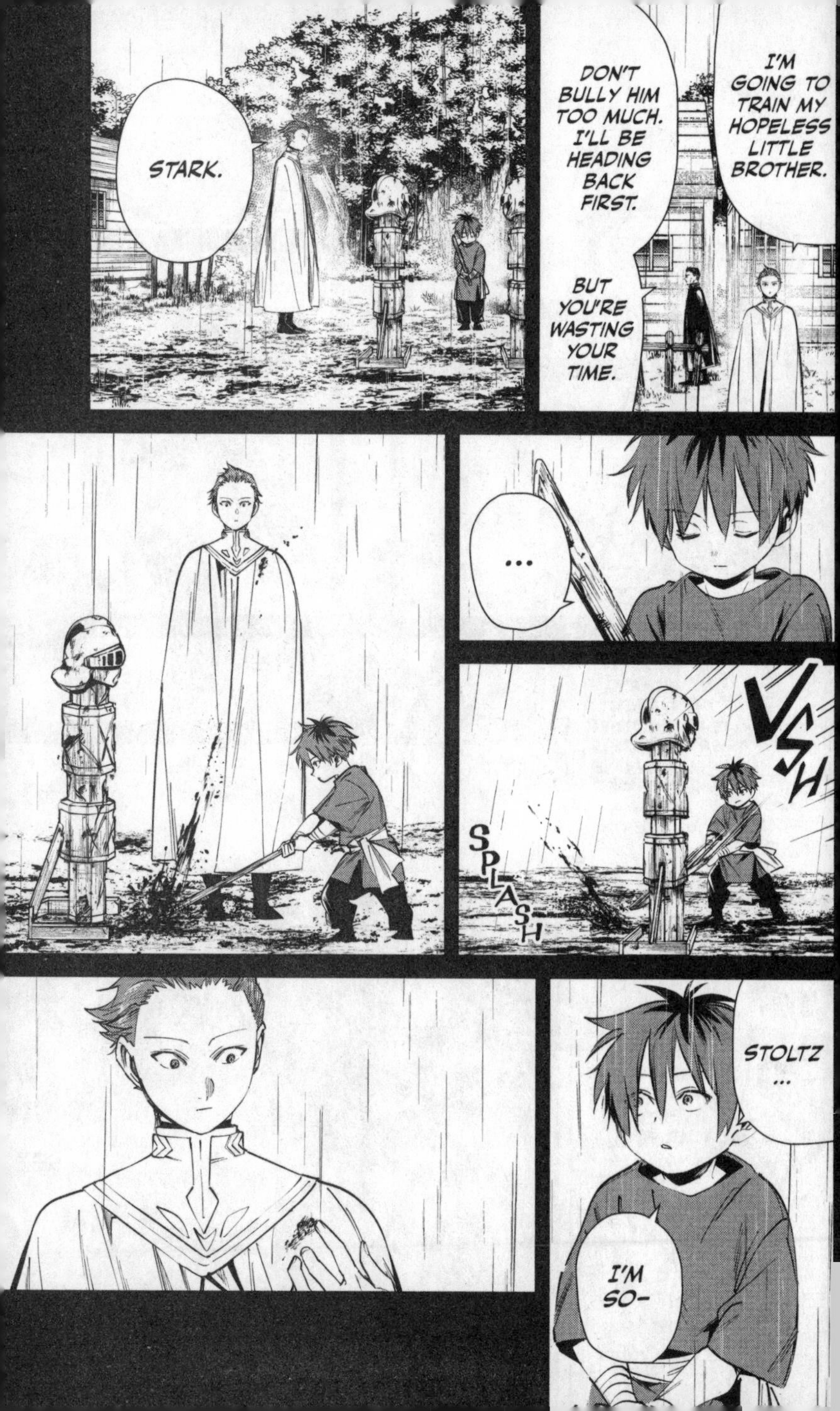
I'M GOING TO TRAIN MY HOPELESS LITTLE BROTHER.
DON'T BULLY HIM TOO MUCH. I'LL BE HEADING BACK FIRST.
BUT YOU'RE WASTING YOUR TIME.
STARK.
...
VSH
SPLASH
STOLTZ ...
I'M SO-

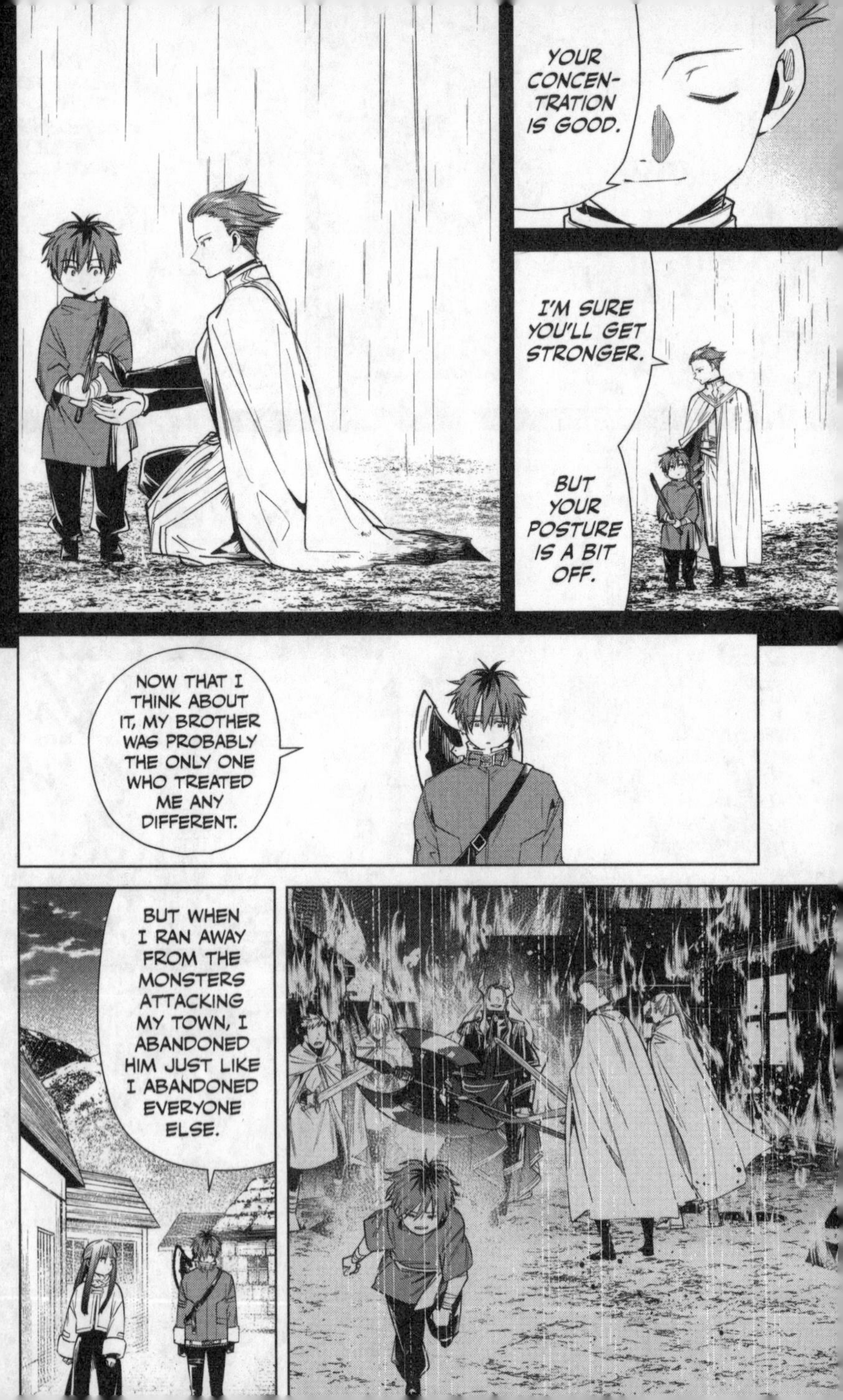
YOUR CONCENTRATION IS GOOD.
I'M SURE YOU'LL GET STRONGER.
BUT YOUR POSTURE IS A BIT OFF.
NOW THAT I THINK ABOUT IT, MY BROTHER WAS PROBABLY THE ONLY ONE WHO TREATED ME ANY DIFFERENT.
BUT WHEN I RAN AWAY FROM THE MONSTERS ATTACKING MY TOWN, I ABANDONED HIM JUST LIKE I ABANDONED EVERYONE ELSE.

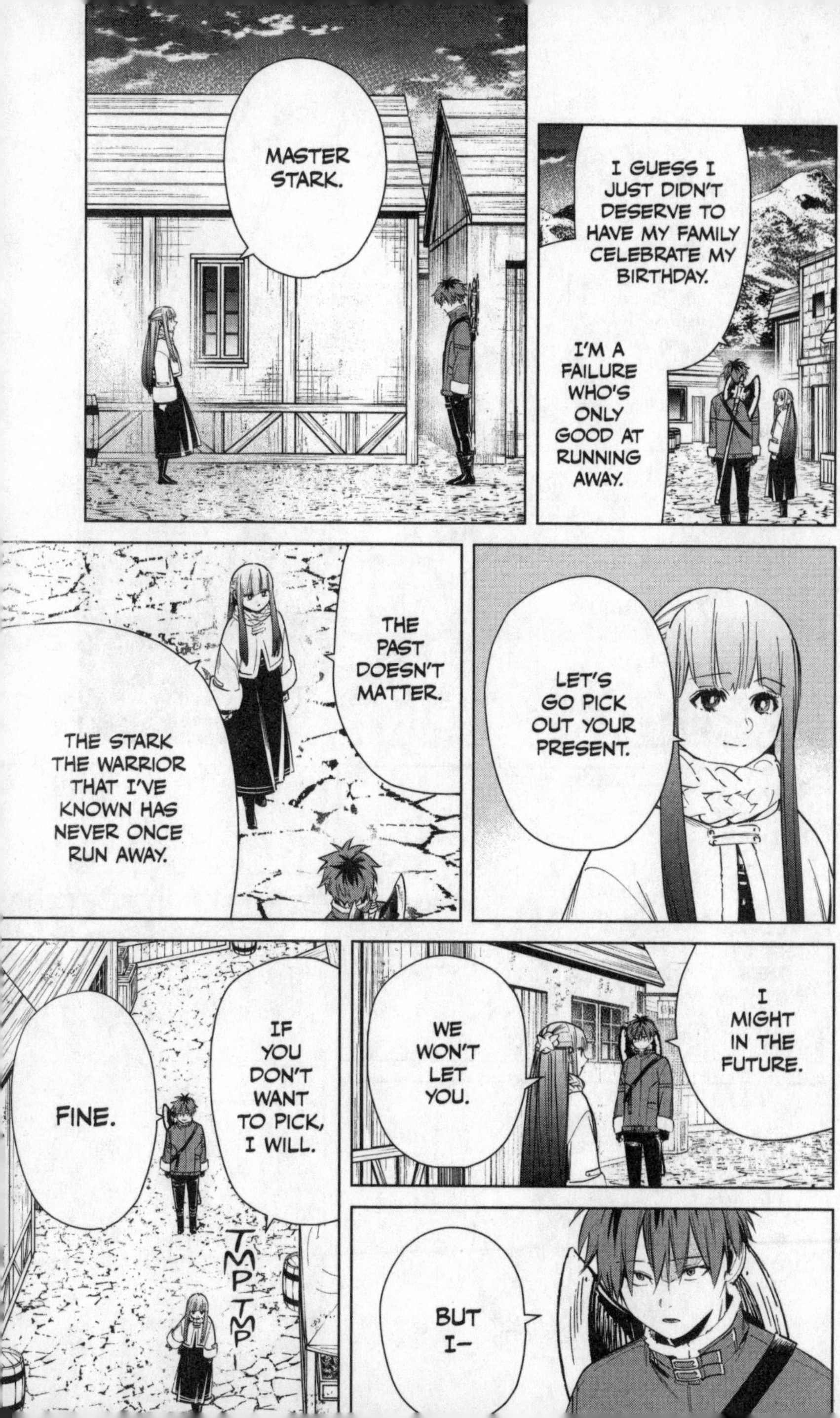
I GUESS I JUST DIDN'T DESERVE TO HAVE MY FAMILY CELEBRATE MY BIRTHDAY.
I'M A FAILURE WHO'S ONLY GOOD AT RUNNING AWAY.
MASTER STARK.
LET'S GO PICK OUT YOUR PRESENT.
THE PAST DOESN'T MATTER.
THE STARK THE WARRIOR THAT I'VE KNOWN HAS NEVER ONCE RUN AWAY.
I MIGHT IN THE FUTURE.
WE WON'T LET YOU.
BUT I—
IF YOU DON'T WANT TO PICK, I WILL.
FINE.
TMP TMP

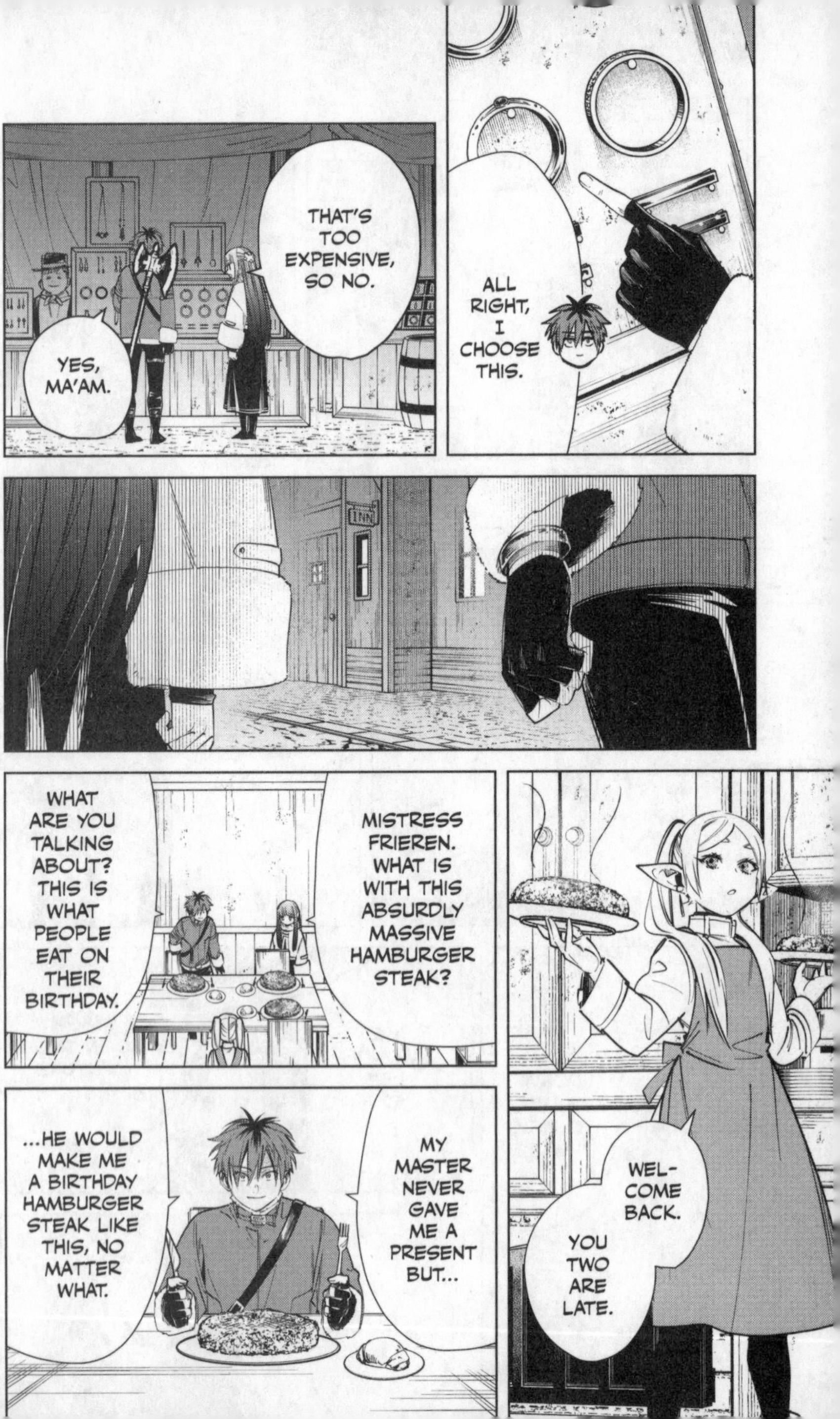
ALL RIGHT, I CHOOSE THIS.
THAT'S TOO EXPENSIVE, SO NO.
YES, MA'AM.
INN
WEL-COME BACK.
YOU TWO ARE LATE.
MISTRESS FRIEREN. WHAT IS WITH THIS ABSURDLY MASSIVE HAMBURGER STEAK?
WHAT ARE YOU TALKING ABOUT? THIS IS WHAT PEOPLE EAT ON THEIR BIRTHDAY.
MY MASTER NEVER GAVE ME A PRESENT BUT...
...HE WOULD MAKE ME A BIRTHDAY HAMBURGER STEAK LIKE THIS, NO MATTER WHAT.

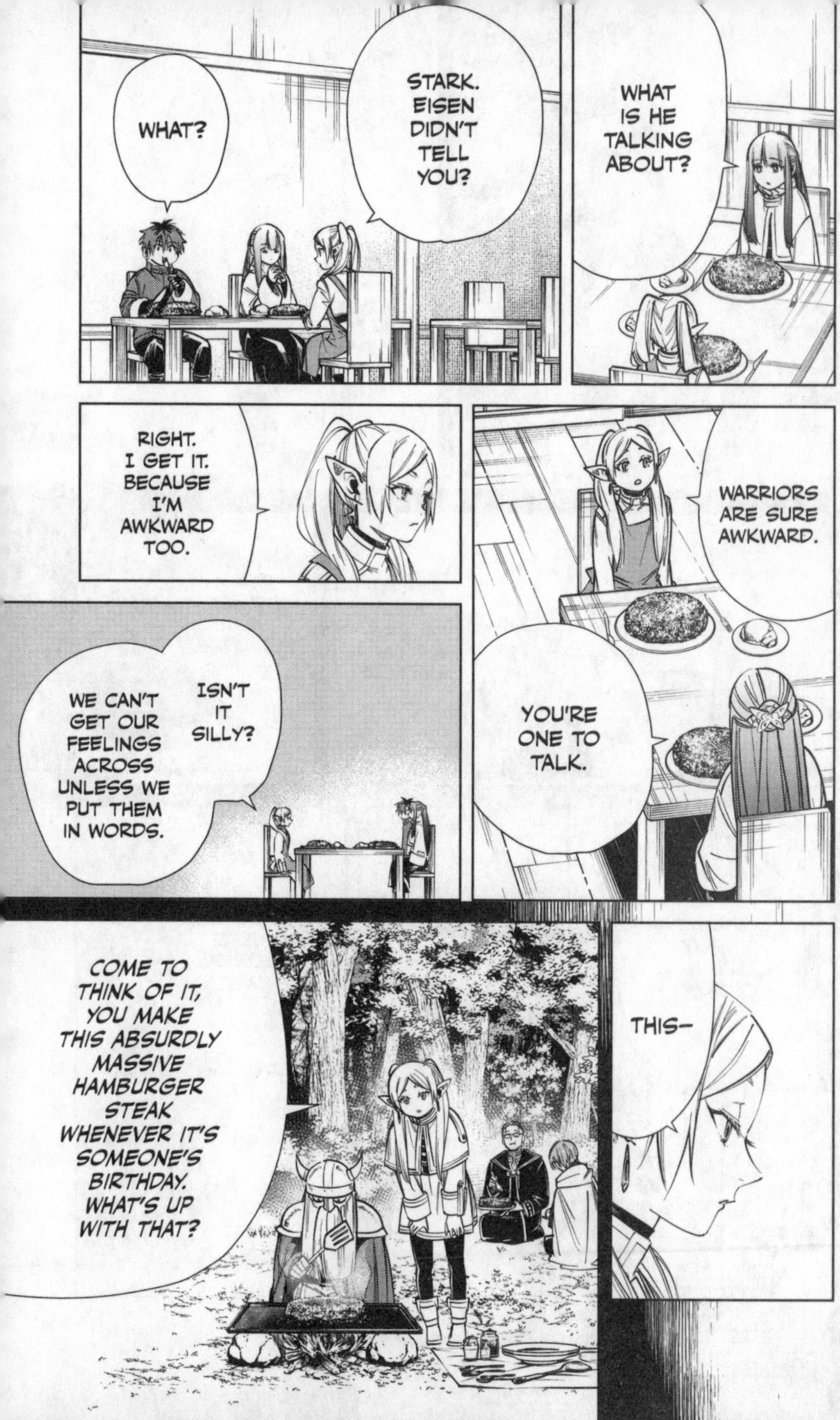
WHAT IS HE TALKING ABOUT?
STARK. EISEN DIDN'T TELL YOU?
WHAT?
WARRIORS ARE SURE AWKWARD.
YOU'RE ONE TO TALK.
RIGHT. I GET IT. BECAUSE I'M AWKWARD TOO.
ISN'T IT SILLY?
WE CAN'T GET OUR FEELINGS ACROSS UNLESS WE PUT THEM IN WORDS.
THIS—
COME TO THINK OF IT, YOU MAKE THIS ABSURDLY MASSIVE HAMBURGER STEAK WHENEVER IT'S SOMEONE'S BIRTHDAY. WHAT'S UP WITH THAT?

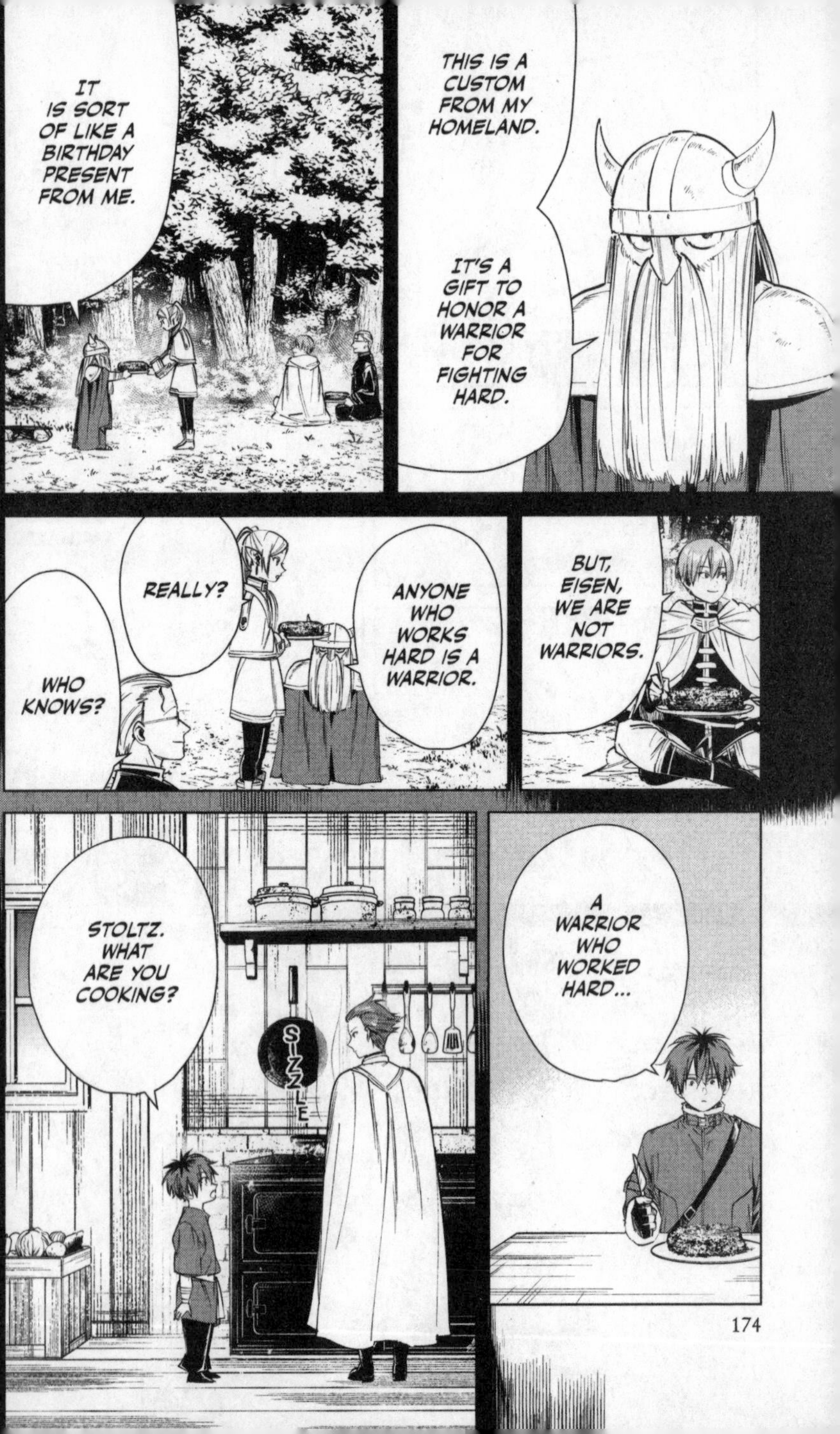
THIS IS A CUSTOM FROM MY HOMELAND.
IT'S A GIFT TO HONOR A WARRIOR FOR FIGHTING HARD.
IT IS SORT OF LIKE A BIRTHDAY PRESENT FROM ME.
BUT, EISEN, WE ARE NOT WARRIORS.
ANYONE WHO WORKS HARD IS A WARRIOR.
REALLY?
WHO KNOWS?
A WARRIOR WHO WORKED HARD...
STOLTZ. WHAT ARE YOU COOKING?
SIZZLE

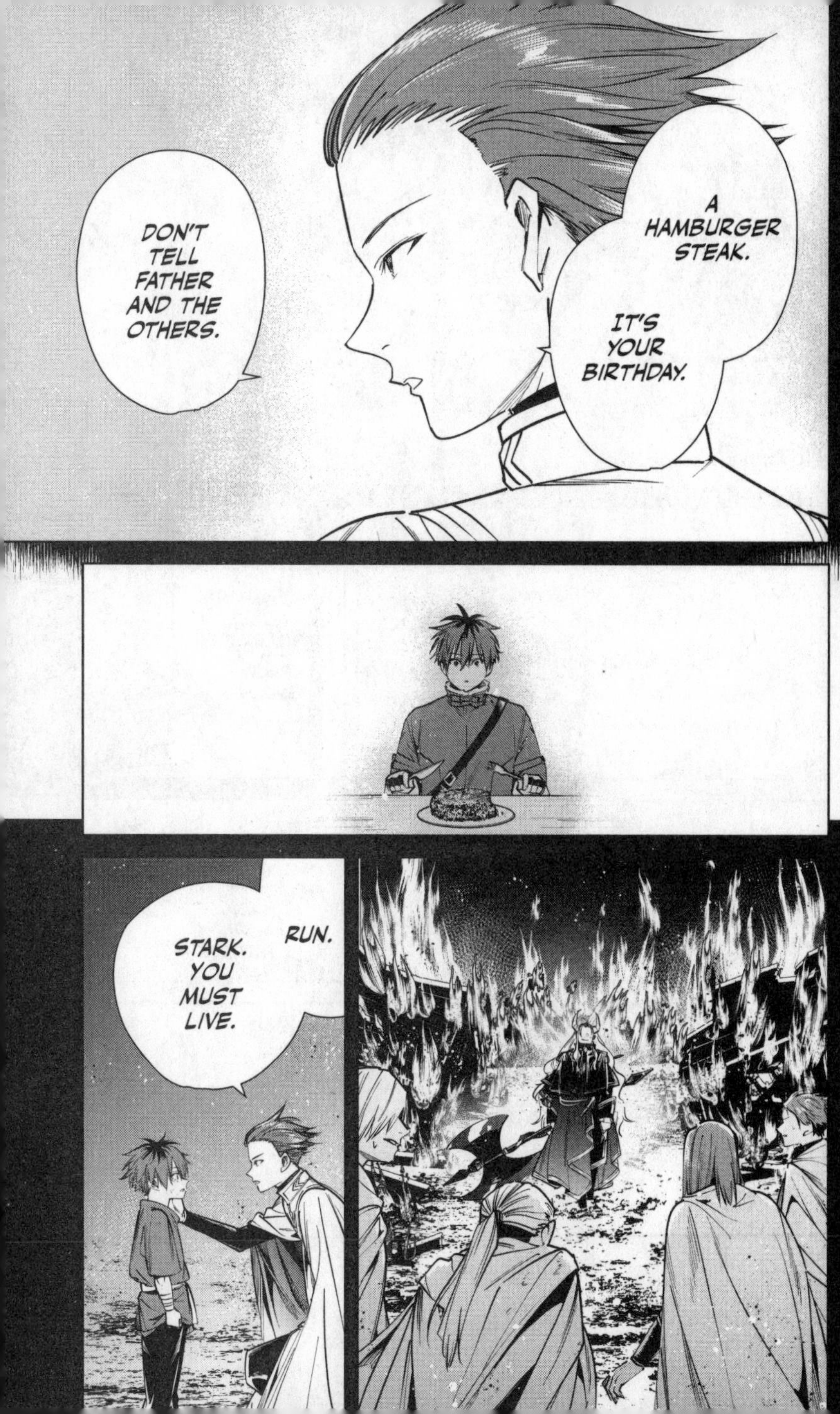
A HAMBURGER STEAK.
IT'S YOUR BIRTHDAY.
DON'T TELL FATHER AND THE OTHERS.
RUN.
STARK. YOU MUST LIVE.

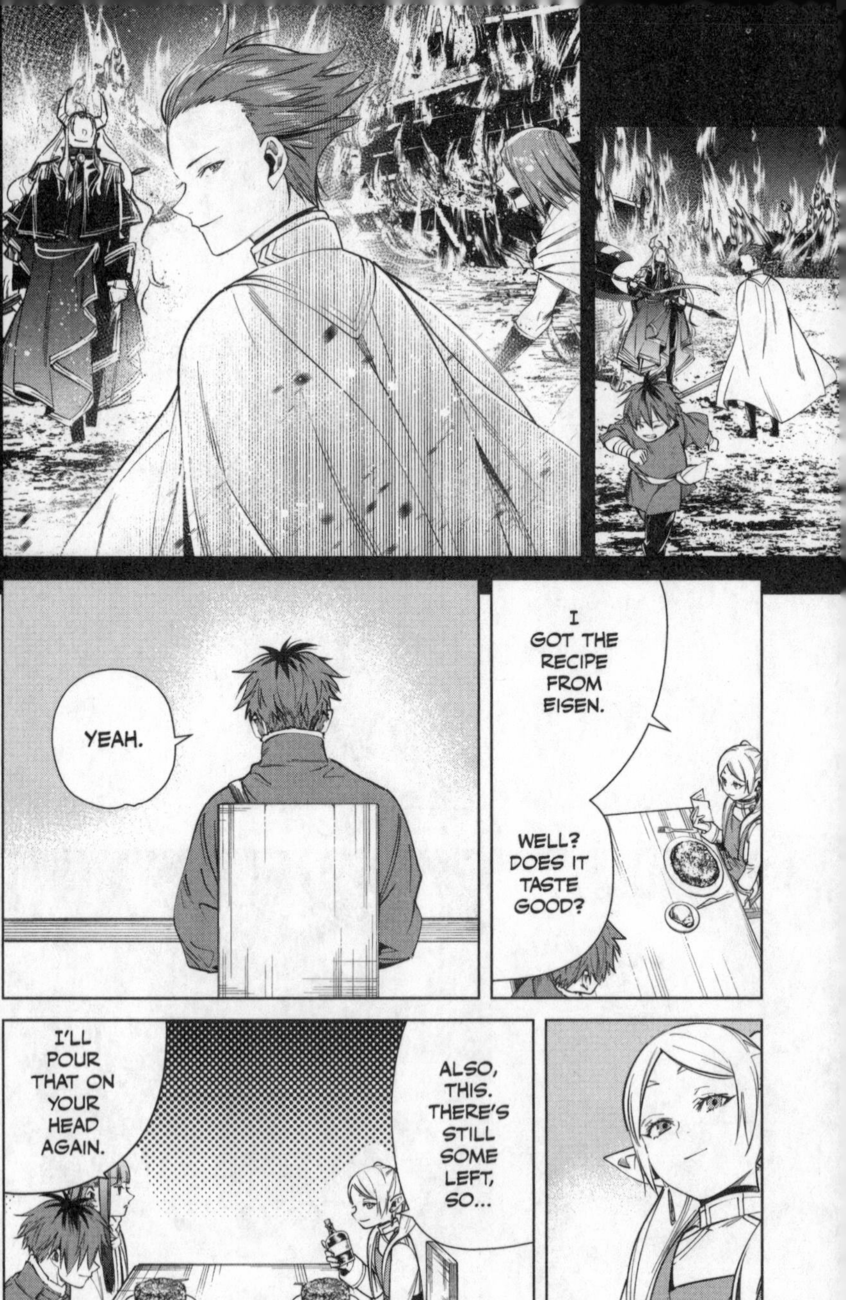
I GOT THE RECIPE FROM EISEN.
WELL? DOES IT TASTE GOOD?
YEAH.
ALSO, THIS. THERE'S STILL SOME LEFT, SO...
I'LL POUR THAT ON YOUR HEAD AGAIN.

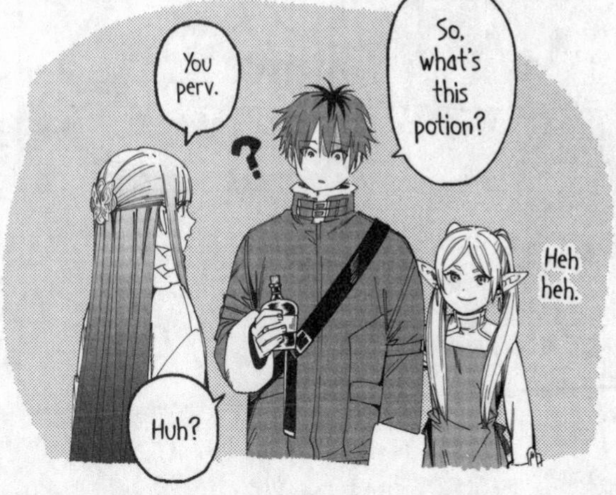
So, what's this potion?
You perv.
Heh heh.
Huh?

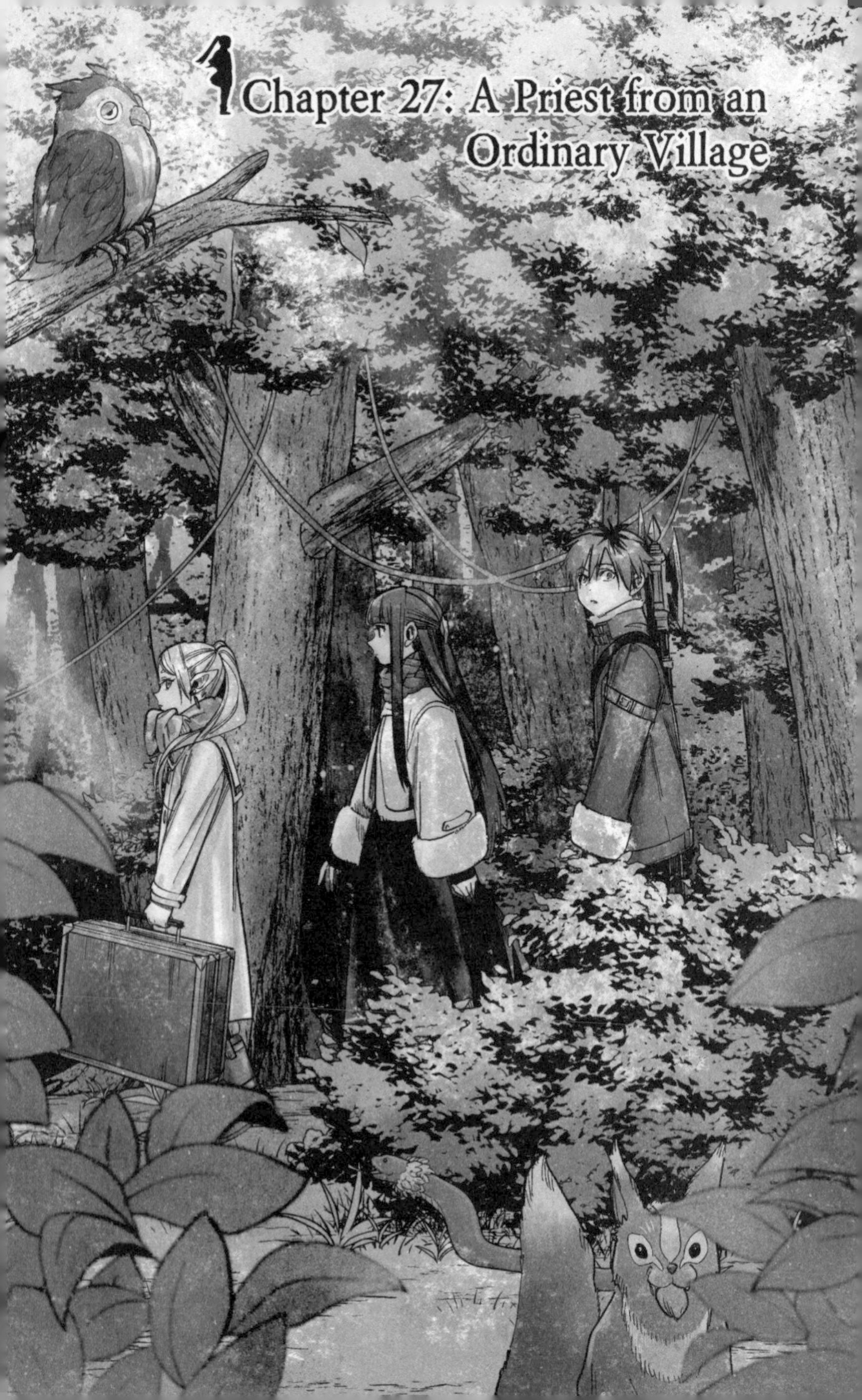
Chapter 27: A Priest from an Ordinary Village

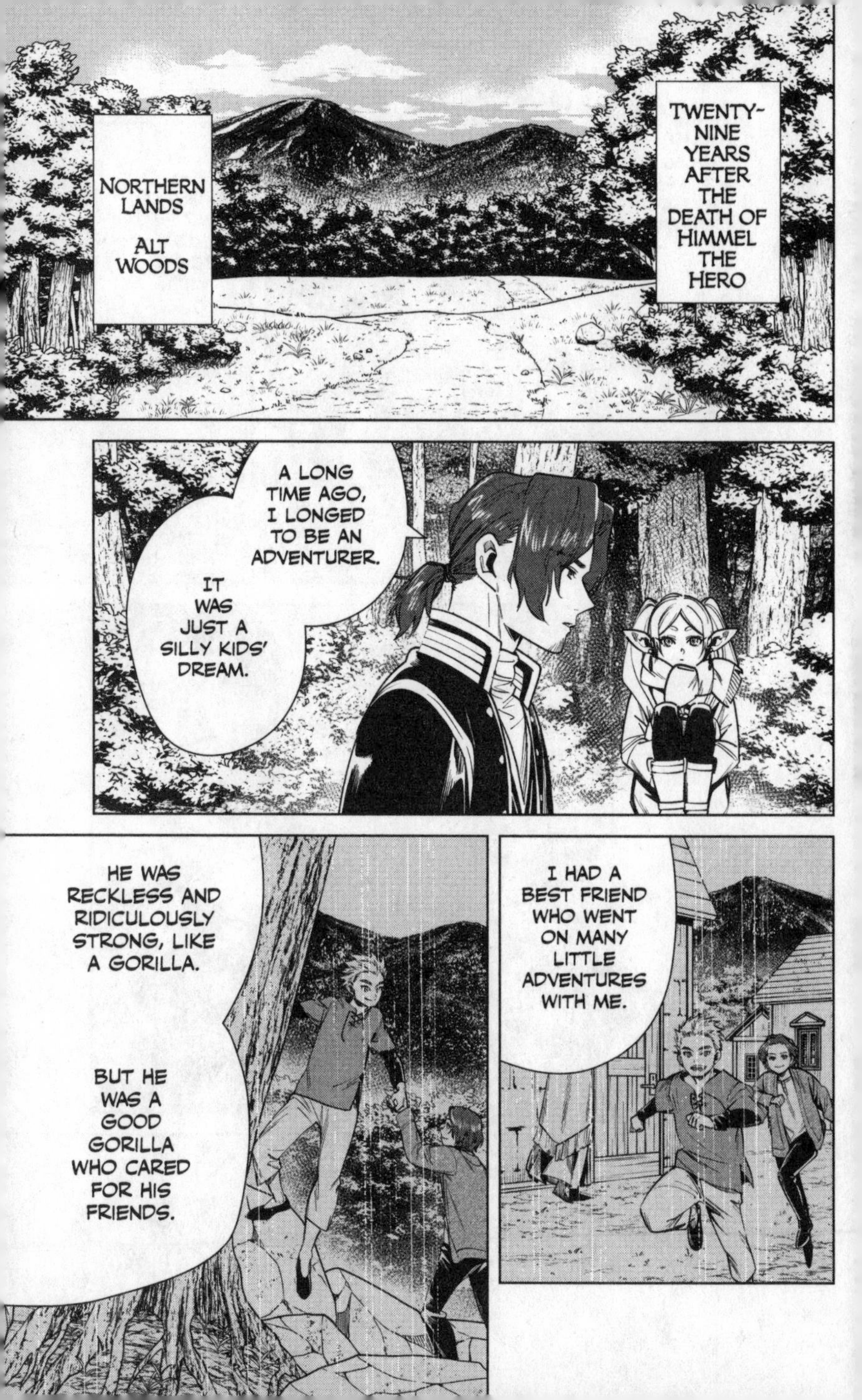
TWENTY-NINE YEARS AFTER THE DEATH OF HIMMEL THE HERO
NORTHERN LANDS
ALT WOODS
A LONG TIME AGO, I LONGED TO BE AN ADVENTURER.
IT WAS JUST A SILLY KIDS' DREAM.
I HAD A BEST FRIEND WHO WENT ON MANY LITTLE ADVENTURES WITH ME.
HE WAS RECKLESS AND RIDICULOUSLY STRONG, LIKE A GORILLA.
BUT HE WAS A GOOD GORILLA WHO CARED FOR HIS FRIENDS.

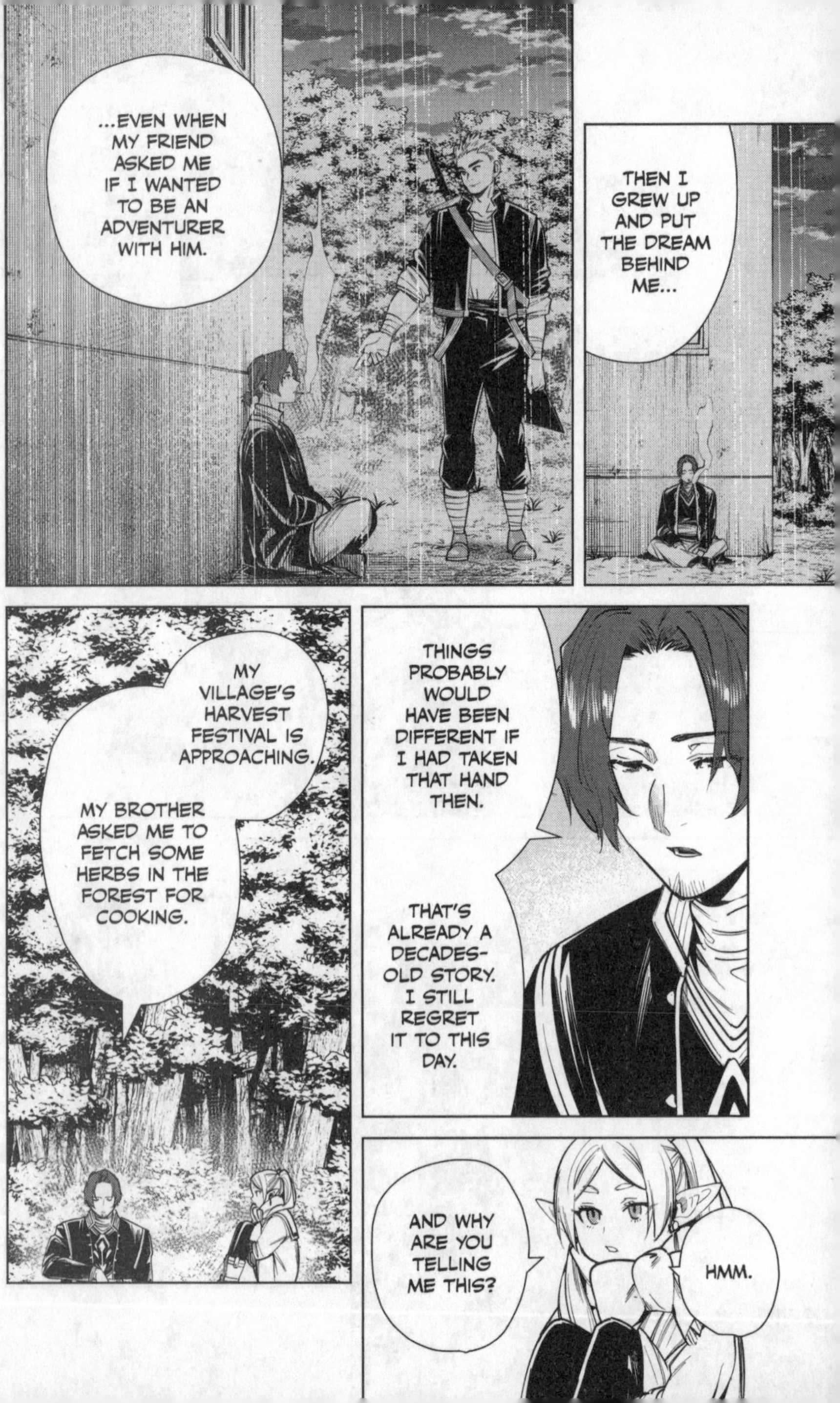
THEN I GREW UP AND PUT THE DREAM BEHIND ME...
...EVEN WHEN MY FRIEND ASKED ME IF I WANTED TO BE AN ADVENTURER WITH HIM.
THINGS PROBABLY WOULD HAVE BEEN DIFFERENT IF I HAD TAKEN THAT HAND THEN.
THAT'S ALREADY A DECADES-OLD STORY. I STILL REGRET IT TO THIS DAY.
HMM.
AND WHY ARE YOU TELLING ME THIS?
MY VILLAGE'S HARVEST FESTIVAL IS APPROACHING.
MY BROTHER ASKED ME TO FETCH SOME HERBS IN THE FOREST FOR COOKING.

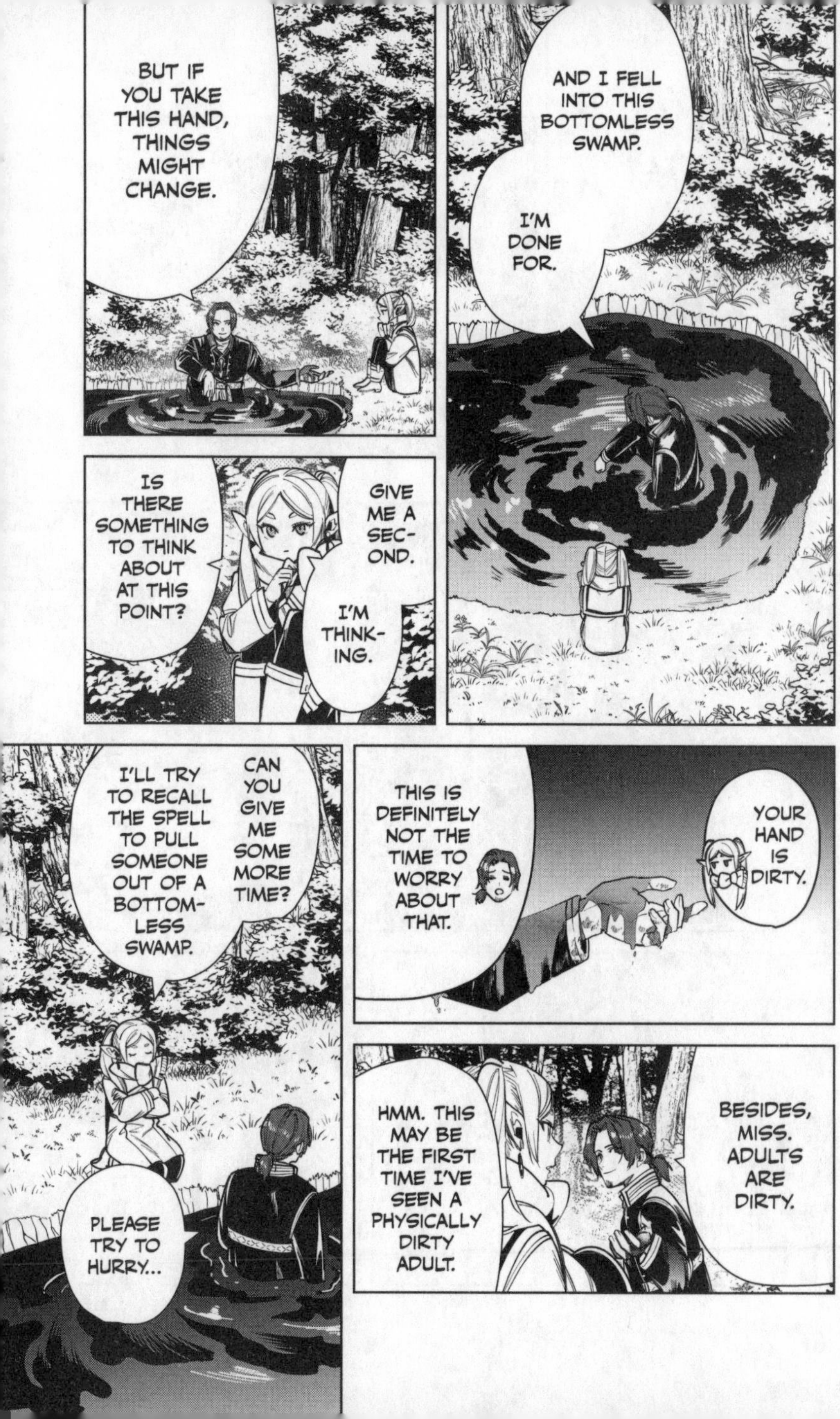
AND I FELL INTO THIS BOTTOMLESS SWAMP.
I'M DONE FOR.
BUT IF YOU TAKE THIS HAND, THINGS MIGHT CHANGE.
GIVE ME A SEC-OND.
I'M THINK-ING.
IS THERE SOMETHING TO THINK ABOUT AT THIS POINT?
YOUR HAND IS DIRTY.
THIS IS DEFINITELY NOT THE TIME TO WORRY ABOUT THAT.
BESIDES, MISS. ADULTS ARE DIRTY.
HMM. THIS MAY BE THE FIRST TIME I'VE SEEN A PHYSICALLY DIRTY ADULT.
CAN YOU GIVE ME SOME MORE TIME?
I'LL TRY TO RECALL THE SPELL TO PULL SOMEONE OUT OF A BOTTOM-LESS SWAMP.
PLEASE TRY TO HURRY...

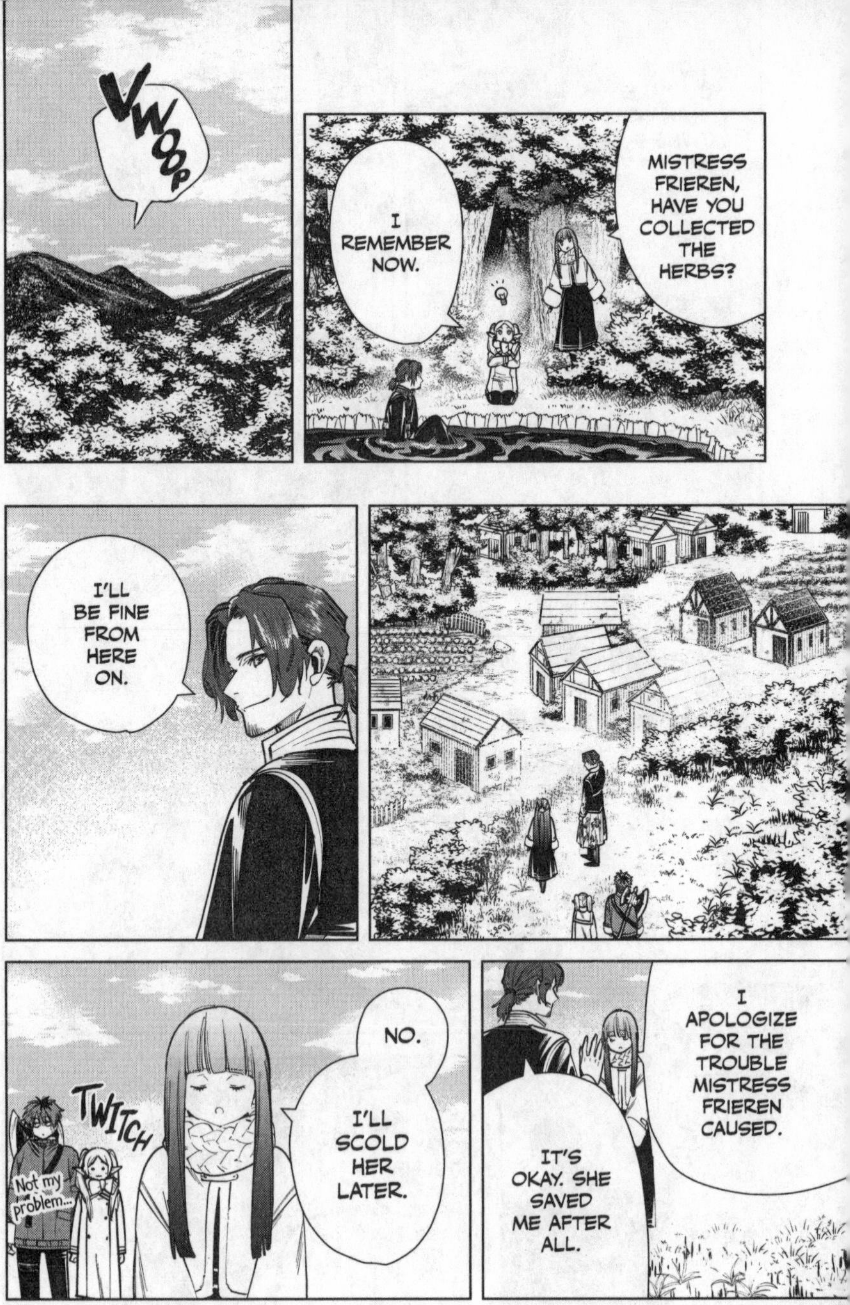
MISTRESS FRIEREN, HAVE YOU COLLECTED THE HERBS?
I REMEMBER NOW.
VWOOP
I'LL BE FINE FROM HERE ON.
I APOLOGIZE FOR THE TROUBLE MISTRESS FRIEREN CAUSED.
IT'S OKAY. SHE SAVED ME AFTER ALL.
NO.
I'LL SCOLD HER LATER.
TWITCH
Not my problem...

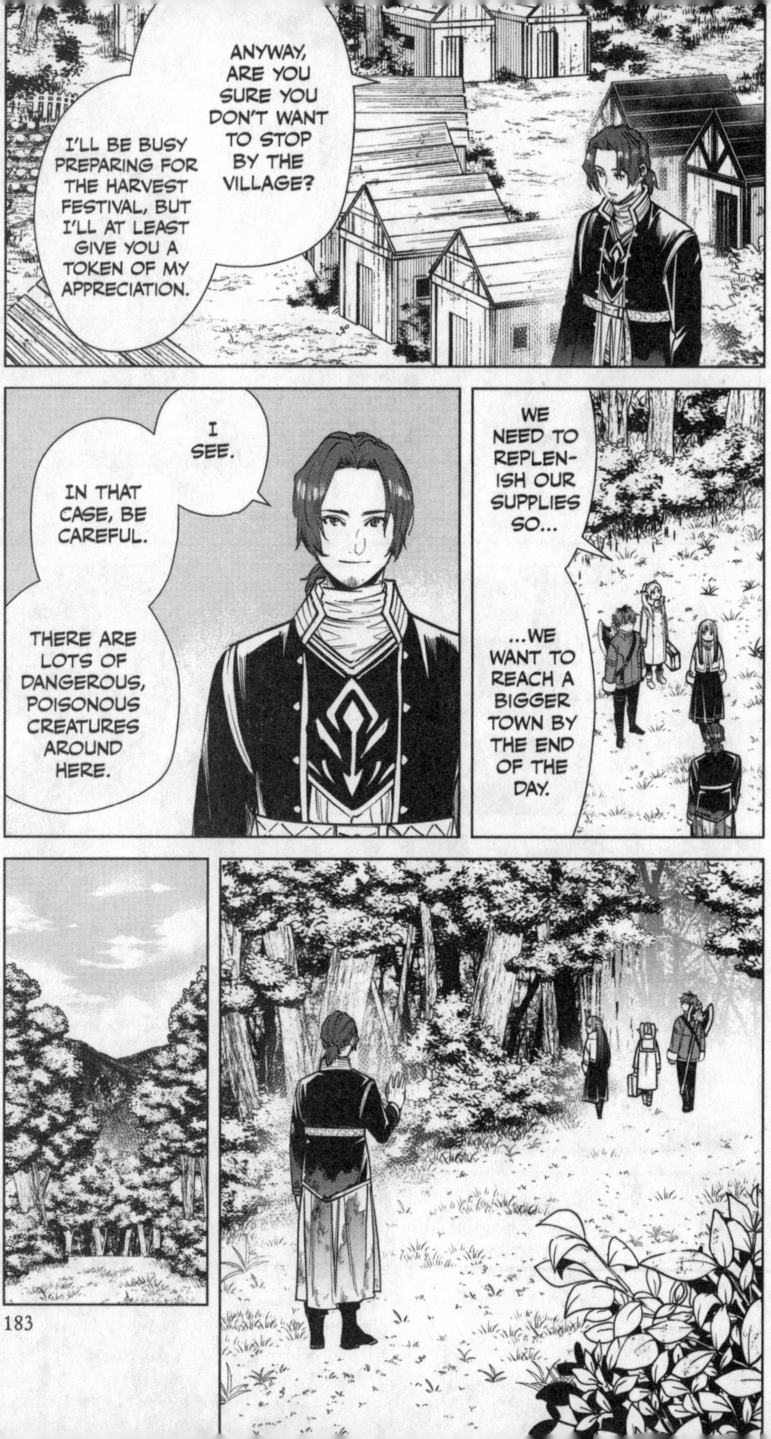
ANYWAY, ARE YOU SURE YOU DON'T WANT TO STOP BY THE VILLAGE?
I'LL BE BUSY PREPARING FOR THE HARVEST FESTIVAL, BUT I'LL AT LEAST GIVE YOU A TOKEN OF MY APPRECIATION.
WE NEED TO REPLEN-ISH OUR SUPPLIES SO...
...WE WANT TO REACH A BIGGER TOWN BY THE END OF THE DAY.
I SEE.
IN THAT CASE, BE CAREFUL.
THERE ARE LOTS OF DANGEROUS, POISONOUS CREATURES AROUND HERE.

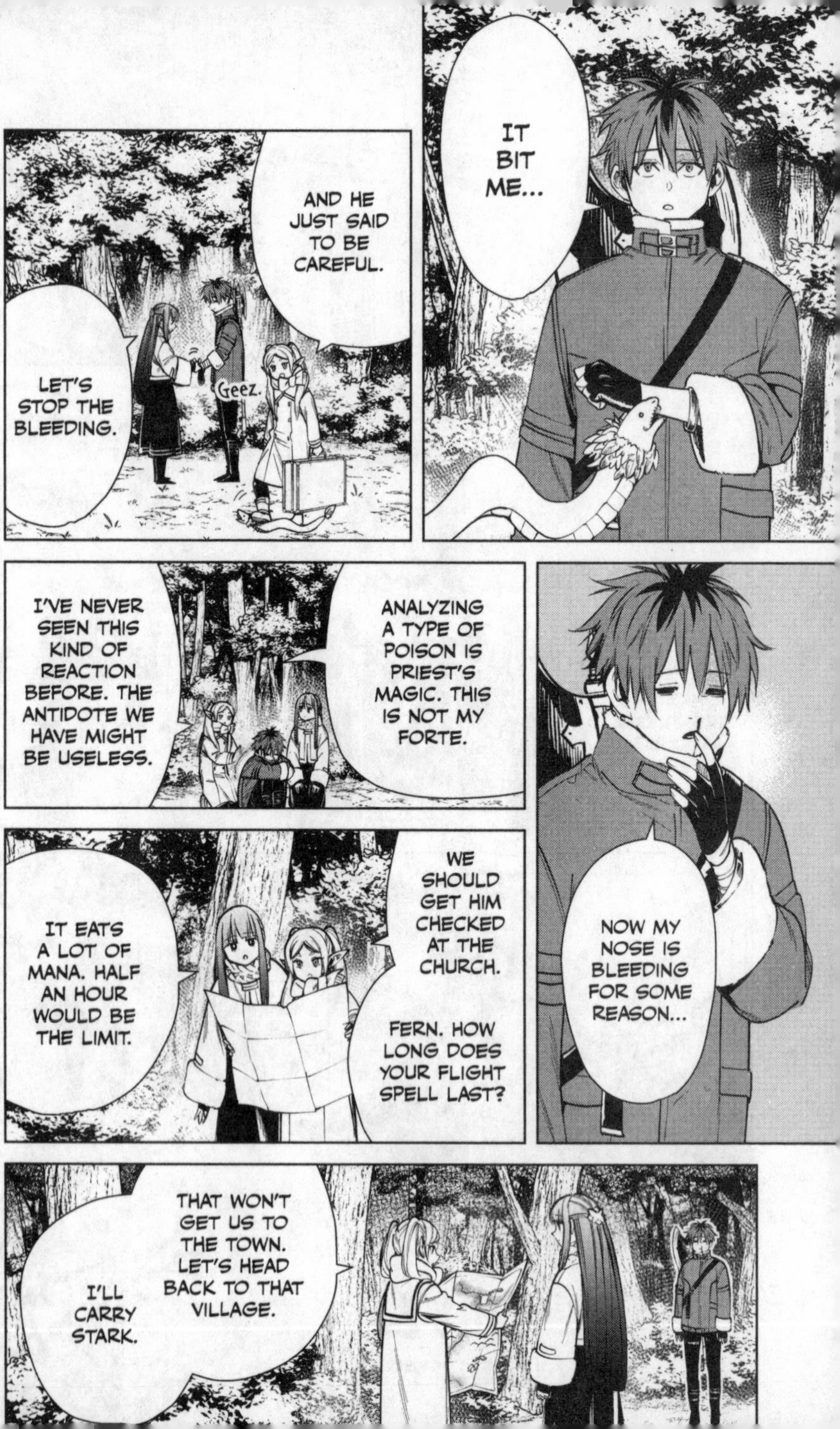
IT BIT ME...
AND HE JUST SAID TO BE CAREFUL.
Geez.
LET'S STOP THE BLEEDING.
NOW MY NOSE IS BLEEDING FOR SOME REASON...
ANALYZING A TYPE OF POISON IS PRIEST'S MAGIC. THIS IS NOT MY FORTE.
I'VE NEVER SEEN THIS KIND OF REACTION BEFORE. THE ANTIDOTE WE HAVE MIGHT BE USELESS.
WE SHOULD GET HIM CHECKED AT THE CHURCH.
FERN. HOW LONG DOES YOUR FLIGHT SPELL LAST?
IT EATS A LOT OF MANA. HALF AN HOUR WOULD BE THE LIMIT.
THAT WON'T GET US TO THE TOWN. LET'S HEAD BACK TO THAT VILLAGE.
I'LL CARRY STARK.

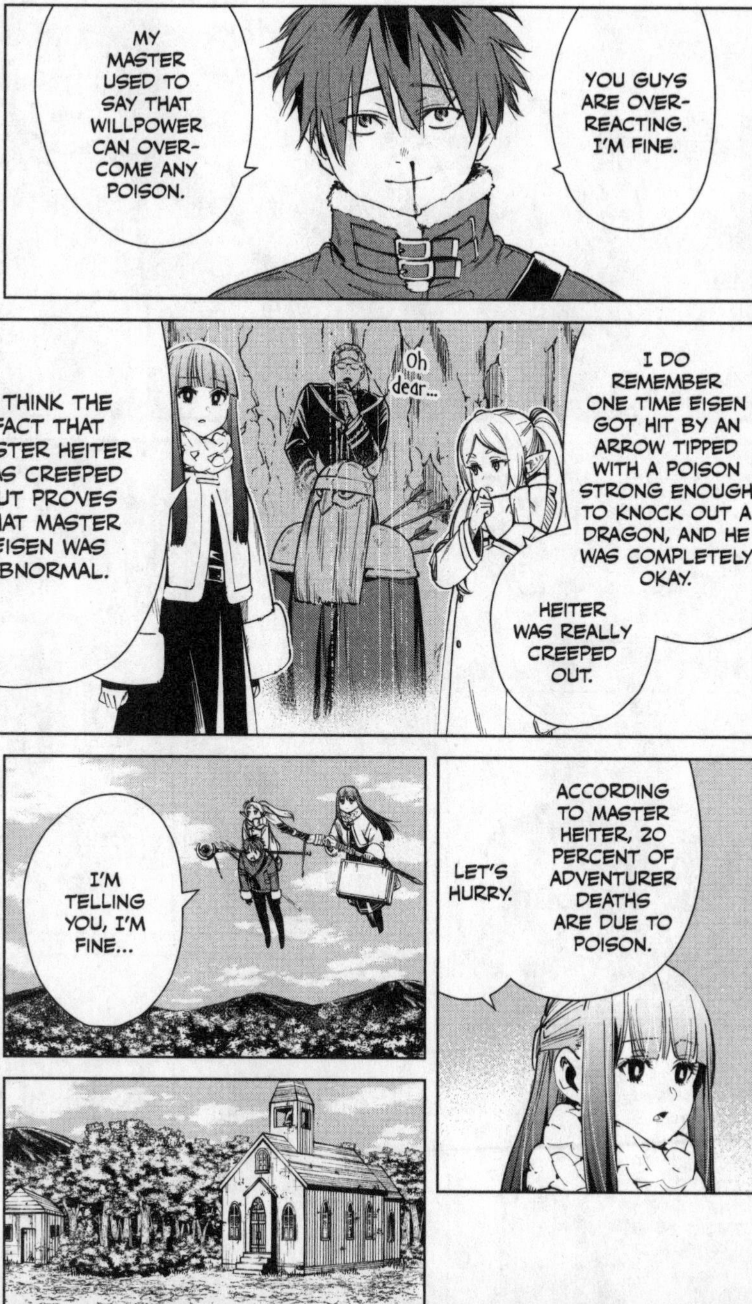
YOU GUYS ARE OVER-REACTING. I'M FINE.
MY MASTER USED TO SAY THAT WILLPOWER CAN OVER-COME ANY POISON.
I DO REMEMBER ONE TIME EISEN GOT HIT BY AN ARROW TIPPED WITH A POISON STRONG ENOUGH TO KNOCK OUT A DRAGON, AND HE WAS COMPLETELY OKAY.
HEITER WAS REALLY CREEPED OUT.
Oh dear...
I THINK THE FACT THAT MASTER HEITER WAS CREEPED OUT PROVES THAT MASTER EISEN WAS ABNORMAL.
ACCORDING TO MASTER HEITER, 20 PERCENT OF ADVENTURER DEATHS ARE DUE TO POISON.
LET'S HURRY.
I'M TELLING YOU, I'M FINE...

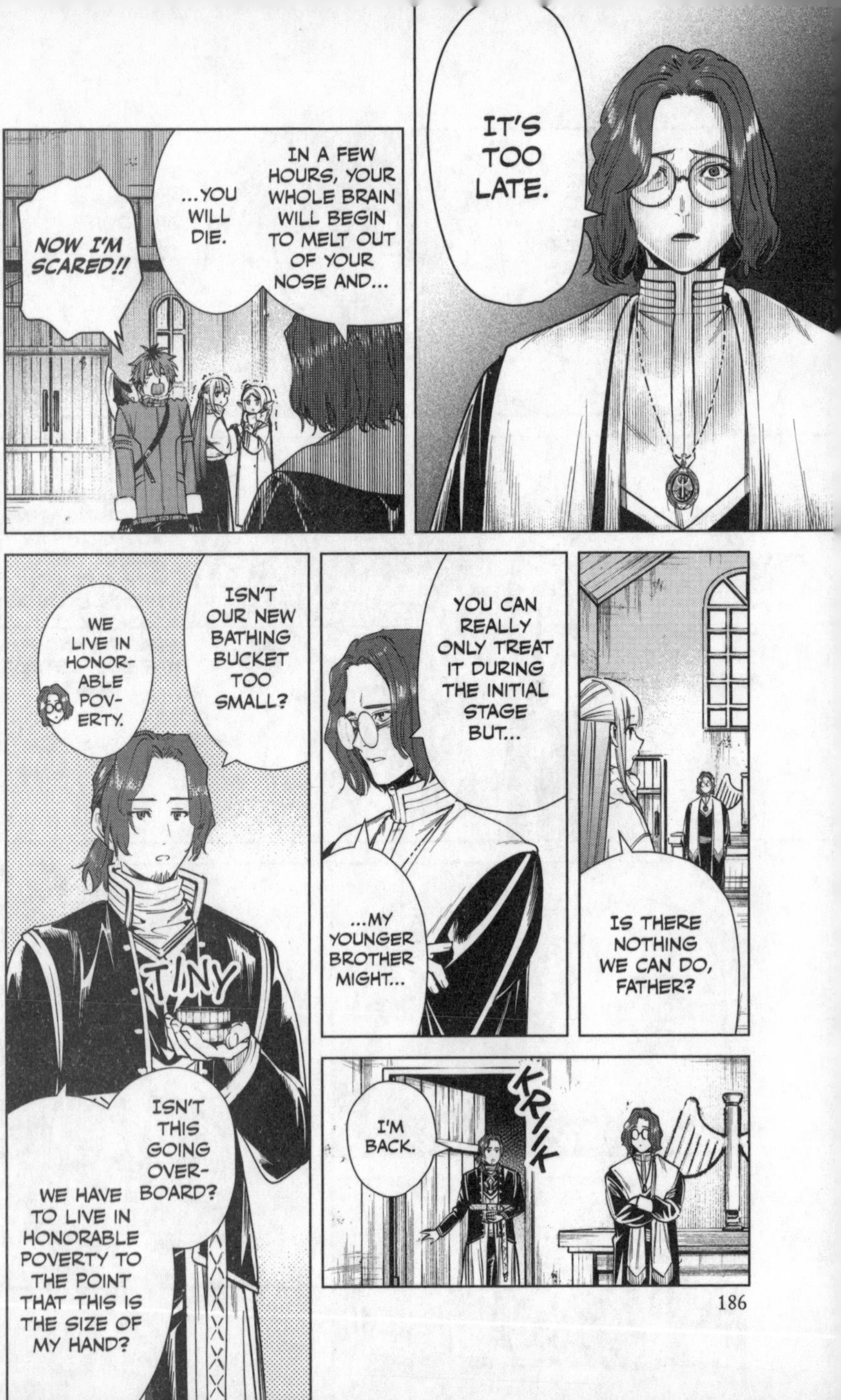
IT'S TOO LATE.
IN A FEW HOURS, YOUR WHOLE BRAIN WILL BEGIN TO MELT OUT OF YOUR NOSE AND...
...YOU WILL DIE.
NOW I'M SCARED!!
IS THERE NOTHING WE CAN DO, FATHER?
YOU CAN REALLY ONLY TREAT IT DURING THE INITIAL STAGE BUT...
...MY YOUNGER BROTHER MIGHT...
KRIK
I'M BACK.
ISN'T OUR NEW BATHING BUCKET TOO SMALL?
WE LIVE IN HONOR-ABLE POV-ERTY.
TINY
ISN'T THIS GOING OVER-BOARD?
WE HAVE TO LIVE IN HONORABLE POVERTY TO THE POINT THAT THIS IS THE SIZE OF MY HAND?

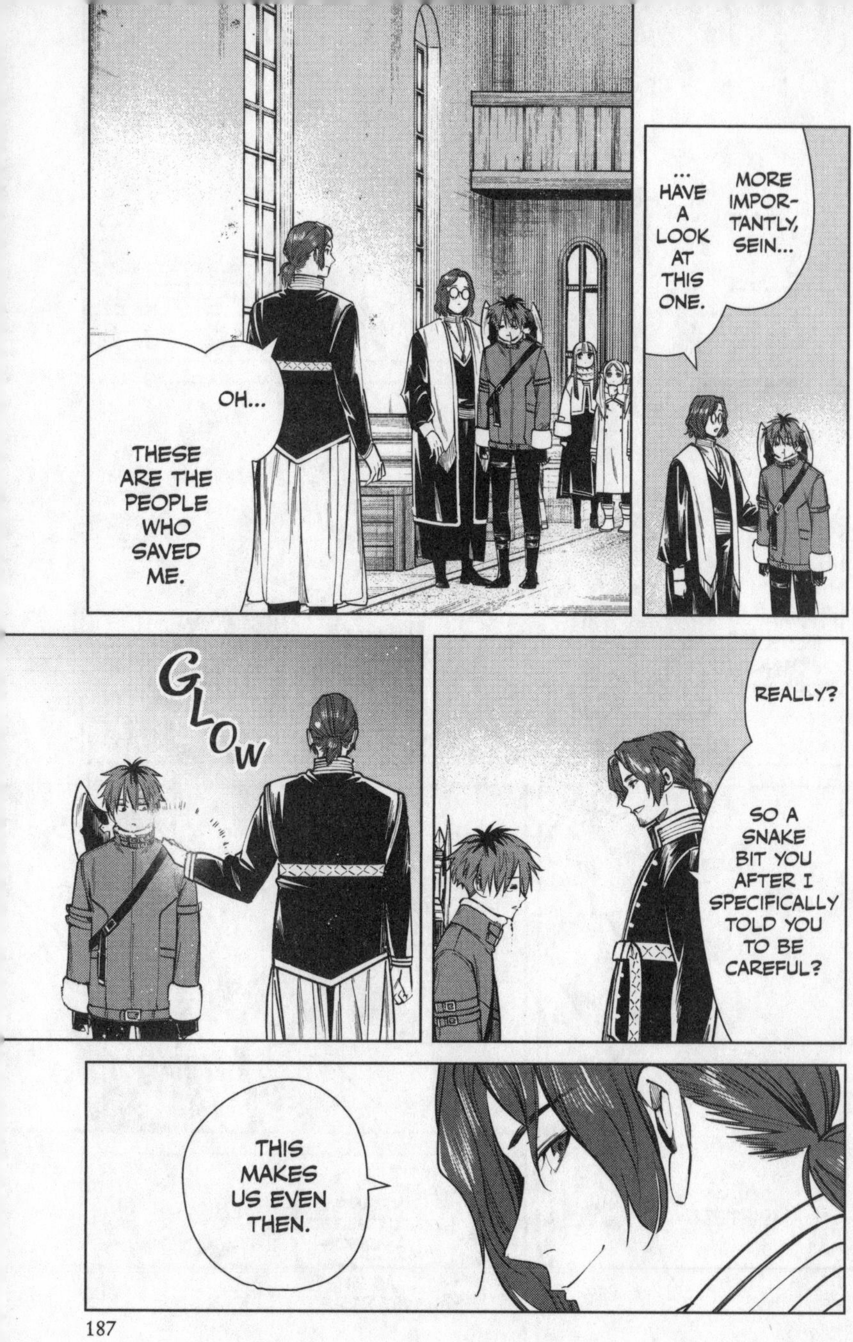
MORE IMPORTANTLY, SEIN...
... HAVE A LOOK AT THIS ONE.
OH...
THESE ARE THE PEOPLE WHO SAVED ME.
REALLY?
SO A SNAKE BIT YOU AFTER I SPECIFICALLY TOLD YOU TO BE CAREFUL?
GLOW
THIS MAKES US EVEN THEN.

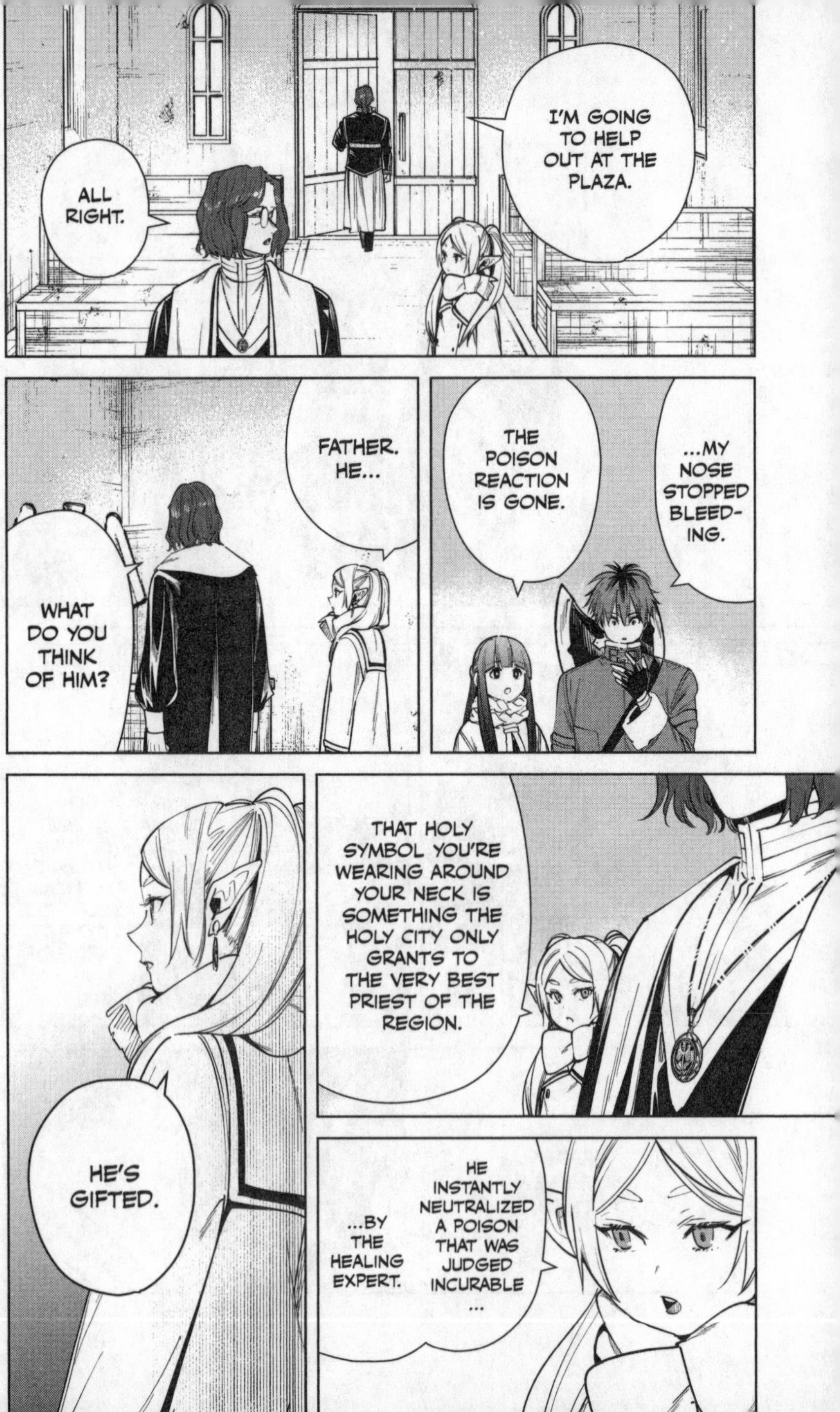
I'M GOING TO HELP OUT AT THE PLAZA.
ALL RIGHT.
...MY NOSE STOPPED BLEED-ING.
THE POISON REACTION IS GONE.
FATHER. HE...
WHAT DO YOU THINK OF HIM?
THAT HOLY SYMBOL YOU'RE WEARING AROUND YOUR NECK IS SOMETHING THE HOLY CITY ONLY GRANTS TO THE VERY BEST PRIEST OF THE REGION.
HE INSTANTLY NEUTRALIZED A POISON THAT WAS JUDGED INCURABLE ...
...BY THE HEALING EXPERT.
HE'S GIFTED.

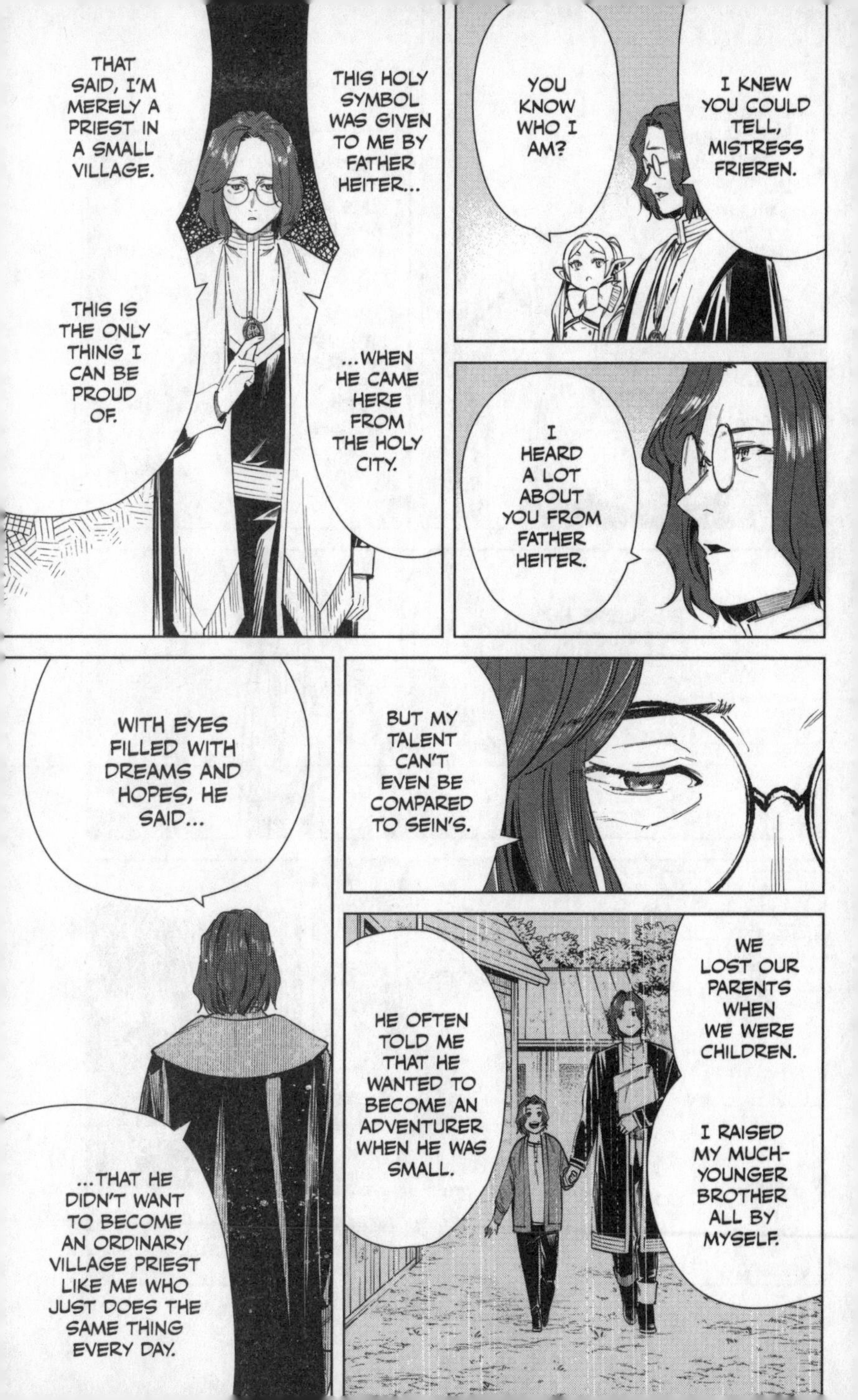
I KNEW YOU COULD TELL, MISTRESS FRIEREN.
YOU KNOW WHO I AM?
I HEARD A LOT ABOUT YOU FROM FATHER HEITER.
THIS HOLY SYMBOL WAS GIVEN TO ME BY FATHER HEITER...
...WHEN HE CAME HERE FROM THE HOLY CITY.
THAT SAID, I'M MERELY A PRIEST IN A SMALL VILLAGE.
THIS IS THE ONLY THING I CAN BE PROUD OF.
BUT MY TALENT CAN'T EVEN BE COMPARED TO SEIN'S.
WE LOST OUR PARENTS WHEN WE WERE CHILDREN.
I RAISED MY MUCH-YOUNGER BROTHER ALL BY MYSELF.
HE OFTEN TOLD ME THAT HE WANTED TO BECOME AN ADVENTURER WHEN HE WAS SMALL.
WITH EYES FILLED WITH DREAMS AND HOPES, HE SAID...
...THAT HE DIDN'T WANT TO BECOME AN ORDINARY VILLAGE PRIEST LIKE ME WHO JUST DOES THE SAME THING EVERY DAY.

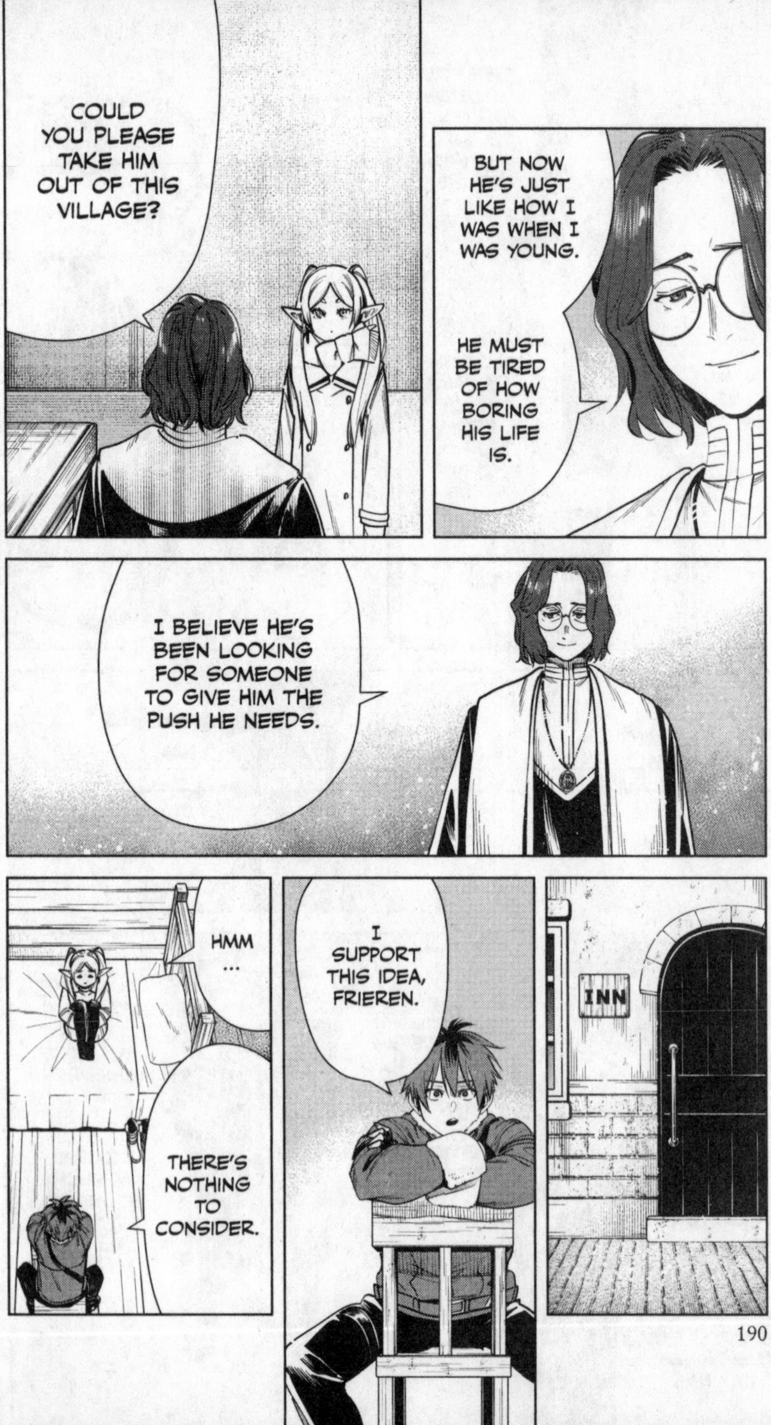

BUT NOW HE'S JUST LIKE HOW I WAS WHEN I WAS YOUNG.
HE MUST BE TIRED OF HOW BORING HIS LIFE IS.
COULD YOU PLEASE TAKE HIM OUT OF THIS VILLAGE?
I BELIEVE HE'S BEEN LOOKING FOR SOMEONE TO GIVE HIM THE PUSH HE NEEDS.
INN
I SUPPORT THIS IDEA, FRIEREN.
HMM ...
THERE'S NOTHING TO CONSIDER.

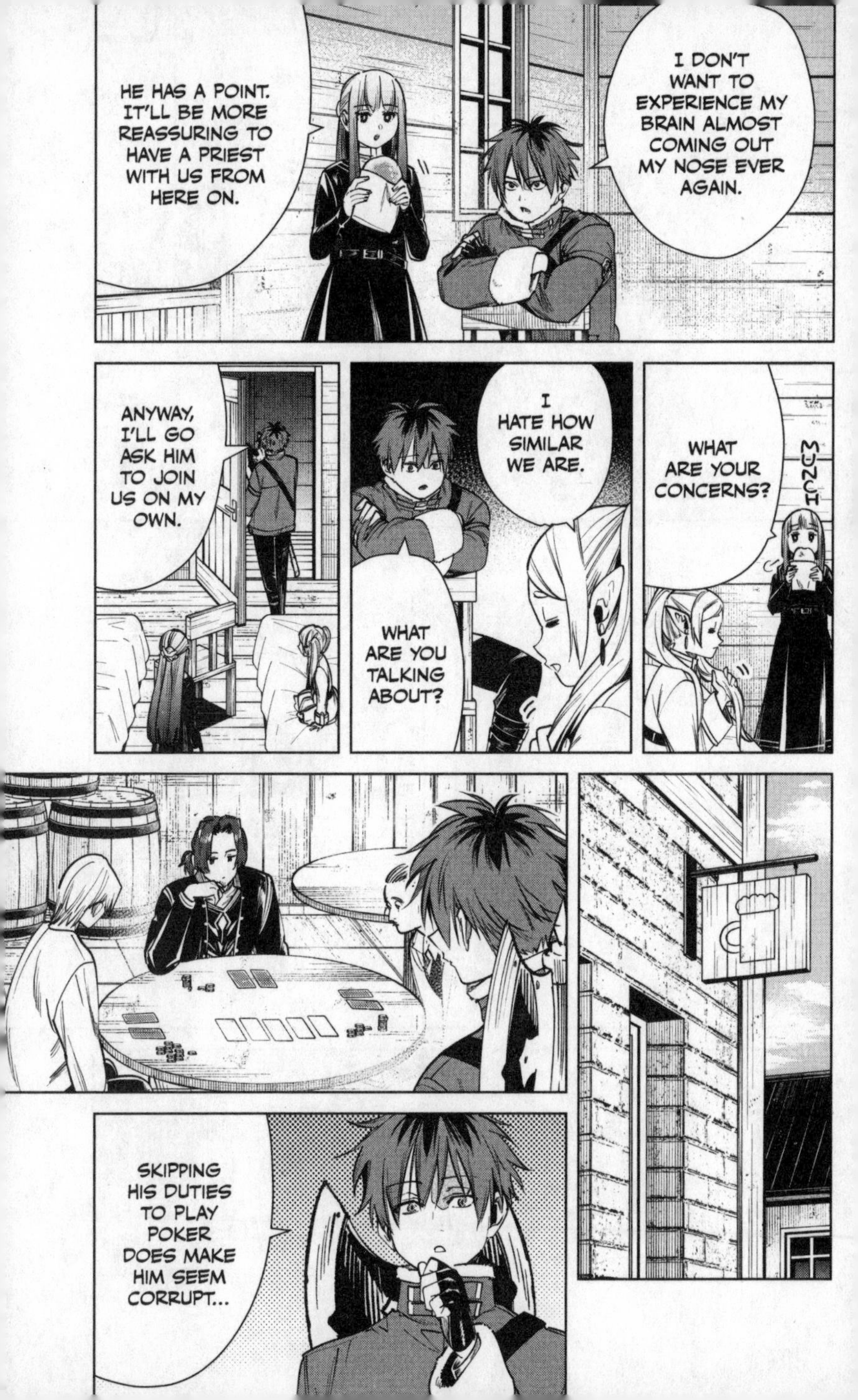
I DON'T WANT TO EXPERIENCE MY BRAIN ALMOST COMING OUT MY NOSE EVER AGAIN.
HE HAS A POINT. IT'LL BE MORE REASSURING TO HAVE A PRIEST WITH US FROM HERE ON.
WHAT ARE YOUR CONCERNS?
MUNCH
I HATE HOW SIMILAR WE ARE.
WHAT ARE YOU TALKING ABOUT?
ANYWAY, I'LL GO ASK HIM TO JOIN US ON MY OWN.
SKIPPING HIS DUTIES TO PLAY POKER DOES MAKE HIM SEEM CORRUPT...

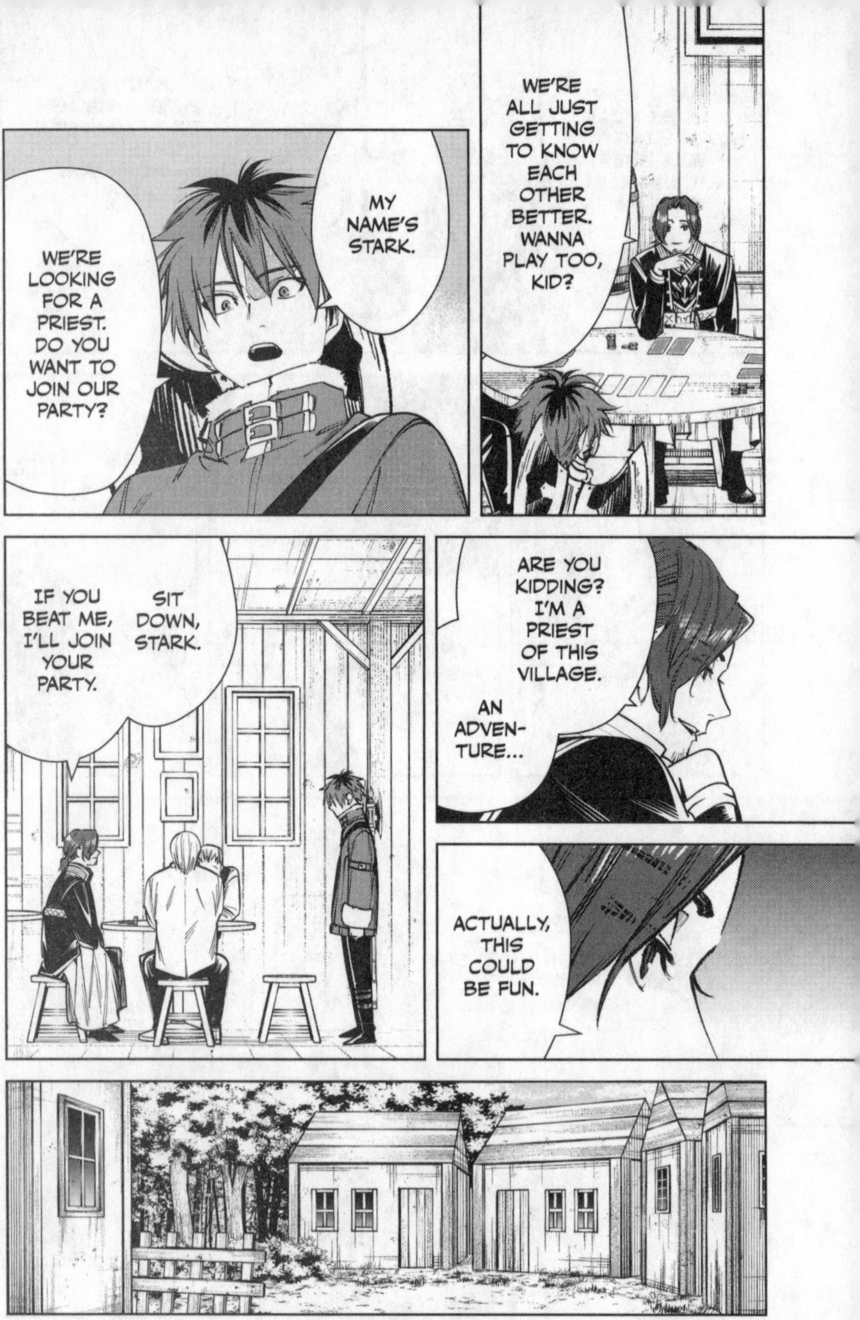

WE'RE ALL JUST GETTING TO KNOW EACH OTHER BETTER. WANNA PLAY TOO, KID?
MY NAME'S STARK.
WE'RE LOOKING FOR A PRIEST. DO YOU WANT TO JOIN OUR PARTY?
ARE YOU KIDDING? I'M A PRIEST OF THIS VILLAGE.
AN ADVENTURE...
ACTUALLY, THIS COULD BE FUN.
SIT DOWN, STARK.
IF YOU BEAT ME, I'LL JOIN YOUR PARTY.

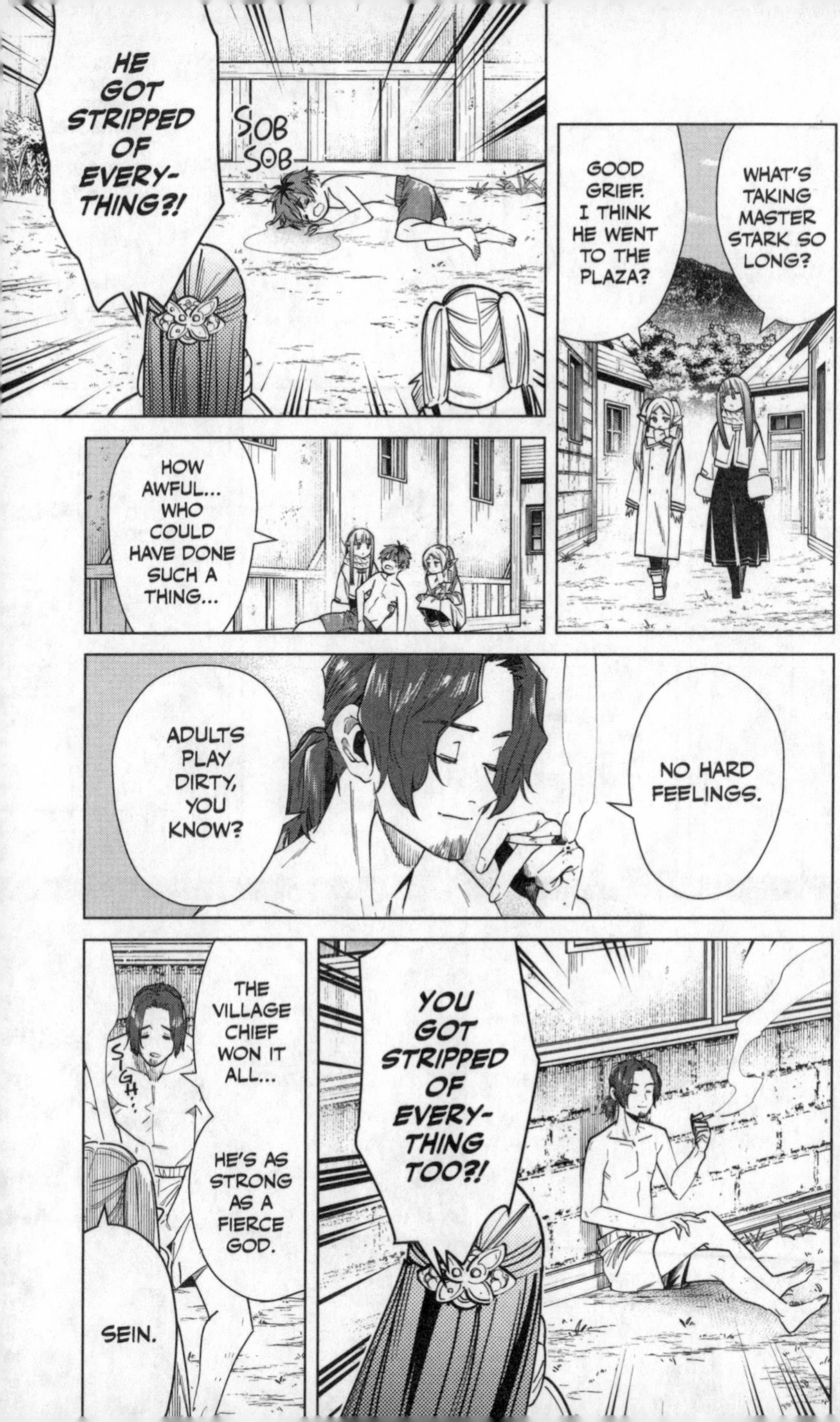
WHAT'S TAKING MASTER STARK SO LONG?
GOOD GRIEF. I THINK HE WENT TO THE PLAZA?
HE GOT STRIPPED OF EVERY-THING?!
SOB SOB
HOW AWFUL... WHO COULD HAVE DONE SUCH A THING...
NO HARD FEELINGS.
ADULTS PLAY DIRTY, YOU KNOW?
YOU GOT STRIPPED OF EVERY-THING TOO?!
THE VILLAGE CHIEF WON IT ALL...
SIGH...
HE'S AS STRONG AS A FIERCE GOD.
SEIN.

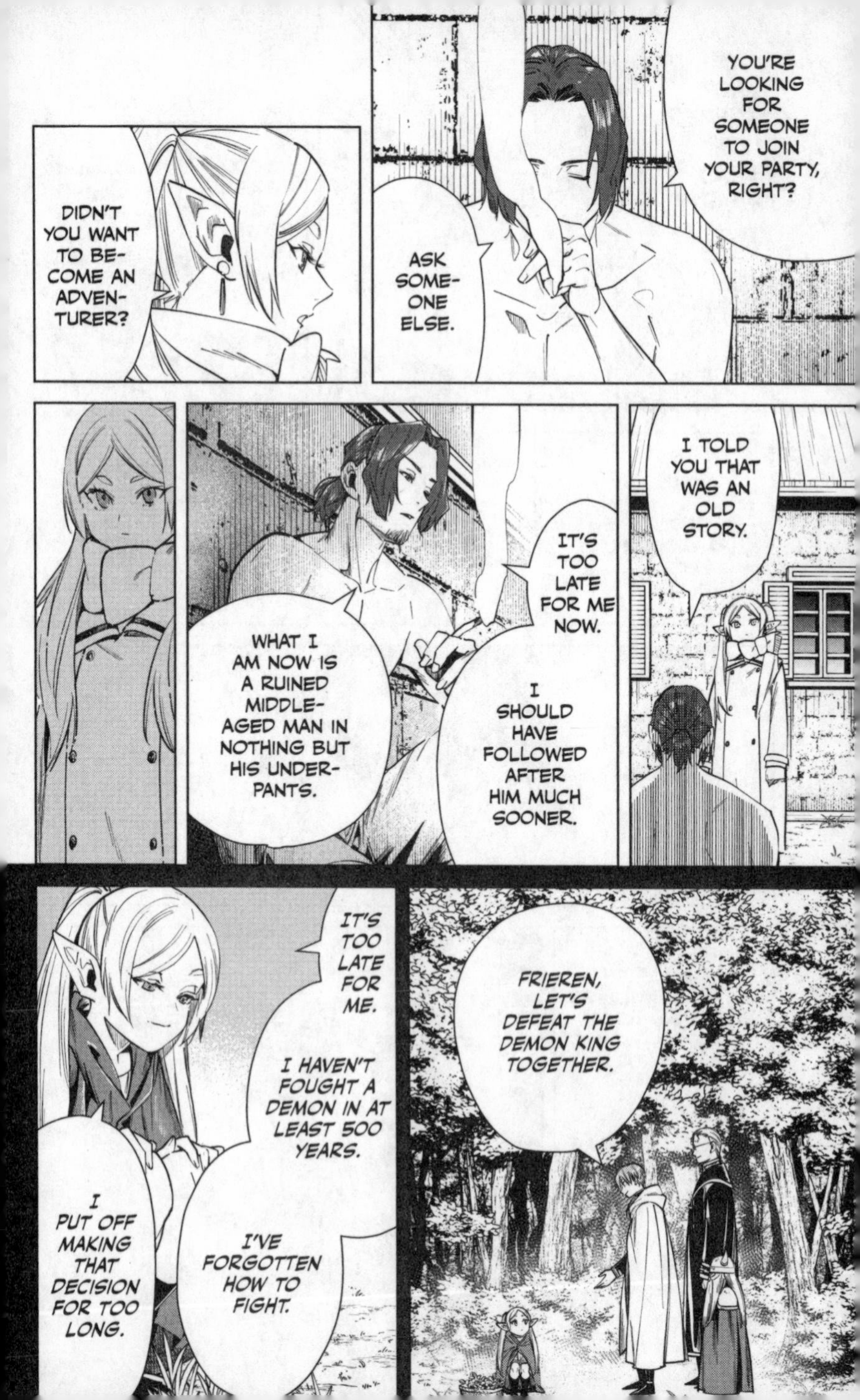

YOU'RE LOOKING FOR SOMEONE TO JOIN YOUR PARTY, RIGHT?
ASK SOMEONE ELSE.
DIDN'T YOU WANT TO BECOME AN ADVENTURER?
I TOLD YOU THAT WAS AN OLD STORY.
IT'S TOO LATE FOR ME NOW.
I SHOULD HAVE FOLLOWED AFTER HIM MUCH SOONER.
WHAT I AM NOW IS A RUINED MIDDLE-AGED MAN IN NOTHING BUT HIS UNDERPANTS.
FRIEREN, LET'S DEFEAT THE DEMON KING TOGETHER.
IT'S TOO LATE FOR ME.
I HAVEN'T FOUGHT A DEMON IN AT LEAST 500 YEARS.
I'VE FORGOTTEN HOW TO FIGHT.
I PUT OFF MAKING THAT DECISION FOR TOO LONG.

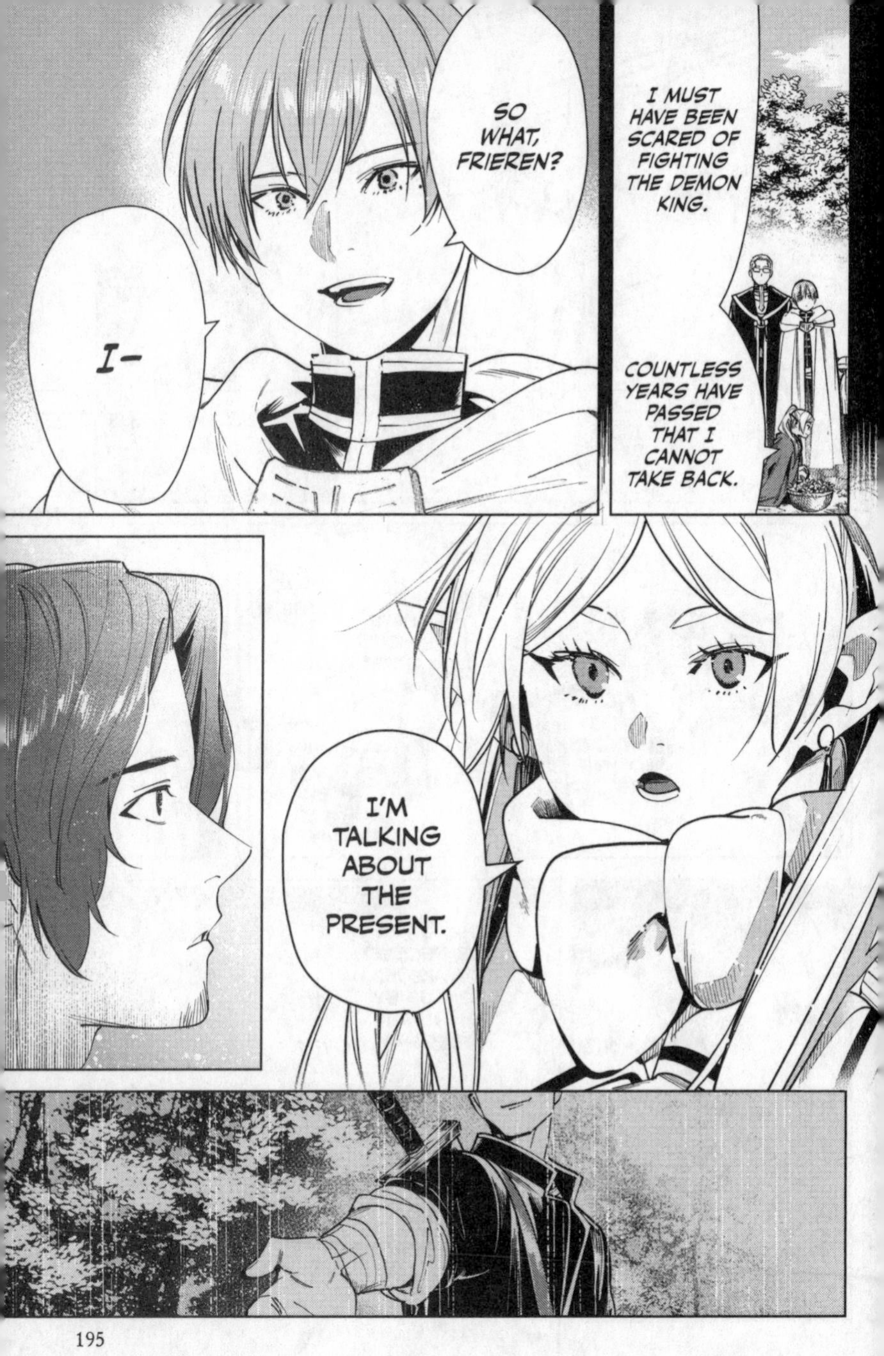
I MUST HAVE BEEN SCARED OF FIGHTING THE DEMON KING.
COUNTLESS YEARS HAVE PASSED THAT I CANNOT TAKE BACK.
SO WHAT, FRIEREN?
I–
I'M TALKING ABOUT THE PRESENT.

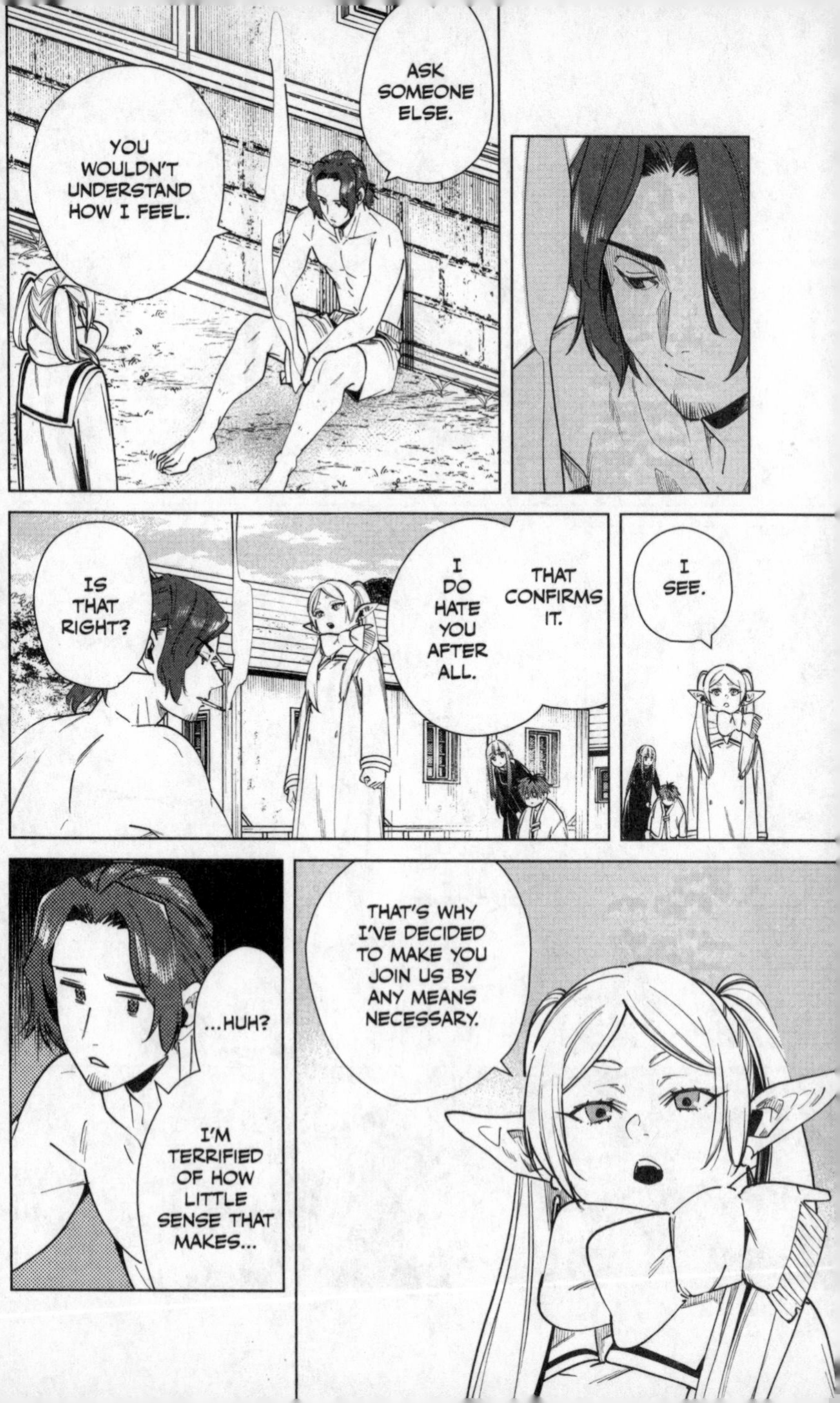
ASK SOMEONE ELSE.
YOU WOULDN'T UNDERSTAND HOW I FEEL.
I SEE.
THAT CONFIRMS IT.
I DO HATE YOU AFTER ALL.
IS THAT RIGHT?
THAT'S WHY I'VE DECIDED TO MAKE YOU JOIN US BY ANY MEANS NECESSARY.
...HUH?
I'M TERRIFIED OF HOW LITTLE SENSE THAT MAKES...

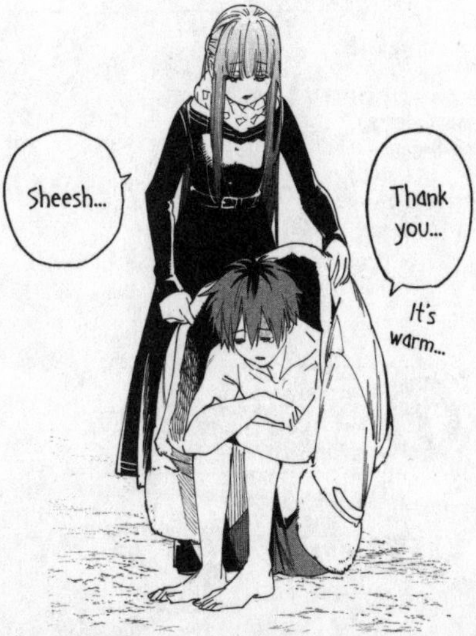
Thank you...
It's warm...
Sheesh...

# Frieren: Beyond Journey's End

## VOLUME 3
### Shonen Sunday Edition

STORY BY
**KANEHITO YAMADA**

ART BY
**TSUKASA ABE**

SOSO NO FRIEREN Vol. 3
Kanehito YAMADA, Tsukasa ABE
© 2020 Kanehito YAMADA, Tsukasa ABE
All rights reserved.
Original Japanese edition published by SHOGAKUKAN.
English translation rights in the United States of America, Canada,
the United Kingdom, Ireland, Australia and New Zealand arranged
with SHOGAKUKAN.

Original Cover Design: Masato ISHIZAWA + Bay Bridge Studio

Translation/Misa 'Japanese Ammo'
Touch-up Art & Lettering/Annaliese "Ace" Christman
Design/Yukiko Whitley
Editor/Mike Montesa

Printed in Canada

Published by VIZ Media, LLC
P.O. Box 77010
San Francisco, CA 94107

10 9 8 7 6 5 4 3 2 1
First printing, March 2022

**VIZ** MEDIA
viz.com

SHONEN SUNDAY
shonensunday.com

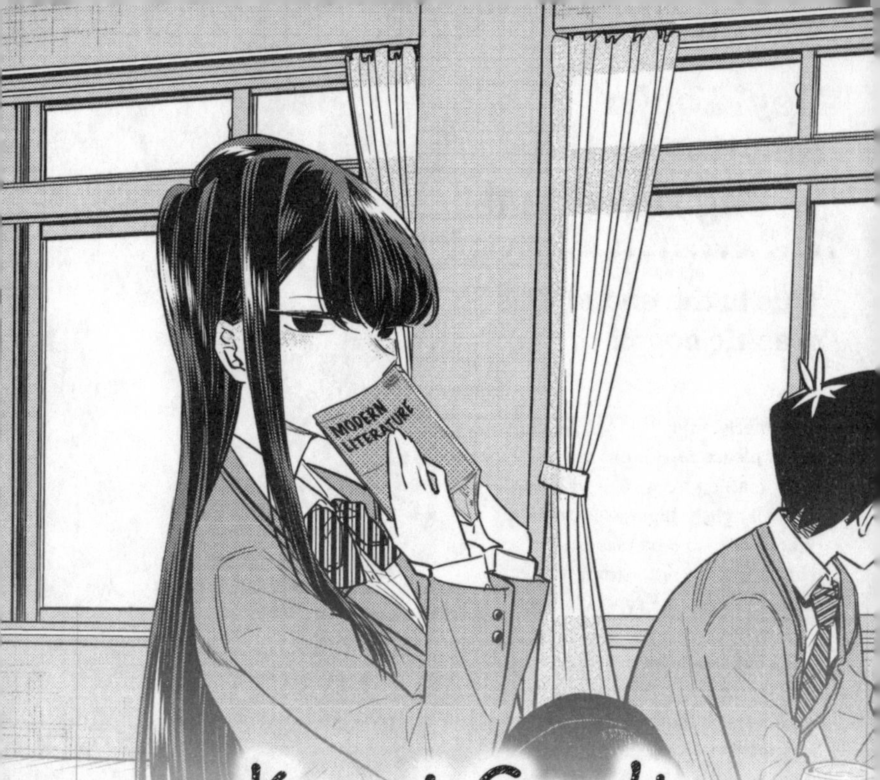
MODERN LITERATURE

# Komi Can't Communicate

Story & Art by Tomohito Oda

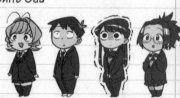

The journey to a hundred friends begins with a single conversation.

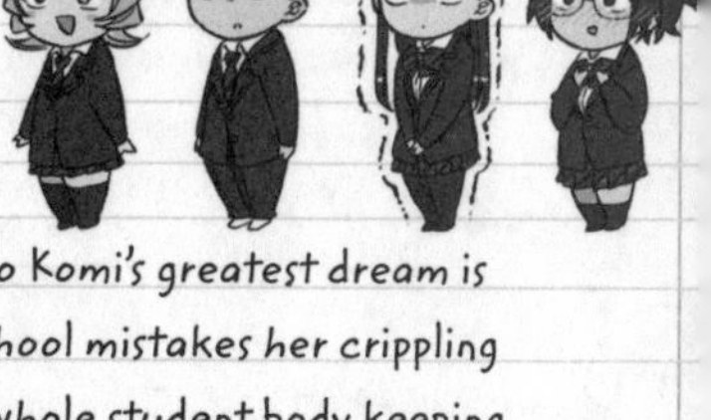

Socially anxious high school student Shoko Komi's greatest dream is to make some friends, but everyone at school mistakes her crippling social anxiety for cool reserve. With the whole student body keeping its distance and Komi unable to utter a single word, friendship might be forever beyond her reach.

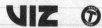

VIZ

# Hey! You're Reading in the Wrong Direction!

## This is the end of this graphic novel!

To properly enjoy this VIZ graphic novel, please turn it around and begin reading from right to left. Unlike English, Japanese is read right to left, so Japanese comics are read in reverse order from the way English comics are typically read.

This book has been printed in the original Japanese format in order to preserve the orientation of the original artwork. Have fun with it!

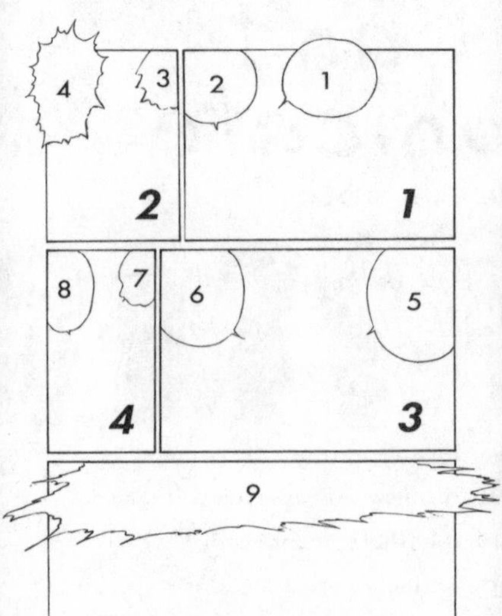
1
2
1
3
4
2
5
6
3
7
8
4
9
5

Follow the action this way

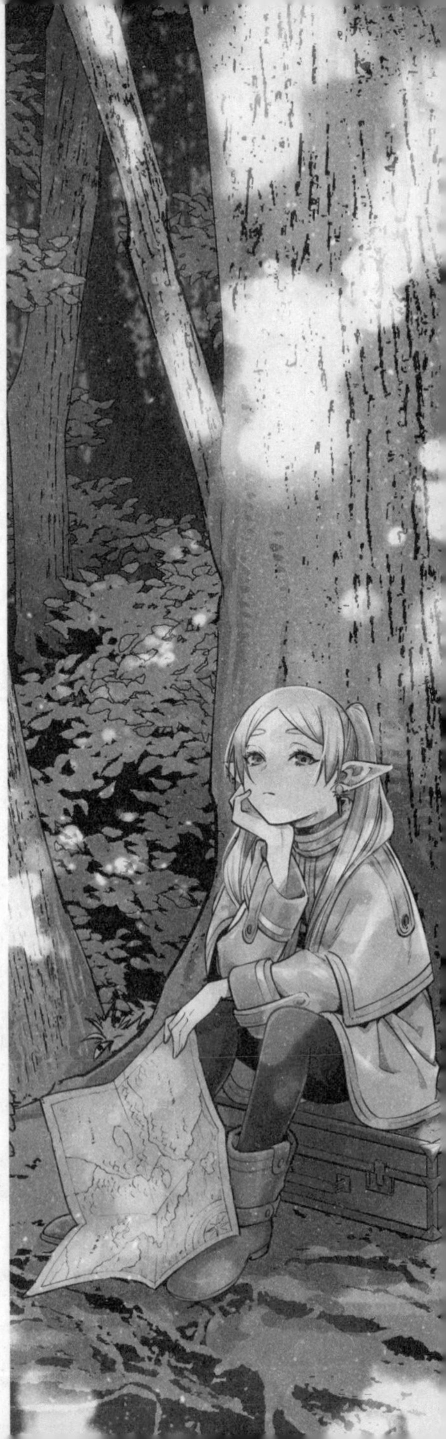